SOME WAYS OF MAKING NOTHING

Before you start to read this book, take this moment to think about making a donation to punctum books, an independent non-profit press

@ https://punctumbooks.com/support

If you're reading the e-book, you can click on the image below to go directly to our donations site. Any amount, no matter the size, is appreciated and will help us to keep our ship of fools afloat. Contributions from dedicated readers will also help us to keep our commons open and to cultivate new work that can't find a welcoming port elsewhere. Our adventure is not possible without your support.

Vive la Open Access.

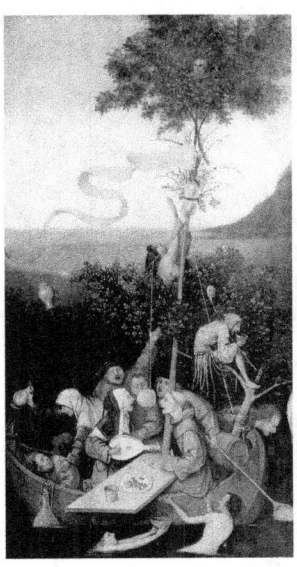

Fig. 1. Hieronymus Bosch, *Ship of Fools* (1490–1500)

First published in 2021 by 3Ecologies Books/Immediations,
an imprint of punctum books.
https://punctumbooks.com

ISBN-13: 978-1-953035-37-0 (print)
ISBN-13: 978-1-953035-38-7 (ePDF)

DOI: 10.21983/P3.0327.1.00

LCCN: 2021931820
Library of Congress Cataloging Data is available from the Library of
Congress

Book design: Vincent W.J. van Gerven Oei. Typeset in Alda OT CEV
10/12 by Berton Hasebe for Emigre and Dislectika by Navid Nuur
Cover image by Jordan Cloninger (drawing of a photograph of some
of the ashes of the burned gallery from Joshua Citarella's *Compression
Artifacts*)

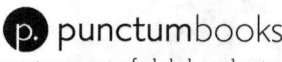

spontaneous acts of scholarly combustion

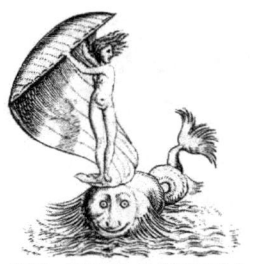

HIC SVNT MONSTRA

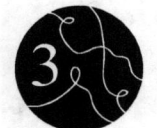

CURT CLONINGER

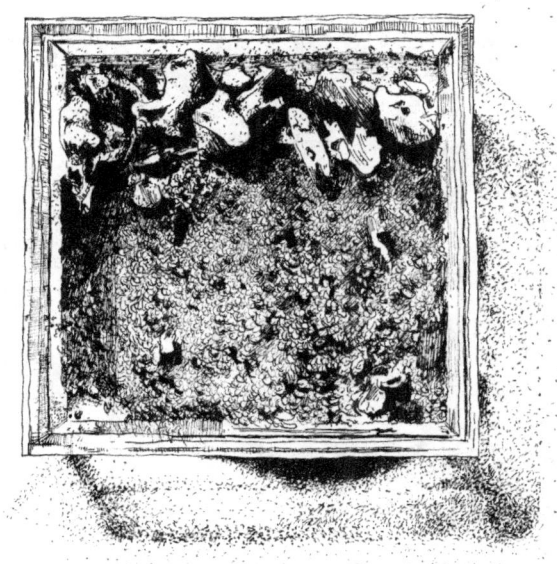

SOME WAYS OF MAKING NOTHING

APOPHATIC APPARATUSES
IN CONTEMPORARY ART

For Kevin Shields (fluff-on-the-needle-izer) and Tony Allen (grindfather): master makers of unforeseen naughts.

CONTENTS

ACKNOWLEDGMENTS

Thanks to my wife Julie for bearing with me as I wrote this book, and for bearing with me in general. Thanks to my eldest son Jordan for doing the illustrations in the book, and to his friend Jeziah MacMillan for helping with their colorization (for the PDF version of the book). Thanks to Haim Steinbach, Joshua Citarella, and Pasqualina Azzarello for letting me ask you a bunch of questions. Thanks to Stephen Hepworth and Peter Katz at the Reversible Destiny Foundation for helping me (more rigorously fail to) get to the bottom of *Mechanism of Meaning*. Thanks to Iain Kerr for introducing me to Whitehead (among many other things). Finally, thanks to Brian Massumi and Erin Manning for encouragement and guidance.

INTRODUCTION

It is an old trick of the contemporary media theorist (and indeed, of the contemporary "interdisciplinary" academic) to take ideas from one discipline and cross-apply them to another discipline. At best the results can be invigorating and generative; at worst the results can seem shoehorned, awkward, irrelevant, and scatological. In this book, I apply ideas from quantum mechanics and negative theology to a small group of contemporary artworks – artworks that succeed by a variety of means to make a variety of flavors of qualitative nothing. From quantum mechanics, the model of an experimental apparatus becomes a useful way of understanding how these particular works of art (and indeed, all works of art) function. And from negative theology, the practice of apophatic writing (a writing that perpetually unsays itself) helpfully informs the goals and tactics of these particular works of art. So, quantum apparatuses apply to all works of art, but apophatic writing only applies to a particular subset of artworks, individual examples of which I analyze here.

I didn't choose quantum mechanics or apophasis for their own novel or culturally current qualities. Indeed, not being all that mathematically gifted, I would have avoided quantum mechanics if at all possible; and apophasis, often associated with both deconstruction and God, is hardly culturally current these days. (Admittedly, the topic of nothing is always hot: a perennial classic.) Instead, I began with the works of art themselves, and tried to let what they were doing inform and determine the way I chose to approach them. Rather than begin with the theory and let the specific examples of artwork stick or fall through the cracks, I have begun with the specific examples of artwork and have let the theory stick or fall through the cracks. The theory that has stuck is surprising and relevant to me, because it addresses long-standing questions that have always bothered my own art practice and research: What is the actual force of language in the real world? How malleable is material? How do humans and objects access each other? In making the truly new, how much agency do I have, and how much of my agency is contingent on the history of the world? How might I halt becoming? If the universe generally tends toward something rather than nothing (Heidegger), and if it always tends toward something new (Whitehead), then what is the ethical value making a new nothing?

In cross-applying these disciplines (physics, philosophy, literary criticism, theology, media theory, art criticism, art history), I hope to avoid a number of pitfalls. Regarding quantum mechanics, it would be a failure if all I accomplished was a "mere" analogizing of quantum mechanical behavior to art apparatuses that aren't really behaving in any way actually relevant to their science laboratory counterparts. In order to avoid this pitfall, I enlist contemporary decoherence theory (from quantum mechanics) and the cosmology of Alfred North Whitehead to provide an explanation of how these works of art are "really" (not just analogically or metaphorically) making nothing. In this sense, "real" does not necessarily mean "scientific." It doesn't even solely mean "actual." But "real" does mean both "actual" and "virtual/potential," both of which comprise the real. All of these concepts will be explained in greater detail in "Chapter 1: Regarding Apparatuses."

Additionally, Chapter 1 makes clear the ways in which scientific apparatuses designed to "measure" quantum behaviors are relevant to art apparatuses. Briefly, quantum-behavior-measuring apparatuses are most notable for creating a specific and intentional cut in the holistic universe which invites the "thing" they are "measuring" (be it proton, electron, or molecule) to manifest a particular, heretofore not-yet-existent "observable" value (position value, momentum value, charge value, spin value). Which type of *observable* is in part determined by the specific "measurement bias" of the apparatus itself. Indeed, the very particle-ness of the "thing" being measured, its thing-, object-, or noun-ness, has arguably yet to emerge prior to the measurement event itself. Philosopher and physicist Karen Barad (following her interpretation of Niels Bohr) usefully refers to this entire congregation (apparatus, measurement event, quarantined system, measured thing) as a singular "phenomenon." Additionally, Whitehead's idea of "negative prehension" and contemporary quantum decoherence theory both take into account the entire rest of the universe which surrounds this cordoned-off "apparatal"[1] phenomenon, and treat it as an implicit component of the overall measurement event.

All well and good, but what has any of this got to do with art? If every work of art acts in some ways like a quantum-behavior-measuring apparatus (and I'm claiming this is true), then a number of relevant observations follow:

1. Works of art don't merely reveal the pre-existent properties of the materials they incorporate. If they did, they would be functioning according to the classical/ Newtonian model of measuring apparatuses, a model

---

1   Here I coin the neologism "apparatal," simply to keep from having to repeatedly say "apparatus-like."

which presumes a world of determined objects that inherently pre-possess measurable properties. Instead, works of art invite material properties to co-emerge as part of apparatal entanglements, and the works of art themselves co-emerge along with these material properties;

2. Works of art don't have a pre-determined outcome. Again, if they did, they would be functioning according to the classical/Newtonian model of measuring apparatuses, a model which presumes a world full of forces acting determinately and inevitably within a knowable system. Instead, works of art collaborate with their materials. The materials enact their own agency which is not wholly pre-determined or ever fully predictable beforehand, and which co-emerges as part of the entire apparatal phenomenon (a holistic phenomenon which includes the art object and any participants, viewers, patrons, users, humans, non-humans determined to be part of the apparatal system);

3. Although the outcome of a work of art is not pre-determined, neither is it fully random. Its outcome is in part contingent on all prior historical "decisions" (by art critics, electrons, weather systems, economic markets, oil paints, and all the other "enduring objects" in the history of the universe), and in part determined by the relevant desire for novelty manifested by all the participants involved in the apparatal phenomenon that is the work of art; and

4. Every art apparatus (in other words, ever work of art) is itself a kind of actualizing provocation that invites (sometimes more courteously, and sometimes more insistently) an evolution, reduction, or change in the universe. These assertions and others will be considered more fully in Chapter 1.

Moving on from quantum mechanics to negative theology, in regards to apophatic writing, it would be a failure if all I accomplished in this book was to approach the actual physical world analogically as if it were itself a "text," the better to apply my readymade literary critical theory to it. A few decades ago, this would have been a standard approach, and it would have failed to take into account the very real and pragmatic decision-making capacity of materials (from photons to oil paints to weather systems). So, although I will address Derridean deconstruction, I will do so mostly to talk about the ways in which deconstruction *differs* from apophatic writing. I will also call upon Mikhail Bakhtin's idea of the utterance, J.L. Austin's classic "speech acts," and Derrida himself (in "dialogue" with John Searle) to account for the ways in which "language" informs and in-forms the actually real. I will also consider Karen Barad's provocative concept of the "discursivity" of materiality, and I will detail the ways in which this concept relates to the theoretical toolset I am attempting to construct. All of these negotiations will occur in "Chapter 2: Regarding Apophasis."

Ultimately this is a book about art. So, another great way I could fail is to reduce the affect and ineffability of art to a kind of utilitarian scientific explanation, or to some sort of literary critical explanation, or to both. In *What Is Philosophy?* (and elsewhere), Deleuze and Guattari propose a cosmology of undifferentiated everything (a.k.a. the plane of immanence, the rhizome, the body without organs) probed and accessed by three major human approaches – science, philosophy, and art. These three approaches all access the same cosmos, but by different means. With quantum mechanics, science has outpaced the other two approaches and found itself in dire need of some philosophy. Sadly, many scientists prove to be awkward, gee-whiz speculative philosophers (when they even dare to try), and many philosophers skimp on the math and head straight toward broad theoretical explanations without attending to the detailed, nuanced implications of the actual experiments. The goal of this book is not to bridge science and philosophy regarding quantum mechanics. Its goal is simply to celebrate and open up a few wonderful works of art. But in order to accomplish this goal, I've had to venture into scientific and philosophical realms. Perhaps by injecting the third approach (art) into the current fracas between science and the more speculative flavors of contemporary philosophy, some clarity or truce will be brokered between the two. But, probably I will just further muddy and problematize the waters, which would be a perfectly acceptable side-effect of a book about making nothing.

The theory I'm proposing may well prove valuable in and of itself. For example, an understanding of how every artwork functions as a kind of apparatus could provide the theoretical foundations of an entire MFA program (if one were so inclined). But the primary goal of my theory is to invent useful ways of opening up and dialoguing with the works of art I wish to discuss. So, in explicating my theory, I will try to be as direct as possible in order to construct a vehicle that does what I need it to do. In so doing, I will necessarily oversimplify Whitehead's rigorously exhaustive speculative cosmology. I will commit myself to certain quantum theories that are still being debated and ironed out. In all of this, I will try to be transparent and straightforward, particularly when I know I'm marginalizing some alternate theory, or oversimplifying some more complex nuance.

Having established a theoretical framework in the first two chapters of the book, the following four chapters discuss particular works of art, and the ways they make various kinds of nothing. My thinking about the pieces of art actually occurred prior to (and then concurrent with) my thinking about the theory, but it makes sense to reverse the order for this book (à la Derrida's *Of Grammatology*). One could read the theory chapters and then stop, but that would be like waxing down your surfboard and not going surfing. Chapter 3 primarily discusses *Mechanism of Meaning* by Arakawa and Gins, contrasting it with Robert Fludd's famous 1617 diagram of the pre-creation void. Chapter 4 discusses the aleatoric animation series *Stop Motion Studies* by the artist David Crawford, comparing it to the (in)famous "delayed choice quantum eraser" experiment. Chapter 5 focuses on two works: Joshua Citarella's *Compression Artifacts* project and William Pope.L's *Black Factory* project. Finally, Chapter 6 considers the shelf-based, found-object ensembles of Haim Steinbach.

After spending four chapters considering these apophatic art apparatuses, some broader conclusions are drawn. "Chapter 7: Toward an Ethics of Nothing" considers why one might want to make nothing in the first place (the last place, or at all).

The figures in this book were draw by my seventeen-year-old son, Jordan. These drawings are in the spirit of physics textbook diagrams. Since I intend to focus less on what these artworks look like and more on the apparatal entanglements and emergences they invite, these drawn diagrams are a way to dampen and de-prioritize the mere visuality of the artworks. Furthermore, some of the works (particularly *Mechanism of Meaning* and *Compression Artifacts*) themselves purposefully problematize their own documentation, so documenting them photographically here in this book as an attempt to clearly "represent" them would either halt their exponential chain of intended problematization, or only awkwardly (at a thrice remove) "illustrate" this chain of intended problematization. The drawn figures are thus meant in the spirit of these artworks to further (d)evolve them, injecting new levels of abstraction into their foregone degradations toward nothingness.

Having delineated what types of failures this book could be, I should mention some ways I hope it will succeed. There is a kind of cosmology which believes the universe is at every instance fully malleable, that individual personal agency abounds, and that every move one makes matters a great deal. This optimistic cosmology is admittedly in short supply these days, but it can still be found amongst sophomore undergraduate art students at liberal arts universities. This kind of cosmology can lead to windmill-tilting, wheel-reinventing, bad art that claims to be mattering more than it actually matters. Yes, everything matters, but some things matter so little to so few so as to more or less not matter all that much to anyone at all. I don't wish to defeat this hopeful cosmology or the idealism that accompanies it. Instead, I want to inject this cosmology with a care and attention to past historical decisions (human and non-human) that have also come to actually matter. There is another kind of cosmology that believes in a universe of bare, utilitarian, pre-determined efficacy. Such a cosmology can lead (and has led) to an array of art so desperate it is largely indistinguishable from direct political action. I don't wish to defeat this realpolitik cosmology or the earnestness that accompanies it, but rather to suggest the possibility that less direct, more speculative flavors of art apparatuses do really, actually matter in the world, in ways beyond mere allegory and analogy.

The goal of this book is to motivate artists to make art that more fully and ingeniously exploits what art apparatuses are actually (capable of) doing. Art apparatuses (a.k.a. "artworks") are still commonly considered as objects and pieces of media, but they are more fruitfully understood as vehicles that collaborate with the universe to co-constitute new becomings. The apophatic art apparatuses considered in this book are unique case studies that particularly foreground this co-constituting function of art. By purposefully refusing to co-constitute much of anything, they open out onto the idiosyncratic contours of nothing at all.

I

REGARDING APPARATUSES AND APOPHASIS

REGARDING APPARATUSES

My goal in this book is to consider some ways of making nothing. In order to do that, I will consider several pieces of contemporary art, each of which ingeniously makes one flavor or another of nothing. These artworks make nothing because they behave as apophatic apparatuses – in other words, they instigate a kind of coherent event that results in the production of nothing. How do they do this? I could simply begin by discussing each art apparatus individually to discern how it functions. But before we dive into the artworks themselves, I want to lay some theoretical groundwork. In this chapter, my goal is to arrive at a general understanding of what an art apparatus is. I will defer to the next chapter my discussion of apophasis, ways of making nothing, and the different kinds of nothing that may be made. In this chapter we will simply concern ourselves with all art apparatuses (whether apophatic or otherwise).

In order to explain what I mean by art apparatuses, I first have to explain the way apparatuses have come to be understood in quantum mechanics. And in order for that explanation to make any sense, I have to explain some of the unique aspects of quantum mechanics. And in order for that explanation to make the sense I feel it needs to make, I have chosen to also consider aspects of the decoherence theory that has arisen within the field of quantum mechanics. And in order for an explanation of all those quantum topics to make the sense I want them to make, I have chosen to begin with a brief explanation of the cosmology of Alfred North Whitehead. So that is quite a tall order for the first chapter of a book that merely intends to talk about a few pieces of contemporary art, but it probably needs to happen. Every piece of art – every painting, sculpture, installation, video, generative software, interactive online environment, ephemeral conceptual provocation, tactical media wearable biotech psychogeographic event, etc. – is an apparatus. So, when I talk about art apparatuses, I am simply talking about art; which is why it is worth spending so much time understanding apparatuses in general.

If this were a book about quantum mechanics, or even about the philosophy associated with it, I would probably begin with a discussion of the seminal double-slit experiment and work my way out and around from there. That would be a kind of inductive approach – begin with the experiment itself, measure the results, and then infer what the results seem to imply. The problem is, the "results" of this particular experiment imply the need for a fundamental re-understanding of experimentation, measurement, results, and inductive reasoning itself. In my own personal chronological history, I began with Whitehead's cosmology, and ran the rest of the voodoo down from there. But Whitehead himself began with (or was at least fully aware of and conversant with) the quantum physics of his time, and so we are not really bypassing quantum physics by starting with Whitehead. Indeed, Whitehead himself cautioned, "Philosophers have worried themselves about remote consequences, and the inductive formulations of science. They should confine attention to the rush of immediate transition."[1]

---

1   Alfred North Whitehead, *Process and Reality* (New York: The Free Press, 1978), 129.

Whitehead's cosmology is more about process than stasis (although it is also about stasis, or at least endurance), more about verbs and events than nouns and objects (although it presents the most reasonable explanation of objects I have ever encountered), more about speculation and adventure than ontological categorization and mathematical proof (although Whitehead was an extraordinary mathematician and, to me, one of the most straightforward and readable philosophers of the twentieth century). He was primarily concerned with the emergence of the new and how it happens.

Whitehead's cosmology has been directly (and painstakingly) correlated with quantum mechanics,[2] but it doesn't merely reduce to a philosophical quantum mechanics. Whitehead speculates about the behavior of the entire universe from an arguably quantum perspective. Whitehead's cosmology, along with discoveries and insights from the (post-Whitehead) field of quantum decoherence will help us bridge the gap (which is not really a gap at all) between delicately prepared and isolated individual electrons and photons, and more complex entities like rocks, plants, dogs, humans, and planets. This bridge will be crucial to my discussion of art apparatuses, since none of the art apparatuses I discuss involve isolated, single electrons. If I intend to claim (and I do) that art apparatuses "really" (and not just metaphorically) behave in some way similar to scientific apparatuses which have been constructed to measure quantum behavior, then I need to explain the relationship between single, isolated electrons in a laboratory, and rocks just lying outside in a field on the ground. Whitehead's idea of "negative prehension" and his overall theory of concrescence, coupled

2   For example: Michael Epperson, *Quantum Mechanics and the Philosophy of Alfred North Whitehead* (New York: Fordham University Press, 2004), and Timothy E. Eastman and Hank Keeton, eds., *Physics and Whitehead: Quantum, Process, and Experience* (Albany: SUNY Press, 2004).

with the theory of quantum decoherence, provides such an explanation.

We will begin with a general explanation of (my idiosyncratic version of) Whitehead's process philosophy. This will lead into a consideration of the dual nature of becoming: 1. the historical contingency to which it is always beholden; and 2. the ongoing, decision-mattering aspects of process which bring the new into the world. We will then consider the concept of quantum decoherence, and the behavior of "large" (better understood as "complex" or "well-decided") objects. Finally, before moving on to apparatuses proper, we will revisit the idea of what "really real" means, what "merely metaphorical" means, and the ways in which prior decisions (least of all human decisions) must be allowed to "actually" matter.

We will next revisit quantum undecidability and "measurement" before (finally) proceeding to apparatuses proper! We will consider the two most famous quantum apparatuses (the original "double slit" and its "which-path" counterpart). We will then proceed to the relevant similarities between quantum-behavior-measuring scientific apparatuses and what I am calling art apparatuses. At that point, we will briefly distinguish our use of the term "apparatus" (as derived from quantum mechanics) from other more media-theoretical uses of the term (in film theory, and by Althusser, Flusser, and Ulmer, respectively). This will be followed by a more detailed consideration of art apparatuses. The chapter will end with a consideration of epochs and futures.

My Condensed and Slightly Modified Whitehead-Derived Cosmology

Whitehead wrote several books explaining his cosmology in detail, the most rigorous of which is *Process and Reality*. My own Whitehead-derived cosmology is supplemented by Gilles Deleuze, (early) Henri Bergson, and Marcel Proust. Whitehead's own cosmology is much more complex than what I am presenting here, but I only need to explain my version of it as will be eventually relevant to my treatment of quantum mechanics and art apparatuses. Any omissions, simplifications, purposefully idiosyncratic modifications, and outright misreadings of Whitehead are solely my own doing.

Instead of starting with a universe full of objects (nouns) with associated properties (adjectives) that occupy space and time (a ground or a stage) and occasionally act upon each other (verbs), Whitehead begins with the actions and events (verbs) and deduces everything else from there (or, more properly, from "then"). Whitehead doesn't concern himself terribly with the question of origins (which came first, the event or the result of the event?). Since the main way the universe proceeds is by a perpetual and ongoing series of becomings, Whitehead just begins in the middle of this perpetual and ongoing series of becomings and unpacks one of these becomings. The becoming event doesn't happen in a void. It is not ahistorical. Indeed, the becoming event (which whitehead calls an "actual entity" or "actual occasion") is preceded by a number of things. The actual entity/occasion is not preceded by "time" (which itself winds up being a byproduct of these irreversible becomings), nor is it preceded by space (which is merely the result of the relationships formed and maintained by these becomings), nor is it preceded by "objects" per se (which are really just themselves the result of all of these becomings). Each actual entity/occasion is preceded by other actual entities (other prior becoming events like itself), and by "eternal objects," which Steven Shaviro describes as the adverbs of Whitehead's scheme ("They are adverbial, rather than substantive"[3]).

My own cosmology modifies and supplements Whitehead's "eternal objects," because I find them problematic. Whitehead means them to be like qualia or potentia which always influence (ingress into) actual entities/occasions, but which are themselves indifferent to and uninfluenced by these actual occasions. Because eternal objects always desire to increasingly complexify the universe via their ingressions, this is one of the ways in which novelty enters the world. Whitehead's concept of eternal objects supplies his cosmology with two requisites: 1. the concept of fundamental potentia; and 2. an explanation for why the world always strives toward newness. I want to keep both of these requisites, but I want to modify "eternal objects" so that they are only responsible for the second requisite. To handle the first requisite, I supplement Whitehead's cosmology with the concept of the virtual from (mostly) Gilles Deleuze.

Whitehead's cosmology contains something called the "extensive continuum," which he describes as, "one relational complex in which all potential objectifications find their niche. It underlies the whole world, past, present, and future."[4] He calls it "the potentiality for division."[5] Although Whitehead's extensive continuum is somewhat analogous to Deleuze's virtual, I find it an awkward analogy without the attendant functioning of Whitehead's eternal objects. So rather than awkwardly attempt to map Whitehead's "extensive continuum" directly to Deleuze's "virtual," I will take the bolder step of altogether replacing Whitehead's eternal objects with Deleuze's virtual. If you like, you might say that Deleuze's virtual combines

3   Steven Shaviro, *Without Criteria: Kant, Whitehead, Deleuze, and Aesthetics* (Cambridge: MIT Press), 38.
4   Whitehead, *Process and Reality*, 66.
5   Ibid., 67.

elements of both the extensive continuum and the eternal objects. Like Whitehead's eternal objects, Deleuze's virtual may still be thought to ingress into actual occasions, but (unlike eternal objects) Deleuze's virtual is also subsequently colored and influenced by all prior actual occasions. I modify the nature of Whitehead's eternal objects here once and for all in order to introduce Deleuze's virtual on its own terms into (my version of) Whitehead's cosmology, without having to perpetually shoehorn it into or awkwardly correlate it with Whitehead's eternal objects.

Whitehead's eternal objects never change. According to Whitehead, "There are no novel eternal objects [...]. The eternal objects are the same for all actual entities."[6] They are like generic qualities without particular instances. They perpetually exist, awaiting particular instantiations in the actual world. They change the actual world, not by ever changing or adding variety to themselves outside of actuality, but by the different *ways in which* they ingress into the actual world. In any theory involving emergence, there is always the nagging problem of how emergence itself emerges. The fact that there is a universe in which emergence and novelty occur at all must in some way be explained (since the universal propensity toward auto-emergence cannot itself have auto-emerged without there already having been a propensity toward auto-emergence in the universe). But Whitehead himself is less concerned with this question of origins. His operative question is not "*Why* is there always something new?" but rather "*How* does the new come about?" Eternal objects play a part in Whitehead's cosmology, his system of how novelty enters the universe. Where or how the eternal objects themselves came about, Whitehead never really explains.

6   Ibid., 22–23.

Unlike Whitehead's eternal objects, Deleuze's virtual *does* change. The virtual is like an unactualized cloud of potentia, conditioned by and contingent upon the ongoing history of the actual world, awaiting ingression into the present actual world. Deleuze's virtual is a two-way street. It both receives from and feeds into the actual historical world. In this sense, Deleuze more successfully displaces the nagging question of origins. The present virtual is conditioned by the past actual, which itself was conditioned by a prior virtual, which was in turn conditioned by a prior actual, backwards toward the dawn of time. Throughout this book, I will substitute Deleuze's virtual for Whitehead's eternal objects.

In addition to all the prior actual entities that have occurred historically, the virtual participates in every immediate actual occurrence (every becoming). The virtual is related to what the medieval scholastic scholars translated into Latin from Aristotle as "potentia." Proust famously describes the virtual as "real without being actual, ideal without being abstract."[7] Not incidentally, Whitehead describes "the future" similarly: "The future is merely real, without being actual; whereas the past is a nexus of actualities."[8] The virtual is not simply anything that could ever possibly happen at any time in any place. It is itself contingent on all prior actual entities (becomings) up to that point. The virtual is not determined, or even pre-formed. It is not like a number of alternate futures all lined up and waiting to be selected. The virtual is more like a cloud of facts that could connect in any number of ways but which have not yet connected in any ways, and may never connect. The total "real" is thus comprised of both the virtual and the actual. "Actually

---

7   Marcel Proust, *Time Regained,* trans. Stephen Hudson (1931; Paris: Feedbooks, 2014), 142, http://www.feedbooks.com/book/1453/time-regained.

8   Whitehead, *Process and Reality,* 214.

real" means historically actualized, having come to pass. Every new historical actualization generates new potentia for the virtual real, which may then (or may never) be subsequently actualized. The virtual is thus never "actually real" (until it has been actualized, at which point it stops being virtual and starts being actual), but the virtual is nonetheless always "real."

It is not such a stretch to swap Deleuze's virtual for Whitehead's eternal entities. Whitehead himself explains:

> The definite ingression [of an eternal entity] into a particular actual entity is not to be conceived as the sheer evocation of that eternal object from "not-being" into "being;" it is the evocation of determination out of indetermination. Potentiality becomes reality [...]. If the term "eternal objects" is disliked, the term "potentials" would be suitable.[9]

Whitehead's term "potentials" is not so far from Deleuze's term "virtual," in the sense that both are "real," just not "actual." There is, however, the important distinction that, whereas Deleuze's virtual both receives from and feeds back into the actual, Whitehead's potentials are a one-way street, always feeding into but never receiving from the actual.

Having injected Deleuze's virtual into Whitehead's scheme, I will continue to explain the scheme. All prior actual entities/occasions color but don't absolutely determine the present actual entity/occasion. The present actual entity decides the way in which it will go based on which prior actual entities it positively prehends, which it negatively prehends, which aspects of the virtual it positively prehends, and which it negatively prehends. From this perspective, we are thinking of the actual occa-

9   Ibid., 149.

sion/entity as a kind of deciding subject-in-the-making, where its decisions will constitute the subject that it becomes. As it decides and prehends, all relevant prior actual entities and all relevant virtual potentia enter into that present tense actual entity, and it emerges as a kind of decided historical entity which then will have a subsequent effect on other actual entities to which it is antecedent. These "prehensions" (from the perspective of the event as subject) and "ingressions" (from the perspective of the rest of the universe as object) all constitute the act of "concrescence" (from both subject and object perspectives). Whereas Whitehead reserves the term "ingression" for eternal objects only, I will simply use "ingression" as the inverse of "prehension." In my use of the term, the virtual may ingress into a present actual entity, and other prior actual entities may also ingress into a present actual entity. The act of concrescence is the immediate event of the actual entity that results in its new availability to be prehended by subsequent actual entities in their own immediate processes. Or, to get inordinately ontological about it, the act of concrescence "is" itself the actual entity/occasion.

Additionally, Whitehead's cosmology includes the concept of "propositions," which are like lures to feeling and becoming. A proposition exerts a kind of affective, aesthetic pull on the actual entity. The proposition's most prized characteristic is not that it is true, but that it is interesting. (Indeed, according to Whitehead, "The importance of truth is, that it adds to interest."[10]) From this perspective, a proposition is less like a "thing" and more like a force. To further modify Whitehead's cosmology, I am going to bracket his use of the term "proposition," and set it aside for later to describe a particular function of the art apparatus itself. Once an art apparatus exists in

10   Ibid., 259.

the world, its very existence becomes a kind of proposition-generator, a lure for future becomings.

If all of these descriptions seem maddeningly vague, it is in part because our language cannot even begin to speak without first presuming a pre-existent subject acting on a pre-existent object. What is required is not merely the linguistic substitution of verbs for nouns, but the rethinking of our fundamental cosmology. Whitehead himself cautions that his cosmology is bound to seems paradoxical and nonsensical

> if you will persist in thinking of the actual world as a collection of passive actual substances with their private characters or qualities [...]. So long as this conception is retained, the difficulty is not relieved by calling each actual substance an event, or a pattern, or an occasion.[11]

And so, we must not merely re-phrase the world, we must re-think the world according to process philosophy.

Whitehead's actual entity/occasion is both subject and object, emerging as a "superject." It is not totally free to determine its own becoming (since it must necessarily respect the prior decisions of other actual entities that have preceded it), but neither is it totally bound and determined to become a certain way. It is able to enact a kind of real-time decision in terms of the way it becomes; and in so doing, it exercises its own agency and causes the new to enter into the world. The becoming of an actual entity/occasion is its concrescence. Whitehead succinctly sums up the dual subject/object nature of the concrescence of each actual entity:

---

11   Alfred North Whitehead, *Symbolism, Its Meaning and Effect* (Cambridge: Cambridge University Press, 1958), 26.

> Every condition to which the process of becoming conforms in any particular instance has its reason *either* in the character of some [other] actual entity in the actual world of that concrescence, or in the character of the subject which is in process of concrescence.[12]

In Whitehead's scheme, all prior actual entities throughout the entire universe are potentially relevant to the decision of every immediate actual entity. Most of these prior actual entities are "negatively prehended": they are simply ignored as not mattering and thus do not ingress into the current actual entity. Nevertheless, according to Whitehead, "If we allow for degrees of relevance, and for negligible relevance, we must say that every actual entity is present in every other actual entity."[13] In being negatively prehended, these prior actual entities don't disappear from the universe. They just remain and await future ingression (or negative prehension) by any subsequent actual entities. The only actual entities that do not play a part (via either ingression or negative prehension) are concurrent actual entities, since they are happening at the same time, and have thus not yet made their decision to become anew, in which case they cannot yet have emerged to become relevant (or irrelevant) to any other actual entities concurrently becoming with them. They can't yet matter (or even not matter). Also, technically, future actual entities are irrelevant to current actual entities; but since virtual potentia are arguably relevant to any future actual entities that have not yet emerged, future actual entities (although non-existent) are implicitly relevant to present tense actual entities via the potentia of the virtual.

The becoming of an actual entity does not always result in radical novelty. As a matter of fact, most becom-

---

12 Whitehead, *Process and Reality*, 24.
13 Ibid., 50.

ings do not lead to radical novelty. Most actual entities choose to negatively prehend the novel options provided them by a universe of prior actual entities coming into contact with virtual potentia. In other words, most actual entities choose merely to prehend and thus replicate the bare facts of the relevant actual entities that preceded them, without adding much novelty to their own concrescences. But to choose to duplicate the past without adding relevant novelty is still an active decision.

Before continuing, a couple of obvious questions naturally arise. Frist, what on earth are actual entities, actually? Give me an example? Actual entities are also known as actual occasions, and to me, they make most sense when thought of as occasions. An actual entity/occasion is a tiny decision. An aggregate number of related actual occasions may accrete over time to form an "enduring object." Electrons, molecules, rocks, animals, humans, and planets are all enduring objects (more or less).

Whitehead considers electrons and humans in this same ontological category, namely that of "[enduring] organisms [with a life-history] which have attained to unity of experience."[14] He explains, "A nexus of many actualities [actual occasions] can be treated as though it were one actuality. This is what we habitually do in the case of the span of life of a molecule, or of a piece of rock, or of a human body."[15] And again, "A historic route of actual occasions, each with its presented duration, constitutes a physical object."[16]

Regarding humans, Whitehead cryptically explains, "Each time [a human] pronounces, 'I am, I exist,' the actual occasion, which is the ego, is different; and the 'he' which is common to the two egos is an eternal object or,

---

14 Whitehead, *Symbolism, Its Meaning and Effect*, 28.
15 Whitehead, *Process and Reality*, 287.
16 Ibid., 321.

alternatively, the nexus of successive occasions."[17] Since I have chosen to remove eternal objects from my adaptation of Whitehead, we are left with his alternative explanation that a persistent human ego (whatever an "ego" even actually is) is a nexus of successive actual occasions. Similarly, regarding very large rocks, Whitehead less cryptically explains, "The Castle Rock at Edinburgh exists from moment to moment, and from century to century, by reason of the decision effected by its own historic route of antecedent occasions."[18] In other words, a rock is a series of historically related and self-similar actual occasions that have accreted over time.

Regarding molecules, Whitehead says:

A molecule [...] is not an actual occasion; it must therefore be some kind of nexus of actual occasions. In this sense it is an event, but not an actual occasion. The fundamental meaning of the notion of "change" is "the difference between actual occasions comprised in some determinate event."[19]

And again:

A molecule is a historic route of actual occasions, and such a route is an "event." Now the motion of the molecule is nothing else than the difference between the successive occasions of its life-history in respect to the extensive quanta from which they arise; and the changes in the molecule are the consequential differences in the actual occasions.[20]

17   Ibid., 75.
18   Ibid., 43.
19   Ibid., 73.
20   Ibid., 80.

So, over the aggregate life-history of an enduring object, the difference between one of its discrete actual occasions and another of its discrete actual occasions constitutes what we would call "change" in that enduring object. Actual occasions aggregate to form what we recognize as enduring objects, but no single actual occasion is itself an enduring object.

Regarding electrons, Whitehead says that "each electron is a society of electronic [actual] occasions, and each proton is a society of protonic [actual] occasions."[21] In other words, although there exist proton*ic* and electron*ic* actual occasions, electrons and protons themselves are not actual occasions. Whitehead comes closest to giving a specific example of an actual occasion in the following passage: "This epoch is characterized [...] by yet more ultimate actual entities which can be dimly discerned in the quanta of energy."[22] So, discrete quanta of energy, the charge differences between an electron's states, "dimly" reveal actual entities/occasions, but these quanta of energy are still not themselves actual entities/occasions.

So, what might an actual occasion actually be? When an isolated photon in a double slit apparatus commits to manifesting a particular observable value, that moment of commitment seems (to me) to be an actual occasion. Or so I infer. Whitehead himself never explicitly states this. He avoids so explicitly correlating his philosophy to quantum mechanics. Indeed, although Whitehead tells us what kinds of objects aggregated actual occasions become over time, and although he explains in detail the becoming process of actual occasions, he never gives us an explicit example of an actual occasion. This is because actual entities/occasions are not really "nouns" or "things" as we understand "things." Over time, actual occasions accrete to become enduring objects that

21 Ibid., 91.
22 Ibid.

we humans "symbolically" (Whitehead's term) interpret as things, but actual occasions themselves are not these things. That the fundamental building-blocks of the universe would not be "blocks" or "stuff" at all, but rather moments of aesthetic decision – this is the radical assertion of process philosophy. According to Whitehead, "'Actual entities' – also termed 'actual occasions' – are the final real things of which the world is made up. There is no going behind actual entities to find anything more real."[23] Personally, I find it thrilling (and terrifying) that the fundamental unit of Whitehead's entire cosmology (and, if he is to be believed, our entire universe) is nothing one can ever explicitly point to and say, "See there? That's it."

So, an isolated electron in a laboratory experiment is not an actual entity/occasion, and a rock in a field is not an actual entity/occasion. Instead, electrons and rocks are enduring objects, societies of actual historical occasions whose unity is due to the persistent relatedness of their individual occasions. The Great Pyramid of Giza is one such enduring object. Each of its actual occasions have decided, moment-by-moment, time-after-time, to (continue to) be, more or less (a bit of sand gained here, a bit of brick lost there), a big giant pyramid.

Why do we humans perceive a world full of persistent enduring objects rather than a world full of fleeting momentary actual occasions? Truth be told, some neurodiverse humans don't perceive a world full of persistent enduring objects. They perceive the world altogether differently. But for me at least, it is easier to pick up a hammer and use it to hammer a nail if I read the hammer and nail as discrete objects rather than as aggregate societies of momentary occasions. But quantum mechanics problematizes our anthropocentric, classical/Newtonian assumption of the present-at-hand object-ness of

23   Ibid., 18.

the world. As Whitehead observes, "Mankind made an unfortunate generalization from its experience of enduring objects. Recently physical science has abandoned this notion."[24] And elsewhere, "We find ourselves in a buzzing world, amid a democracy of fellow creatures; whereas, under some disguise or other, orthodox philosophy can only introduce us to solitary substances, each enjoying an illusory experience."[25]

Another obvious question is, how on earth can an occasion "decide" anything? This question arises from the inherent subject/object divide built into our language, and from a kind of anthropocentrism that associates "decision" with "human decision." But according to quantum mechanics, a single isolated electron, when "invited" by a particular apparatus (double-slit, pre-which-path) to "commit to" a definite position, is left largely to its own devices to "decide" where it might land. Granted, it is not totally free to land anywhere. It is (somehow) constrained by the quantum waveform equation. But within the range of the predictable waveform pattern of position probabilities, each individual electron may land anywhere it chooses. In other words, once the predictive waveform pattern has done its generalized predicting, there is no further predicting exactly where that exact particle position might be.

So "decide" turns out to be a fairly decent word to describe such human-undecidable behavior. Whereas Newtonian (classical) mechanics claimed that the exact measurement of an object's position could be determined if only we had enough input data, quantum mechanics (or at least the most convincing interpretations of it) claims that we can have all the data available in the universe about an isolated particle's observable "properties" (and indeed we do, in the quantum waveform), and still

24   Ibid., 35.
25   Ibid., 50.

we are not able to predict beforehand the precise value of those properties. This is because the "properties" do not yet exist until the particle (having been insistently invited by the measuring apparatus to do so) "decides" what those properties are.

Another obvious question is, how exactly does a "prehension" function? Whitehead explains, "I have adopted the term 'prehension,' to express the activity whereby an actual entity affects its own concretion of other things."[26] According to Whitehead's cosmology, there are two kinds of prehensions: conceptual prehensions and physical prehensions. Physical prehensions happen when a present-tense actual occasion simply incorporates into itself the bare, factual data that are the other prior actual occasions relevant to it. Conceptual prehensions involve novelty and virtual potentia. Conceptual prehensions imagine how things may have been otherwise. They affect the quality, the affective *ways in which* physical prehensions occur. They involve what whitehead calls "mentality," but this is by no means an exclusively human mentality related to conscious human thought, any more than Whitehead's term "decision" is an exclusively human action related to conscious human will.

Whitehead explains, "Here I am using the term 'mind' to mean the complex of mental operations involved in the constitution of an actual entity. Mental operations do not necessarily involve consciousness."[27] He elaborates:

A single [actual] occasion is alive when the subjective aim which determines its process of concrescence has introduced a novelty of definiteness not to be found in the inherited data of its primary phase. The novelty is introduced conceptually and disturbs the inherited

26   Ibid., 52.
27   Ibid., 85.

"responsive" adjustment of subjective forms. It alters the "values," in the artist's sense of that term.[28]

And finally:

Each actuality [actual occasion] is essentially bipolar, physical and mental, and the physical inheritance is essentially accompanied by a conceptual reaction partly conformed to it, and partly introductory of a relevant novel contrast, but always introducing emphasis, valuation, and purpose. The integration of the physical and mental side into a unity of experience is a self-formation which is a process of concrescence.[29]

As I interpret these passages, actual occasions inject a kind of aesthetic choice (a desire, a valuation of options, a preferential opinion) into their own self-becomings; and in so doing, they add novelty to the world. Novelty is injected not by the lockstep repetition of prior data, but by the aesthetic arrangement of prior data into new constellations. These new aesthetic arrangements emerge as their own new data, to be further "remixed" (my term, not Whitehead's) by subsequent actual occasions. Novelty enters the world not by means of the noun, or even by means of the verb, but by means of the adverb, the how, the way-in-which. Or, as Brian Massumi concisely asserts, "To explain away the qualitative factors of experience is to explain away potential."[30]

Whitehead, more rigorous and specific than I, describes his own philosophy best in the following passages [my comments in brackets]:

28 Ibid., 104.
29 Ibid., 108.
30 Brian Massumi, "Virtual Ecology and the Question of Value," in *General Ecology: The New Ecological Paradigm*, ed. Erich Hörl (London: Bloomsbury, 2017), 350.

Regarding starting with becomings (verbs) rather than objects (nouns), he states:

> The philosophies of substance [Newtonian-based philosophies] presuppose a subject which then encounters a datum, and then reacts to the datum. The philosophy of organism [Whitehead's philosophy] presupposes a datum which is met with feelings, and progressively attains the unity of a subject.[31]

Regarding the defining role that process plays in reality: "Nothing is finally understood until its reference to process has been made evident."[32] And again, "Existence' (in any of its senses) cannot be abstracted from 'process'."[33]

Regarding the dual role that prior historical decisions (permanence) and immediate novel decisions (flux) play in reality:

> In the inescapable flux, there is something that abides; in the overwhelming permanence, there is an element that escapes into flux.[34]

> The creativity transcends the world already actual, and yet remains conditioned by that actual world in its new impersonation.[35]

> Order entering upon novelty; so that the massiveness of order does not degenerate into mere repetition; and so that the novelty is always reflected upon a background of system.[36]

---

31 Whitehead, *Process and Reality*, 155.
32 Alfred North Whitehead, *Modes of Thought* (New York: The Free Press, 1968), 46.
33 Ibid., 96.
34 Whitehead, *Process and Reality*, 338.
35 Ibid., 237.
36 Ibid., 339.

Finally, there are two ultimate types of existence im-
plicated in the creative process, the eternal forms with
their dual existence in potential appetition and in realized fact, and realized fact with its dual ways of existence as the past in the present and as the immediacy
of the present. Also, the immediacy of the present har-
bours an appetition towards the unrealized future.[37]

Freedom, givenness, potentiality, are notions which
presuppose each other and limit each other.[38]

Whitehead's cosmology does indeed provide a kind of
exciting freedom (a sense of adventure) from an overly
deterministic Newtonian universe, but the freedoms
Whitehead posits are always contingent upon the prior
decisions that the rest of the universe has made, decisions which were themselves also contingent upon prior
decisions, etc. The entire universe simply takes its own
self into account from an infinite number of different
perspectives, moment by moment by moment.

To think of it from a particularly human perspective
(since humans are themselves ever-becoming enduring
objects in the universe), If an immediate decision of mine
is to become actually real, if it is to actually matter in the
universe, then it must have some bearing on subsequent
decisions made by subsequent actual entities in the universe. My immediate decision may be ignored (negatively
prehended) or factored into (prehended by) a future actual occasion in some remote way as to be practically inconsequential, but it must be an actual part of the overall
environment of the universe, an environment which is
itself collaboratively and perpetually being made by the
immediate decisions of all the actual entities in the universe. Just as my immediate decision must be given care

37 Whitehead, *Modes of Thought*, 84–85.
38 Whitehead, *Process and Reality*, 133.

by those subsequent to me (however remotely, obliquely, or even negatively), I too must necessarily give care to all of the immediate decisions of others (and myself) made prior to me (however remotely, obliquely, or even negatively). According to Whitehead's cosmology, that is the way the universe proceeds.

Fortunately, "giving care" to all the prior immediate decisions in the universe doesn't happen human-consciously. That would be an impossible and exhausting ethical task. For "me" as a human (a "human" being a large, clumped, well-decided, ongoing society of actual occasions), most of the immediate decisions "I" enact in micro-second actual occasions never reach the level of my consciousness.

Contingency upon History

The contingency of immediate actual entities upon past actual entities cannot be overemphasized. Arguably, this contingency aspect of Whitehead's process philosophy is the least sexy, least novel, least experimental, least liberating aspect of the concrescence event. It seems like some drab and deterministic holdover from the world of Newtonian cause-and-effect law. Experimenting with isolated particles in well-prepared and shielded apparatal environments measuring brave new quantum superposition behaviors, one is tempted to believe that all electrons inherently want to remain in undecided states of quantum superposition, and if we would just stop imposing our human will on them by forcing them through our scientific apparatus obstacle courses, a much more malleable universe would emerge. Unfortunately (and fortunately), this is simply not the case.

The majority of rocks that have become rocks didn't become rocks solely because of human observation, measurement, or interference. They themselves decided to become rocks (in their own rocky and particulate way of "deciding"). Most of the molecules in a rock are not perpetually desiring to be free of their aggregated rock state. Indeed, moment by moment, actual occasion by actual occasion, most rock molecules choose to ignore the opportunity to be elsewhere and instead choose to remain in their molecular societies within their larger rocky societies. The size, scale, and singular position of a rock are a byproduct of prior decisions made by the society of occasions that are the rock, in collaboration with the rest of the (observing, semi-ingressing, mostly negatively prehended) universe. The successive actual occasions in any society known as rock choose to remain relevant to each one another, and subsequently grow, coalesce, cool, and compress – all depending on the past activities of the rock and its collaborations with the rest of the universe via the process of moment-by-moment concrescence. I may do what I want with a rock (throw it, break it up, use it to build a monument), but I may not return it to its elementary particles simply by replacing my old Newtonian cosmology with a more accurate quantum cosmology. The rock has its own history (one which does happen to include me, however obliquely, at least for the past few decades since I've had my own history in our shared universe), and the universe impels "me" to attend to the rock's history.

Even in the scientific laboratory, most experiments which mean to "measure" quantum behavior must carefully prepare their own initial states. For example, in certain experiments, pairs of photons are initially entangled via spontaneous parametric down conversion so that their polarizations become correlated. This is achieved by sending a laser beam (itself already a kind of prepared photon entanglement) through a beta-barium borate crystal. Thus, in most cases, for quantum behavior to be experimentally "observed," a kind of ideally "measurable," neutral, non-contingent, "coherent" initial state must be created. Particles must be disentangled from any prior, relevant, contingent histories they have developed with other entities, themselves, and the rest of the universe, in order to afford them the kind of free agency that quantum-behavior-measuring apparatuses intend to measure. Once that ideal initial state is achieved, all sorts of surprising and novel "quantum" behaviors become measurable. By "measurable," I simply mean that the particles and the measuring apparatus prehend and are prehended by one another, and this mutual prehension itself constitutes the act of "measurement." Once this new prehension occurs, in order for any of those same particles to be re-measured (with any "meaningful" "measurement" outcome), they must again be re-prepared in a newly quarantined "initial state."

These experimental initial states are rarely found readymade, unshielded, unentangled, and cohered in the universe proper. They must be carefully prepared. If this preparation were not so vital and precarious to "observable" quantum behavior, we would have already easily developed a powerfully functional quantum computer. Since these initial states must themselves be prepared, they are not technically "initial." They are initial to the overall phenomenal context of the measuring apparatus, but beyond that context, they themselves are also contingent to the prior decisions of the other actual entities in the universe. If this were not so, their quarantined self-cohesion would not have to be purposefully prepared from a prior state of entanglement with the rest of the universe.

Once these initial experimental states have been prepared, Karen Barad may indeed claim that "relata do not preexist relations; rather relata-within-phenomena emerge through specific intra-actions."[39] But, prior to a prepared experimental state, it may not be claimed that

39 Karen Barad, *Meeting the Universe Halfway* (Durham, North Carolina: Duke University Press, 2007), 140.

relations precede relata, else there would be no need for the preparation of a coherent "initial" experimental state. All the universe would be a ready-made laboratory of pure potentia and pure relations (prepositions, if you will) waiting to manifest themselves in subsequent relata (nouns). Instead, according to Whitehead, all of the prior actual entities/occasions and decisions in the universe come to bear and are relevant upon each new, immediate act of concrescence. Prior actual entities do not fully determine each new act of concrescence, but neither are they irrelevant to each new act of concrescence. If prior actual entities were irrelevant, if their historically concresced relations (their chosen societies) had no bearing or precedence on new, immediate decisions being made by other actual entities/occasions, then electrons out in a field of rocks would be completely free, always and perpetually, to determine whether or not they manifested themselves as having momentum or position; we would live in a world of perpetually undecided and superimposed waves/particles; and each present decision would be eternally reversible – fully malleable and thus fully inconsequential.

Whether or not, at the dawn of time, the universe itself began with relations (prepositions) or relata (nouns) is a chicken or egg question of cosmological origins which we will briefly address (and fail to answer) later in this chapter. But whichever came first cosmically and historically, the two have been cycling into one another ever since: prior relata (past actual entities) ingressing into new relations (immediate actual entities/occasions) which themselves then emerge as new relata (recently accreted actual entities and communities of entities) which are then further ingressed into new relations (the next wave of immediate actual entities/occasions), etc. According to Whitehead,

It must be remembered that just as the relations modify the natures of the relata, so the relata modify the nature of the relation. The relationship is not a universal. It is a concrete fact with the same concreteness as the relata.[40]

Martin Savransky further elucidates:

It's not just, then, that the world is relational, that relationality is original whereas societies are derivative [...]. Rather, to resist the danger of relational reductionism, I suggest we must come to terms with a world made, dynamically, of the shifting modes of mattering of societies-and-relations all the way down, all the way back. Paying close attention to those modes or manners, and to their dynamic natures, becomes, thus, the task of an ethics concerned [...] with the fragile and dynamic problem of co-existence of the many modes of mattering that compose the world in its becoming.[41]

For a contemporary artist, it is standard operating procedure to take into account the prior history of her materials, and to purposefully prepare the initial states of her materials (or to purposefully leave their initial states unprepared, depending on the conceptual goals of the artwork). Materials have their own agency, as the saying goes. I may not simply impose my human will on them at will. I may cut against the grain of wood if I wish, but my blade will get some push-back from the wood. The common admonition to the contemporary artist is to "let matter matter." The more nuanced Whiteheadian version might be: "let the prior decisions of the rest of the

---

40 Alfred North Whitehead, *Adventures of Ideas* (New York: The Free Press, 1967), 157.
41 Martin Savransky, "Modes of Mattering: Barad, Whitehead, and Societies," *Rhizomes: Cultural Studies in Emerging Knowledge* 30 (2016): 8–9.

universe matter, and co-negotiate with these decisions, keeping in mind that 'matter' is less of a noun object and more of an accreted series of collaborative events." Not quite as catchy, but this fine-grained awareness of matter as an ongoing series of accreting, concrescing events will become important as we begin thinking about art apparatuses. Without a care for the prior decisions of actual entities/occasions, I risk acting with a sense of faux-agency, believing in a universe more malleable than it actually is (or malleable in ways it simply is not), and I risk a kind of discourtesy toward the prior historical decisions of actual entities.

Before proceeding to the much more exciting and theoretically radical aspects of the concrescence event (namely the immediate act of decision made during the actual occasion), I must here allow Whitehead a few final, clarifying comments on historical contingency and its relationship to novel creation: "The process creates itself, but it does not create the objects which it receives as factors in its own nature."[42] "No event can be wholly and solely the cause of another event. The whole antecedent world conspires to produce a new occasion."[43] "In the full concrete connection of things, the characters of the things connected enter into the character of the connectivity which joins them."[44] And, relevant even to prepared and quarantined individual photons, "There is no element in the universe capable of pure privacy."[45]

Immediate Decisions That Matter

Fortunately, the act of concrescence is not wholly dependent upon and totally determined by the prior histor-

42 Whitehead, *Adventures of Ideas*, 179.
43 Whitehead, *Modes of Thought*, 164.
44 Ibid., 58.
45 Whitehead, *Process and Reality*, 212.

ical decisions of prior actual entities; for, as Whitehead explains, "'Decided' conditions are never such as to banish freedom. They only qualify it. There is always a contingency left open for immediate decision."[46]

Whitehead occasionally uses the term "decision" when describing the freedom of actual entities to positively prehend and negatively prehend that which ingresses into them and thus creates the new. From an artistic, curational, and DJ/remix perspective, these types of "decisions" seem most analogous to creative curatorial remix choices which, when integrated in a rigorous, fine-grained way, result in a novel output that becomes more than the mere sum of its sources. From this remix culture perspective, such prehensions and ingressions are "aesthetic" choices. If the terms "decision" and "aesthetic" seem problematically anthropocentric when applied to non-human entities, then Whitehead's regular use of the terms "zest," "appetition," and "feeling" will seem even more problematic. But, in the same way that Niels Bohr inherited terms from classical Newtonian physics ("cause/effect," "object," "property," "observable," "particle," "wave," "measurement," "outcome") and was forced to re-apply them in new ways to describe radically new quantum behaviors, Whitehead is simply using terms that have historically been applied to humans and re-applying them to describe behaviors not previously attributed to non-human entities.

So, for instance, Whitehead (re-)defines "appetition" as "the feeling of determinate relevance to a world about to be."[47] He describes actual entities as having "a zest for the enhancement of some dominant element of feeling."[48] Elsewhere he refers to "the form of blind zest."[49] He de-

46 Ibid., 284.
47 Ibid., 163.
48 Ibid., 188.
49 Ibid., 163.

scribes the act of concrescence as an event whereby "a feeling appropriates elements of the universe, which in themselves are other than the subject; and absorbs these elements into the real internal constitution of its subject by synthesizing them in the unity of an emotional pattern expressive of its own subjectivity."[50]

To rightly understand the role that immediate decision plays in concrescence/becoming, it is essential to understand that, in Whitehead's cosmology, the universe and all of its actual entities are perpetually striving for novelty. The universe inherently wants to become new. Whitehead describes the entire universe as "a creative advance into novelty."[51] In order for this advance to happen, real difference must actually be allowed to differ. The "subjectivity" of the actual entity enters into play and makes novel decisions that are truly unforeseeable. These decisions result in its own self-constitution.

In the following passage, Whitehead explains the free-ranging subjectivity that "any one actual entity" has in the exercising of its own immediate prehensions:

Any item of the universe, however preposterous as an abstract thought, or however remote as an actual entity, has its own gradation of relevance, as prehended, in the constitution of any one actual entity: it might have had more relevance; and it might have had less relevance, including the zero of relevance involved in the negative prehension; but in fact it has just that relevance whereby it finds its status in the constitution of that actual entity [...]. In the constitution of an actual entity: whatever component is red, might have been green; and whatever component is loved, might have been coldly esteemed.[52]

50   Ibid., 275.
51   Ibid., 28.
52   Ibid., 148–49.

To rephrase this passage from the perspective of DJ/re-mix culture, each actual entity of the universe samples and remixes into itself those prior aspects of the universe it finds most relevant.

Whitehead further elaborates on this subjective appropriation-as-(self-)becoming process: "Dead datum" from the past is met and "universalized into a character of creativity by the vivifying novelty of subjective form selected from the multiplicity of pure potentiality."[53] (Here "pure potentiality" might be interpreted to correspond with Deleuze's "virtual.") Whitehead continues, "They are the creation of their own creature [...]. The actual entity, in a state of process during which it is not fully definite, determines its own ultimate definiteness."[54] "What was received as alien, has been recreated as private."[55]

To proceed with the DJ/remix analogy (and in all earnestness), it is as David Bowie observes, "I am the DJ / I am what I play." Or, as composer and musician Ornette Coleman noted regarding the elements which emerge during improvisational free jazz performances, "None of these forms existed before their relation to each other."[56] In *Difference and Repetition*, Gilles Deleuze speaks of "that precise point at which the determined maintains its essential relation with the undetermined."[57] In Whitehead's cosmology, that point is the creative act of concrescence. What emerges each time is a novel actual entity/occasion, which is immediately added back the universe from whence it has just emerged. By this ongoing process of

53 Ibid., 164.
54 Ibid., 255.
55 Ibid., 213.
56 Ornette Coleman, liner notes of *Naked Lunch: Music from the Original Motion Picture Soundtrack*, Milan America, 1992, quoted in Timothy S. Murphy and Daniel W. Smith, "What I Hear is Thinking Too: Deleuze and Guattari Go Pop," *ECHO: A Music-Centered Journal* 3, no. 1 (Spring 2001): 9.
57 Gilles Deleuze, *Difference and Repetition*, trans. Paul Patton (New York: Columbia University Press, 1994), 47.

concrescence, novelty is perpetually added to the universe.

Even immediate decisions to remain more or less the same are never decisions to remain exactly the same. With every new actual entity (even one that decides to remain the same), the universe itself is always made new, if for no other reason than that it is now comprised of one additional actual entity that has decided to remain the same. Like Melville's Bartleby, actual entities may prefer not to decide, but they cannot avoid deciding that they would prefer not to. As Marjorie Perloff observes of Gertrude Stein's prose, "Repeat the same and it is no longer the same."[58]

According to Whitehead's cosmology, then, how to actualize the virtual is no great pressing ethical issue, because the virtual is being actualized non-stop. I can't help but actualize the virtual, always already and evermore. The more pressing ethical question is: how to actualize the virtual in ways that matter (and to whom)? Sometimes the most ethical decision is simply to endure and remain. Yet even this seemingly "conservative" decision must be "progressively" made (and remade and remade) in an ongoing series of immediate decisions which continually make anew the same enduring society of entities (this rock, this tree, this swamp, these frogs, these humans, this home, this Large Hadron Collider).

Decoherence and Negative Prehension

According to quantum mechanical experimental results, certain properly prepared and isolated particles are deduced to be in a state of undecided superposition. They are undecided as to any specific "observable" "property"

---

58 Marjorie Perloff, "'Grammar In Use': Wittgenstein/Gertrude Stein/ Marinetti," *South Central Review* 13, nos. 2–3 (Summer–Autumn, 1996): 42.

– position and momentum being the most famous of the observables. In this properly prepared state, an electron, a photon, and sometimes even fairly large molecules have not yet committed to being in any particular position. Some people like to think they are in all possible positions simultaneously, but even that interpretation seems a bit too "decided." This raises the relevant and quite fair question, can a particle without a particular position even be considered a particle? Is a noun, thing, or object which is not yet located any single "where" even a noun yet? Furthermore, in the absence of any other environmental particles, to whom would it even be a noun? To itself?

More questions immediately arise. If these tiny particles are the fundaments of larger particles, then is this undecided superposition state the fundamental way in which larger particles behave? This must certainly not be the case, since all the rocks I have observed are in single, decided states rather than several superpositions simultaneously. Why? Maybe the rocks are really in multiple positions just like the isolated electrons, and my consciousness just makes them seem like they are in a singular state to me? No, that's hermetic solipsism, and stupid. (I have just dismissed the "many minds" interpretation of quantum behavior in a single sentence!) Perhaps we should return to our isolated and prepared electron and experiment on it a bit more. We discover that, if we construct the proper apparatus to measure electrons for rock-like behavior, that apparatus causes(?) the electrons to behave more like rocks. So, given this experimental result, maybe when I look at the rocks, my "measurement/ observation" of them causes them to immediately decide to settle down and commit to a single position. No, that's anthropocentric, human-consciousness magic, and stupid. (I have just dismissed the consciousness collapse interpretation of quantum mechanics in a single sentence!) Maybe each one of the myriad of possible rock superpositions does actually, ontologically exist in a myriad number of simultaneous, alternate, and perpetually multiplying and diverging worlds, and "I" just happen to be one of many alternate versions of myself, the one who just happens to be residing in this particular world. No, that's too mathematically convenient, and just plain stupid. (I have just dismissed the many worlds/universes interpretation of quantum mechanics in a single sentence!) Maybe there is no real quantum superposition state and we just think there is because we haven't yet discovered some currently hidden variables which would explain this behavior in terms of more normal (classical/Newtonian) physics. No, because increasingly sophisticated quantum-behavior-measuring experiments continue to indicate an increasingly definitive "no." (I have just dismissed the De Broglie–Bohm hidden variables interpretation of quantum mechanics in a single sentence!)

So what explanations remain? Maybe there is some discrete, universal, built-in, limit law on this type of superimposed behavior related to size, and once objects get above a certain specific size, they are forced to decide upon a singular position. No, because experiments on the border of microcosmic sizes and macrocosmic sizes (the "mesocosmic border") show no clear-cut line above which superposition stops (and things commit to being in one place) and below which superposition continues to be present. (I have just dismissed the scale-induced collapse interpretation of quantum mechanics in a single sentence!) Maybe these superpositions just sort of spontaneously decide of their own volition to collapse into a single position? No, because decoherence experiments are able to discern particular environmental factors which increase and decrease rates of decoherence. (I have just dismissed the spontaneous collapse interpretation of quantum mechanics in a single sentence!)

The remaining (satisfactory) explanation is known as decoherence theory, an explanatory theory to which I subscribe. I will describe my understanding of it in terms of Whitehead's cosmology, and in terms that will become particularly relevant to our pending consideration of art apparatuses. I begin with an explanation of "the measurement problem" in quantum mechanics; followed by a general philosophical observation that is not exactly from Whitehead, nor is it part of decoherence theory proper, but it is simply my own attempt to connect the two via some personal observations.

In quantum mechanics, there is something called "the measurement problem." The "problem" is that you can't measure a quantum entity without "causing" it to behave a certain way. You don't cause it to manifest a specific measurement outcome value (to land in a single specific position, for example). If you did, then scientific "measurement" (and, by extension, "science") as we have known it since Newton would be irrelevant, since outcomes would be completely subjective depending on the measuring apparatus you chose to use. Quantum behavior doesn't eradicate scientific measurement altogether, but it does change our fundamental understanding of "measurement." If I choose one type of apparatus, I cause the particle on which I am experimenting to manifest one observable (for example, position). If choose another type of apparatus, I cause the particle to manifest its complementary observable (the complementary observable of position is momentum). I can even set up a single apparatus which is able to measure the position of a particle with 75% certainty and its momentum with 25% certainty, or vice-versa, or 50/50, 60/40, etc. But if I am able to measure a particle's position with 100% certainty, I am 0% certain of its momentum.

This uncertainty is not the result of me being ignorant of inherent properties that the particle already possesses but which I am unable to fully measure (that would be the old Newtonian understanding of probability). This uncertainty is instead based on the fact that

the "particle" has not itself decided on its own properties until my measurement apparatus "invites" it to do
so, however gently (as in the 50% certain position/50%
certain momentum measuring apparatus) or insistently
(as in the 100% certain position/0% certain momentum
measuring apparatus). Neither is this uncertainty due to
the clumsiness of the apparatus itself. The apparatus is
not physically, mechanically, or thermodynamically (in
an old Newtonian sense) disrupting the particle. My uncertainty is not simply a technical problem of apparatus
construction and set-up (although it is often also that).
My uncertainty is a novel, quantum-specific, non-Newtonian kind of "problem." The cause of my uncertainty is
neither solely ontological (what is the nature of the thing
I am observing?) nor solely epistemological (what is the
nature of the way in which I am observing?). The cause of
my uncertainty is both ontological and epistemological
at the same time. According to prior philosophical models of substance, identity, property, space, and time, I'm
not supposed to have a single problem that is both ontological and epistemological at the same time. So, the fact
that my problem is truly ontico-epistemological implies
that the prior philosophical models which classified certain topics as ontological and others as epistemological
were based on prior, Newtonian-esque understandings of
subject/object, cause/effect, thing/event – understandings which need revisiting and revising.

Having said all that, I propose that the "measurement
problem" arises as a "problem" at all because to "measure"
is necessarily to break off a part out of a continuously
flowing and ever becoming holistic unity (the universe).
No measurement, no problem. If we could step outside of
the universe (a model Newtonian physics inherently presumes), we would be able to observe it as a holistic system
without having to take a cut out of it. But, since we can't
get outside of the universe, the best we can do is cut into
it from where we are within it, and then make mathemat-

ical and philosophical allowances for the fact that we are ourselves a part of the thing into which we are cutting. As science writer Jim Baggott observes, "We obviously have no way of observing an observer-independent reality."[59] The best we can hope for as human quantum scientists is to negotiate and account for the subject–object (super-ject) entanglements that arise within whatever particular chunk of the universe (i.e., the contextual phenomenon comprised of our apparatus, our measured particle, our contained system, and the surrounding universal environment) we choose to cut out and observe.

The problem gets even more difficult because (per Whitehead) the universe is verb-centric rather than noun-centric. If the unity of the universe were noun-based (comprised of discrete static objects), the measurement problem would merely be ontological. We could stand on one part of the universe as we cut out and observed another part of the universe. But since the unity of the universe is fundamentally verb-based (an ongoing, interconnected, holistic event/process of becoming), in order to carve out a "part" of it and "observe" that "part," we have to enact a measurement event that itself then immediately becomes a decision-making occurrence which immediately enters the rest of the holistic universe and becomes relevant to all of it, including the "part" we are trying to measure. You can stand on one part of a noun in order to observe and measure another part of the same noun without too much difficulty, but you cannot so easily stand on one part of an event in order to observe and measure the same event that you are measuring (an event which is, itself, your very act of measurement).

It would almost seem that quantum-behavior-measuring apparatuses would have to freeze time in order to

---

59 Jim Baggott, *Beyond Measure: Modern Physics, Philosophy, and the Meaning of Quantum Theory* (Oxford: Oxford University Press, 2004), 118.

make accurate measurements. But this won't do either, because "time" is not really a continuous, flowing, durational container which contains sequential events (that is the old Newtonian understanding of time). Instead, "time" itself is actually the byproduct, creation, result (and thus not merely the "container") of irreversible decision events (immediate actual entities) themselves. So, it is a tautology to appeal to time to resolve the measurement problem, since "time" itself is the result of irreversible decisions, one of which is "measurement" (by definition).

The point of thinking through these implications of a cosmology which considers the universe to be a contained holistic system in process is to foreground the important and fundamental fact that the measurement problem only emerges as a "problem" when we divide the holistic universe into sub-systems. Noted physicist and key developer of decoherence theory Wojciech H. Zurek observes, "In the absence of systems [...] the problem of interpretation [how to explain why the act of measurement forces certain observables to emerge] seems to disappear. There is simply no need for "collapse" [of the quantum wave function and its superposition of states] in a Universe with no systems."[60]

Physicist Maximilian Schlosshauer takes up Zurek's point and elaborates, "Moreover, terms like "observation," "correlation," and "interaction" will naturally make little sense without a division into systems. [Physicist and "father" of decoherence theory H. Dieter] Zeh has suggested that the locality of the observer defines an observation in the sense that any observation arises from the igno-

---

60 Wojciech H. Zurek, "Decoherence, Einselection, and the Quantum Origins of the Classical," *Reviews of Modern Physics* 75, No. 3 (2003): 718, doi:10.1103/RevModPhys.75.715. [Bracketed comments are mine.]

rance of a part of the universe, and that this locality also defines the "facts" that can occur in a quantum system."[61]

Schlosshauer goes on to cite mathematician N.P. Landsman for further clarification: "The essence of a "measurement," "fact" or "event" in quantum mechanics lies in the non-observation, or irrelevance, of a certain part of the system in question [...]. A world without parts declared or forced to be irrelevant is a world without facts."[62]

In other words (and to reiterate): no measurement, no problem. Here is Schlosshauer again, this time on the mathematics involved in a quantum-behavior-measuring apparatus: "Once the measurement axioms (and thus the trace rule [the mathematical trick which crosses-out all the "negatively prehended" potentia of the rest of the universe]) are dropped, we are left with a global entangled system-environment state that, according to the standard [quantum mechanical] interpretation, does not allow us to say anything about the physical state of the system or to assign a particular outcome (i.e., a definite value of a physical quantity) to the system."[63]

Returning now to Whitehead (indeed, I already took the liberty of inserting his concept of negative prehension into the preceding citation), a measurement made by a quantum-behavior-measuring apparatus might be said to constitute a nexus of actual entities/occasions wherein apparatus, particles, and sub-system all prehend one another and ingress into one another in an

---

61 Maximilian Schlosshauer, *Decoherence and the Quantum-To-Classical Transition* (Berlin: Springer, 2010), 102. [Bracketed comments are mine.]

62 N.P. Landsman, "Observation and Superselection in Quantum Mechanics," *Studies in History and Philosophy of Modern Physics* 26, no. 1 (1995): 45–46, quoted in Schlosshauer, *Decoherence and the Quantum-To-Classical Transition*, 102.

63 Schlosshauer, *Decoherence and the Quantum-To-Classical Transition*, 333. [Bracketed comments are mine.]

irreversible event. During this singular "measurement" event, all of the possible measurement outcomes (even the bizarre and logically contradictory ones) other than the actual(ized) measurement results are negatively prehended ("traced over" in quantum mathematical terms), and thus a specific concrescence occurs. According to Whitehead, "The togetherness of things involves some doctrine of mutual immanence. In some sense or other, this community of the actualities of the world means that each happening is a factor in the nature of every other happening."[64]

All well, good, and cosmic, but what still needs accounting for is all those rocks out sitting in that field! We didn't measure them with our scientific apparatuses in a way that helped actualize their singular, stable positions, so why are they sitting still? Why have they committed to a single, non-superpositional position? The answer which decoherence theory provides is that we humans and our scientific apparatuses are not the only things in the universe with magical "measuring" powers. Different parts of the universe take other parts of the universe into account perpetually. As Karen Barad profoundly and poetically observes, "Only part of the world can be made intelligible to itself at a time, because the other part of the world has to be the part that it makes a difference to."[65] In this sense, the universe effectively auto-measures itself, part by part. "Measurement" then, becomes kind of a silly, human-science-specific term for this process of taking-into-account. Whitehead's much more rigorous and precise words would be "prehension" (from the perspective of the immediate actual entity and what it decides to take into account as mattering in that moment), "negative prehension" (from the perspective of the immediate actual entity and what it decides to not take into account

64 Whitehead, *Modes of Thought*, 164.
65 Barad, *Meeting the Universe Halfway*, 432.

as mattering in that moment), "ingression" (from the perspective of those other prior actual entities which are taken into the account by the immediate actual entity as mattering in that moment), and finally "concrescence" (the name of this entire "measuring" event).

According to Zurek,

> Quantum theory has simultaneously deprived the "conscious observer" of a monopoly on acquiring and storing information: Any correlation is a registration [...]. Moreover, even a minute interaction with the environment, practically inevitable for any macroscopic object, will establish such a correlation: The environment will, in effect, measure the state of the object, and this suffices to destroy quantum coherence.[66]

I am inclined to call this measuring event a "taking-into-account," or more precisely (and more Appalachian) – a "reckoning." Not "reckoning" in the sense of a final, summative, doomsday tally, because these concrescent reckonings are happening every micro-second and lead into subsequent reckonings which lead into subsequent reckonings "to the crack of doom"[67] (in Whitehead's evocative prose). Instead, "reckoning" in the sense of being asked, "Would you like some of this pie?" and answering, "I reckon I would." In this kind of reckoning event, I take a reckoning of my appetite for pie at that moment; I eyeball and reckon the potential tastiness of the pie; I reckon I don't have too many chores left to accomplish that day; I reckon whether or not my waistline can handle the blow; I re-reckon the potential tastiness of the pie and reckon that I don't care about my waistline right now; and ultimately I decide that I would like to take that piece of pie

---

66 Wojciech H. Zurek, "Decoherence and the Transition from Quantum to Classical – Revisited," *Los Alamos Science* 27 (2002): 105.
67 Whitehead, *Process and Reality*, 228.

into my mouth and make it a part of me. Of course, this drawn out description of micro-reckonings actually occurs (more or less) as one single instantaneous reckoning. And of course, in this particular example, I'm describing a human-involved measuring event which would include some form of human consciousness; although, the more tasty-looking and tasty-smelling the pie, the more this particular reckoning event heads toward the proto-conscious, visceral, and affective.

But humans are not the only ones who may reckon. To Whitehead, consciousness is just the apex of being, but most things are "decided" in a human without ever reaching the level of consciousness. And in this Whiteheadian sense, particles, air molecules, rocks, and stomachs may also decide and reckon. It is curious that my reckoning of the pie would somehow make the pie a part of "me" before I ever even "physically" ate the pie. Newton would not be happy about this curiosity (all apple puns aside). But in the universe of quantum reckonings, everything takes everything else into account. Why was my reckoning of the pie not required in order to stabilize the position of the pie? Because different parts of the pie had already "self-reckoned" other parts of the pie all the way down to the molecules in the chemical ingredients used to make the pie.

Philosopher Michael Epperson's Whiteheadian interpretation of Quantum Mechanics (*Quantum Mechanics and the Philosophy of Alfred North Whitehead*) seems to suggest that all of these quantum reckonings "really" do affect the "potentia" of every other entity in the universe (recall that potentia are "real" but not "actual" in a Proust–Bergson–Deleuze sense), but that such quantum reckonings don't yet affect the "actual" real of every other entity in the universe. So, my reckoning of the pie has changed the virtual real relevant to the pie and myself. Some things are now able to happen in the world that were not able to happen prior to my reckoning of the pie; and (equally as important) some things are now *not* able to happen in the world. Furthermore, some things are more likely to happen; some things are less likely to happen; and most things in the universe will remain pragmatically (almost totally and utterly, but never wholly) indifferent to my reckoning of the pie. True, my immediate reckoning of the pie has not yet changed my waistline, because I have not yet actualized (in a Newtonian, thermodynamical sense) the ingression of the pie into my stomach. But my hankering for the pie has been actualized, whether or not I ever proceed to eat the pie. My hankering is no longer virtual potential. It is now actual potential.

The fact that virtual changes do *really* matter, even if they may never come be actualized, is a challenging concept from a Newtonian perspective. Prior to discovering and confirming quantum superimposition behavior, one could think of the real world as being solely comprised of that which is actual. The virtual was not real. There was no virtual. Any single outcome in the actual real world was bound and determined to actually happen. If you had enough actual real-world data, you could exactly predict any such single outcome, but your prediction would not determine the outcome. If you lacked enough actual real-world data, you could make a range of predictions based on the limited data you had, but the outcome was already going to happen regardless of your estimated range. Your probabilistic (non-deterministic, non-real) range would not affect the outcome. But according to quantum mechanics, the virtual probabilities accounted for in the quantum wave function are no longer non-real guesses. They are, instead, understood as a determined range of possible outcomes. An outcome in the overall range is bound to happen, but which single outcome will actually happen in each individual instance is impossible to pre-determine (even with all the data in the universe), because the exact outcome is not decided until that individual instance. The virtual (in the form of the quantum wave function) is actualized in each actual instance of decision. To me, such instances of immediate decision are examples of Whitehead's actual occasions/entities.

Newton underestimated the "reality" of the virtual because he misunderstood what "measurement" actually is. Measurement is cutting out one part of an ongoing, holistic universe event, and inviting it to return a specific measurable result. The "result" of the event is better understood as the concrescence, outcome, or having-become of a new actual occasion. As with all other actual occasions/entities in the universe, this "measurement" event is co-determined by its constituent participants. In the case of a laboratory measurement event, the participants are: the experimental apparatus, the quarantined sub-system, the participant particles, and the (negatively prehended) rest of the universe. It is wrong-headed to think that the experimental apparatus alone is solely responsible for the results. This would be uber-anthropocentric. It would mean we humans and our scientific apparatuses solely make the world. But it is also wrong-headed to think that the particles being "measured" alone are solely responsible for the results.

This latter flavor of wrong-headedness (attributing all the agency to the objects being measured) was Newton's mistake, and it is easy to see how he made it. Newton was (mostly) measuring complex, well-decided, apple-pie-type objects which had already measured themselves and been measured by their environment a billion times over. These objects had already experienced quantum decoherence. They had already chosen (and chosen and chosen) to remain together as enduring objects. Newton was not "freshly" measuring them in isolated, carefully prepared, pre-measurement states. He "ignored" the effect which his measuring apparatuses were having on these already well-decided, measured, and reckoned (societies of) entities because his measuring apparatuses were having a negligible effect on them. By "overestimating" the agency of the entities he was measuring, he was actually courteously "respecting" all of the prior decisions they had already made. Newton's objects sure seemed like they already knew what they wanted to be and do. A rock didn't need to be "invited" by a scale apparatus to know what it wanted to weigh. It already weighed what it weighed. At its well-decided, rock-level of entanglement and concrescence, its superpositional days were (almost entirely) over.

Newton's least forgivable (but still perfectly understandable) mistake was to impute these well-decided, rock-level characteristics to less decohered particles (like quantum-behaving photons) which were not so well decided. Yes, a rock seems to be a noun, with adjectival, preexistent properties. But a photon of light is not so much a noun with pre-existent, adjectival properties; as it is a particle/wave, verb/noun, entity/occurrence that still has all sorts of decisions to co-make with the rest of the universe regarding which property values it might even manifest at all. It took the development of quantum-behavior-measuring apparatuses (both gedanken and physical) to properly reckon what measurement itself even is.

What else must be said about decoherence theory? A proper definition might finally be in order: "The practically irreversible delocalization of phase relations into the composite system-environment state induced by inevitable and ubiquitous environmental monitoring constitutes precisely the process of decoherence."[68] Zurek most concisely defines decoherence as "environment-induced superselection." He explains, "Decoherence destroys superpositions. The environment induces, in effect, a superselection rule that prevents certain super-

---

68 Schlosshauer, *Decoherence and the Quantum-To-Classical Transition,* 69.

positions from being observed."[69] I would modify "being observed" to "actually existing," because I don't believe that the other unobserved superposition options are being observed in alternate universes, or by alternate states of mind. If the eigenstates (possible but as of yet unmanifested states) of the quantum waveform fail to ultimately manifest during environmentally induced superselection (i.e., decoherence), then they are nowhere else being "observed" by anyone or anything. They simply "remain" within the virtual real.

It is important to reiterate that decoherence is not solely (and certainly not inherently) based on an object's size or scale. Whether or not decoherence occurs, and even the rate at which it occurs, are contingent upon a number of actual factors. The size and number of particles in the environment which does the "measuring" do indeed factor into the rate of decoherence of the "measured" particle. But these are not the only factors. For example, it has been experimentally observed that "cryogenic temperatures suppress decoherence."[70] The colder the temperature, the larger an object can exist without decohering, so much so that "a cryogenic version of the Weber bar – a gravity-wave detector – must be treated as a quantum harmonic oscillator [exhibiting a quantum superposition of wave states] even though it may weigh a ton."[71] In 2002, Zurek and Harold Ollivier even devised an experimental means of measuring the relative quantumness (superpositional quantum behavior) vs. quasiclassicality (superselected and decohered "classical" behavior) of a single system.[72] Such experimental results on the "mesocosmic border" (the border between the microcosmic and the macrocosmic) indicate that deco-

---

69 Zurek, "Decoherence and the Transition from Quantum to Classical – Revisited," 105.
70 Ibid., 98.
71 Ibid., 88. [Bracketed comments are mine.]
72 Ibid., 95.

herence is a contingent and gradual (although, in most cases, near-immediate) process. In other words, there is no static, magical dividing line between quantum and classical behavior.

Still, as stated earlier, if quantum superposition happened all the time and all over the place at all scales, it would be quite easy to shield large objects from the effects of decoherence, and we would already have a working quantum computer. It is not and we don't. Yes, we live in a quantum world, all the way up and all the way down. But no, once decoherence has occurred, I can't treat a rock which has decided to decohere as if it could at any time be in a state of quantum superposition. Actually (or rather, virtually), there does exist a near-infinitely remote possibility that a rock sitting in a field could immediately change its position without anybody kicking it or throwing it in a Newtonian fashion, but this possibility is so remote as to be pragmatically nil.

An additional point to be made is that decoherence is itself a kind of quantum mechanical behavior. Thus, decoherence theory is not really a philosophical "interpretation" of quantum mechanical behavior. As explained by Schlosshauer, "Since decoherence is simply a consequence of a realistic application of the standard quantum formalism, it cannot by itself give an interpretation or explanation of this formalism."[73] As with a child perpetually asking "why?" about every subsequent answer she is given, eventually, all explanations of quantum mechanical behavior arrive at one of two places: 1. circular/tautological explanations ("it is this way because the abstract math by which we have chosen to understand it works out this way"); or 2. fundamental mystery and wonder

---

73 Maximilian Schlosshauer and Kristian Camilleri, "What Xlassicality? Decoherence and Bohr's Classical Concepts," *American Institute of Physics Conference Proceedings* 1327 [International Conference on Advances in Quantum Theory] (2011): 30.

("it behaves this way, but we don't know why"). Scientists are historically hesitant to accept result #2 without first rigorously researching all the unknown hidden variables until they discover a deeper layer of why. But when you finally get all the way to the bottom of physical behavior, and there are no more hidden variables, sometimes all you are left to do is speculate and wonder.

It is fascinating to me the particular kind of inexplicable wonder left standing when one pursues decoherence theory to its limits: namely, the wonder that measurements should have any outcomes at all. Again, I defer to Schlosshauer for a clear and concise explanation of this situation:

> The measurement problem, and the more general problem of the quantum-to-classical transition, is composed of three main issues:
>
> — The preferred-basis problem (what determines the preferred physical quantities of our experience?).
> — The problem of the nonobservability of interference (why is it so hard to observe interference effects?).
> — The problem of outcomes (why do measurements seem to have outcomes at all, and what selects the particular observed outcome?).
>
> [...] It is reasonable to conclude that decoherence is capable of solving the first two problems, whereas the third problem is intrinsically linked to matters of interpretation that are mostly outside of the scope of decoherence.[74]

Problem #1 (the preferred-basis problem, i.e., in the wild universe, beyond the quantum physics laboratory, why

---

74 Schlosshauer, *Decoherence and the Quantum-To-Classical Transition*, 112–13.

does the position observable manifest itself more readily than the momentum observable?) is particularly relevant to art apparatuses, because it pertains to the role apparatuses play in the overall collaborative measurement event. A quantum-behavior-measuring apparatus does not get to determine the particular measurement value (the particular momentum of the particle, or the particular position of the particle). But the apparatus does get to determine (with greater or lesser degrees of insistence) which of these two complementary observables (momentum or position) emerges. The quantum-behavior-measuring apparatus plays a part (the nature of what to measure), and the particle plays a part (the value of the actual measurement result).

But (asks the child) why? Why does the universe, when it goes to measure or observe other parts of itself, beyond the shielded and prepared environment of the quantum-behavior-measuring apparatus, always seem to prefer the position observable over the momentum observable? In other words, why do we live in a universe of mostly solid objects rather than a universe of mostly ephemeral events? Decoherence theory provides the circular, tautological explanation: During the decoherence event, the preferred-basis of "position" (usually) decoheres more quickly than the preferred-basis of "momentum." But why? And here decoherence theory is at a loss, and we arrive at fundamental mystery or wonder: The universe seems to want to behave this way (usually, at human-scale, in our corner of the universe), but we don't know why.

Problem #2 (the problem of nonobservability of interference, i.e., why do rocks in a field remain in a single position instead of bouncing around in superpositional flux?) is also relevant to art apparatuses, because it suggests that we must be careful and courteous toward our materials. Materials themselves measure each other and are measured by each other in ways that cause them to decohere and thus stop exhibiting interference effects (i.e., superpositionality). This is the answer that decoherence theory provides. But why? And here, decoherence theory is at a loss, and must turn to Whitehead, and to quantum consistent-history theories: Because immediate, actual occurrences/entities, when they prehend and negatively prehend the rest of the universe, make irreversible historical decisions which must be honored by all subsequent actual occurrences/entities. But why? Because, in the words of process philosopher and theologian George Hartshorne, "An actual world cannot be all possible worlds [...]. To be actual is to exclude some possibilities."[75] But why? Because the universe seems to want to behave this way, but we don't know why.

Problem #3 (why do measurements have outcomes at all, and what chooses these outcomes?). This is such a rich and peculiar question. I grudgingly admire the discipline of science for coming to the bottom of itself and arriving at such an unlikely, post-structuralist type of question. I suppose Whitehead would answer that it is because actual entities have appetitions and affections and affinities, and that they respond to lures and provocations in novel and original ways. But why? Because the universe seems to want to be new, but we don't know why.

Well-Decided Objects (Societies of Entities)

Whitehead has a special category for actual entities that have formed societies and endured. They are special not because they are large or even because they have decohered, but because they are (and this is my own term) "well-decided." With every new immediate actual occasion, each of these occasions has decided to continue to-

75 Charles Hartshorne, "Bell's Theorem and Stapp's Revised View of Space-Time," *Process Studies* 7, no. 3 (1977): 188, quoted in Epperson, *Quantum Mechanics and the Philosophy of Alfred North Whitehead*, 144.

gether as a society. More technically, each of these actual occasions has decided to attend to and replicate prior forms of being inherited from the bare factual, physical pole of antecedent actual occasions; rather than injecting novel inflections of being, via the mental pole, which could have been ingressed from the fecund potentia of the virtual. A rock is a society of entities, a human is a society of entities, and there is no special qualitative dividing line that makes one of these societies categorically different than the other. In other words, Whitehead didn't coin a new ontological category to describe a human; he kept using the same rock category. In his own words, "An ordinary physical object, which has temporal endurance, is a society."[76]

Of course, there are qualitative differences between these two enduring societies (rocks vs. humans), but as Martin Savransky explains:

> Societies are not grouped together just because they happen to have common characteristics, and their contrast with actual entities is not simply a matter of scale, or of mere quantity, but of organizational complexity – of modes of existence.[77]

Whitehead himself lists some of these different modes of existence:

> There is the animal life with its central direction of a society of cells, there is the vegetable life with its organized republic of cells, there is the cell life with its organized republic of molecules, there is the large-scale inorganic society of molecules with its passive acceptance of necessity derived from spatial relations, there

76 Whitehead, *Process and Reality*, 35.
77 Savransky, "Modes of Mattering," 7.

is the infra-molecular activity which has lost all trace of the passivity of inorganic nature on a larger scale.[78]

Although Whitehead refers to scale, the "actual" differences are relational rather than volumetric. Indeed, one could say that "size" is simply the byproduct of a well-decided and well-committed society of occasions, occasions that share a common history.

If decoherence theory explains the ways in which isolated individual entities lose their quantum superpositional behavior and enter into a kind of concrescent collaboration with the rest of the (observing) universe, then the theory of quantum mechanical "histories" explains the way a sequence of those decohered occasions persist as a single enduring object. In a sense, enduring societies of entities share a common history which continues to persist and endure due to an ongoing series of collective re-honorings of these common prior decisions. Or, in Whitehead's own words, "A vegetable is a democracy."[79] Let us return to the rock lying in the field. Each new occasion of the enduring object known as rock is not deterministically bound to honor the prior occasions of the rock; but ordinarily, in an enduring object like a rock, most new occasions do choose to re-honor these prior histories. To put it another way (in keeping with my Whitehead–Deleuze amalgamated cosmology), although each present-tense rock occasion could always be lured into activating its mental pole and ingressing novel potentia from the virtual into the concrescence of its own actual self-becoming, most rock occasions simply attend to the physical pole of the prior, actual, historical rock occasions, prehend them into itself, ignore (negatively prehend, fail to ingress) the novel virtual options, and perpetuate (more or less) the consistent history of

78 Whitehead, *Modes of Thought,* 164.
79 Ibid., 24.

the rock. To humans, such a series of ongoing decisions to re-up and re-integrate prior decided actual occasions without injecting virtual novelty into the present occasion appears exactly like a rock remaining in a field. But according to Whitehead's cosmology (and to quantum mechanics), a rock remaining in a field is actually a series of active decisions; whereas, according to Newtonian physics, the same rock remaining in a field exhibits an inert absence of action.

Whitehead's way of thinking is a very non-Newtonian way of thinking about large objects, particularly organic objects. But, to Whitehead, macroscopic and microscopic objects all participate in the same moment-by-moment process of concrescence. Michael Epperson describes the concrescence process from a "quantum histories" perspective: "A macroscopic material object [...] becomes characterized most fundamentally as a history of evolutions of discrete facts or events – evolutions from actuality to potentiality to actuality."[80] Epperson later describe the same process from (his version of) a Whiteheadian perspective:

> Classically described objects are more fundamentally described as historical routes of atomic events, where past events influence but do not determine future events. The universe is a multiplicity of such events, each of which evolves or becomes via a process of prehending and integrating all the antecedently actualized events (data) that the universe comprises. Some data are, of course, more relevant than other data; and indeed, most data once brought together by prehension are further integrated largely by elimination.[81]

---

80 Epperson, *Quantum Mechanics and the Philosophy of Alfred North Whitehead*, xii.
81 Ibid., 107.

How do these larger societies of entitites (rocks and such) stay together? By (mostly) ignoring all of the virtual potentia available, moment-by-moment, to each of their immediate actual entities, individually and collectively. They decide to remain and endure. But this is not a one-time decision. It is actively re-made moment-by-moment. Which means a variant decision may be made at any time, albeit contingent upon all prior actual entities in the universe. The new, variant decision may not vary wholly from the prior decisions. True, it is not slavishly bound to simply repeat the prior decisions exactly, but neither is it free to radically veer from the path of the prior decisions. The particular quality, flavor, and amount of novel potentia it may inject and inflect into its own present-tense self-becoming is itself conditioned by prior actual occasions on two counts: 1. because the present-tense occasion in question must begin with and can only "launch or veer from" the prior actual occasions leading up to it; and 2. because the virtual potentia itself (according to Deleuze's scheme, not Whitehead's) is conditioned by the prior actual history of the entire universe. Each present-tense actual occasion is constrained in these two ways, locally (from whence it begins, in the actual, according to its physical pole) and universally (from whence the rest of the universe begins at the time of its concrescence, in the virtual, according to its mental pole). Each present-tense actual occasion may be said to have a modicum of freedom and agency, which is directly derived from, contingent upon, and made possible by its own inherent conformity to the prior actual histories of "itself" and of the rest of the universe.

By ethical implication, then, to imagine that a rock (society) somehow desires to return to the primordial indeterminate state of its individual electrons, and that I (a human society) am its ethical ally in helping it return to that "liberated" state of increased undecidability, is to discourteously ignore the prior, historical (co-)affections/decisions of the (society known as) rock. Indeed, I will have to work hard against the rock to return it to that dis-integrated state. An isolated electron, on the other hand, is more playfully indifferent (open?) to my experimental interferences.

"Entity" in Whitehead's sense doesn't really mean "thing" in any sort of noun-y, Heideggerian sense (however orthodoxically or inventively Heidegger is interpreted). "Entity" means close to what Barad calls "phenomenon," and aspects of that phenomenon.[82] So, the noun-ness of the "entity" is not the issue. Indeed, to Whitehead, entities are mostly occasions (although they are also sometimes ideas and sometimes societies of occasions, both of which may be thought of as noun-y things). The noun-ness of entitites matters less to Whitehead than what Barad might call agential cuts – entangled historic ingressions. These ingressions must be respected, because they have historically occurred, in the actual real (and not just the virtual real).

A brief word about humans. Because humans are also well-decided, enduring objects, and because books like this are usually written by and for humans, we humans tend to have a kind of vested interest in ourselves. I have and will continue to use "actual entities" and "actual occasions" interchangeably, occasionally combining them into "actual entities/occasions." Each term describes the same "thing," but there is a kind of anthropocentric tendency, when talking about humans, to shift toward "actual entities" and away from "actual occasions." Thinking of myself as an enduring society of actual entities is destabilizing enough; thinking of myself as an enduring society of actual occasions is even more disturbing. But in Whitehead's scheme, both terms (entity and occasion) mean exactly the same thing. Toward the beginning of

---

82 Barad's "phenomenon" should be distinguished from the much more human-centric "phenomenon" of Husserl and company.

Creative Evolution, Henri Bergson states, "We change without ceasing."[83] Similarly, toward the beginning of *Relationscapes,* Erin Manning states, "We are going, always already."[84] These becomings that "I" am perpetually becoming won't be halted by "my" cognitive inability to comprehend them.

Indeed, as mentioned earlier, consciousness to Whitehead is merely the apex of experience. A rock doesn't need "consciousness" to decide to remain a rock (or to decide to become a rock), and my body doesn't need "consciousness" to decide most of the things it decides either. In Whitehead's own words, "Consciousness flickers; and even at its brightest, there is a small focal region of clear illumination, and a large penumbral region of experience which tells of intense experience in dim apprehension. The simplicity of clear consciousness is no measure of the complexity of complete experience. Also, this character of our experience suggests that consciousness is the crown of experience, only occasionally attained, not its necessary base."[85] "Intellectual feelings are not to be understood unless it be remembered that they already find at work 'physical purposes' more primitive than themselves. Consciousness follows, and does not precede, the entry of the conceptual prehensions of the relevant universals."[86]

I myself suspect that "consciousness" is just a stand-in word for something that we don't really understand yet, like "instinct." "Consciousness" is involved in writing, so whenever humans write books they tend to overvalue consciousness in their books. (Fortunately, art apparatuses are not books.)

83 Henri Bergson, *Creative Evolution,* trans. Arthur Mitchell (New York: Henry Holt, 1911), 12.
84 Erin Manning, *Relationscapes: Movement, Art, Philosophy* (Cambridge: MIT Press, 2009), 14.
85 Whitehead, *Process and Reality,* 267.
86 Ibid., 273.

Real (Not Metaphorical) Art Apparatuses vs.
Rivers of Fundament

Why is any of this important to an understanding of art
apparatuses (a.k.a. works of art)? Because if I want to be
efficacious in my art making, I need to take into account
the real world, in all of its actuality and virtuality, in all of
its quantum-behaving undecidedness and its quasi-New-
ton-behaving well-decidedness. It would be a mistake to
conclude that my art work (my art apparatus) was merely
passively receiving the materials I was using, and rigorously arranging them to accurately represent some fact
which then emerged as a true measurement of reality (as
if it were some sort of Newtonian scientific apparatus).
Of course, nobody in their right mind would think like
this about a painting anymore, and even few of Newton's
contemporaries would have thought of painting in this
way. Many people in the 1800s did think of the photographic camera as a kind of scientific Newtonian apparatus, but most 20th century theorists of photography have
tended to challenge and problematize that interpretation
(Barthes, Sontag, and Flusser, to name just three). But it
would also be an oversimplification to conclude that my
art work (my art apparatus) was behaving as an actual,
literal, physical, quantum-behavior-measuring apparatus, observing my materials as if they were isolated and
prepared individual photons in a shielded laboratory environment. So, what is the proper way to think about my
art apparatus?

   If matter is meant to actually matter (as it is and must
in contemporary art), then I am not authorized to treat
quantum behaviors (such as superposition and indeterminacy) as fundamentally relevant to contemporary art
criticism, contemporary media theory, or contemporary
artmaking practices simply because these behaviors are
"fundamental" to all matter. What does that mean, fundamental to all matter? Fundamental in what ways? Un-

der what conditions? In what contexts? The soles (funda-ments) of my shoes are made of rubber, but that doesn't mean that my standing and my locomotion are radically and fundamentally indebted to the chemical properties of rubber. My standing and my locomotion in these shoes are indeed in some oblique capacities entangled with the chemical properties of rubber, but the specific nature of those entangled capacities is going to require some rigor-ous working through. Humans could choose to radically alter the entire infrastructure of their city's transporta-tion systems based on the fundamental chemical prop-erties of rubber, but that would probably be a bad idea. Fundament is as fundament does, to those for whom the fundament is fundamental.

A fundament can only matter "all the way up" (from quarks to quasars, as the saying goes) to the exact de-gree that it remains relevant to those actual entities/occasions that themselves remain relevant all the way up. Whitehead gives us a cosmology of concrescence, a process philosophy, that is relevant all the way up and down. His cosmology is admittedly speculative, but he still means it to be taken as real (and not metaphorical). An actual entity is to be understood as actually real, not as some subjective, human-invented phylum or class. As Whitehead explains: "The appeal to a class to perform the services of a proper entity is exactly analogous to an ap-peal to an imaginary terrier to kill a real rat."[87] Granted, due to the very real and universal effects of decoherence, superpositional behavior and quantum indeterminacy themselves do *not* remain all that relevant all the way up (at least to a human observing a field of rocks). And yet (according to Whitehead's cosmology), ongoing im-mediate prehensions and negative prehensions and reck-onings *do* still remain relevant all the way up and down. Indeed, this ongoing process of perpetual reckoning and

87   Ibid., 228.

deciding, occasion by occasion, is the very description of how anything becomes and remains relevant to anything else at all, always already, in the first place and evermore. The beginning of each concrescence event is primed by the inheritance of prior actual occasions along the physical pole. These occasions suggest propositions and invoke lures for new ingressions of virtual potentia along the mental pole. The result of this concrescence event is a newly emerged and fully formed actual occasion/entity (a bare fact) that itself feeds forward into subsequent present-tense concrescence occasions. This process of concrescence is not only fundamental; more importantly, it is all-pervasive. And well-decided histories, those enduring societies of actual entities/occasions (per both Whitehead and theories of quantum histories) are inherently relevant (and indeed, relevance-preserving) aspects of this all-pervasive process by which relevance is perpetually manufactured.

So, even though art apparatuses (works of art) are better understood in terms of quantum-behavior-measuring apparatuses than in terms of Newtonian apparatuses, this is not due to the all-pervasive authority of quantum fundament. Quantum mechanics alone is not sufficient for a proper theory and practice of the art apparatus (the work of art), much less is it sufficient for a holistic cosmological understanding of the universe. Quantum superposition may indeed always be mathematically occurring in some near-infinitely miniscule degree to large, well-decided entities throughout the entire universe, but to whom does this fact really matter? To mathematicians and theoretical physicists, it may matter a lot. To the materials with which I am pragmatically engaged as an artist, it matters remotely little. I can't make the facts of quantum undecidability matter any more than they actually matter in any particular material engagement simply because they are supposed to "fundamentally" matter. Those facts and forces and processes have to work their way into and through the histories of the materials with which I am engaging, and they have to persist as relevant in those materials, in order for them to be relevant to my artwork's apparatal engagement with those materials.

For a practicing contemporary artist, what actually winds up mattering depends on the nature of my materials and the way in which I construct my apparatus (as any proper study of quantum-behavior-measuring apparatuses says it should). For example, if my material is fabric, I must understand that my fabric is already well-decided in terms of the properties it wishes to exhibit. But I may enter into a kind of collaborative dialogue with these properties and modulate them. I may wish to consider (to reckon, to prehend) the history of the fabric I have chosen to use. If the fabric is cotton, and I am an artist in the southeastern United States, such historical considerations enter into an entanglement of slavery, factories, child labor, women's labor, men's and women's fashions, technological ginning apparatuses, crop rotation practices, plantation economics, the gender-determined roles of German artisans and its effect on the marriage of Josef and Anni Albers, the Albers's respective pedagogical roles at the Bauhaus and Black Mountain College, and the subsequent influence of Anni Albers on the perceived legitimacy of fabric arts in a contemporary gallery setting. Note that, as a practicing artist, I am led to reckon all of these historical considerations because they are still virtually real to the actualized bolt of cotton I intend to use.

True, according to decoherence theory, by the time I am holding the bolt of cotton in my hands, it is *not* behaving quantum-mechanically (in any way relevant to my apparatal collaboration with it). I may not engage with it electron by electron by electron. Quantum mechanics *alone* does not directly legitimize or authorize my engagement with these prior-decided histories of cotton. But neither am I constrained to apply quantum mechanics to artmaking "merely" metaphorically or analogically. To do so would risk being discourteous to the actual historical decisions cotton has made in collaboration with the rest of the universe up to the immediate apparatal event which is my artwork. In order to get from quantum mechanics to a properly courteous treatment of my materials, I must go by way of Whitehead's cosmology of concrescence, by way of decoherence theory, and by way of Deleuze's (Aristotle's, Proust's, Bergson's, Massumi's) virtual potentia. I must allow the ingressed and decohered quantum histories of the material I am using to really matter, actually and virtually, at the well-decided and well-inhered "scale" (level of complexity) at which we are both collaborating, keeping in mind that the way in which I construct my art apparatus will also come to (really) matter in the resultant artwork, concrescence, "measurement" which eventually emerges.

Martin Savransky's reading of Karen Barad is particularly insightful and relevant to these issues of fundament, scale, and historical contingency:

> What is at stake, I think, is that even though, as Barad argues, we should not confine the potential lessons of Bohr's quantum mechanics to some "microscopic" scale beyond which Newtonian (meta)physics may prevail unchallenged, we also should not be too quick to reduce the requirements of other practices to the lessons of supposedly "more fundamental issues of principle" (*Meeting the Universe Halfway* 110). We must honor Bohr's lessons, but not as something that the entire world must comply with as a matter of principle. Rather, if an attention to relationality is such a lesson, we must take the risk of extending it, of proposing it, as a question to which each practice has to find its own mode of response, for which each practice has to learn how to become responsible.[88]

---

88   Savransky, "Modes of Mattering," 6.

According to Deleuze and Guattari (in *What Is Philosophy?*), there is just one universe, one undifferentiated plane of immanence. There is just one real (actual and virtual). It is traversed by philosophy, science, and art, but it is the same plane of immanence. No approach has a monopoly of access to the plane; each approach finds its own way, not in isolation from the other approaches, and not subservient to them, but in correlation with them, contingent to the reality of the plane itself.

Matter must be allowed to matter to those entities for whom it matters in the ways in which it decides to matter. I can't constrain matter to perpetually matter in a quantum or exact way any more than I can constrain it to matter in a Newtonian or approximate way. But I may construct apparatuses that invite matter to collaborate in various ways. Such is the object lesson (no pun intended) of quantum-behavior-measuring apparatuses.

And now, we continue our descent into fundament, beyond the (imaginary) classical–quantum divide, further down and further in.

Indeterminacy

Quantum "indeterminacy" or "undecidability" or "complementarity" or "uncertainty" has been touched upon throughout this chapter, but it bears solid reiterating here, because it is the one truly radical and novel "challenge" that quantum physics poses to "western" philosophy. A prepared and isolated particle prior to "measurement" (whether measurement by a human-designed quantum-behavior-measuring apparatus, or measurement by some other part of the universe) exists in a state of superposition. Said particle is not an entity containing properties. It has no properties. It may only be assigned a mathematical "waveform" function (which is not itself a physical wave) from which its properties will eventually be derived. But no properties exist prior to measurement. It is not solely the case that no measurement *values* of properties yet exist (although this is also the case). Until the particle is invited to manifest a particular property (i.e., an "observable"), that property itself doesn't even exist.

For example, in the case of complementary spin states (spin is one kind of quantum observable), W.H. Zurek explains, "The states of the two spins in [a quantum-entangled two particle system] are not just unknown, but rather they cannot exist before the "real" measurement."[89] Werner Heisenberg unfortunately chose to called this indeterminate complementarity "uncertainty," but we are not merely uncertain about the value of a property that already exists; prior to measurement, there is nothing about which to be certain or uncertain. As Karen Barad insightfully clarifies, "We can't know something definite about something for which there is nothing definite to know."[90]

The measurement apparatus (or the "measuring" environment, if no apparatus is present) invites the particle to manifest one property or its complement, depending on the particular nature of the apparatus (or environment). The particle itself then manifests a measurement value of that property, observable according to the measurement "bias" of the apparatus. Position and momentum are complementary observables. A single apparatus may measure both, but it may not measure both with 100% certainty. This is not because there is anything technically deficient with the state of our current technical apparatuses. This is because the particle simply cannot manifest both complementary observables simultaneously with 100% commitment.

89 Zurek, "Decoherence and the Transition from Quantum to Classical – Revisited," 93. [Bracketed comments are mine.]
90 Barad, *Meeting the Universe Halfway*, 118.

Famous Quantum Apparatuses

The two most famous quantum experiments are the double-slit experiment, and the related which-path double-slit experiment. Physicist Richard Feynman famously and regularly said that the double-slit experiment "contains the *only* mystery"[91] of quantum mechanics. The double-slit experiment was initially performed with light by Thomas Young in 1801, well before the advent of quantum mechanics. It has since been performed with single photons (of light) as well as single electrons (of matter). It has even been performed with large molecules comprised of numerous atomic particles.

Having taken the time in this chapter to establish a Whiteheadian cosmology inspired by the behavior exhibited in these experiments, they should not seem as "weird" to us as they did to those who initially observed them, namely, scientists coming from the perspective of Newtonian physics. Since the behavior manifested by these apparatal configurations confounds Newtonian physics, even the basic, generic, functional language one uses to describe these experiments can't help but belie the chosen interpretive perspective of the person doing the describing. Indeed, the terms "object," "apparatus," "measure," "property," "experiment," "interact," and "observe" belie one (more classical) perspective; while the terms "apparatal phenomenon," "particle," "observable," "manifest," "intra-act," "invite," and "detect" belie an entirely different (more "quantum") perspective. And even then, there are numerous individual interpretive models within quantum mechanics. Is the particle a "wave/particle"? Is the particle following a "pilot wave"? Does the

---

91 Richard P. Feynman, "Lecture 37: Atomic Mechanics," in *The Feynman Lectures on Physics,* Volume I: *Mainly Mechanics, Radiation and Heat* (Pasadena: California Institute of Technology, 2013), 1–1: Atomic mechanics, http://www.feynmanlectures.caltech.edu/III_01.html.

"waveform collapse"? Does it "decohere"? Do we simply see one particular history or eigenstate while others are manifesting in alternate universes, alternate worlds, or alternate mental states? The fundamental way in which our very descriptive language is so indebted to a Newtonian way of thinking about the universe plays havoc with even the simplest descriptions of these (decidedly non-Newtonian) phenomena. I will not bother to explain these apparatal experiments from alternate interpretive perspectives, but will instead explain them from the perspective of decoherence theory (the interpretive perspective I have been following thus far).

One final note: the quantum behavior described below is not inherently "weird." One might fairly ask, "Weird to whom?" Nor is it any more inherently "amazing" than the fact that humans are able to isolate a single proton or a single electron at all, or that a single experiment may be made to return consistent results, or that any given experiment may be made to return any measurable results at all. As G.K. Chesterton observers, "A child of seven is excited by being told that Tommy opened a door and saw a dragon. But a child of three is excited by being told that Tommy opened a door."[92] When it comes to the double-slit experiment, we humans are more like the three-year-old.

The Double-Slit Experiment
(The Quintessential Quantum Apparatus)

A single particle (a photon or, more "weirdly," a single electron) is shot toward a barrier with a single slit. If it passes through that barrier (some don't, and are bounced back off the barrier), it moves on toward a second barrier with two slits spread a particular distance apart from each other. If it passes through that barrier, it winds up being

92 Gilbert K. Chesterton, *Orthodoxy* (New York: Dodd, Mead & Co., 1908), 34.

detected in a single particular location behind the second barrier. A bunch of particles are passed through this apparatus, one at a time. Eventually, when all the individual locations are examined together, they form a "diffraction" pattern (See Fig. 1). This diffraction pattern seems weird, because if we were shooting tennis balls toward a barrier with two holes, we would expect to find a big clump of marks behind one of the holes, and a big clump of marks behind the other one of the holes. We wouldn't expect to find any marks behind the barrier between the two holes. And yet most of the marks in the diffraction pattern are behind this middle barrier. The diffraction pattern is actually what we would expect to find if we sent a wave of water through the two holes in the barrier. The water would split up and go between both holes, and then on the other side of the barrier, the water from one hole would interfere with the water from the other hole, and a diffraction pattern would be detected when this pair of interfering waves hit the far detector. But (and this is important) the apparatal arrangement didn't send the particles through all at the same time. They went through one at a time. So unlike well-decided, macrocosmic, Newtonian-behaving waves at the beach, the one-at-a-time individual particles couldn't have physically interfered with each other. Each one decided where to land independently of the other ones being sent. And only after we looked at all of these individual decisions together did we see a wave(-like) pattern.

Some people like to interpret this behavior as each single particle splitting up, going between both holes, and then interfering with itself. But if we are going to leave Newtonian physics behind (and we must), then the particle is not really required by the two slits to manifest itself as a physical wave any more than it is required by the two slits to manifest itself as a physical particle. The particle is not a physical wave, although neither is it a decohered, well-decided, tennis-ball-type of particle. (As we previ-

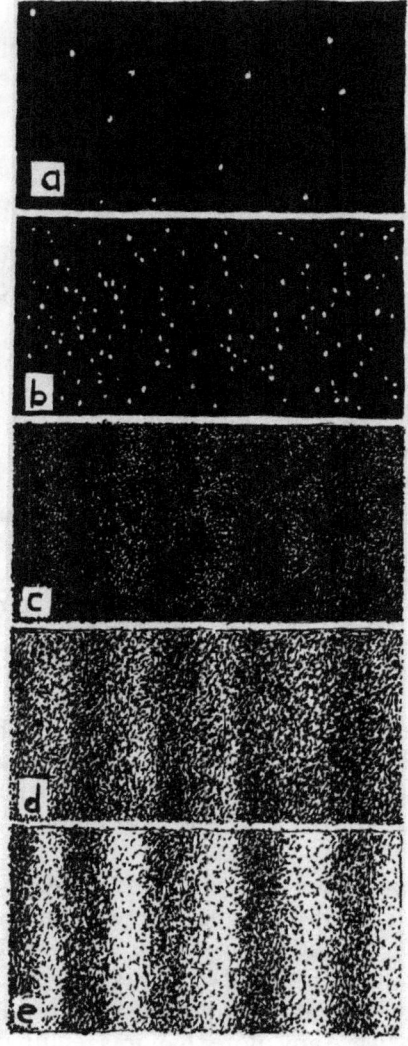

Fig. 1: A gradually accreting diffraction pattern. Drawing by Jordan Cloninger.

ously mused, is a particle without any decided position even properly considered a "particle?" But we must call it something if we are to keep talking about it, so I will continue using the noun "particle.") The particle is in a state of quantum superposition, the probability distribution of which happens to form a wave-like pattern. The particle may be predicted to land somewhere along that wave-like pattern, but where exactly it lands is up to each single particle.

The two slits (gently, but not insistently) invite the superpositioned particle to semi-commit to a kind of partial, wave-patterned proto-decision. This gentle, two-slit invitation is the reason why we don't see a big clump of marks detected behind each slit (which we would see if this were a less gentle, more insistent, single-slit invitation).[93] "And" (not "then," because the entire apparatal event is more holistic than micro-sequential) the final far-detector "wall" (not really a wall, but a position-measuring device behind the two-slit wall) more insistently invites the particle to commit to a single ("superselected" is Zurek's term) position. Thus, in this particular apparatal configuration, each particle is gently invited to semi-commit to a kind of wave-patterned distribution behavior which manifests in the permanent, irreversible commitment (particle by particle) to a single, specific location.

According to my application of Whitehead's cosmology to quantum mechanics, each of these discrete measurement events (particle by particle), is its own actual occasion/entity.

---

93 "Gentle invitation" and "insistent invitation" are my own terms, not actual terms from the field of quantum mechanics.

The Which-Path Double-Slit Experiment
(The Plot Thickens)

The same basic apparatal set-up is constructed, but this time a (non-physically interfering) mechanism is added which is meant to detect which of the two slits the particle went through, or whether it went through both slits at the same time. With this which-slit detector in place, the particle is insistently invited by the entire apparatus to commit to one slit or another. As a result, the particle *does* commit to one slit or another (but never both), and is detected by the far detector "wall" in tennis-ball-like fashion, appearing behind one slit or the other. Once a bunch of particles are shot through the apparatus, one at a time, the aggregate pattern that emerges is one big clump behind one slit, and one big clump behind the other slit (in "normal," "quasi-classical" fashion). The prior diffraction pattern is no longer detected. In other words, the distribution pattern detected by the far detector "wall" is now entirely different than it was in the gentler, less insistent, non-which-path apparatus. This new which-path apparatus still does not determine where exactly each particular particle is detected. According to my own interpretation, that particular specific decision is still made by each individual particle. But this new which-path apparatus (the whole entire apparatal configuration) more insistently invites each particle to semi-commit to a non-wave-like, decidedly clump-like distribution pattern. And then, as before, the far detector "wall" quite insistently invites each particle to commit to a single, permanent, irreversible position.

The Delayed Choice Quantum Eraser Experiment
(Too Much Too Soon)

The so-called "delayed choice quantum eraser" experiment is the mind-blower of all quantum-behavior-measuring experiments. It serves to problematize our prior ideas of "time" altogether. I will thus defer discussion of it until Chapter 4, where we will consider it in conjunction with David Crawford's equally time-problematizing *Stop Motion Studies* project. Both apparatuses (the delayed choice quantum eraser apparatus and Crawford's aleatoric, micro-animation art apparatus) will be considered from an apophatic perspective as mechanisms of deferment.

Some Implications of Quantum-Behavior-Measuring Apparatuses

> *"The oddness of a quarry whose species does not preexist its capture, a prey whose determinate existence results from the casting of the hunter's net."*
> – Brian Massumi[94]

What to make of these two experiments – the double-slit experiment and its which-path counterpart? Karen Barad emphasizes a key interpretation of both: "It is important to realize that in the absence of an experimental arrangement that gives meaning to the notion of "which-slit" – that is, an experimental arrangement that makes it possible to determine which slit a particle goes through... – this information is not just unknown; it is ontologically indeterminate."[95] When the nuanced differences between "unknown" and "indeterminate" are not merely semantic but are experimentally demonstrated, enacted, elucidated, and enunciated, then we are authorized to pragmatically and "really" revisit and examine our habitual usage of these terms, and to revisit and examine

---

94 Brian Massumi, "Introduction: Like a Thought," in A *Shock To Thought: Expression after Deleuze and Guattari*, ed. Brian Massumi (London: Routledge, 2005), xx. [Regarding the arbitrary nature of Louis Hjelmslev's concept of "purport."]
95 Barad, *Meeting the Universe Halfway*, 268.

our habitual ways of thinking about the universe based on these terms (and not only the terms "unknown" and "indeterminate," but also the terms "ontology," "information," "experiment," and "knowledge.")

As we move toward art apparatuses, let us take with us from these quantum-behavior-measuring apparatuses three key interpretations, each intrinsically related to the others. Karen Barad's insights and her careful and original reading of Niels Bohr prove indispensable to these interpretations.

I. The apparatal phenomenon is holistic.

The best way to understand the "measurement results" of a quantum-behavior-measuring apparatus is to consider the entire apparatus (the way in which it is arranged, the materials from which it is made, and the materials it is "measuring") as a single, holistic phenomenon. According to Barad, "The boundary between the "object of observation" and the "agencies of observation" is indeterminate in the absence of a specific physical arrangement of the apparatus."[96] "A condition for objective knowledge is that the referent is a phenomenon (and not an observation-independent object)."[97]

Conditioned by Newtonian physics, we are prone to think about "the experiment" in parts: a measuring device, a measured particle, an inherent property of that particle, the value of that property, a measurement event, and a measurement outcome. In actuality, the entire assemblage is itself a holistic phenomenon, and that holistic, singular occurrence (that apparatal phenomenon) enacts the "measurement outcome."

96 Ibid., 114.
97 Ibid., 198.

2. Human intention alone is not enough to determine which type of observable is observed. Material intervention is required.

As a scientist, I can't simply "look" and subjectively decide to see a particle's position or its momentum, since these have yet to be determined. I must meticulously construct a specific material apparatus in a specific material way so that the apparatus invites the particle to manifest or make one or the other kind of complementary "observable" I wish to observe. The apparatus doesn't invite the exact, singular, specific measurement value (that is up to the particle), but it does invite (more or less insistently) a particular kind of observable (or a particular ratio of complementary commitment – for example, 25% position certainty/75% momentum certainty). In other words, all relevant material aspects of the holistic apparatal phenomenon matter – not just the "material" of the particle, but also the material configuration of the "measuring" apparatus, and both in relation to the surrounding "environment" of the rest of the universe.

Schlosshauer explains:

> Measurements must be of such a nature as to establish robust records, that is, the system-apparatus correlation ought to be preserved in spite of the inevitable interaction with the surrounding environment [...]. The 'user' cannot choose the observables arbitrarily, but must design a measuring device whose interaction with the environment is such as to ensure stable records (which, in turn, defines a measuring device for this observable).[98]

Barad herself states:

---

98 Schlosshauer, *Decoherence and the Quantum-To-Classical Transition*, 334.

Given a particular measuring apparatus, certain properties *become determinate,* while others are specifically
excluded. Which properties become determinate is
not governed by the desires or will of the experimenter
but rather by the specificity of the experimental apparatus.[99]

Furthermore, "The nature of the observed phenomenon
changes with corresponding changes in the apparatus."[100]
When the double-slit apparatus is modified to become
the which-path double-slit apparatus, and an entirely different set of "outcomes" is "observed."

3. Apparatuses are made to mean, and they mean what they have become.

The "measurement outcome" of each holistic apparatal
phenomenon (the reckoning of the "particle" by the
"measuring" device, *and* vice versa) is itself the "meaning"
of that singular phenomenon. This is a difficult concept
to explain, because we are used to Newtonian subject/ob-
ject distinctions, where an active subject acts upon a pas-
sive object and the result is a predicated outcome. This
Newtonian kind of thinking fails to get at what is actually happening in an apparatal phenomenon. Karen Barad's
neologism for describing this new quantum relationship
between measuring device, particle, and surrounding environment is "intra-action." Not "interaction," because
the key involved entities ("measuring" device and "measured" particle) are neither fully determined "subjects" or
"objects" prior to their "intra-action."

What exactly is the "measurable outcome" of any giv-
en holistic apparatal phenomenon? In the case of the two
double-slit experiments above, the particle leaves a mark
on a detector. Is this mark "knowledge" or "information?"

99   Barad, *Meeting the Universe Halfway,* 19.
100 Ibid., 106.

Or is it both? A "measurable" outcome may be defined as a (not necessarily human-)legible, singular, irreversible, and thus "meaningful" outcome. So then, one way of "making meaning" is by reckoning, valuing, including (via prehension), and excluding (via negative prehension) that which matters and that which doesn't matter. Such meaning-making is done by the holistic apparatal phenomenon itself prior to (and indeed, apart from) any humans reading any meters or observing any results. Returning to and slightly modifying our David Bowie lyric, "I am the DJ / I mean what I play."

The result of this apparatal process of measurement doesn't *have* a meaning (something which must be semantically and interpretively deduced and supplied post-facto). The measurement itself *is* the meaning. It means what it has become. It is its own meaning. The apparatal phenomenon has intra-actively, collaboratively decided to mean itself.

So then, in terms of an art apparatus (a.k.a. a work of art), here is how to make a work of art mean something: you simply get some materials and make a work of art. As long as the material entities involved are apparatally invited to take part in their own intra-active becoming, the work of art will mean what it has collaboratively decided to become. (Granted, how to make an *apophatic* work of art mean or become nothing rather than mean or become *something* is a bit trickier; but one step at a time!)

The work of art "means" what it has become (and likewise, the measurement outcome of an apparatus "means" what it has become), because "measurement" and "meaning" are, by definition, the very act of cutting yourself out from the holistic universe, and then reckoning another part of the universe from your cut-out part of the universe. You reckon that other part of the universe by prehending it into yourself, and in so doing, you become something new. Here "you" can mean "you human," but it can also mean "you apparatus," or "you work of art." Because we are all societies of actual entities/occasions.

"Meaning" is not merely *contingent* upon the results of reckoning (i.e., "measurement"), meaning itself *is* the act of reckoning. This is true not only for humans, but for our stand-in apparatuses. As Whitehead makes clear:

> However far the testing of instruments is carried, finally all scientific interpretation is based upon the assumption of directly observed unchangeability of some instrument for seconds, for hours, for months, for years. When we test this assumption we can only use another instrument; and there cannot be an infinite regress of instruments.[101]

Barad likewise observes, "A 'measuring instrument' cannot characterize (i.e., be used to measure) itself."[102]

So then, apparatuses cannot step outside of the holistic universe and look back on it "objectively." The best they can do is purposefully cut into different parts of the universe in different ways. Since apparatuses are made to mean, and since they mean what they become, the ways in which I construct my art apparatus (my work of art) matters a great deal. Art apparatuses are not merely objective divining rods pointing toward permanently decided materials with permanently decided properties. Art apparatuses and their materials co-decide what winds up mattering. Furthermore, the entire art apparatus is itself that which comes to matter. It means what it becomes.

On this particular point (and countless others), Whitehead and Barad are so close (although Barad, in her seminal text *Meeting the Universe Halfway*, never once cites Whitehead). Whitehead writes, "How an actual entity becomes constitutes what that actual entity is; so that the

---

101 Whitehead, *Process and Reality*, 127.
102 Barad, *Meeting the Universe Halfway*, 274.

two descriptions of an actual entity are not independent. Its 'being' is constituted by its 'becoming'."[103] This is so similar to Barad's idea that the apparatal phenomenon means what it becomes. Whitehead writes, "The word 'decision' does not here imply conscious judgment [...]. The word is used in its root sense of a 'cutting off'."[104] This is so similar to Barad's idea of "agential cuts" as irrevocable, meaning-making decisions. These similarities are presumably due to the fact that both thinkers are engaging theoretically with the same quantum phenomena.

From Quantum-Behavior-Measuring Apparatuses to Art Apparatuses

From our consideration of quantum-behavior-measuring apparatuses, it is apparent that "reckoning" and "measuring" are not as far from "collaborating" and "making" as is generally thought. From a classical/Newtonian perspective, scientists were merely objectively measuring phenomenon, but from a quantum mechanical perspective, it turns out scientists were really intra-acting and co-making all along. This paradigm shift involves a change from measuring to making.

Historically, artists have experienced a similar paradigm shift, but in the opposite direction. Artists (of the mostly white, male, European flavor) have transitioned from the "artist as hero" Renaissance paradigm (where humans were the measure of all things and material was wrested into the form the artist desired by his determined will), toward a paradigm where the artist is in a kind of collaborative dialogue with her materials, respecting and minding their material-ish contributions and propensities. In this sense, artists have moved from making to-

103 Whitehead, *Process and Reality*, 23.
104 Ibid., 43.

ward a kind of reckoning or measuring. Both shifts (the scientific shift toward making and the artistic shift toward measuring) meet somewhere in the middle, at a place where materials collaboratively become along with other materials, contextual environments, and humans; a place somewhere between reckoning and making. This middle ground is the ground of the apparatus as a singular, holistic phenomenon. This apparatal middle ground is a place between discovery and creation. It demands a lifelong practice (one apparatus at a time) of invention; but also of attention, listening, and respect toward prior historical decisions (both human decisions, material decisions, and entangled human/material decisions), so that what emerges may somehow matter better.

As Martin Savransky asserts:

> Mattering always entails taking risks. Thus, in order to entertain the challenge of an ethics of worlding, we need to attend to the specific manners of creating delicate contacts between the mode of mattering of an entity and the mode of invention of a practice, so that the obligations posed by the former may be inherited in a way that forces the practice to invent a way of becoming responsible for it.[105]

Such attention to actually real historical decisions necessarily demands a recognition of the real and relevant differences between quantum-behavior-measuring apparatuses and art apparatuses. One relevant difference is not just in "scale" (per se), but in the well-decided, "societal" nature of most art materials (clay, oil, wood, felted wool) vs. the superpositioned proto-nature of most quantum particles (photons, electrons, and even c70 fullerene carbon molecules). The manifested behaviors, propensities, tendencies, and appetitions of more well-decided, endur-

105 Savransky, "Modes of Mattering," 10.

ing societies of entities (from rocks to wool to planetary ecosystems) are materially relevant and may not be ignored (although they may be induced, lured, tempted, teased out, modulated, and negotiated).

Each apparatal arrangement or engagement demands its own unique treatment and approach. In the same way that I can't simply feed felted wool into a double-slit apparatus and expect meaningful results, I can't make an installation from felted wool and claim that it behaves like a quantum-behavior-measuring apparatus simply by analogy. Again, Savransky cautions:

> The mode of relationality that characterizes an experimental practice cannot simply be extended *by analogy*. Rather, the relational proposition needs to be posed as a question to which practices of social inquiry [and I would add, practices of art] must find their own way of responding.[106]

Each apparatal configuration demands its own kind of attention, including attention to the ways in which the construction of that apparatus is influenced by the goals of the discipline in which it finds itself (art, science, sociology, culture theory, philosophy), as well as attention to the ways in which that apparatus in turn influences the future development and goals of that discipline. Of all these disciplines (these human-invented ways of accessing the immanently real universe), art and science are unique in that they both construct physical apparatuses which are meant to engage directly with physical materials. Both art and science apparatuses enact apparatal cuts, and in so doing, they carve out apparatal contexts from the rest of the universe. Both art and science apparatuses are surrounded by unique external "environments" – the laboratory and the studio, the cryogenic chamber and the

106 Ibid., 11. [Bracketed comments are mine.]

art gallery. So, the similarities and differences between these particular, actual types of apparatuses (scientific and artistic) must be treated with particular, actual, non-metaphorical care.

So, for instance, not all scientific apparatuses are the same. There are scientific apparatuses for measuring the emergent position of individual photons (for example, a double-slit apparatus), and scientific apparatuses for measuring the weight of individual rocks (for example, a scale). It follows, then, that one relevant *difference* between a scale for weighing rocks and an art apparatus (i.e., any work of art) is that the scale is constructed to be pragmatically unconcerned with the infinitesimal influence it is having on the infinitesimal quantum superpositional behavior of the already well-decided and well-decohered rocks it is measuring; whereas the art apparatus is purposefully constructed to enter into an intra-active phenomenon with its materials so that new outcomes collaboratively emerge. The rock-measuring scale intends to extract value from the measurement intra-action without contributing to it, whereas the art apparatus intends to dialogue with, modulate, and be modulated by its materials via intra-action. In this sense, the art apparatus has more in common with the double-slit apparatus than it does with the rock-weighing scale, because the double-slit apparatus is invited by the diffractive behavior of its "measured" particles to become aware of its own intra-action with said particles, whereas the rock-weighing scale is constructed to be largely indifferent to the intra-active influence it has on its rocks. (The rock-weighing scale is not totally indifferent, however. Indeed, the measurement value of the weight of the rock *is* itself the exact "difference" to which the scale cannot be indifferent.)

One relevant *similarity* between the rock-weighing scale and the art apparatus is that both are (usually) dealing with well-decided, well-decohered societies of entities (like rocks) at a level of abstraction courteous toward and relevant to the well-decided histories of those entities. (In this sense, the art apparatus has less in common with the double-slit apparatus than it does with the rock-weighing scale). All that to say, if matter is meant to matter (and it means to), then it must be allowed to matter as it means.

Another exciting similarity between artistic and scientific apparatuses is that both instigate actual phenomena. Both apparatuses (when implemented) are more than mere thought experiments. They have actually been instantiated in the world in real ways that have actually come to matter. The best scientific and art apparatuses stay with you, and they invite you to stay with them, to consider and reconsider them. They gnaw at you. You keep returning back to them, working them through, trying to figure and fold them into your daily world, your own cosmology. They oblige you to account for them, to reckon with them, however casually or insistently.

The goal of an art apparatus is in some sense the goal of a scientific apparatuses – not necessarily to demonstrate or explain why something occurs, but simply to cause something to occur. This is a primary function of both artistic and scientific apparatuses – not necessarily to establish new paradigms of thought (although that could also happen), but to persist as undeniable provocations that must then be chewed on and wrestled with, explained away or embraced, but which insistently refuse to be ignored as having not actually happened. Artistic and scientific apparatuses may not be fully understood, but they have undeniably occurred.

The Individual Work of Art as a Singular Apparatus vs. Generic Media as Apparatus

I am claiming that each individual work of art functions as its own kind of apparatus. I am borrowing the concept of apparatus from laboratory science, and more particularly from quantum mechanics. The term "apparatus" has been used in media studies before to describe the overall behavior of an entire medium as it relates to the culture in which it is situated. Louis Althusser introduced the concept of an ideological state apparatus; Vilém Flusser uses the term apparatus to describe not only the photographic camera but the entire cultural regime it enforces; and Gregory Ulmer has also used the term to delineate and describe differences in particular historical media regimes. "Apparatus theory" in film studies is similarly related to the ways in which the apparatus of the film camera itself enforces and informs a particular kind of human reception of film as a medium. Media historian Jussi Parikka has even suggested a "new apparatus theory" of media be developed based on Karen Barad's interpretations of quantum apparatuses, while noting that theorists "from Jonathan Crary to Henning Schmidgen" have already interpreted laboratory apparatuses in the context of media history.[107]

All of these theoretical projects address media in a broad sense, from the perspective of media theory and its relevance to human culture. I have no problem with the use of the term "apparatus" to describe and analyze the general ways in which media function to define and modulate eras of human culture, but that is not my own particular project with this book. Instead, I mean to ad-

---

107 Jussi Parikka, "Apparatus Theory of Media à la (or in the wake of) Karen Barad," *Machinology: Machines, Noise, and Some Media Archaeology*, July 16, 2009, https://jussiparikka.net/2009/07/16/apparatus-theory-of-media-a-la-or-in-the-wake-of-karen-barad/.

dress singular art apparatuses, one at a time, across a variety of different media – each work of art understood as a single, functional apparatus. Will the singular art apparatuses I choose to examine necessarily be influenced by the media materials with which they engage? Of course. Will these local apparatal engagements be relevant to broader contemporary human cultures? One would certainly hope so. Will these local apparatal engagements be entirely constrained and defined by the media materials they use? One would certainly hope not. Could these local apparatuses be so influential that they alter the course of media studies, art history, and the way in which humans and materials collaborate in the future? With the construction of every new art apparatus, this possibility is always implicitly assumed.

A singular art apparatus may indeed move its own era past a state change threshold and into a new era, but only by itself being well aware of its own materials, their histories, and their surrounding cultural context(s). Marcel Duchamp's (R. Mutt's) *Fountain* and John Cage's 4'33" eventually breached their eras. They were the double-slit and which-path apparatuses of their time. And like Thomas Young's original 1801 double-slit apparatus, none of their contemporaries knew quite what to make of them.

According to my local/individual use of the term, an art apparatus is a singular, contrived event with a delimited boundary. Where the artist chooses to draw the boundary in part determines the event. Although the art apparatus must certainly be aware of the human and material histories involved in its contrived phenomenon, the goal of an art apparatus is not merely to problematize or deconstruct the media genre in which it has been produced (a de rigueur move at this point in art history). Instead, the goal of an art apparatus is to generate an apparatal situation in the world that results in something more (or less) than the material sum of its parts.

So, for instance, I am more hopeful than Flusser (which may not be saying much). In *Towards a Philosophy of Photography*, Flusser suggests that all one can do with a photographic apparatus is exhaust its possible combinatory outputs within the prescribed program defined by the apparatus of the camera, like playing a variable but pre-defined game. I am suggesting that an ethical apparatal art practice co-makes a new game, together with its media materials, one apparatus at a time. Flusser asserts, "[Apparatuses'] intention is not to change the world but to change the meaning of the world. Their intention is symbolic."[108] I am asserting something slightly (but fundamentally) different: Any art apparatus worth its materials actually does change the world, and this actual change of the world is itself an immediate change in the meaning of the world.

The Art Apparatus (The Work of Art) Proper

Turning fully to the art apparatus proper (but not yet fully to the particular type of art apparatus known as apophatic), I will just reiterate that every work of art, from Michelangelo's *David* to a Dan Flavin neon light installation may be considered an art apparatus. The medium, genre, historical era, and social context of the work of art are of course relevant to the functioning of the apparatus, but all works of art may still be understood to function as apparatuses. Even many works like Andrei Rublev's *Christ the Redeemer* icon from the 1400s, which we now consider to be "artworks" but which at the time were more like mechanisms for contemplation and worship, may usefully be considered as art apparatuses. My point is not to flatten the entire fields of art history, criticism, and

---

108 Vilém Flusser, *Towards a Philosophy of Photography*, trans. Anthony Matthews (London: Reaktion Books, 2012), 25.

theory; or to neutralize the nuance of their various and relevant insights. Instead, I simply want to initially approach all art from this broader apparatal perspective, so that I may then focus in on a particular apophatic (nothing-making) type of art apparatus.

Having established a relationship between art apparatuses and scientific (particularly quantum-behavior-measuring) apparatuses, I now pivot from Alfred North Whitehead and Niels Bohr to Gilles Deleuze, Deleuze and Guattari, and philosopher (and Deleuze scholar) Elizabeth Grosz. In pivoting to Deleuze, I never really leave Whitehead, since Deleuze's cosmology is in constant implicit and explicit contact with Whitehead's cosmology (as well as with Henri Bergson's and Marcel Proust's). Deleuze (and Deleuze and Guattari) focus more specifically than Whitehead on art, which is why Deleuze's perspective becomes particularly relevant here. To me, Deleuze is the philosopher of the analog synthesizer — not simply because he applied his philosophy to the workings of the analog synthesizer, but because his entire cosmological model of deterritorializations and reterritorializations proceeds and behaves like a philosophical version of an analog synthesizer. An analog synthesizer is a machine which renders the waves of the universe sensory (and thus sensible). It generates, gathers, modulates, folds, and outputs the chaotic forces of the universe. An analog synthesizer is thus a kind of apparatus (although Deleuze doesn't explicitly use that term to describe it) for modulating the standing waves and forces of the universe. It acts as a kind of lightning rod or divining rod for these forces, and then acts as a rigorous modulation machine of them. It bears mentioning that oscillators and wave-generating devices are a regular part of the experimental arsenal of those decoherence-exploring physicists working at mesoscopic scales, intent on "observing" quantum superposition behavior at increasingly larger scales.

Rather than simply describe the ways in which a work of art functions as an apparatus, I will proceed instead by explaining to a(n imaginary) practicing artist the best ways to take advantage of the apparatal nature of the works of art she is making. I will draw on Deleuze throughout.

1. Make your art apparatus more about what it causes to happen than what it looks like or "represents."

Even when your work does look like something (and it will almost always have some visual appearance), the ways in which this look affects what the work is actually causing to happen is more relevant to the overall apparatal phenomenon (the artwork) than the look in and of itself.

Deleuze, in conversation with Richard Pinhas (experimental musician and former student of Deleuze), states, "You don't live in the same manner according to whether you develop a form or you find your way in relations of speeds and slownesses among particles, or things functioning as particles, insofar as you distribute affects. It's not the same mode of life at all."[109] Elsewhere, regarding Francis Bacon, Deleuze states, "In art [...] it is not a matter of reproducing or inventing forms, but of capturing forces."[110] Finally, Deleuze and Guattari on art after Romanticism: "The postromantic turning point: the essential thing is no longer forms and matters, or themes, but forces, densities, intensities."[111]

109 Gilles Deleuze and Richard Pinhas, "Vincennes Seminar Session, May 3, 1997: On Music," trans. Timothy S. Murphy, *Discourse: Journal for Theoretical Studies in Media and Culture* 20, no. 3 (Fall 1998): 9.

110 Gilles Deleuze, *Francis Bacon: The Logic of Sensation*, trans. Daniel W. Smith (London: Continuum, 2003), 56.

111 Gilles Deleuze and Félix Guattari, *A Thousand Plateaus: Capitalism and Schizophrenia*, trans. Brian Massumi (Minneapolis: University of Minnesota Press, 1987), 343.

If you proceed by attending to the nature of your materials rather than solely according to the resultant forms you are creating, you will more fully take advantage of the art apparatus of which you are a part. What are your materials already doing? What might they want to be invited to do? Deleuze exhorts, "It's not enough to make moving shadows on the wall. You have to construct images that can move by themselves."[112]

It is not enough to merely stage your materials to behave "as if" they are metaphorically related to the form or content of your art. The materials themselves should be more fine-grainedly, intrinsically intra-active with the entire function of your holistic art apparatus. For example, (post-)internet artist Jon Rafman had a large solo show of several installation stations at the Stedelijk Museum in Amsterdam.[113] Part of Rafman's practice is finding marginal, subcultural online video content and re-editing it into affectively disturbing video collages. In the Stedelijk show, each video collage was screened inside of an installation environment which metaphorically (albeit affectively) enacted some aspect of the video. So, for example, a video with sinking elements was looped above a ball pit in which you gradually sank while you watched the video. A video with bondage elements was to be watched while sitting in a row of claustrophobic sofa seats. A video about the isolation of video game addiction was projected inside of a private viewing booth modeled to look like a desktop computer. Each of these stations proceeded by metaphor, and each added (somewhat, but not terribly much) to the already strong video work screened within these viewing environments.

---

112 Gilles Deleuze, "Mediators," in *Negotiations: 1972–1990,* trans. Martin Joughin (New York: Columbia University Press, 1995), 122.

113 The show was wonderfully entitled *I have ten thousand compound eyes and each is named suffering.*

The most successful viewing station in the entire show (if both video and viewing environment were judged together and considered as a single holistic apparatus) was comprised of a video with jarring jump-cuts projected onto a large wall in front of a fairly free-swinging, single-person swing hung from the ceiling and several yards away from the video wall. While merely standing on the floor watching the video, its jump-cuts were not all that disturbing; but while swinging on the swing, the entire experience was terribly disruptive. On the swing, you could never acquire a stable frame of reference. The projection on the wall was large enough that, while swinging, all four edges of the video never quite came into full view. Each jump-cut in the video thus became massively disruptive, because on the swing you were trying to stabilize yourself via a steady ground-plane frame of reference, which forced you to more fully throw yourself cognitively into the video in search of some steadying frame of reference, which then placed you in an even more vulnerable and vertiginous cognitive position where the violence of the jump-cuts was able to bodily enact its full force. The whole apparatus was made even more disturbing by the fact that the swing simply looked like an ordinary swing you would find on a playground. Since it was a single-seat swing at a large and well-visited art museum, everyone had to wait their turn. And so, prior to getting on the swing, you were able to watch other people swinging; and from the ground, the whole apparatus looked fairly benign and even slightly banal. This apparent simplicity of the apparatus made your affective experience all the more disturbing once you finally took your own turn on the swing.

With this particular viewing station (as opposed to the others in the show), the swing set was in no way a metaphor of the filmic jump-cut. The swing set was not literally sharp. It did not move jerkily (indeed, it moved quite continuously and smoothly). It intensified the af-

fective instability of the filmic jump-cuts by collaboratively, intra-actively participating in an overall, holistic,
apparatal project of instability. This swing set viewing
station apparatus created a jump-cut experience in the
viewer's body. The viewer's body entered into an apparatal relationship with the swing and the video, the wall,
the space, and the rest of the viewers waiting in line and
wondering. I don't even remember what the "content" of
the video "represented." I don't remember what the video
was "about." Instead, it became "about" what the entire
apparatus was doing. This is not to say that a successful
art apparatus can only be an abstract installation involving moving parts and harshly edited video. The Rothko
Chapel is a successful art apparatus. Seurat's *A Sunday
on La Grande Jatte* painting is a successful art apparatus.
Rublev's *Christ the Redeemer* icon is a successful art apparatus. But the right move to be made is always beyond
what the art work "represents" and toward what it causes
to happen.

2. Your art apparatus should open out onto universal
   forces and invite them into itself.

A particularly successful art apparatus will seek to gather
universal anomalies, those actual entities and potentialities of the universe that usually fail to ingress with other
actual entities, those things which get traced-over and
normalized(-out), those not quite orthogonal, not quite
orthonormal, yet nonetheless potential vectors (to borrow some mathematical terms from quantum mechanics). Your art apparatus should suck the universe into
itself in ways that cause the improbable and unlikely to
ingress into the actual real. Your art apparatus should fail
to negatively prehend (and thus positively prehend, however fractionally) some unlikely, oblique, prior actual en-

tity. According to Deleuze and Guattari, "The artist opens up to the Cosmos in order to harness forces in a 'work'."[114]

An art apparatus which takes full advantage of its apparatal nature is one that is able to make much of things (forces, entities, potentia) that are "usually" (in our current era) negatively prehended. Not to "exploit" these anomalies for utilitarian use or gain, but to give them their own place at the concrescence table, to invite them to matter in new ways normally denied them. This invitation occurs by means of amplification – constructing an apparatus that will amplify the influence of a force not normally influential. According to Elizabeth Grosz, the goal is "above all to generate excess, further vibratory forces, more effects, useless effects, qualities that can't be directly capitalized."[115]

As an artist who purposefully constructs art apparatuses, you are most efficacious and ingenious when you see yourself not as a forger of forms or a maker of metaphors, but as a harnesser and modulator of forces. Deleuze and Guattari even suggest a new job title:

> The modern figure is not the child or the lunatic, still less the artist, but the cosmic artisan [...]. To be an artisan and no longer an artist, creator, or founder, is the only way to become cosmic, to leave the milieus and the earth behind. The invocation to the Cosmos does not at all operate as a metaphor; on the contrary, the operation is an effective one, from the moment the artist connects a material with forces of consistency or consolidation.[116]

---

114 Deleuze and Guattari, *A Thousand Plateaus*, 337.
115 Elizabeth Grosz, *Chaos, Territory, Art: Deleuze and the Framing of the Earth* (New York: Columbia University Press, 2008), 54.
116 Deleuze and Guattari, *A Thousand Plateaus*, 345.

The cosmic artisan does not bother constructing a meta-phor which offers a means by which humans may under-stand a world which already exists. Instead, the cosmic artisan constructs apparatal invitations which entice uni-versal forces to become involved in new configurations which themselves come to actually matter and make a world newly altered by these holistic art apparatuses.

3. Open up the holistic process of your art apparatus to purposefully invite humans into it (if humans are in-deed your "intended" "audience," however primarily or fractionally).

You are not creating a black box apparatus which obscures its process and only affords an input hole for materials and an output hole for the completed art object. Never-theless, mind that you do not create a stilted, awkwardly staged "interactive" apparatus which so constrains hu-man participation as to render their decisions largely pre-determined and inconsequential. This is the pitfall of most self-declared "interactive" art. Just because there is a forking narrative or a pushable button does not mean that you have automatically achieved the goal of inviting the human to participate in your apparatus. Oftentimes an awkwardly staged invitation for a "user" to "interact" with your work is actually just one more way to overde-termine and artificially stage their ingression into the work. As Jacques Rancière insists throughout *The Eman-cipated Spectator,* a painting hanging on a wall in a gallery may prove more truly "interactive" than a purposefully "interactive," computer-centric, new media installation.

Process Art as a genre becomes one way to invite the "viewer" into the process of the creation of the "artwork," whereby the artwork becomes more about the process of its own emergence than about the output of a singular art object. Performance Art as a genre becomes another means in which an art apparatus may be explicitly constructed to play out, a phase at a time, in relation to its human "audience." Because Process Art and Performance Art involve the "audience" in the apparatal process early or throughout, there is a potential for their human audience members to more integrally ingress into the holistic apparatal event. But there are other ingenious, non-Process-Art, non-Performance-Art means of extending the holistic phenomenon of the overall apparatal process out into the last-mile, "art object meets art patron" phase of the art apparatus.

The standard advice is to make sure that some element of the resultant art object reveals the means of its own creation. But there are better, more fine-grained ways to imbue an art object with the process of its own production than simply "revealing" an aspect of the production process via some cheeky visual clue in the resultant art object. Better to stop thinking of the art apparatus as an "art object" altogether. The art apparatus thus continues beyond the resultant "art object" to include the event of experience that the human art patron has with the art object. What kinds of "inclusion" do I mean? I do not simply mean the final, summative conclusion of interpretive completion, à la Marcel Duchamp. Duchamp famously asserted, "The creative act is not performed by the artist alone; the spectator brings the work in contact with the external world by deciphering and interpreting its inner qualifications and thus adds his contribution to the creative act."[117] I'm less interested in the role of the "spectator" as a kind of semiotic "reader" or "interpreter" of the signifying "meaning" of the work. Instead, I understand the "spectator" to be a part of the entire, holistic, actually real art apparatus. The "spectator" not only "looks" and then consciously invents some cognitive interpreta-

117 Marcel Duchamp, "The Creative Act," in *The Essential Writings of Marcel Duchamp*, eds. Michel Sanouillet and Elmer Peterson (London: Thames and Hudson, 1975), 140.

tion. Instead, the "spectator" intra-acts with the entire configuration of the art apparatus and is herself changed as a result. She herself now "means" something different. The best art apparatuses (even those apparatuses that are "merely" paintings) approach their human audiences not as semiotic readers who tie-off and finalize the creative act with their conscious interpretations, but as enduring objects which are themselves involved in the holistic apparatal configuration.

Your art apparatus is able to accomplish results that a philosophy apparatus is simply not able to accomplish, and you (as a cosmic artisan) should take advantage of these strengths. Because the art apparatus deals in materials, it has access to the affective base of human bodily experience which Whitehead describes. This experiential base is not necessarily proto-conscious or even the Freudian subconscious, because such affective bodily experiences may never wind up influencing the conscious (or subconscious) at all. Indeed, most do not. But neither are these affective bodily experiences explicitly a-conscious, because they may indeed ultimately fold into consciousness, depending on their particular, eventual relevance to consciousness.

Learning to play the drums makes quite plain the ways in which such embodied "knowledges" are indifferent toward (or at least not contingent upon) conscious "knowledge." You can read all the books you want on drumming, but without bodily playing the drums on a regular basis, you will never actually "know" how to play the drums. As Henri Bergson explains, "It is one thing to understand a difficult movement, another to be able to carry it out. To understand it, we need only to realize in it what is essential, just enough to distinguish it from all other possible movements. But to be able to carry it out, we must besides have brought our body to understand it. Now, the logic of the body admits of no tacit implications. It demands that all the constituent parts of the movement shall be set forth one by one, and then put together again. Here a complete analysis is necessary, in which no detail is neglected, and an actual synthesis, in which nothing is curtailed."[118]

The best art apparatuses purposefully invite their human "audiences" to bodily, affectively intra-act with them, not just to consciously interpret them. Grosz speaks of "the non-functional perceptual immersion in things and qualities that art generates."[119] Elsewhere she describes "the rendering sonorous of forces, ultimately the forces of chaos itself, that are themselves nonsonorous."[120] She asks, "How does the work of art bring about sensations, not sensations of what we know and recognize, but of what is unknown, unexperienced, traces not of the past but of the future, not of the human and its recognized features, but of the inhuman?"[121] As the cosmic artisan, it is your job to answer this question, to invent art apparatuses that entangle marginalized actual occasions, virtual potentia, and immediate, immanent human bodies.

4. Proceed with care.

Experimental does not mean slack. Quite the opposite. This is not to say that a rigorous artistic practice need necessarily be "scientific," but it should proceed with care – care toward materials and their histories, and care toward the construction of an art apparatus that might most matter. Deleuze and Guattari counsel, "Sobriety, sobriety: that is the common prerequisite for the deterritorialization of matters, the molecularization of material,

---

118 Henri Bergson, *Matter and Memory*, trans. Nancy Margaret Paul and W. Scott Palmer (New York: Zone Books, 2005), 112.

119 Elizabeth Grosz, "Bergson, Deleuze and the Becoming of Unbecoming," *parallax* 11, no. 2 (2005): 9.

120 Grosz, *Chaos, Territory, Art*, 57.

121 Ibid., 60.

and the cosmicization of forces."[122] They quote composer
Karlheinz Stockhausen: "Work with very limited materials and integrate the universe into them through a continuous variation."[123]

5. Trouble Things Up!

Cause trouble within the apparatus. Continually modulate and vary. Tweak the heck out of stuff (with great
care). Construct apparatuses meant to trouble, irk, bother, and provoke your materials. Otherwise, only normal-
ized, expected, and already-enacted results will (re-)oc-
cur. No truly experimental scientific apparatus would
waste its time re-confirming some already known behavior. In experimental science, you are trying to conduct an
experiment that solves some unknown problem or con-
firms some unproved hypothesis. More often than not, by
rigorously attending to the unknown problem, your constructed scientific apparatus accidentally creates a new
problem worth exploring. With an art apparatus, you can
just cut straight to creating the new worthwhile problem,
but always with attention and rigor, or the problem will
wind up being not all that worthwhile.

It was Albert Einstein's own intellectual problems and
objections with quantum mechanics, and his rigorous
and careful concern in posing them, that led to the pursuit, construction, and verification of a number of worthwhile, actual apparatuses (which subsequently wound up
further confounding and problematizing Einstein's original problems and objections). It was Bertram Russel's and
Alfred North Whitehead's rigorous pursuit of a contra-
diction-free, hermetically airtight mathematical system
that led to the proof that no such system could ever ex-

122 Deleuze and Guattari, *A Thousand Plateaus*, 344.
123 Karlheinz Stockhausen, interviewed in *Le Monde*, July 21, 1977, quoted in Deleuze and Guattari, *A Thousand Plateaus*, 551.

ist, which then led to Whitehead's pursuit (invention?) of speculative philosophy (a flavor of philosophy worth having) and Russel's pursuit (invention?) of analytic philosophy (another flavor of philosophy worth having, I suppose). Musician, producer, and artist Brian Eno and painter Peter Schmidt collaborated on a series of cards meant to provoke inventive solutions. They called the series "Oblique Strategies: Over One Hundred Worthwhile Dilemmas." One of your goals as a cosmic artisan is to create art apparatuses that generate worthwhile dilemmas. Worthwhile to whom? In what ways? To what futures? These are your operative motivational questions.

The nature of your art apparatus may be derived from certain theoretical questions, or it may be derived from the results of prior apparatuses. The outcomes of your apparatuses (that which emerges from your apparatal cuts into the universe) may confirm or disconfirm prior theories, but these binary confirmations or disconfirmations in and of themselves are largely irrelevant. The best art apparatuses give rise to new theoretical interpretations, which then lead to new theoretical questions, which then lead to the creation of new apparatuses. Your apparatuses may be created based on hunches, questions, or wild conjectures (all carefully pursued). They may be created by speculatively treating one thing as if it were another thing, just to see what concrescences might emerge. Art apparatuses lead to new speculative questions which provoke the construction of new art apparatuses which lead to new speculative questions, etc. This ongoing, forward-feeding art practice is never hermetically sealed, but always in continuous dialogue with materials and their histories in the actual world. If you listen aright, the materials themselves will pose many of the questions.

Constantly remember, all this experimental troubling must nonetheless be done with care and rigor. Deleuze:

"A very lengthy preparation, yet no method, nor rules, nor recipes."[124]

The construction of your art apparatus may initially be driven by a theoretical question or provocation, but it must immediately become open to the directions in which the provocation itself begins to lead (even, especially, if it begins to lead away from an immediate and tidy resolution of the provocation). Filmmaker and theorist Trinh T. Minh-ha cautions, "A creative event does not grasp, it does not take possession, it is an excursion."[125]

As cosmic artisans, we are authorized to borrow our methods of experimental troubling from other disciplines, particularly from speculative philosophy. According to Deleuze and Guattari, the process of inventing concepts (i.e., philosophy) "implies a sort of groping experimentation and its layout resorts to measures that are not very respectable, rational, or reasonable. These measures belong to the order of dreams, of pathological processes, esoteric experiences, drunkenness, and excess."[126] Note: rigor does not exclude irrationality. There is a kind of rigorous irrationality that is particularly relevant to an art practice (and not to a scientific practice).

Following Artaud, Deleuze and Guattari continue:

Thought as such begins to exhibit snarls, squeals, stammers; it talks in tongues and screams, which leads it to create, or to try to. If thought searches, it is less in the manner of someone who possesses a method than that of a dog that seems to be making uncoordinated leaps. We have no reason to take pride in this image

124 Gilles Deleuze and Claire Parnet, *Dialogues II*, trans. Hugh Tomlinson and Barbara Habberjam (New York: Columbia University Press, 2007), 8.

125 Trinh T. Minh-ha, *When the Moon Waxes Red: Representation, Gender, and Cultural Politics* (New York: Routledge, 1991), 26.

126 Gilles Deleuze and Félix Guattari, *What Is Philosophy?*, trans. Hugh Tomlinson and Graham Burchell (London: Verso, 2009), 41.

of thought, which involves much suffering without glory and indicates the degree to which thinking has become increasingly difficult: immanence.[127]

Note: rigor does not imply a smooth, coordinated procession of inquiry. There is a kind of rigorous irregularity that is particularly relevant to an art practice (and not to a scientific practice).

6. Purposefully open your art apparatus out onto the rest of the universe, so that your apparatus may act as a proposition-generator, a lure for future feeling and becoming.

I mentioned earlier that I was bracketing and deferring Whitehead's concept of "propositions" in order to later apply it directly to the art apparatus itself. Here we are. Your art apparatus is a proposition-generator, a lure for feeling. The purposeful, particular way in which you construct it acts as a procedure for drawing out this lure. Once your art apparatus has done its work (one human "patron" at a time), it remains in the universe as a perpetual proposition-generator. Your artwork has caused something to actually, historically occur in the world, and now that occurrence becomes a real proposition which attracts, entices, lures, and provokes future becomings. Your art apparatus doesn't *prove* anything; it lures future things to become. Your art apparatus doesn't end at itself. It throws itself forward toward future becomings.

Regarding propositions, Whitehead explains, "A proposition is a new kind of entity. It is a hybrid between pure potentialities and actualities. A 'singular' proposition is the potentiality of an actual world including a definite set of actual entities in a nexus of reactions involving the hy-

---

127 Ibid., 55.

pothetical ingression of a definite set of eternal objects."[128] "A proposition is a complex entity which stands between the eternal objects and the actual occasions. Compared to eternal objects a proposition shares in the concrete particularity of actual occasions; and compared to actual occasions a proposition shares in the abstract generality of eternal objects."[129] Again, here I will substitute Deleuze's "virtual potentia" for Whitehead's "eternal objects/pure potentialities;" but otherwise, Whitehead's explanation is explicitly relevant to my claims. While the purely physical pole in an actual occasion is busy merely prehending the bare facts of prior actual data, what entices, awakens, and lures the mental pole to consider the ways in which things might become otherwise? Propositions. It is essential to note that Whitehead's propositions mostly occur at the a-conscious level. Rocks and electrons may "mentally" entertain propositions. Whitehead himself clarifies, "Finally, it must be remembered that propositions enter into experience in other ways than through judgment-feelings."[130] "Propositions intensify, attenuate, inhibit, or transmute, without necessarily entering into clear consciousness, or encountering judgment."[131] And finally, "A verbal statement is never the full expression of a proposition."[132] Art apparatuses don't generate Whiteheadian propositions by positing written artist statements. Rather, their apparatal engagements with the world are purposefully constructed to generate affective propositions that lure the world into being other than it has been before.

Purposefully orient your art apparatus outward and forward, that it may most efficaciously entice, snare, and entangle future becomings. Deleuze and Guattari advise

128 Whitehead, *Process and Reality*, 185–86.
129 Ibid., 197.
130 Ibid.
131 Ibid., 263.
132 Ibid., 192.

us to "produce a deterritorialized refrain as the final end of music, release it in the Cosmos—that is more important than building a new system. Opening the assemblage onto a cosmic force."[133] Artist and Deleuze scholar Simon O'Sullivan observes, "Art is ontologically difficult. It is not made for an already constituted audience but in fact calls its audience into being."[134] Construct your art apparatus in such a way that it may propose, invite, entice, invoke, and lure new audiences and new epochs into being.

Epochs and Futures

Art apparatuses are mechanisms which instigate actual concrescences which lead the world to be created anew. But, according to Whitehead, any and every actual occasion/entity creates the world anew, always already. So, there is nothing so very special about creating the new. Indeed, it is very difficult if not impossible keep from creating the new (as the rest of this book will explore). The actual occasions generated by quality art apparatuses differ from other "ordinary" actual occasions in that they create a new that might somehow be better than the new that creates itself by default. Some art apparatuses are so ingenious at creating the new that the new they create leads to an entirely new epoch. What defines a new epoch? According to my understanding of Whitehead, when the usual modes of change themselves change, that meta-change constitutes the beginning of a new epoch. More on this definition later.

I already mentioned that John Cage's *4'33"* and Marcel Duchamp's *Fountain* created a new artistic epoch. Quantum-behavior-measuring apparatuses also created a new

133 Deleuze and Guattari, *A Thousand Plateaus*, 350.
134 Simon O'Sullivan, *Art Encounters Deleuze and Guattari: Thought Beyond Representation* (London: Palgrave Macmillan, 2006), 68.

scientific epoch. They foregrounded fundamental, heretofore unknown behavioral regularities (like superposition) that initially seemed like impossibilities. Scientists
were gradually forced to interpret the implications of
these behaviors, implications which necessitated a re-
consideration of the nature, function, and boundary of
the scientific apparatus itself. Due to quantum-behavior-measuring apparatuses, we have been forced to re-
interpret the meaning of measurement, the meaning of
an object, the meaning of a property, the meaning of a
behavior, the relationship between objects and their environments, the meaning of causality and irreversibility,
and the meaning of time. So, the double-slit apparatus is
a radical apparatus that re-defined our understanding of
an apparatus itself. The best art apparatuses do the same.

Marcel Proust's intelligent description of the way in
which art epochs change is worth citing in full:

> To succeed thus in gaining recognition, the original
> painter, the original writer proceeds on the lines ad-
> opted by oculists. The course of treatment they give us
> by their painting or by their prose is not always agree-
> able to us. When it is at an end the operator says to us:
> 'Now look!' And, lo and behold, the world around us
> (which was not created once and for all, but is created
> afresh as often as an original artist is born) appears to
> us entirely different from the old world, but perfectly
> clear. Women pass in the street, different from what
> they used to be, because they are Renoirs, those Renoir
> types which we persistently refused to see as women.
> The carriages, too, are Renoirs, and the water, and
> the sky: we feel tempted to go for a walk in the forest
> which reminds us of that other which when we first
> saw it looked like anything in the world except a for-
> est, like for instance a tapestry of innumerable shades
> but lacking precisely the shades proper to forests. Such
> is the new and perishable universe which has just been

created. It will last until the next geological catastrophe is precipitated by a new painter or writer of original talent.[135]

New epochs don't emerge from nowhere, but from the epochs which precede them. According to Deleuze and Guattari, "In a sense, everything we attribute to an age was already present in the preceding age."[136] Thus, new epochs are never created simply by ignoring prior historical decisions (whether human-made or material-made), but, on the contrary, by closely (and experimentally) attending to them.

Karen Barad insightfully observes that apparatuses play an integral part in codifying the disciplinary distinctions of a particular epoch: "Apparatuses are neither neutral probes of the natural world nor social structures that deterministically impose some particular outcome. Significantly, [...] the notion of an apparatus is not premised on inherent divisions between the social and the scientific, the human and the nonhuman, nature and culture. Apparatuses are the practices through which these divisions are constituted."[137] Similarly, if the implications of an apparatus are radical enough, prior disciplinary distinctions may be modulated and redistributed, resulting in entirely new epochs. Indeed, according to Elizabeth Grosz's reading of Deleuze, philosophy itself is "the becoming-artistic of scientific knowledge and the becoming-scientific of artistic creation."[138] The instigation of such cross-disciplinary becomings may rightly be considered the implicit charge of Deleuze's cosmic artisan.

135 Marcel Proust, *The Guermantes Way*, trans. C. K. Scott-Moncrieff (1925; Paris: Feedbooks, 2014), 296, http://www.feedbooks.com/book/1449/the-guermantes-way.
136 Deleuze and Guattari, *A Thousand Plateaus*, 346.
137 Barad, *Meeting the Universe Halfway*, 169.
138 Grosz, "Bergson, Deleuze and the Becoming of Unbecoming," 12.

An epochal shift occurs when the usual modes of change themselves change. Whitehead declares that "laws of change are themselves liable to change,"[139] and when they do, we have entered a new epoch. Whitehead explains, "The form of process is not wholly dependent upon derivation from the past. As epochs decay amid futility and frustration, the form of process derives other ideals involving novel forms of order."[140] "Entities with new relationships, unrealized in our experiences and unforeseen by our imaginations, will make their appearance, introducing into the universe new types of order."[141] Himself a renowned mathematician, Whitehead offers this (wonderfully self-deprecating) example: "There is no difficulty in imagining a world – i.e., a cosmic epoch – in which arithmetic would be an interesting fanciful topic for dreamers, but useless for practical people engrossed in the business of life."[142] According to her own original cosmology, Karen Barad proposes a very similar process, "Matter's dynamism is generative not merely in the sense of bringing new things into the world but in the sense of bringing forth new worlds, of engaging in an ongoing reconfiguring of the world."[143]

The one thing that doesn't change, according Whitehead, is the general propensity of the universe to always strive toward novelty. The modes of change may radically change from epoch to epoch, but the fundamental propensity toward change itself will never change. We (and those who survive us) will never find ourselves permanently marooned in a new epoch that has changed so much it has discarded change altogether and refuses to ever change again into the next epoch.

---

139 Whitehead, *Modes of Thought*, 95.
140 Ibid., 103.
141 Whitehead, *Process and Reality*, 288.
142 Ibid., 199.
143 Barad, *Meeting the Universe Halfway*, 170.

The potential of provoking such epochal shifts is exciting, but it is not without a very real element of danger, by definition. Following Artaud, Jacques Derrida explicitly formulates, "Danger as Becoming."[144] Elsewhere he explains, "The future can only be anticipated in the form of absolute danger. It is that which breaks absolutely with constituted normality and can only be proclaimed, presented, as a sort of monstrosity."[145] Whitehead himself soberly observes, "When fundamental change arrives, sometimes heaven dawns, and sometimes hell yawns open."[146] An ethics of rigorous care coupled with experimental daring is required if we are to invite epochal changes that will come to matter to those future societies of entities (human, material, other) that will come.

Fortunately (and unfortunately), for the cosmic artisan, the main challenge is not how to avoid accidentally unleashing something hellish, monstrous, and worse onto the world. The main challenge is how to unleash anything into the world that matters much at all one way or another. Yes, all art apparatuses can't help but make something new, but making a flavor of new that matters much demands a lifelong practice of rigorous, ongoing experimentation.

Here ends our consideration of the artwork as art apparatus, its relationship with the scientific apparatus, and how a cosmic artisan might use an art apparatus to make a new world. If you are the type of cosmic artisan who intends to make something, feel free to stop reading now and begin making your next something-making art apparatus. If, however, you are the type of cosmic artisan that intends to use your art apparatus to make nothing (or if

144 Jacques Derrida, *Writing and Difference*, trans. Alan Bass (London: Routledge, 2005), 239.
145 Jacques Derrida, *Of Grammatology*, trans. Gayatri Chakravorty Spivak (Baltimore: Johns Hopkins University Press, 1997), 5.
146 Whitehead, *Modes of Thought*, 95.

you are just curious), further inquiry is required – inquiry which leads into the shining darknesses of apophasis.

2

REGARDING APOPHASIS

Historically, apophasis is a kind of writing about God that purposefully undermines itself in order to avoid the heresy of overdetermining God by reducing him to language. It functions in conjunction with kataphatic writing, which is writing about God that straightforwardly declares God's nature and attributes. Without kataphatic writing, apophatic writing would have nothing to unsay. Without apophatic writing, kataphatic writing would quickly reduce God to a series of assertive truth statements. Apophatic writing is found in a number of religious traditions. It is associated with mysticism, and often finds itself at the boundary of orthodoxy in each of these traditions, since the tenets defining any orthodoxy must necessarily be expressed as assertive creeds, and apophatic writing is always eating away at the edges of credal assertion.

Before I get too far into an explanation of apophatic writing, I should clarify why I am even (re-)opening the notoriously problematic can of worms that is apophasis, and how I mean to appropriate apophasis for my own project. The goal of this book is to analyze some worthwhile ways of making nothing. Initially, it seems like "making nothing" should be as simple as abstaining from making something. Just quit your job making art apparatuses, and you will have succeeded at making

nothing. There is, however, an important difference between abstaining from making something and purposefully making nothing.

According to Alfred North Whitehead and process philosophy, something is always made. Indeed, one cannot
refrain from making something. Even my death brings
something new into the world, and my subsequent and
ongoing absence from the world is negatively prehended
by all future actual occasions (becomings) of the world.
Thus, to refrain from making art apparatuses (as most
non-artists already do) is still to make something. Even
when Marcel Duchamp took his famous hiatus from making art in order to focus on playing chess, he was nonetheless making something in the world. Had Duchamp
been an auto mechanic instead of an artist, and had he
decided to take an obscure hiatus from car repair to focus
on playing chess, he would still have been making something in the world. But in neither case would Duchamp
have been making an apophatic art apparatus – an art
apparatus with the express intention of making nothing.

It turns out that, since everything is always already
becoming something new (moment by moment by moment), there is really no way to make a permanent nothing. In Whitehead's own words, "You cannot approach
nothing; for there is nothing to approach."[1] To make a
permanent nothing would amount to a kind of radical,
holistic nihilism. I don't think such permanent, holistic
nothings are possible; and even if they were, I wouldn't
advocate purposefully heading toward them. When I talk
about making nothing, I am really talking about deferring (however fractionally) the inevitable, headlong rush
of the universe toward something new. I am talking about
a kind of braking, munging up, and confounding (howev-

---

1   Alfred North Whitehead, *Process and Reality* (New York: The Free
     Press, 1978), 93.

er fractionally) the inevitable becomings of the universe – the perpetual concrescences that are bound to proceed.

As in cooking, the pace at which and the order in which things come together is often of crucial importance. Gradually turning down the boil is not at all the same as throwing something immediately from a boiling pot into a bath of ice-chilled water. In both cases, room temperature is eventually reached, but the pragmatic effects are qualitatively (and often radically) different. Shock blanching something at high heat for thirty seconds is not at all the same as mildly simmering something on low heat for hours, even if the same quantitative amount of heat is imparted in each instance. Such qualitative differences in speed and sequence are never inconsequential, and rarely even incidental. In the overwhelmingly noun-centric history of philosophy, nouns and the adjectives that describe their qualities have generally been foregrounded; whereas verbs and the adverbs that describe their qualities have generally been marginalized. Likewise, the history of art has skewed toward noun-centricity. "Oh, you're an artist! Do you paint or sculpt?" Whereas the nothings we are pursuing here are not nouns with adjectival qualities. Instead, they are (jarring or confounding) adverbial arrests in verb-centric becomings that result in the deferred emergence of anything at all (whether subsequent nouns, subsequent verbs, or the noun–verbs that Whitehead calls "actual entities/occasions").

So why slam on the brakes of concrescence, actualization, and becoming? What is the ethical efficacy of such a seemingly punk rock, nihilistic sabotage of emergence? I address this question more fully in the final chapter, where I approach an ethics of nothing. But a preliminary answer here may make my incorporation of apophasis more followable and sensible. In a world where everything is always already hurtling forward into new becomings, the challenge is not how to make something new, but how to make something new that might matter. Slowing the emergence of things has been advocated (by conservation-minded folks), and accelerating the emergence of things has also been advocated (by accelerationists and capitalists alike). Both approaches can be relatively useful or relatively impotent (depending on the contexts in which they are deployed). I am simply advocating a third approach of full-on braking (for however brief an instant), in order to qualitatively modulate whatever eventually emerges subsequent to the braking.

I lived in northern Montana for a year, and I had a friend there from northern Saskatchewan who drove deftly (but cavalierly) on ice. He used his emergency brake to steer. Being from south Alabama where there is never any ice, his driving terrified me. But he was actually a safer driver than his more cautious southern counterparts who were only comfortable gradually accelerating or decelerating. His emergency brake was a normal part of his driving apparatus. By rigorously engaging it and disengaging it at strategic moments during his driving process, he was more effectively able to steer on ice. This modicum of seemingly nihilistic and jarring stoppage was actually just one more tool in his driving toolbox, one that better equipped him to co-navigate (and in a sense, surf) the trajectory that emerged from his engagement with both ice and car.

In our current era of broadly entangled and accelerated co-emergence, we are all driving on ice. This is particularly true given that most of our current cosmological models of explanation are noun-centric and event-agnostic (if not altogether event-blind). And probably, the entire history of the universe has always been a kind of driving on ice, co-deciding and co-emerging along a perpetually recalibrating vector, toward a moving future target-on-wheels which our ongoing becomings are continually repositioning. This is not a bad thing. It is (becoming) what it is (becoming). But if this is indeed the way the universe actually unfolds, then adding a nothing-making brake mechanism to our ethical and aesthetic tool box seems less like nihilistic theoretical wankery, and more like a kind of pragmatically useful safe-driving practice. I am interested in apophasis because it suggests a means of developing such a braking mechanism.

What I term braking, Whitehead himself might term "hesitation" or "indecision." In a sense, hesitation and indecision during the actual occasion are what lead to the activation of the mental pole and to the ingression and actualization of the virtual into the actual. Hesitation and indecision are ultimately what lead to conscious human thought. Whenever something can't either be dismissed out of hand (incompatible opposition negatively prehended) or prehended as bare fact without modulation (perfect concordance positively prehended), whenever there is "contrast" rather than mere incompatible opposition or perfect concordance, then there is hesitation and (potential) ingression of the virtual. Whitehead explains that during the actual occasion, things may proceed according to "yes-form" feelings, "no-form" feelings, or "suspense-form" feelings.[2] Only suspense-form feelings (may) lead to the ingression of the virtual. During the actual occasion, Whitehead says that there are judgments of belief, judgments of disbelief, and "suspended judgments." Suspended judgements allow "concentration of attention involving increase of importance."[3] In other words, when binary judgments are suspended, qualitative increases or decreases in valuation become possible. These re-valuations or re-reckonings are what reconfigure the prior actual, actualizing virtual potentia. From a similar perspective, according to Brian Massumi, "'Indecision' between activity and passivity is a positive re-

2   Ibid., 270.
3   Ibid., 273.

source for the theory of value."[4] Indecision makes a space for non-binary, affective re-valuation to occur. Returning to Whitehead, suspended judgments allow the actual occasion to prehend "information which is neither included nor excluded by our direct perception," according to an "indifference to truth or falsehood."[5] Indeed, as previously mentioned, according to Whitehead, the main importance of truth is simply that "it adds to interest."[6] Elsewhere, Whitehead explains that, "eternal objects, and propositions, and some complex sorts of contrasts, involve in their own natures indecision."[7] Whitehead says that appetition (being lured by a proposition) includes in itself "a principle of unrest, involving realization of what is not and may be."[8] To be unrestful, to hesitate, is to leave the door cracked to what is not yet but may yet become. Braking is the means by which apophatic art apparatuses invite (however insistently or courteously) such promising hesitations.

Art apparatuses that make nothing never simply create an absence, a vacuum, or a void (all impossible "somethings"). Instead, an apophatic art apparatus might enact a kind of hesitation, an indecision, a deer-in-the-headlights freeze. In so doing, the apophatic art apparatus makes nothing by arresting (however briefly) the ongoing process of becoming. Or, an apophatic art apparatus may make nothing by confounding the presence or absence binary inherent in classical human thinking, triggering a kind of back-and-forth arche-nothing that refuses to arrive at the resolved "something" of mere presence or absence. Whatever the tactics employed, apophatic art

4   Brian Massumi, "Virtual Ecology and the Question of Value," in *General Ecology: The New Ecological Paradigm,* ed. Erich Hörl (London: Bloomsbury, 2017), 354.
5   Whitehead, *Process and Reality,* 275.
6   Ibid., 259.
7   Ibid., 29.
8   Ibid., 32.

apparatuses actively make phenomena that lure and en-snare their participants (both human and material) into experiences of nothing that mere abstinence from something (don't view the artwork; don't make the artwork) could ever achieve.

Just as there are significant qualitative differences between making nothing and abstaining from making something, so too are there significant qualitative differences between making nothing and simply undoing something. "Undoing" acts on that which is already done; but undoing itself is just another new instance of doing. Since the decisions of actual occasions are irreversible, nothing can really be undone. So, for instance, mere iconoclasm does not inherently equal visual apophasis. Iconoclasm doesn't return the world to a historical state prior to the existence of icons; it just makes a new world of destroyed icons.

Furthermore, there is an important functional difference between something that is indifferent to enacting signification and something that succeeds at signifying a lack of signification. Critics Leo Bersani and Ulysse Dutoit characterize Samuel Beckett's unique understanding of failure: "To fail does not mean to represent successfully existential failures or existential meaningless; it means to fail to represent (either meaninglessness or meaning)."[9] Apophatic art apparatuses never attempt to signify a lack of signification, but sometimes they do flirt with enacting a failure to signify. Generally, however, the goal of an apophatic art apparatus is not to elude capture by human systems of signification (an impossible and tired goal), but to make nothing(s). Since everything can always be captured and put to use as a signifier by a human (even silence, even "absence," even "nothing"), apophatic art apparatuses are often indifferent toward their eventual

9   Leo Bersani and Ulysse Dutoit, *Arts of Impoverishment: Beckett, Rothko, Resnais* (Cambridge: Harvard University Press, 1993), 14.

and inevitable capture by semiotic systems. Sometimes apophatic art apparatuses purposefully attempt to defer their own semiotic capture as long as possible, and then to confound this capture when it does inevitably happen. But apophatic art apparatuses are always doing something more in the world that merely confounding human semiotic systems. The something more that they are always doing is making nothing by braking becoming.

Finally, apophatic art apparatuses are not simply literary apparatuses culled from the historical tradition of apophatic writing. Instead, they are art apparatuses which produce an apophatic occurrence or phenomenon. In the same way that I am not merely taking the concept of apparatus from quantum mechanics via analogy (since art apparatuses are legitimately functioning apparatuses), I am not merely taking apophatic tactics from literary apophasis via analogy (since apophatic art apparatuses produce actual apophatic effects, whether or not they employ human language). It is important to note that uttered human language (whether read or heard) is an actual occurrence in the world; it does not stand removed from the world. So, an apophatic art apparatus that does happen to employ human language (like Arakawa and Gins's *Mechanism of Meaning*) is not merely talking "about" the world so much as exerting an actual force in the world. It is also important to note that materials in the world already "mean" (if not always human-linguistically). So, an apophatic art apparatus that does not employ human language (like David Crawford's *Stop Motion Studies*) is still actually uttering and meaning. Both apparatuses (*Mechanism of Meaning* and *Stop Motion Studies*) (do not) mean what they (fail to) become.

I won't attempt apophatic writing in this book (although the previous sentence comes close), but I will analyze some classic examples of it. I am admittedly offering a kataphatic explanation of apophatic writing. I will use the term "God" and refer to God in the third person singular masculine as "him." Apophatic writing would quickly unsay both of these terms. As per the ways in which Jacques Derrida practiced deconstruction, it was almost always counter-productive for him to give a clear definition of deconstruction. Derrida's deconstructive practices differed from text to text, as determined by the contours of the texts he was deconstructing. I mention Derrida here because, since the emergence of deconstructive practices, deconstruction has often been associated with apophasis. I will argue that this association is not altogether fair to either practice. At any rate, I am not Derrida, and I am not even writing an apophatic text (much less practicing deconstruction). I am not even writing a book about apophatic writing. I am writing a book about apophatic art apparatuses – art apparatuses that behave apophatically. Since using an art apparatus to pragmatically make nothing is already tricky enough, I will not make it any more complicated by treating this book as if it were itself an art apparatus trying to make nothing. I will simply proceed as straightforwardly as possible.

I will first present a more expanded definition of apophasis and analyze some instructive examples of apophatic writing. This will be followed by some relevant similarities and differences between apophasis and deconstruction, in order to salvage (for my own particular purposes) what may be salvaged from deconstruction, and to distinguish the ways in which apophasis differs from deconstruction. Next, I will consider the ways in which language is real (both actually and virtually); and what "real," "actual," and "virtual" mean in regards to language. This will involve an explanation of literary critic Mikhail Bakhtin's concept of the utterance, and a brief return to Whitehead and Deleuze. I will acknowledge the sense in which the perpetual becomings of matter are themselves "discursive" (Karen Barad's term), but this recognition alone will not be enough to account for the particularly unique behaviors of human language. I will then consider the ways in which human language is itself a force in the world, but this recognition alone will not be enough to account for all that matter comes to mean. It turns out matter and language both mean and matter, but differently. Ultimately, we will arrive at an understanding of language that strongly opposes both: 1. the reduction of the universe to a giant text that awaits human interpretation; and 2. the concept that there is any such thing as direct phenomenological access to immediate meaning which would overcome the shortcomings of mediated human language.

Having thought through language and its functions in the world, I will return to apophatic language proper and extract some of its tactics for use in our apophatic art apparatuses. In particular, we will consider the sister tactics of perpetual deferral (no ending) and the arche-trace (no beginning), the powerful (hard-braking) tactic of indifference, and the immobilizing (confounding) tactic of aporia. Finally, I will consider why art might be more suitable for apophasis than writing, and think through some salient differences between apophatic art and what might be understood as deconstructive art.

A Kataphatic Explanation of Apophatic Writing

Apophatic writing is a way of talking about God that seeks to properly revere him by not overly delimiting him. "Apophasis" is negation and "kataphasis" is affirmation. Since God is beyond all we can affirm about him, in order to more accurately describe him, we must balance our affirmations with reverent negations. Theologian Bruce Ellis Benson explains, "One affirms something but denies it, because to affirm it too strongly would be heretical and to deny it completely would also be heretical."[10] In the Greek, Kataphasis means something like "toward assertive speaking" and apophasis means something like "away from assertive speaking."

By definition, it might seem that any art which refrains from using human language is apophatic. But apophatic writing doesn't simply move away from "language" (on the contrary, it traffics in the medium of language); instead, it more specifically moves away from assertive, declarative language – away from the copula of equation. Whereas kataphatic language would freely assert something like "God is love," apophatic language would never couple or equate God with anything. So visual art that traffics in non-linguistic media (as much visual art does) has not yet overcome the copula (the "is") of equation and representation. A realistic painting of a pear that is meant to represent a pear is still operating in the realm of kataphatic assertion, even if the painting lacks a human language title ("This is a Pear"). Magritte's paintings and titles playfully and ingeniously trouble this space between pictographic and linguistic assertion, but they are still probably not yet apophatic art apparatuses.

Regarding the coupling function of the "is" and its (non-)relation to apophatic writing, Jewish philosopher Jacob Taubes explains:

> In the realm of the "is"-assertion, there is no place for God. With an "is"-assertion, an object is referred to and described. The sum of "is"-assertions constitutes science. What is not an object is not knowable, cannot enter the realm of knowledge, and must be declared by science as null. But "God is not" is also the assertion of theology. For theology has always denied that God

---

10   Bruce Ellis Benson, *Graven Ideologies: Nietzsche, Derrida & Marion on Modern Idolatry* (Downers Grove: InterVarsity Press, 2002), 153.

is an object and agrees in this with atheism, and with science grounded on atheism.[11]

From this perspective, apophatic writing doesn't "unsay" language per se, but rather it "unsays" the linguistic copula, the linking verb "is" of equation, in order to avoid overly reducing God to mere ontological presence.

Indeed, "disontology" is the name given by literary historian Michael Sells to the kind of apophatic writing that refuses to reduce God to an ontological thing. Disontology is not simply an alternative way of practicing ontology. Instead, it opposes the ontological project altogether, (ab)using language in order to undermine and confound its ontological presumptions.

In the Greek, "ontology" means something like "the study of being." Ontology assumes that there even is such a thing as "being," and that being is made up of noun-ish things. Ontology tries to understand the "nature" (the essences and qualities) of these noun-ish things – what are they like individually and how do they relate to each other? Indo-European languages (including English) presume an ontological understanding of being. To ask, "What is being?" is already to presume that being is some kind of "thing" that has a "nature." Once "being" (or "the world," or "immanence," or "the real") is instead understood as a series of becomings and events in perpetual flux (à la Whitehead), this alternate understanding of being and becoming is not simply a new *kind* of ontology, but an entirely different "thing" altogether. This new way of thinking requires a new way of speaking which avoids the presuppositions of ontology – a kind of disontological speaking. Apophasis is one such way of disontologically speaking. In *Twilight of the Idols,* Nietzsche writes, "I'm afraid we're not rid of God because we still

11 Jacob Taubes, "Notes on an Ontological Interpretation of Theology," *The Review of Metaphysics* 2, no. 8 (1949): 102–3.

believe in grammar."[12] Apophasis attempts to approach a non-ontotheological, disontological God who exceeds the strictures of grammar.

The God of apophasis is a uniquely thorny entity when it comes to ontology, particularly if he is to be understood as the giver of being who himself precedes being. This giver and source of being may then subsequently choose to participate in being, but he is hardly reducible to being. It is worth noting that Whitehead's cosmology contains a God, but Whitehead's God is more like the creative force immanent to the universe itself. Whitehead's God is intrinsically bound up with Whitehead's eternal entities, and since I have chosen not to follow Whitehead into the nuances of his eternal entities, I am not bound to wrestle with the subtle nuances of his God. I'm not so much substituting the God of apophasis for Whitehead's God, because my cosmological amalgam of Whitehead and Deleuze doesn't really require (or forbid) a God, per se. But the God of apophasis must (initially) become central to my focus on apophatic writing, since the original and primary function of apophatic writing is to properly revere the apophatic God.

In a nutshell, Whitehead's God is too small to be the God of mystical apophatic writing. Whitehead's central concern is not, "Why is there always something new?" but rather "How is there always something new?" So, Whitehead's God is not the originary creator of the universe; but instead, he is a wholly immanent entity within the functional mechanisms of the universe, as contingent upon the actual real as the actual real is upon him.[13] Whereas the God of apophasis exceeds being altogether. Humans may speak kataphatically about God only inso-

---

12 Friedrich Nietzsche, *Twilight of the Idols: Or, How to Philosophize with the Hammer*, trans. Richard Polt (Indianapolis: Hackett Publishing Company, 1997), 21.

13 See particularly Whitehead, *Process and Reality*, 225, 348–49.

far as God has revealed himself to humans. In the words of (Pseudo-)Dionysius (the Areopagite), arguably the greatest Christian apophatic writer, "It alone could give an authoritative account of what it really is."[14] But humans can never speak ontologically about God as if he were some sort of categorizable thing ("He is nothing. He is no thing."[15])

It is crucial to note that, in apophatic writing, negation never takes primacy (for then it would turn into another kind of affirmation), nor does it "cancel out" the affirmative. Instead, negation and affirmation work hand-in-hand, cycling back and forth, as we try to reverently speak about God. Catholic philosopher Jean-Luc Marion explains, "Negation and affirmation bear upon the same attributes, only envisaged from two points of view. Instead of neutralizing one another, they reinforce one another with a properly unthinkable tension."[16] This back-and-forth process of affirmation and negation has been called "negative theology" (after a phrase from Dionysius's classic apophatic text *The Divine Names*), but Marion rightly points out that, "Dionysius uses nothing that might be translated as 'negative theology.' If he speaks of 'negative theologies,' in the plural, he does not separate them from the 'affirmative theologies' with which they maintain [their] relation."[17] So, although I will continue to refer to this way of writing as "apophatic," it is more properly understood as "kataphatic/apophatic."

Pseudo-Dionysius himself further reminds us that God is necessarily beyond even this kataphatic/apophatic way of thinking: "We should posit and ascribe to it all the affirmations we make in regards to beings, and more appro-

---

14 Pseudo-Dionysius, "The Divine Names," in *The Complete Works*, trans. Jean Leclercq (Mahwah: Paulist Press, 1987), 50.

15 Ibid., 103.

16 Jean-Luc Marion, *The Idol and Distance: Five Studies*, trans. Thomas A. Carlson (New York: Fordham University Press, 2001), 148.

17 Ibid., 145.

priately, we should negate all those affirmations, since it surpasses all being. Now we should not conclude that the negations are simply the opposites of the affirmations, but rather that the cause of all [God] is considerably prior to this, beyond privations, beyond every denial, beyond every assertion."[18] In other words, even the new resultant kataphatic knowledge gained by the kataphatic/apophatic way of saying/unsaying must itself be apophatically unsaid ad infinitum. Unlike some sort of Hegelian dialectic which seeks (through thesis, antithesis, and synthesis) to perpetually evolve concepts throughout history, the kataphatic/apophatic dance means to elude any synthesis (however historically temporary) and any evolution (however ongoing). Neither kataphasis nor apophasis ever get the last word. There is no last word, because any God worthy of the role necessarily eludes any sort of reduction. Apophasis means to perpetually confound, undermine, and mung up any linguistic attempt to reduce and capture the living God. It is this emphasis on the perpetual deferral of reduction (the extra-linguistic version of "reduction" might be understood as "becoming") that we mean to port from apophatic writing into our apophatic art apparatuses. A successful apophatic art apparatus is a work of art that resists (however fleetingly) the inevitable move toward becoming.

Apophatic writing shares certain affinities with many forms of experimental writing: Dadaist absurdity, Zen mysticism, Oulipian pataphysics, Korzybskian general semantics, and Derridean deconstruction, to name a few. (The specific relationship between apophatic writing and deconstruction will be explored later in this chapter.) But apophatic writing is its own unique form of literature. Importantly, apophatic writing is not simply illogical, irrational, random, arbitrary, or generic. On the contrary,

18 Pseudo-Dionysius, "The Mystical Theology," in *The Complete Works*, 136. [Bracketed comments are mine.]

apophatic writing is rigorous, non-arbitrary, and quite specific. Michael Sells explains, "The apophatic paradoxes are constructed upon a foundation of conventional logical distinctions; the more highly tuned the rationality of the kataphatic context, the more successful will be the apophatic paradox."[19] This practice of rigorous unsaying that is in meticulous dialogue with the specific contours of the kataphatic assertions which it unsays makes apophasis a particularly suitable tactic for any art apparatus that means to "make nothing" (brake the becoming) of the well-decided materials with which it is in dialogue.

Before we proceed to some specific examples of apophatic writing, it is important to understand that any apophatic experience ultimately exceeds the generic confines of "literature" and "writing." As philosopher and literary theorist William Franke clarifies:

> The experience of apophasis, as an experience of not being able to say, is quintessentially linguistic: the experience itself is intrinsically an experience of the failure of language [...]. And yet the experience in question is not fundamentally experience of language or of any other determinable object, for this could be adequately expressed. The experiencing subject is affected by "something" beyond all it can objectively comprehend, something engendering affects that it cannot account for nor even be sure are its own.[20]

Successful apophatic writing must always ultimately exceed any tidy reduction to writing, speaking, human language, and even non-human discursivity; because the

19 Michael A. Sells, *The Mystical Languages of Unsaying* (Chicago: University of Chicago Press, 1994), 212.
20 William Franke, "Apophasis as a Mode of Discourse," preface to *On What Cannot Be Said: Apophatic Discourses in Philosophy, Religion, Literature, and the Arts*, ed. William Franke, vol. 2 (Notre Dame, Indiana: University of Notre Dame Press, 2007), 3.

goal of apophasis is to confound reduction. So, although we have chosen to begin with the historical genre that is apophatic writing, apophasis itself is an affective experience, not merely a style of linguistic formulation. As such, apophatic experiences can be (and are) triggered by a variety of non-linguistic materials.

Some Examples of Apophatic Writing

Without much accompanying analysis or commentary, here are some historical examples of apophatic writing. I've tried to select passages of extreme apophasis in order to foreground the very limits of the genre. I've chosen passages written by Pseudo-Dionysius (c. 500 CE) and Meister Eckhart (1260–1328 CE), both Christians famous for their apophatic writing. Apophatic writing occurs across most religions (there is a particularly strong strain within the Sufi tradition of Islam), and even (arguably) in various genres of philosophy, but it seems to me that apophasis is forced to be at its most extreme when faced with kataphatic assertions that are most straightforward and clearly formulated. Christianity, with its specific claims of a particular, incarnate, historical messiah presents apophatic writers within the Christian tradition with a particularly acute challenge, and Dionysius and Eckhart ingeniously rise to that challenge in the following passages.

Regarding God

God is not some kind of being. No. [...] He was not. He will not be. He did not come to be. He is not in the midst of becoming. He will not come to be. No. He is not. [...] He is not contained in being. [...] He has every shape and structure, and yet is formless and beautyless. [...] He is nothing. He is no thing.[21]

God is therefore known in all things and as distinct from all things. He is known through knowledge and through unknowing. Of him there is conception, reason, understanding, touch, perception, opinion, imagination, name, and many other things. On the other hand, he cannot be understood, words cannot contain him, and no name can lay hold of him. He is not one of the things that are and he cannot be known in any of them. He is all things in all things and he is no thing among things. He is known to all from all things and he is known to no one from anything. This is the sort of language we must use about God.[22]

It is not soul or mind, nor does it possess imagination, conviction, speech, or understanding. Nor is it speech per se, understanding per se. It cannot be spoken of and it cannot be grasped by understanding. It is not number or order, greatness or smallness, equality or inequality, similarity or dissimilarity. It is not immovable, moving, or at rest. It has no power, it is not power, nor is it light. It does not live nor is it life. It is not a substance, nor is it eternity or time. It cannot be grasped by the understanding since it is neither knowledge nor truth. It is not kingship. It is not wisdom. It is neither one nor oneness, divinity nor goodness. Nor is it a spirit, in the sense in which we understand that term. It is not sonship or fatherhood and it is nothing known to us or to any other being. It falls neither within the predicate of nonbeing nor of being. Existing beings do not know it as it actually is and it does not know them as they are. There is no speaking of it, nor name nor

21 Pseudo-Dionysius, "The Divine Names," 98–103.
22 Ibid., 108–9.

knowledge of it. Darkness and light, error and truth – it is none of these. It is beyond assertion and denial.[23]

Whoever perceives something in God and attaches thereby some name to him, that is not God. God is above names and above nature.[24]

God is nameless because none can say or understand anything about Him.[25]

As he is simply one, without any manner and properties, he is not Father or Son or Holy Spirit, and yet he is a something that is neither this nor that.[26]

You should know Him without image, without means, and without semblance.[27]

Regarding Mystical Practices

It is not God's intention in his works that man should have in himself a place for God to work in. Poverty of spirit is for a man to keep so free of God and of all his works that if God wishes to work in the soul, he himself is the place in which he wants to work... Man should be so poor that he should not be or have any place in which God could work. When man clings to place, he clings to distinction.[28]

---

23 Pseudo-Dionysius, "The Mystical Theology," 141.

24 Meister Eckhart, *Meister Eckhart: The Essential Sermons, Commentaries, Treatises, and Defense,* trans. Bernard McGinn (New York: Paulist Press, 1981), 204.

25 Meister Eckhart, *The Complete Mystical Works of Meister Eckhart,* trans. Bernard McGinn (New York: Crossroad, 2009). 463.

26 Meister Eckhart, *Meister Eckhart: The Essential Sermons,* 181.

27 Meister Eckhart, *The Complete Mystical Works of Meister Eckhart,* 464.

28 Meister Eckhart, *Meister Eckhart: The Essential Sermons,* 202.

What is the final end? It is the hidden darkness of the eternal Godhead, which is unknown and never has been known and never shall be known. God abides there unknown in Himself, and the light of the eternal Father has ever shone in there, and the darkness does not comprehend the light.[29]

Lead us up beyond unknowing and light, / ...in the brilliant darkness of a hidden silence.[30]

We pray to enter within the super-bright gloom, and through not seeing and not knowing, to see and to know that the not to see nor to know is itself the above sight and knowledge.[31]

Leave behind you everything perceived and under-stood, everything perceptible and understandable, all that is not and all that is... By an undivided and abso-lute abandonment of yourself and everything, shed-ding all and freed from all, you will be uplifted to the ray of the divine shadow which is above everything that is.[32]

As we plunge into that darkness which is beyond intel-lect, we shall find ourselves not simply running short of words but actually speechless and unknowing.[33]

* * *

---

29 Meister Eckhart, *The Complete Mystical Works of Meister Eckhart*, 283.
30 Pseudo-Dionysius, "The Mystical Theology," 135.
31 Pseudo-Dionysius, "Mystic Theology," in *The Works of Dionysius the Areopagite*, trans. John Parker (London: James Parker and Co., 1897), 133.
32 Pseudo-Dionysius, "The Mystical Theology," 135.
33 Ibid., 139.

My goal in citing the above examples is not to lay out any sort of particular theological propositions. Any such propositions would be beyond the scope of this book. Among other things, the God of mystical apophatic writing is a kind of limit-case study of an entity who refuses to ever finally and reductively resolve into any stable or static thing. The God of Pseudo-Dionysius and Meister Eckhart is useful to us not because he is a typical example of the kinds of enduring objects we will encounter in our art apparatuses (apophatic or otherwise). Far from it. Rather, the ways in which these mystical writers are forced to approach such an anomalous entity causes them to invent rigorous braking strategies, linguistic ways of making nothing, which will become useful to our own apophatic art apparatuses as we attempt to brake (however temporarily) the eventually inevitable self-becoming of ordinary actual occasions.

It is important to note that Dionysius and Eckhart aren't purposefully obfuscating the issues or deceptively muddying the waters with tangentially vague, abstract language. Apophatic writing is not mere sophistry. Instead, it rigorously traces the contours of its subject to the point at which the representational, denominating, explicative, kataphatic function of language itself is exhausted. This exhaustion doesn't affirm or deny the "being" or "existence" or "immanence" or "transcendence" of God. It merely enacts the inability of language to reduce God to any one of these states. Such extreme apophatic writing initially invites and then requires and enforces a kind of intellectually athletic (and often contortive) performative reading. The texts above do indeed denotatively mean what they say (they are not mere babble), but their main goal is not simply to clearly assert truths (that would move them toward the realm of kataphasis). Instead, these texts mean to lead their readers away from the realm of assertive truth statements. The apophatic experience that the reader has while being led away from assertion is itself the "meaning" of the texts. The texts "mean" the performative intellectual contortions that they instigate. Of course, the same could be said of all texts. All texts "mean" the performative readings that they instigate; it's just that kataphatic texts instigate less contortive readings than apophatic texts. According to this understanding, then, all texts (whether kataphatic or apophatic, denotative or poetic, sensible or absurd) function as apparatuses. All texts invite an utterance phenomenon (whether heard or read) to occur. More relevant to our interests, the particular apophatic passages above function as *apophatic* apparatuses. But they are not yet apophatic *art* apparatuses. To make apophatic art apparatuses, we either need materials other than text, or additional materials in conjunction with text, or we need to treat text as a different kind of supra-semiotic material.

Relevant Similarities and Differences between Apophatic Writing and Deconstruction

Much has already been written on both apophasis and deconstruction. A fair amount has even been written on the relationship between the two. Derrida himself has written about their relationship. Is deconstruction merely a contemporary form of apophatic writing, or is apophatic writing an ancient form of deconstruction? Or are the two mutually exclusive? Or do the two exist in some other more oblique and complicated relationship? Since apophatic writing and deconstruction are both means of troubling stable ontologies, it has proved (and will continue to prove) inherently difficult to construct stable, reductive ontologies about what these two practices are and are not. I will argue that apophatic writing and deconstruction are mostly different, with certain overlapping similarities and goals. In order to make my case, I must first briefly describe my understanding of deconstruction – an infamously slippery task since, like apophasis, deconstruction inherently resists reduction to resolved, assertive definitions.

Before I tackle a gloss of deconstruction, here is a quite apophatic passage by Derrida himself which could have resided comfortably above amongst the Eckhart and Pseudo-Dionysius passages:

> Of him there is nothing said that might hold [...] –Save his name [...] – Save the name that names nothing that might hold, not even a divinity, nothing whose withdrawal does not carry away every phrase that tries to measure itself against him. "God" "is" the name of this bottomless collapse, of this endless desertification of language.[34]

Derrida is quite familiar with the mystical traditions of negative theology and the historical practices of apophatic writing practiced within them. Arguably, deconstruction has its precedence in the historical traditions of apophatic writing; but deconstruction is (usually) not, technically or even functionally, apophatic writing.

Derrida purposefully resists regularly and clearly defining deconstruction. He even resists regularly using the noun "deconstruction" as the moniker of his philosophical project. Derrida makes most sense to me as a kind of post-phenomenological philosopher, and less sense to me as a literary theorist. His goal is to read philosophical texts deconstructively, one by one; not to establish a new form of literary criticism known as "deconstruction." However (in the context of a "dialogue" with analytic phi-

---

34 Jacques Derrida, "Post-Scriptum: Aporias, Ways and Voices," trans. John P. Leavey, Jr., in *Derrida and Negative Theology*, eds. Harold Coward and Toby Foshay (Albany: State University of New York Press, 1992), 300.

losopher John Searle), Derrida does come fairly close to defining deconstruction in the following passage:

> The structure of the area in which we are operating here calls for a strategy that is complex and tortuous, involuted and full of artifice: for example, exploiting the target against itself by discovering it at times to be the "basis" of an operation directed against it; or even discovering "in it" the cryptic reserve of something utterly different.[35]

Deconstruction first reads a text according to the contours of the text's own fault lines, and in so doing discovers these fault lines (implications of the text not overtly stated in the text, weaknesses of the text which the author has attempted to marginalize, prior assumptions that the text has made which work against the very assertions the text is trying to make). According to Derrida, "The movements of deconstruction do not destroy structures from the outside. They are not possible and effective, nor can they take accurate aim, except by inhabiting those structures."[36] Deconstruction then writes its own text in dialogue with the source text. The deconstructive text proceeds according to the logic of the source text, and like a mathematical proof, eventually comes to the aspects of the source text that are inconsistent, revealing them. Unlike a mathematical proof, nothing is reductively proved or disproved by the deconstructive text. Instead, the deconstructive text is itself immediately open to subsequent deconstructive readings. Indeed, if the deconstructive text is truly deconstructive, it openly invites such future readings.

---

35 Jacques Derrida, *Limited Inc.*, trans. Alan Bass and Samuel Webber (Evanston: Northwestern University Press, 1988), 55.

36 Jacques Derrida, *Of Grammatology,* trans. Gayatri Chakravorty Spivak (Baltimore: Johns Hopkins University Press, 1997), 144.

"Deconstruction" is not a philosophy that asserts its own truth, but more like a way of proceeding. As literary theorist Jonathan Culler explains, "Deconstruction has no better theory of truth. It is a practice of reading and writing attuned to the aporias that arise in attempts to tell us the truth."[37] In this sense, deconstruction is similar to apophatic writing. Both "feed off" the kataphatic truth assertions of their source texts.

Each deconstructive reading will be different – tactically, formally, rhetorically, tonally. The way in which the deconstructive text proceeds will depend largely on the way in which the source text proceeds. And, according to Culler, "Paradoxically, the more powerful and authoritative an interpretation [i.e., a source text], the more [deconstructive] writing it generates."[38] Again, this is similar to apophatic writing. The more specific the kataphatic assertion, the more necessarily contorted the apophatic writing must be. And, as with deconstruction, there is no single, rote formula or method for the ways in which apophatic writing may be done. Each apophatic approach varies depending on the particular contours of the source kataphatic assertion, and thus both approaches (deconstruction and apophasis) are contingent upon the existence of some prior kataphatic assertion. In this sense, deconstructive readings and apophatic writings are like quantum-behavior-measuring apparatus: each relies on a prepared initial state. Art apparatuses also rely on a prepared initial state: their source materials (in whatever media).

The main differences between apophatic writing and deconstruction lie in their ethical goals, however obliquely these must be inferred. The goal of apophatic writing is to undermine ontological language (language based on

---

37 Jonathan Culler, *On Deconstruction: Theory and Criticism after Structuralism* (Ithaca: Cornell University Press, 1985), 80.
38 Ibid., 47.

presences, essences, identities, and assertions of truth) *as it attempts to describe God* (note: the uniquely anomalous nature of God as subject matter is essential) in order to perhaps mystically be encountered by the God who is beyond "there/not there," beyond "is/is not." The goal of deconstruction (as I understand it) is to undermine ontological language *as it attempts to describe any and everything at all* in order to give difference its due – to reveal difference (rather than presence, essence, or identity) as the actual means by which all meaning in the world emerges.

The fact that apophasis unsays texts about God whereas deconstruction deconstructs texts about any topic whatsoever may seem minor, but it actually puts apophasis and deconstruction in two different philosophical camps. Apophasis would not deny the positivist elements of the universe itself. Attributes, behaviors, and characteristics of actual entities do not arise merely as the result of pure difference. Positivist characteristics are real and in the immanent world. Apophasis does not deny any of this. It would only add a, "Yes, and... the God about which we write also exceeds all immanence." Apophasis doesn't claim that *everything* (or indeed, any other thing) exceeds immanence. The apophatic God alone flashes in and out of immanence at whim and will. Whitehead is intent upon keeping all outside, transcendental forces from being smuggled into his wholly immanent cosmology. Contrarily, apophasis asserts that there is one (and only one) especially unique entity who is not constrained by immanence, being, entity-ness, thingness, or anything else. There is one (and only one) exception to the constraints of immanence: God.

Deconstruction's project is altogether different in respect to positivist forces, entities, and God. The goal of deconstruction is not to unsay meaning itself, but to dethrone the idea that meaning is the result of originary essences and identities (nouns with inherent qualities and properties), and to replace this idea with a demonstration of how meaning is actually the result of ongoing (non-originary) differences. So, for example, green means green not because there is some fundamental, originary, foundational essence of greenness in the world, but because there are all sorts of differences in the world between colors (always already), and the "meaning" of green arises from these differences. The difference between red and green is not derived from an essential property of redness and an essential property of greenness. Instead, red and green are themselves derived from the difference between themselves (and all other colors). Deconstruction means to foreground and enact difference (as opposed to essence, presence, or identity) as constitutive of meaning, so deconstruction always downplays and undermines essence, presence, or identity as originary. This approach of undermining essence as foundational and originary is not applied to God alone, but to everything in the universe.

Apophasis, on the other hand, means to give God (alone) his due by enacting the failure of language to reduce him to an ontological meaning. Deconstruction is primarily concerned with difference in and of itself (wherever that concern may lead, as long as it doesn't permanently and statically lead back to difference as a new originary presence). Apophasis is primarily concerned with God himself (wherever that may lead, as long as it doesn't permanently and statically lead back to assertive or reductive declarations about God). Deconstruction undermines presence to get at difference. Apophasis undermines meaning altogether to get at God. Deconstruction and apophasis each make a kind of nothing, but deconstruction attempts to make an ongoing nothing of everything, which (according to Whitehead's cosmology of perpetual process) is simply not sustainable for very long. Deconstruction makes nothing of the primacy of presence and arrives at a vibrant (but ultimately unmoored) world of differences differing. Apophasis makes nothing of all meaning (whether identity-derived or difference-derived) and arrives at God-only-knows-where. The implicit faith wager involved in apophasis is that God may manifest himself, but there can never be any guarantee of this. Apophasis rigorously descends or ascends into nothing and waits to be found by God (or not).

Just as deconstruction requires ontological language in order to have something to deconstruct, so apophasis requires kataphatic language in order to have something to unsay. But these two relationships are not perfectly analogous. The former relationship is much more antagonistic; the latter much more resigned. Apophatic writing doesn't need to deconstruct kataphatic writing in order to achieve its goals. Indeed, without kataphatic assertions perpetually remaining to balance the apophatic project, apophatic writing risks heresy (as Meister Eckhart tragically discovered).

The differences between apophasis and deconstruction become particularly acute when one attempts to read apophatic texts deconstructively. It becomes like applying one kind of sulfuric acid to another. Apophatic texts are not your normal presence-presuming texts, defenselessly and naively awaiting deconstruction. Consequently, when Derrida himself attempts a deconstructive reading of Pseudo-Dionysius (in "How to Avoid Speaking: Denials"[39]), it is with such rigor and care that Derrida becomes maddeningly indirect and circuitous, with occasional flashes (due to exhaustion?) of uncharacteristic directness and an (almost) biographical or confessional tone. It is as if Pseudo-Dionysius's "The Mystical Names" is itself exhausting Derrida's own deconstructive reading of it. Derrida can't avoid assertively imposing his

39 Jacques Derrida, "How To Avoid Speaking: Denials," trans. John P. Leavey, Jr., in *Derrida and Negative Theology*, eds. Harold Coward and Toby Foshay (Albany: State University of New York Press, 1992), 73–142.

overarching concern with difference onto a text that has itself already moved beyond the identity–difference dichotomy in relation to God.

For our purposes, apophasis is more suitable than deconstruction for the creation of art apparatuses that make nothing, because apophasis is able to work within Whitehead's cosmology of becoming. Apophasis doesn't need to undermine all presence for all time under all circumstances everywhere forever. It simply needs to make local and temporary naught of presence in the exceptional and singular case of God. What we are porting from apophasis, then, is not a nihilistic approach that would break the entire universe, or even an ethics of (arche-) primary difference that would undermine every and all essences everywhere forever. Indeed, apophasis is flexibly indifferent to the battle between identity and difference regarding all other entities save one (God). Indeed, even in the case of God, apophasis doesn't ever permanently side with difference or absence against identity or essence. It merely performatively and cyclically enacts the role of difference in conjunction with its identity-centric counterpart, kataphasis. Thus, apophasis is a better, less universal, more locally applicable tool than deconstruction for our art apparatuses. We don't need to break the universe, we only need to brake a part of the universe, and follow wherever such braking may lead.

Language as Actual/Virtual via Mikhail Bakhtin's "Utterance"

It turns out that tactics from apophatic writing are directly applicable to art apparatuses in actual ways and not by mere analogy. This is not because the world itself is a text (that would require shoehorning all material in the world to fit into human linguistic structures); nor because human language is merely an ordinary and usual form of material discursivity (that would require diluting, flattening, and dishonoring the unique and complex historical accretions that have resulted in human language being in the world). There is a third way to think about human language and its actual functions in the world which will help us more clearly understand the relevance and applicability of apophatic writing tactics to art apparatuses intent on making nothing. This third understanding comes via Mikhail Bakhtin's concept of the utterance, and its relevance to Deleuze's virtual/actual model of the real as applied to Whitehead's cosmology of concrescence.

Prior to unpacking Bakhtin's concept of the utterance, here are some explanations from Bakhtin himself:

> Language enters life through concrete utterances (which manifest language) and life enters language through concrete utterances as well. The utterance is an exceptionally important node of problems. [...] Only the contact between the language meaning and the concrete reality that takes place in the utterance can create the spark of expression. It exists neither in the system of language nor in the objective reality surrounding us. Thus, emotion, evaluation, and expression are foreign to the word of language and are born only in the process of its live usage in a concrete utterance.[40]

An "utterance" event could be spoken words uttered at a particular historical time, but it could also be an instance of reading a book at a particular historical time. What it can't be is simply a book sitting on a shelf unread. The book on the shelf unread contains the syntactic, system-

---

40 Mikhail Bakhtin, "The Problem of Speech Genres," in *Speech Genres and Other Late Essays*, trans. Vern W. McGee (Austin: University of Texas Press, 1986), 63, 87.

atic, grammatical side of human "language," but that is only one side. I propose that the book on the shelf unread is akin to (but not exactly like) Deleuze's virtual real. It may be instantiated and read (aloud or quietly) in history at any time, in which case it then becomes actualized, it becomes actually real as it ingresses into all of the actual occasions that take place during that particular utterance occurrence. If humans suddenly stop talking and reading and go extinct on the earth in actual history, the human "language" in the book on the shelf freezes and loses its ongoing, becoming relationship with the rest of the universe. The physical book itself (as a material object) is still prehended as an enduring object by any relevant actual occasions, and even the language within the book is arguably negatively prehended, but the language itself has a negligible effect on the actual real.

However, as long as humans are alive on the planet, talking and reading, even if we ourselves never open that particular book, the words used in that book continue to change over the years through ongoing usage in actual utterance events (changes that feed into and condition the potentia of the virtual real), so that when we finally do open the book and read it (prehending it into a series of actual occasions), our human understanding of certain words in that book will be different now than it was ten years ago. Artist and theorist Joseph Grigely even adds the supplemental idea that when an author pens a text, that historical event of writing (or typing or dictating or whatever) is itself an utterance. It is by no means the defining or final utterance of that particular series of words, but it still qualifies as an actual utterance.[41]

The speaker of written language speaks once by writing. Her speech is then archived and time-shifted. It is translated into a potential future event that is only com-

41 See particularly Joseph Grigely, *Textualterity: Art, Theory and Textual Criticism* (Ann Arbor: University of Michigan Press, 1998), 113–17.

pleted (performed) upon its subsequent reading. Further-more, with each new reading (even by the same "listen-er") a new utterance event occurs. Because the writer has already completed her single utterance performance (the initial writing) by the time her book is read (re-uttered), the event-contingent aspect of this two-part process (writing and reading) is often overlooked and superseded by an inordinate emphasis on the static words them-selves, what they signify, and how they fit into a syntac-tic or semiotic system. This calcification of the written word, this inordinate emphasis on its denominational, denotative aspects, is what Bakhtin's theory of the utter-ance seeks to counteract. Bakhtin's theory of the utter-ance properly accounts for the importance of the lived, bodily, actual affect of the utterance event (what might simply be described as "context") on the "meaning" of human language.

Bakhtin's concept of the utterance may be further sup-plemented with Roland Barthes's concept of intertextu-ality, the idea that any single text is actually itself a tissue of citations of prior texts (whether explicitly footnoted or not). And yet, according to Bakhtin, without lived, his-torical, actually real utterance events (whether they occur via speaking or listening or writing or reading), human "language" remains hermetically sealed. Without real-time historical utterance events (which occur millions of times a day all over the world, and have occurred, day af-ter day, for thousands of years), virtual human language (unread written language in a book on a shelf) is impo-tent to exert its influence on the actual real. Furthermore, without ongoing historical utterance events, this same virtual language is unable to receive new meanings and connotations that evolve from the particular inflections, affects, timbres, typefaces, lighting, or contexts of each specific, actually real, historical utterance. This two-way transfer of meaning is why Bakhtin calls the utterance event "an exceptionally important node of problems."

This second aspect (the flow of lived actual language into virtual language) is particularly important. The utterance is the way in which "the world" gets into "language." For example, imagine you are reading this paragraph in a coffee house. The way your coffee tastes and the music to which you are listening and the sunlight through the window and the condition (and media) of your edition of the book and the typeface in which the book is set are all affectively modulating the language you are reading (in subtle but actually real ways). Subsequent to this utterance event (your reading of this paragraph), the next time you think and use and read and speak any of the words in this paragraph, those words have changed for you (however subtly) based on this particular reading (utterance) of the paragraph. Furthermore, if you read this same paragraph again two days later in a different setting (or even in the same setting), that second reading constitutes a completely new utterance event. All of human language may thus be usefully understood as an ongoing and evolving dialogue amongst all humans throughout all history, but a dialogue totally contingent upon and entangled with the real historical instances (and the non-human materials involved in those instances) in which each word has been uttered. Language itself cannot evolve without the actual utterance event.

To give another example, suppose that I bodily meet a friend with whom I have previously corresponded online but have never met "in real life." We talk and spend time together. Those utterance events which occurred throughout our bodily meeting have now altered our subsequent online communication. That fact is obvious enough. But each of those utterances has now also altered all of our future communication with other humans (whether online or off), and has also altered (to however subtle a degree) the history of the English language (assuming we are speaking English). Furthermore, there is nothing magical about us having met bodily (although obviously there are important qualitative differences between online and offline utterances). The online correspondences that my friend and I had prior to our bodily meeting also qualify as actual utterances. Bakhtin's utterance doesn't prioritize the spoken voice, or bodily presence, or any particular form of text. The utterance simply has to happen in lived, historical time. It has to be an actual event.

To Bakhtin, the event of any single conversation between two people is an extension of a larger, ongoing historical conversation. Each utterance is a speech act in response to another utterance, going backwards through time. It is not merely that we all inherited the syntax of a common language system. Instead, we are all inheritors of every preceding conversation that has actually happened historically. Our current, nuanced understanding of language is subtly colored by every utterance anyone has ever made. In Bakhtin's own words:

> Any speaker is himself a respondent to a greater or lesser degree. He is not, after all, the first speaker, the one who disturbs the eternal silence of the universe. And he presupposes not only the existence of the language system he is using, but also the existence of preceding utterances – his own and others – with which his given utterance enters into one kind of relationship to another [...]. Any utterance is a link in a very complexly organized chain of other utterances.[42]

All utterances are thus vehicles of transmutation which are simultaneously dependent on their immediate, subjective contexts and on a history of previous contexts. From the perspective of Whitehead's cosmology, this makes perfect sense. Each utterance is comprised of a series of actual occasions. Each one of these actual occa-

---

42 Bakhtin, "The Problem of Speech Genres," 69.

sions prehends all prior actual occasions (whether negatively or positively) and ingresses the positive prehensions into itself.

Granted, Bakhtin's utterance does prioritize a kind of
human subject, but Bakhtin is writing his theory prior to
object oriented ontology and its anthropocentric warn-
ings. Might we imagine cross-species utterances ("Las-
sie, come here girl!")? Might we imagine animal, plant, or
even rock utterances? Of course.

According to Bakhtin's theory of the utterance, uttered
human language is always already doing much more than
merely describing the real world (although it is doing that
too). Uttered language is actually altering the history of
the world. Language is itself a part of (not apart from) the
actual world; it is an actual force in the actual world. Language is not merely descriptive or syntactical; it is also an
enacted and context-contingent event. Human language
operates as a force in the actual world via any entity able
to access its virtual reservoir. Most humans are such entities, and humans are not the only ones with such access.

Photographer Hollis Frampton famously observed,
"Photography is not a substitute for anything." Art historian Liz Kotz later proposed the radical corollary, "Language is not a substitute for anything."[43] The implication is that language, like photography, is freed from the
burden of re-presentation, to develop as its own artistic
medium. Language does not simply declare, define, or
describe. As such, language is less usefully understood
solely from the Saussurean perspective of signifier and
signified and better understood as a holistic relationship
between a virtual language system and an actual uttered
historical event, one feeding into the other in an ongoing, unfolding progression. Meaning is never solely dis-

---

43 Liz Kotz, *Words To Be Looked At: Language in 1960s Art* (Cambridge:
MIT Press, 2007), 188.

embodied and propositional, but always context-dependent and enacted. To revisit Bakhtin's own explanation:

> The natural meaning of the word applied to a particular actual reality under particular real conditions of speech communication creates a spark of expression [...]. Only the contact between the language meaning and the concrete reality that takes place in the utterance can create the spark of expression.[44]

To reiterate, apart from a lived, historical utterance event, any "meaning" that exists in an abstract linguistic system remains quarantined, bereft, and contextless.

Notably, something akin to Bakhtin's concept of the utterance is suggested in the writings of Derrida. Derrida is frequently mischaracterized as one who seeks to reduce the entire material world into a kind of text, but as literary theorist Claire Colebrook argues, "Derrida is not, we are coming to understand, a textualist; he does not endorse a narrowly linguistic idealism."[45] In *Limited, Inc.*, Derrida begins with the speech-act theory of J.L. Austin, which famously observes that certain kinds of "performative" utterances enact what they say. (For example, the utterance, "I promise," actually makes a promise.) Austin distinguishes these kinds of performative utterances from ordinary "constative" (declarative) utterances. For example, according to Austin, an utterance like, "The sky is blue," is constative and not performative. Yet even Austin is haunted by the implication that "mere" constative utterances are themselves performative. In his seminal text *How To Do Things with Words,* Austin confesses:

44 Bakhtin, "The Problem of Speech Genres," 86–87.
45 Claire Colebrook, "Matter without Bodies," *Derrida Today* 4, no. 1 (2011): 3.

Clearly any, or almost any, perlocutionary act [the changing of a listener's mind] is liable to be brought off, in sufficiently special circumstances, by the issuing, with or without calculation, of any utterance whatsoever, and in particular by a straightforward constative utterance (if there is such an animal).[46]

But Austin fails to develop this insight toward its more radical conclusion. Derrida expands Austin by claiming that all utterances (whether declarative or explicitly performative) are themselves performative. This is true because all utterances cause something to happen in the world. In Derrida's own words, "The promise is not just one speech act among others; every speech act is fundamentally a promise."[47]

Austin is concerned with the intention of the speaker, as if what the speaker means to convey is somehow essential in determining the particular genre of the speech act. But Derrida is unconcerned with the intention of the speaker, since the force and effect of an utterance are never solely determined by the speaker's intentions. And Bakhtin is more concerned with the context of the utterance, since saying "I promise" as an actor in a theater performance would not be the same as saying it as a groom during a wedding ceremony.

Elsewhere, Derrida introduces the idea of "the unconscious text" which seems very similar to what I am calling the "virtual real" aspect of Bakhtin's utterance theory. In *Writing and Difference,* Derrida explains, "The unconscious text is already a weave of pure traces, differences in which meaning and force are united—a text nowhere present, consisting of archives which are always already

46 J.L. Austin, *How To Do Things with Words* (London: Oxford University Press, 1962), 110. [Bracketed clarifications are mine.]
47 Jacques Derrida, "The Villanova Roundtable," In *Deconstruction in a Nutshell: A Conversation with Jacques Derrida*, ed. John D. Caputo (New York: Fordham University Press, 1997), 22–23.

transcriptions. Originary prints. Everything begins with reproduction. Always already: repositories of a meaning which was never present."[48] The utterance event would thus be the occurrence which takes these "non-present texts" (proto-meanings, differences differing, possibilities of new meanings yet to emerge) and prehends them into actual history.

It will be useful now to pause and connect our current understanding of the utterance back to art apparatuses. It would seem that if the utterance itself is a kind of actual phenomenon, then it must necessarily involve humans; and indeed, it usually does. But the utterance does not solely involve humans as reflective, disembodied, thinking cogitos who use language as a once-removed means of abstractly understanding the world, or even as a kind of Machiavellian means of socially controlling other human behavior within a sociologically sequestered, human-centric "culture" that never quite manages to touch the "physical" world of "nature." The problem is not with Bakhtin's utterance model of human language and its relationship with the actual world, but with our understanding of what humans are doing in the actual world when we utter human language.

It is true that humans do not directly and immediately control objects with incantatory spells, causing rocks to levitate by verbally commanding them to do so. The effects of human language on rocks are less direct but no less actual. Land deeds, quarry rights, construction blueprints, town hall dialogues, blog essays about housing shortages, and thousands of other human language utterances have contributed to the eventual and actual levitation of many rocks into many buildings. Because humans are part of the "natural" world and are themselves enduring objects within the world, human language is an actual force in the actual "physical" world. We need not

---

48 Derrida, *Writing and Difference*, 265–66.

even take recourse in the argument that certain behavioral patterns of animals constitute a legitimate kind of language (although this is true), or that all materials in the world make "discursive" decisions (à la Barad) that come to mean what these materials have decided to become (although this is also true). It is enough to note that human language causes many actual, physical events to occur in the world. This is because language is always doing more than merely re-presenting the world.

Some of the apophatic art apparatuses we examine will use human language, and some will not. Most of our apophatic art apparatuses will involve humans, but this fact is not shameful or inordinately anthropocentric, as long as materials from the world are also included and given their own say. We will even take time to speculatively consider certain kinds of art apparatuses which do not involve humans, but these will be exceptional.

Because we mean to examine art apparatuses that actually make nothing (instead of merely illustrating "nothing"), it becomes useful to make a case for the actual efficacious force of human language in the world. If ordinary, descriptive human language can be shown to always already have an actual force in the world, how much more of a force will the purposefully disontological, intentionally affective language of apophasis have on the world? It is from this affectively forceful language of apophasis that our art apparatuses import their tactics. Bakhtin's model of the utterance makes a case for the actual, efficacious force and function of any and all human language in the world. Having preliminarily associated the functioning of language with the functioning of the art apparatus, let us return to examining the utterance in a bit more detail.

Bakhtin is useful for our purposes because he recognizes that *all* forms of utterance are tinged with contextual affect, not just spoken utterances. He writes:

Each text (both oral and written) includes a significant number of various kinds of natural aspects devoid of signification [...] but which are still taken into account (deterioration of manuscript, poor diction, and so forth). There are not nor can there be any pure texts. In each text, moreover, there are a number of aspects that can be called technical (the technical side of graphics, pronunciation, and so forth).[49]

Proust echoes these sentiments when he writes:

Books, [...] through the way their cover opens, through the quality of the paper, can preserve within themselves as vivid a memory of how I then imagined Venice or of the wish I had to go there, as the sentences themselves.[50]

Not just human-centric vocal tone and bodily gesture may inflect utterances and infect meaning, but also material-centric typefaces, paper thicknesses, screen resolutions, and font sizes.

Media theorist N. Katherine Hayles has acutely recognized many of the ways in which the material affects of computer-based media inflect and inform their textual "content." In her seminal essay, "Print Is Flat, Code Is Deep," she writes, "We can no longer afford to pretend that texts are immaterial or that text on screen is the same as text in print. The immateriality of the text

---

49 Mikhail Bakhtin, "The Problem of the Text in Linguistics, Philology, and the Human Sciences: An Experiment in Philosophical Analysis," in *Speech Genres and Other Late Essays*, trans. Vern W. McGee (Austin: University of Texas Press, 1986), 105.

50 Marcel Proust, *Time Regained*, trans. Stephen Hudson (1931; Paris: Feedbooks, 2014), 152, http://www.feedbooks.com/book/1453/time-regained.

has ceased to be a useful or even a viable fiction."[51] Not only does the materiality of the medium color the text's meaning, but Hayles radically argues that the materiality of the medium is in turn colored by the meaning of the text. "Materiality is reconceptualized as the interplay between a text's physical characteristics and its signifying strategies, a move that entwines instantiation and signification at the outset."[52]

The idea that the "meaning" of a text cannot be easily separated from its material instantiation suits Bakhtin's utterance theory well. The semiotic meaning of language (from the virtual realm) combines in the utterance event with the affective "meaning" of the material instantiation of that particular utterance (whether live human voice, recorded human voice, algorithmically generated synthetic [faux-]human voice, printed type on paper, computer-generated font on screen, etc.). The utterance is always a nexus of two-way exchange. Not only does the affective timbre of the voice inform the meaning of the text, but (and this seems the more radical notion) the meaning of the text informs the affective timbre of the voice. Signifying words, far from being cerebral and removed from bodily affect, actually create their own kind of bodily affect. In the utterance event, semiotic meaning ingresses into the physical world (via reading eye, listening ear, speaking voice, writing pen); at the same time, affective force (timbre, typeface, shadow, paper thickness) enters into and colors the virtual (yet real) meaning of words. The actual real informs the virtual real which informs the actual real and so on. Likewise, affect informs meaning which informs affect and so on. This actual/virtual way of understanding the holistic real becomes a useful tool for overcoming the false dichotomy between

51 N. Katherine Hayles, "Print Is Flat, Code Is Deep: The Importance of Media-Specific Analysis," *Poetics Today* 25, no. 1 (2004): 87.
52 Ibid., 67.

affect and meaning, experience and idea, physical world and human language.

Regarding the utterance, Whitehead himself observes, "There is not a sentence, or a word, with a meaning which is independent of the circumstances under which it is uttered."[53] And, "There is always a tacit reference to the environment of the occasion of utterance."[54] In White-head's text *Symbolism,* language is understood as a human cognitive means of abstracting (and thus filtering) bodily affect (so that humans don't get overwhelmed by pure affect). But language itself is then returned to the world (as a new entity now itself in the world), and it begins to have its own affective influence. Rather than seeing human language as a problem to be solved or philosophically overcome, Whitehead admires it. In *Modes of Thought* he writes, "Language is the triumph of human ingenuity, surpassing even the intricacies of modern technology."[55]

Deleuze also understands human language, not as a means of reducing and representing a universe "out there," but rather as a kind of affective force within the universe. In discussion with Lyotard, Deleuze says, "A text, for me is nothing but a little cog in an extra-textual machine."[56] In *A Thousand Plateaus,* Deleuze and Guattari theorize "a new 'pace' produced by the imbrication of the *semiotic* and the *material*."[57] The world is not a text, and human language is not the master key to accessing it. In-

53 Alfred North Whitehead, "Immortality," in *Essays in Science and Philosophy* (New York: Philosophical Library, 1947), 96.

54 Whitehead, *Process and Reality,* 264.

55 Alfred North Whitehead, *Modes of Thought* (New York: The Free Press, 1968), 31–32.

56 Gilles Deleuze and Jean-François Lyotard, et al., "Discussion," after the presentation of Lyotard's "Notes sur le retour et le Kapital," and Deleuze's "Pensée nomade," in *Nietzsche AuJourd'hui, 1: Intensités* (Paris: Union Générale D'Éditions, 1973), 186.

57 Gilles Deleuze and Félix Guattari, *A Thousand Plateaus: Capitalism and Schizophrenia,* trans. Brian Massumi (Minneapolis: University of Minnesota Press, 1987), 337. [Italics appear in the original text.]

stead, human language is just one more plateau that has historically accreted in a world full of a thousand other accreted plateaus.

Another advantage of Bakhtin's utterance model is that it foregrounds language's contingent relationship with actual history. Human language has never been and can never be ahistorical. Media theorist Alexander Galloway even makes the compelling argument that math is now historically contingent. *"After software has entered history, math cannot and should not be understood ahistorically* [...] after cybernetics, after the mathematization of the genome, after Google's page rank algorithm, after the industrialization of the social graph, after the growing chasm of the digital divide, any talk of math's unmediated discourse with reality comes off as disingenuous or in poor taste."[58] As Galloway insightfully observes, even math is an affective historical force in the actual world. Again, this is because humans are actual entities in the actual world, and their use of math actually changes the world.

Philosopher Eugene Thacker eloquently describes the relationship between language and affect when he writes, "Literature and life are connected not as form to matter but as mutually deforming and unforming activities."[59] And Elizabeth Grosz radically contends:

Altogether new conceptions of corporeality [...] need to be developed, notions which see [...] animate materiality and the materiality of language in interaction, which make possible a materialism beyond physicalism (i.e., the belief that reality can be explained in terms of the laws, principles, and terms of physics), a

58 Alexander R. Galloway, "The Poverty of Philosophy: Realism and Post-Fordism," *Critical Inquiry* 39 (2013): 360, 362. [Italics appear in the original text.]

59 Eugene Thacker, "APOPHATIC ANIMALITY: Lautréamont, Bachelard, and the Bliss of Metamorphosis," *Angelaki: Journal of the Theoretical Humanities* 18, no. 1 (2013): 96.

materialism that questions physicalism, that reorients physics itself.[60]

Bakhtin's model of the utterance event provides a useful way of understanding both the influence of language on physical material, and the influence of historical utterances on the meaning of language; not as separate binary entities, but as Thacker's "mutually deforming and unforming activities."

Linguistically Generated Affect That Escapes Linguistic Recapture

It is important to understand the mechanisms of the utterance event and the ways in which human language systems and actual lived affect feed back and forth into each other, but this closed-circuit model of meaning-generation is not the end of the story. There is always a surplus of affect in the world that escapes (re-)capture by language systems, yet which nonetheless continues to "mean" something in the world. To whom does it mean something? To the rest of the non-human entities in the world, and even to those parts of a human that "know" without linguistically knowing. Recall that, according to Whitehead, consciousness (that which is able to traffic in linguistic representation and understanding) is merely the apex of being. "Humans" ongoingly experience and participate in all sorts of actual occasions apart from their conscious awareness of them.

Human language, once uttered, always has affective results. I see a stop sign, read it as signifying my need to stop, and already my physical body is in motion as a result of this linguistic encounter. But the converse is not

---

60 Elizabeth Grosz, *Volatile Bodies: Toward a Corporeal Feminism* (Bloomington: Indiana University Press, 1994), 22.

always true. Not all affect in the world has a de facto linguistic meaning. My increased pulse at becoming aware of the stop sign does not necessarily "signify" anything linguistically. Nor does it refuse to signify anything. It is simply indifferent to its own potential recapture (or lack thereof) by linguistic systems of signification. All affect, all material, every occurrence in the world may be described and understood using human language. But (and this is essential), not all events in the world are so described and understood. Yes, all becomings in the world mean something, just not necessarily linguistically; they *mean* the very thing that they have become, to themselves and to the rest of the universe in all of its future becomings.

Apophatic language in particular seeks to supersaturate the utterance event with an embarrassment of affective surplus, returning as little assertive meaning as possible. Poetry seeks a kind of back and forth dance between meaning and aesthetic affect, ultimately arriving at a surplus of affect that purposefully exceeds (but never fully drowns out) the denotative "meaning" of the poem. Even a letter to the editor calling for empathetic action involving the construction of new buildings to counter a housing shortage is not merely a declarative utterance. Its goal is to incite a surplus of affective passion that will lead to humans levitating stones into buildings.

Affective surplus always escapes linguistic recapture because all language is inherently polysemic. No single word ever means one single thing. So even when a writer is trying to be as straightforward as possible (as in the case of clear construction instructions for a housing project), there will always be some slippage between what the writer intends and what is understood. A surplus of material affect escapes into the world whenever such slippages occur. The slippage between intention and understanding is not merely an occasional accident caused by carelessly worded language, but an inherent property of all language. To put this in information-theoretical terms, there is no such thing as a pure signal. No signal is ever possible without a modicum of noise as the background from which it may arise and be recognized as signal.

Rather than attempting to overcome such slippages between "intention" and "understanding," the cosmic artisan celebrates and exploits them. Indeed, a primary goal of all contemporary artists (and indeed, all artists) is to turn systems of signification into affective surplus. Elizabeth Grosz is adamant in championing such artistic production of affect. In *Chaos, Territory, Art: Deleuze and The Framing of the Earth,* she posits, "Art is the art of affect more than representation, a system of dynamized and impacting forces rather than a system of unique images that function under the regime of signs."[61] Later, she calls for "the generation (and never the reproduction or repre-sentation) of sensations."[62] Finally, parenthetically citing Deleuze and Guattari, she proposes that "artworks... do not signify or represent ('no art and no sensation have ever been representational' [*What Is Philosophy,* 193]): they assemble, they make, they do, they produce."[63] An artwork need not even purposefully evade being interpreted as "meaning" something. (Indeed, every entity in the world is defenseless at every moment to being interpreted as "meaning" something.) The goal of the cosmic artisan is not to avoid being reduced to language any more than it is to create linguistic meaning via material affect. In-stead, the cosmic artisan means to create a surplus of ma-terial affect, via language and any other forces she finds lying around.

Creating a surplus of material affect via human lan-guage is not difficult, because human language is always

---

61 Elizabeth Grosz, *Chaos, Territory, Art: Deleuze and the Framing of the Earth* (New York: Columbia University Press, 2008), 3.

62 Ibid., 17.

63 Ibid., 75.

slipping, refracting, and diverging during every utterance event. Whitehead was a keen theorist of the affect-generating function of language. Conveniently for our purposes, he even takes the time to analyze the affect-generating function of a particular language-centric art apparatus (in this case, a Hamlet soliloquy): "It is difficult to believe that all logicians as they read Hamlet's speech, 'To be, or not to be:...' commence by judging whether the initial proposition be true or false, and keep up the task of judgment throughout the whole thirty-five lines. Surely, at some point in the reading, judgment is eclipsed by aesthetic delight. The speech, for the theatre audience, is purely theoretical, a mere lure for feeling."[64]

Not only does Whitehead recognize and analyze the affective surplus created by human language, he rightly recognizes that the inherent ambiguity of language is its cause. He observes, "The vagueness of verbal statements is such that the same form of words is taken to represent a whole set of allied propositions of various grades of abstractness."[65] He calls attention to "the hopeless ambiguity of language,"[66] but rather than lamenting this ambiguity or trying to overcome it, Whitehead resignedly accepts ambiguity as inherent to language. At times, he even seems amused by language's ambiguity: "Language, as usual, is always ambiguous as to the exact proposition which it indicates. Spoken language is merely a series of squeaks."[67] The ambiguity of language allows (indeed, forces) language to do more than merely denotatively "mean" any single representative thing. Instead, human language is able to function affectively and bodily, in addition to and in excess of any cognitive signifying that it may also incidentally be doing.

---

64 Whitehead, *Process and Reality*, 185.
65 Ibid., 193.
66 Ibid., 196.
67 Ibid., 264.

Karen Barad, from her own unique "agential realist" perspective, reinforces Whitehead's concept of signifiers as propositional lures to feeling: "Representations are not (more or less faithful) pictures of what is, but productive evocations, provocations, and generative material articulations or reconfigurings of what is and what is possible."[68] Indeed, representations act as apparatuses, even if they claim not to, regardless of their 'accuracy.' Thus, even the most realistic photographic representation of a forensic crime scene, regardless of any objective accuracy it claims to achieve, is actually functioning as a meaning-generating apparatus.

Note that it is not necessary for signification to cease functioning altogether before a surplus of affect may occur. Oftentimes it is quite the opposite. As with apophatic writing, the more kataphatic the denotative assertions, the stronger the apophatic affect. Likewise, the more a speaker is trying to clearly convey her exact meaning, oftentimes the more affective surplus is generated. Marcel Proust talks about "an increasing profundity of sound."[69] Anthropologist Kathleen Stewart describes Roland Barthes's concept of the "third meaning" of language (a meaning resulting from a surplus of affect) as "Immanent, obtuse, and erratic, in contrast to the 'obvious meaning' of semantic messages and symbolic signification... Their significance lies in the intensities they build."[70] And Gilles Deleuze evocatively describes what happens when signifying representation becomes aware of its affect-generating capacities: "When representation discovers the infinite within itself, it no longer appears

---

68 Karen Barad, *Meeting the Universe Halfway* (Durham: Duke University Press, 2007), 389.

69 Marcel Proust, *The Captive,* trans. C. K. Scott-Moncrieff (1929; Paris: Feedbooks, 2014), 220, http://www.feedbooks.com/book/1451/the-captive.

70 Kathleen Stewart, *Ordinary Affects* (Durham: Duke University Press, 2007), 3.

as *organic* representation but as *orgiastic* representation: it discovers within itself the limits of the organised; tumult, restlessness and passion underneath apparent calm. It rediscovers monstrosity."[71]

Deleuze's own acute and idiosyncratic interest in art makes his writings (and the subsequent theories they have inspired) particularly relevant to our project of making nothing via apophatic art apparatuses. Deleuze's original analysis of the radical artwork and theory of Antonin Artaud leads us deeper into some specifics of how language may become exceedingly affective.[72] Artaud prescribes, "One may invent one's language, and make pure language speak with an extra-grammatical or a-grammatical meaning, but this meaning must have value in itself, that is, it must issue from torment."[73] Artaud critiques Lewis Carroll's experimental language (in poems like "Jabberwocky") as failing to issue from bodily torment, and thus resulting in a dearth of affective surplus. It is not enough, then, to merely avoid speaking denotatively. One must do it in a way that somehow incites, hooks into, and lures bodies.

Elsewhere, writing about the novels of Pierre Klossowski, Deleuze recognizes "the shifting function of language which now expresses only intensities."[74] Klossowski himself describes "fluctuations of intensity [...] which

---

71   Gilles Deleuze, *Difference and Repetition*, trans. Paul Patton (New York: Columbia University Press, 1994), 42. [Italics appear in the original text.]

72   I come to the following two examples by way of Brian Massumi own insightful analysis in "Introduction: Like a thought," in *A Shock To Thought: Expression after Deleuze and Guattari*, ed. Brian Massumi (London: Routledge, 2005), xiii–xxxix.

73   Antonin Artaud, "Letter to Henri Parisot," in *Lettres de Rodez* (Paris: G.L.M., 1946), quoted in Gilles Deleuze, *The Logic of Sense*, trans. Mark Lester (New York: Columbia University Press, 1990), 84.

74   Deleuze, *The Logic of Sense*, 294.

correspond to the thought of everyone and no one."[75] Regarding these fluctuations, Deleuze adds, "At the same time that bodies lose their unity and the self its identity, language loses its denoting function (its distinct sort of integrity) in order to discover a value that is purely expressive, or, as Klossowski says, 'emotional.'"[76] Perhaps, then, art apparatuses may be used to break down human identities (and even human bodies) in order to help language move beyond mere signification and begin trafficking in exceedingly affective intensities. Arakawa and Gins's apophatic art apparatus *Mechanism of Meaning* proceeds along such lines.

What other types of slippages and misreadings may be invited and exploited by art apparatuses in order to cause a surplus of affect? To choose just one example, the creation of a purposefully noisy channel between instruction and implementation in something as standard as a dance performance could lead to radically new forms of bodily motion. "Misinterpreted" or "misread" instructions to a dancer never entirely inhibit the dancer from proceeding to move. This is because all language is polysemic. Something can always be performed in the world as a result of instructive utterances, however "misinterpreted." Billions of things can be performed. And each different performed thing qualitatively differs from the other things that could have been performed.

In this particularly constructed apparatal context (dance instructions relayed along a noisy channel to a dancer), language begins to acts as a kind of affective, analog force on human bodies. Even with very simple instructional language systems, an almost infinite number of interpretations and resultant behaviors are possible.

---

75 Pierre Klossowski, "Oubli et anamnèse dans l'expérience vécue de l'éternel retour du Même," in *Nietzsche, Cahiers de Royaumont* (Paris: Minuit, 1967), 233, quoted in Deleuze, *The Logic of Sense*, 299.

76 Deleuze, *The Logic of Sense*, 299.

These variable possibilities increase due to the fact that the apparatal context we have created is itself embedded in an overlappingly complex and telescoping series of contexts (contexts of human etiquette, art historical contexts of performance and dance, contexts of (de-) skilled athletic performance, gendered body movement contexts, modestly contexts, etc.). Not every uttered instruction is completely arbitrary and open to any meaning whatsoever; but the shades of subtle differences in interpreted meaning can be almost infinitely fine-grained and nuanced (depending on telescoping contexts, interpretations of tone, bodily affect, prior human relationships between speaker and dancer, etc.). As Jonathan Culler profoundly observes, "Meaning is context bound, but context is boundless."[77]

Before we leave our focus on human language and proceed to forms of a-linguistically generated meaning, it is crucial to remember that human language is a strange, unique, wildly refracting force in the world. Human language is prehended by actual occasions (as is every other force in the world), but by means usually involving human-centric utterance events; and humans are peculiarly anomalous enduring objects in the world. To deny the anomalous nature of human consciousness (whatever "human consciousness" is) is to deny the well-decided and well-accreted actual histories of humans and their languages. By no means does the world reduce to human language (that would be anthropocentric, solipsistic, and silly), but neither does human language flatten into just one more ordinary, material-discursive force in the world. Human language is far too complex and historically well-accreted, entangled, and decided to ever be meaningfully accessed via such molecular-theoretical means. Yes, the world is by no means contingent upon

---

77 Culler, *On Deconstruction*, 64.

humans, but neither are humans just one more ordinary thing in the world.

The good news for the practicing contemporary artist (Deleuze's cosmic artisan) is that she is not an ontologist of rhetoric, linguistics, semiotics, grammar, or affect. She need not commit to a Saussurean, Peircean, Whiteheadian, Derridean, Bakhtinian, or even Baradian model of language. Setting aside the vast complexities of human language for a moment, to even theorize about the bare ways in which plain old inorganic rocks create rocky material-meaning for other inorganic rocks requires all sorts of complicated speculative gymnastics. When the well-decided and well-accreted plateau of human language systems are unleashed onto the world, wild and complex refractions begin to resound, far too complex and fine-grained for any single theoretical model to pin down. Bakhtin himself proposed a taxonomical project of identifying and labeling every type of speech genre that might ever occur in any utterance context, but was wise enough not to take up the project himself. It would have proved a fool's errand. Fortunately, our cosmic artisan need only modulate, intensify, complicate, and bother these wildly refracting relationships between material-meaning, human language, oblique incantatory force, consciousness, bodily affect, virtual linguistic potential, and actual pragmatic efficacy. She simply needs enough understanding of language and meaning to trouble the waters and see what arises.

My main reason for getting into the quagmire of human language theory at all is simply to show that tactics from apophatic writing need not be merely metaphorically or analogically adapted in the creation of an apophatic art apparatus. Since language is itself a force in the world, apophatic writing itself is already a kind of actual, non-metaphorical apparatus. It is simply a literary-genre apparatus rather than an art-genre apparatus. But as an apparatus, its functions are more or less the same.

A-linguistically Generated Meaning

Although human language participates in the actual world of actual meaning, it is responsible for only a small fraction of all the meaning-making that goes on in the world. Why do most humans, when they choose to theorize about the world, place such an inordinate priority on human language? Because, as a human, to philosophically theorize about the nature of the world is to inherently traffic in human language. But there are other, less linguistic ways that human consciousnesses may involve themselves in the world. One such way is through the creation of art apparatuses.

The material universe is forever making meaning. Indeed, the ongoing, becoming process of the universe is itself what the universe comes to mean, moment by moment, to all the various parts of the universe that are perpetually attending to (or negatively prehending) all the other parts of the universe. This is the broad and fundamental definition of "meaning." Meaning has occurred prior to human language, it currently occurs alongside it, and it will continue to occur after it. Indeed, human language, according to our Whiteheadian model of actual occasions/entities, is a form of material meaning – not via any simple analogy, but via very complex forms of ingression that are almost impossible to unpack in any meaningful way at a moment-by-moment analytical pace.

In a sense, our prior treatment of quantum-behavior-measuring apparatuses in Chapter 1 was itself already an analysis of one kind of a-linguistically generated meaning. Art apparatuses themselves may generate a-linguistic meaning, although they are rarely thought of as doing so. The reason is because everything in the actual world may be described using human language. Art apparatuses are (almost always) created by humans for (almost always) other humans in (almost always) human-institutional contexts, and so art apparatuses are prime candidates for reduction to human language. Indeed, every commercial artist who shows work in a Chelsea gallery is hoping for her art apparatuses to be linguistically reduced, preferably via a favorable review in *Artforum Magazine* or *The New York Times*. But art apparatuses themselves involve materials, and do not always involve human language; and thus they may well (theoretically, at least) create a-linguistically generated meaning that never gets reduced to human language. For example, artwork created by a non-speaking outsider artist who never gets "discovered" may qualify as purely a-linguistic.

Whether or not a work of art or an affective material experience is or is not subsequently reduced to human language, such an artwork or experience nevertheless always also creates its own a-linguistic "meaning." Humans who work with materials have affective relationships with those materials that are always in some ways a-linguistic. Mark Twain as a steamboat pilot on the Mississippi river was always looking for "signs" in the river and sky (rough water, a certain color sunset). These "signs" only become linguistic signs when he writes about them in *Life on the Mississippi*; but as he is actually piloting, these signs are experienced by him more as affective bodily instincts or urges, moving across a large range of qualia, never binarily shifting from signifying "safe" to signifying "dangerous" in a single instant, but known, felt, and apperceived by a racing heart and a rush of adrenalin prior to (and often without ever needing to be put into) words. For a riverboat pilot, the current in a river may cause a qualitative bodily experience that simply means what it eventually becomes. This kind of a-linguistic meaning may also be caused by an art apparatus. Actually, such material "meaning" can't help but be caused by an art apparatus, regardless of what subsequent linguistic meaning may or may not emerge.

As a matter of fact, such material meaning only rarely results in conscious linguistic meaning. The eruption of material meaning into conscious linguistic meaning is never inevitable. It is an anthropocentric mistake to assume that all phenomena are proto-linguistic; that they all eventually lead to a second-order linguistic difference. Phenomena are indifferent to human language. They may or may not lead to human language. A craftsman may spend his whole life on a lathe in an affective "dialogue" with wood – a "dialogue" which is altogether a-linguistic, and one which he may never choose to put into words (or even think in words). This is unlikely, but theoretically possible. Meaning is always already "made" by all material becomings in the world, indifferent to capture by human language. Indeed, "meaning" is not even "made," so much as: that which is made comes to mean what it has become.

Some Things That Apophatic Art Apparatuses Are Not

Keeping these understandings of language, affect, material, and meaning in mind, let us return to our apophatic art apparatus which means to make nothing (i.e., brake becoming), and let us disqualify some apparatal approaches that only superficially seem to make nothing, but actually do not. It is not enough for our apophatic art apparatus to simply avoid human language in order to reveal the "bare phenomenological being" which remains. The world doesn't need human language to make meaning; and more to the point, the mere avoidance of linguistic meaning doesn't constitute the making of nothing. If mere a-linguistic affect qualified as overcoming meaning, which in turn qualified as making nothing, then all art that avoided the use of human language would be apophatic. This way of thinking is too facile. Linguistic meaning is hardly the only flavor of "something." "Nothing" is not merely the absence of linguistic meaning. Thus, constituting a regime of "phenomenological presence" which is indifferent to the regime of human language is not enough. For nothing to be made (for the brakes to be applied), even this regime of phenomenological presence must be somehow apophatically (performatively) confounded. Phenomenological presence itself must be deterritorialized (to use Deleuze and Guattari's term), and deterritorialization proceeds differently depending upon the strata we mean to deterritorialize. Deterritorializing the linguistic representation of presence and deterritorializing phenomenological presence itself are two very different things. How might the deterritorialization of phenomenological presence proceed?

Post-figurative painting is not inherently apophatic, nor is abstract expressionism. Just as avoiding a typographic signifier does not inherently make nothing, neither does avoiding a pictographic signifier. Jackson Pollock's paintings generate all sorts of affective somethings, whether or not they are semiotically legible as representing any particular, noun-ish, figurative something. Certain flavors of abstract expressionism (Rothko's chapel, for example, according to Bersani and Dutoit) arguably do create a kind of impasse and poverty of affect that might qualify as apophatic. But this interpretation of Rothko's work is in almost direct opposition to what Rothko (and Clement Greenberg) thought his work was accomplishing. Was Rothko making luminous darknesses; or was he making lures toward something which then immediately barred our entrance into anything much at all? Only the latter might qualify as apophatic art: Rothko as trompe l'oeil painter of the void.

Another facile move would be to simply do away with material in our art altogether. If we move toward performance art and away from the art object, then certainly our performance art will constitute an apophatic art apparatus, since we have done away with the "something" of material. If this were true, then all performance art (and all "digital" art) would be apophatic art. But, as Whitehead reminds us, all material is actually an accreted series of occasions. From this perspective, all art – from the heaviest Michelangelo marble sculpture to the most ephemeral Allan Kaprow happening – is performance art. So, process philosophy won't allow us to consider events as "nothing." On the contrary, according to Whitehead, all material is actually just a series of ongoingly enacted and decided events.

Art that simply mixes language and materials does not yet constitute an apophatic art apparatus. Nor does art that treats language as a kind of material. Neither of these approaches are *excluded* from apophatic art apparatuses, but they do not in themselves constitute the making of nothing.

"Conceptual" art is not inherently apophatic. To enact a tautology via art (however dematerialized) is not inherently to make nothing. Depending on how the tautology is enacted, such conceptual art may simply be a denotative object lesson, or a kataphatic model of aporia. There is a difference between actually inhibiting processes of becoming and merely representing such inhibitions. The former qualifies as apophatic; the latter does not.

Furthermore, there is no clear and easy (meta)physical separation between "concepts" and "materials." In the words of the experimental art collective Spurse, "The narrative of conceptual art history is wrong. You cannot dematerialize things to get concepts. Ideas are embodied practices."[78] William James implies something similar when he asserts, "[Consciousness] *is fictitious, while thoughts in the concrete are fully real. But thoughts in the con-*

---

78 Spurse, *Time Drills: A Series of Exercise Scores* (Omaha: Bemis Center for Contemporary Art, 2009), Glossary: "Enaction."

crete are made of the same stuff as things are."[79] If concepts themselves are already things, then foregrounding concepts by de-emphasizing physical materials does not yet make nothing. It just shifts the emphasis toward a less solid kind of something.

Minimalism itself is not inherently apophatic. At its worse, minimalism may actually function as a quest for essentialism and pure phenomenological presence, the very things that apophatic art means to problematize.

Nor is apophatic art merely psychedelic art or op art that attempts to affectively and phenomenologically disrupts human perception. Trippy confusion alone is not vacuous enough to qualify as nothing. (It may be a start toward nothing, if rigorously pursued.)

If dematerialization of solidity and avoidance of human language are not enough to make nothing, then how does the apophatic art apparatus make nothing? As expected, it depends on the specific nature of each apophatic art apparatus. In the following chapters, we will examine several particular ways of making nothing, one artwork at a time. Prior to that, let us take some time to extract a few general tactics from apophatic writing apparatuses and port them to apophatic art apparatuses.

Tactics from Apophatic Writing Apparatuses Ported to Apophatic Art Apparatuses

In extracting tactics from apophatic writing apparatuses and applying them to apophatic art apparatuses, I should be clear that it is not at all my intention to "critique" or "deconstruct" art apparatuses by using apophatic writing. This book is not an apophatic text, and it would be (and

79   William James, "Does 'Consciousness' Exist?" in *Essays in Radical Empiricism* (New York: Longmans, Green, and Co., 1912), 37. [Italics appear in the original text.]

historically has been) a kind of scatological exercise to write critically about artworks in a deconstructive manner. Similar to Derrida's failed attempts to deconstruct Pseudo-Dionysius, writing apophatically about any art apparatus (particularly about apophatic art apparatuses) would be like applying one kind of corrosive acid to another kind of corrosive acid. Perhaps something curious would emerge, but that is not my goal. The apophatic art apparatuses discussed in this book are themselves already making much more interesting and alluring nothings than could ever be produced by my making a kind of textual nothing of them. I actually intend to accomplish the opposite: to make a reverent textual something of their ingenious artistic nothings.

Similarly, my goal is not at all to reduce art to a kind of text in order for me to then write critically about it via some form of literary apophasis. Instead, I mean to examine art apparatuses that themselves make nothing of materials and presences and becomings, just as apophatic writing makes nothing of kataphatic linguistic assertion. The "writing" aspects of apophatic writing are less crucial to my project than the "making nothing" aspects of apophatic writing.

Since the universe is always already at every moment making something new, apophatic art apparatuses do not naively seek to escape altogether from this perpetual process of becoming. Such an escape would be impossible. Instead, apophatic art apparatuses seek to rigorously interrupt, stall, defer, or at least doggedly perturb this perpetual process of becoming. If quantum-behavior-measuring apparatuses create phenomenal entanglements that mean what they become, then apophatic art apparatuses create phenomenal entanglements that forestall, stymie, hinder, trouble, problematize, or defer (however temporarily) any resolved, assertive becomings (and thus any emergent meanings). Apophatic art apparatuses fail to mean what they have not (yet) become, in one way or another, by one means or another. According to their various ways and means, apophatic art apparatuses make nothing (by temporarily braking the inevitable becoming of something).

An Apophatic Tactic:
Perpetual Deferral – No End/No Source

One general way in which apophatic art apparatuses make nothing is via the act of perpetual deferral. Deferral and refusal of resolution are a standard tactics in the perpetual cycling back and forth between kataphatic assertion and apophatic denial. Deferral of resolution works forwards and backwards in lived historical time. Deferral is not only a refusal to resolve future becomings, but a refusal to resolve and establish the prior origins of present becomings as foundational and fundamental. According to our understanding of apparatuses and actual occasions, each becoming must inherently begin with some prior state. But this prior state itself required a prior state before it, and so on. Rather than attempt to track down and resolve which comes first – the assertion or the denial –, kataphasis and apophasis adopt a kind of *in medias res* approach as they continue to cycle back and forth between each other. Since this cycling is interminable, and its origins are indefinite, there is no end and no source. Apophatic art apparatuses don't seek to establish "nothing" as the ground of everything, once and for all. On the contrary, the making of nothing (the braking of something) must perpetually defer and unground any and all subsequent attempts to establish nothing as an originary ground. Making nothing thus becomes an ongoing performance rather than a once-and-for-all accomplishment.

H.P. Lovecraft's apophatic-esque prose provocatively evokes (or rather, fails to evoke) a few such groundless nothings. He writes of "no trace save destruction itself."[80] He describes a God-pronounced decree whereby a human entity "must not only cease to be, but must cease ever to have been."[81] Of the destruction of every entity in a prior cosmos, Lovecraft says, "Nothing survived to tell that they had been and gone, been and gone, always and always, back to no first beginning."[82] There is always the potential of terror lurking in any rigorously made nothing.

Of course, the apophatic tactic of perpetual deferral not only defers the founding of an originary ground, but it also defers the resolution of a present becoming. Deleuze suggests a kind of topological means of deferral via the baroque process of folding. "The Baroque invents the infinite work or process. The problem is not how to finish a fold, but how to continue it, to have it go through the ceiling, how to bring it to infinity."[83] Such topological foldings are not concerned with the deconstructive deferral of linguistic meanings. Instead, Baroque material foldings actually intend to defer the resolution of materials themselves by continuing a process of perpetual deformation. Similarly, apophatic art apparatuses make present nothings by remaining in the flux of process, by perpetually deferring future resolved becomings.

---

80 H.P. Lovecraft, "The Lurking Fear," in *The Dreams in the Witch House and Other Weird Stories,* ed. S.T. Joshi (New York: Penguin Books, 2004), 64.

81 H.P. Lovecraft, "The Case of Charles Dexter Ward," in *The Thing on the Doorstep and Other Weird Stories,* ed. S.T. Joshi (New York: Penguin Books, 2001), 126.

82 H.P. Lovecraft, "The Dream-Quest of Unknown Kadath," in *The Cthulhu Tome,* ed. Anthony Uyl (Woodstock: Devoted Publishing, 2016), 411.

83 Gilles Deleuze, *The Fold: Leibniz and the Baroque,* trans. Tom Conley (London: Athlone Press, 1993), 34.

An Apophatic Tactic:
Indifference (Utter? Toward What?)

Another general way in which apophatic art apparatuses make nothing is via an attitude of indifference. The apophatic art apparatus must remain indifferent to a number of different agendas (for example, the agenda to manifest presence, but also the agenda to actively deconstruct presence) in order to avoid being sidetracked by any particular agenda. Apophatic art apparatuses don't even actively oppose being hijacked by these tangential agendas, because to oppose them is also to be reactionarily derailed and sidetracked by them. Apophatic art apparatuses simply remain indifferent to these agendas. They give themselves over to these agendas while always simultaneously exceeding them.

Apophatic art apparatuses are indifferent toward resolving differences between subject and object, self and other. They are indifferent toward resisting or not resisting their own subsequent reduction to linguistic signification. They do not actively court or actively resist linguistic interpretation. Some apophatic art apparatuses (like William Pope.L's *Black Factory*) are purposefully not indifferent toward their own subsequent archiving, canonization, institutionalization, and communication. The *Black Factory* does purposefully work to sabotage its own subsequent insertion into art history. But all apophatic art apparatuses (even Pope.L's *Black Factory*) are largely indifferent to their own subsequent capture by linguistic systems of assertive meaning. This indifference is precisely what allows apophatic art apparatuses to always affectively far exceed linguistic reduction.

Derrida's *différance* (difference and deferral) and "indifference" are neither antonyms nor synonyms of each other. They are just two different responses to the assertive project of kataphatic language. *Différance* attempts an ethical escape from kataphatic assertion by shifting the emphasis of such language from likeness and presence to difference and absence. *Différance* attempts a strong escape from kataphatic language via a kind of weak engagement with it.

Indifference, on the other hand, is simply indifferent to either engagement or disengagement with human language. As such, indifference can be a very powerful tactic. Difference (between what is actually in the world and the language that describes it, between one thing and another, between one word and another) seeks to subsume all (the primacy of primacy, the presence of presence, the becoming of being). But indifference eludes the all-encompassing embrace of difference. Indifference is not anti-difference (simply another form of difference) or alter-difference (yet another form of difference). Indifference is simply indifferent to difference, to identity, and to the difference and play between difference and identity. Indifference enacts a rigorous letting be of such signifying (anti-signifying, alter-signifying, even a-signifying) concerns.

In *Writing and Difference,* Derrida imagines "an existence that refuses to signify, [...] an art without works, a language without trace."[84] But apophatic art apparatuses are indifferent to Derrida's deconstructive agenda. They don't refuse to signify; they are simply indifferent to signification. They don't bother camouflaging themselves; they are (usually) recognizable as "works of art."

In the nastiest and most unfortunate version of "the linguistic turn," "phenomenological experience" is thought of as an inherently pre-linguistic condition, as if all actual occasions in the world are destined to eventually arrive at some sort of linguistic reduction. But most actual occasions are never reduced to or translated into words or even conscious human thoughts. Not that actual occasions are inherently anti-linguistic, or even a-

---

84 Derrida, *Writing and Difference,* 219.

linguistic; they are simply altogether indifferent to human linguistic capture and reduction. Apophatic art apparatuses are also indifferent to human linguistic capture and reduction. They neither court it nor resist it. At most, they sometimes purposefully and playfully bother troubling it (as in the case of Arakawa and Gins's *Mechanism of Meaning*).

Apophatic art apparatuses are indifferent to the "sensible/intelligible" ontological dichotomy. They do not resist capture as intelligible. They do not seek to solely traffic in the sensible or sensory. Nor do they seek to deconstructively undermine this dichotomy by prioritizing the sensible over the intelligible. Nor do they seek to supplant the regime of the intelligible by declaring that all meaning is wholly sensible. Apophatic art apparatuses do not identify as sensible or intelligible, nor do they refuse to identify as sensible or intelligible.

In Chapters 4 and 5 of *A Thousand Plateaus,* Deleuze and Guattari recognize human language not as some all-totalizing, all-binding force to be escaped and overcome at all cost, but as just one among many well-decided historical accretions of territorialized strata (some other strata being geology, biology, economics, politics, music, ethology, etc.) Deleuze and Guattari don't seek to deconstruct language, nor do they seek to write their own language in a way impervious to deconstruction. This is because there are always plenty of other relevant and exciting, extra-linguistic strata at play in the world, waiting to be modulated, deterritorialized, and reterritorialized onto other strata and into entirely new strata. And infusing all strata, there awaits the teeming plane of undifferentiated immanence which obeys no single strata, least of all the strata of human language. Like Deleuze and Guattari, apophatic art apparatuses are usually indifferent toward human language and its deconstruction. Apophatic art apparatuses have bigger nothings to fry.

An Apophatic Tactic:
Cognitive Aporia

A third general way in which apophatic art apparatuses make nothing is by manufacturing cognitive aporia. Cognitive aporia enacts an impasse. It halts, blocks, stymies, and confounds cognitive resolution. Cognitive aporia is a particular kind of perpetual deferral involving human thinking. Apophatic art apparatuses purposefully make a place for their human "audiences" within the apparatal phenomenon that they engender. Apophatic art apparatuses lure human thinking to crash, but in a very particular way.

(Not that human "consciousness" is reducible to human brains, and not that human brains operate at all like computers, but) by analogy, there are several ways software can crash. One kind of crash returns an error message alerting its user that there has been a crash. A bit less courteous, but still gentle, is the software crash where the software stops functioning and shuts down. The thorniest kind of software crash is created by an endless internal loop within the software that hangs the software up. The software is still running, working, making, becoming, and meaning; often even using an excess of processing energy to do so. But it is trapped within its present process. No result or outcome will ever be returned. Apophatic art apparatuses crash human thinking in a similar way. They do not return the error message "nothing." They do not shut down and make a weak nothing by failing once and for all to make a conclusive something. Instead, apophatic art apparatuses perpetually hang up any conclusive, summative becomings. In so doing, they continuously and perpetually make nothing.

Why Might Apophatic Art Be Better Than Apophatic Writing?

Why bother porting apophatic tactics from writing to art? What might art be able to accomplish apophatically that writing cannot? One difference between the aesthetics of writing and the aesthetics of art is that, ever since Kant proposed his version of the sublime, the idea of cognitive aporia (achieved by one's being overwhelmed by the sublime) has been part of the fundamental theoretical understanding of visual aesthetics. One way to achieve aesthetic impact is by ordered beauty; the other is by appeal to an overwhelming sublime. Although apophatic writing predates Kant by many centuries, apophatic writing has always remained at the fringes of most historical forms of writing, as an extreme form of mystical practice. Kataphatic assertive writing has almost always taken center stage. From this perspective, artists have had more historical experience using apophatic tactics (if never explicitly labeled "apophatic") than writers; and contemporary art audiences are (arguably) more open to engage with apophatic art that contemporary readers of literature are open to engage with apophatic writing (although within certain sub-genres of experimental literature, this claim is debatable). Contemporary artists may find a wider audience (and thus a wider influence) for their apophatic art than contemporary writers may find for their apophatic texts. As literary theorist Stanley Fish snidely observes, "Although the 'textual' or the 'discursive' is [...] a crucial site of social contestation, the people who study that site are not crucial players in the contest."[85]

If apophatic tactics are currently more intrinsic to contemporary art than to contemporary writing, why did these tactics first appear historically in writing? My

85 Stanley Fish, *Professional Correctness: Literary Studies and Political Change* (New York: Oxford University Press, 1995), 123–24.

guess is that human language was so inherently bound by kataphatic assertion that apophasis was most desperately needed there first; and that once it appeared, it was most recognizable as a generic anomaly there.

In shifting from human-instigated apophatic writing to human-instigated apophatic art, I am not shifting straight out into the total, phenomenal universe. I am merely moving sideways from one form of human activity to another. It is not incumbent upon me to make a case for how the "non-human" world-in-itself enacts apophatic tactics and creates apophatic apparatuses, because humans are (almost) always an intrinsic (although by no means sole) component in the creation of apophatic art apparatuses. The difference between apophatic writing and apophatic art is that materials from the world get introduced into apophatic art apparatuses in more direct, less oblique ways than they get introduced into apophatic writing apparatuses. Yes, materials in the world do enter written apophatic language via the utterance event, but this utterance ingression is a particularly unusual, nuanced, human-consciousness-contingent type of occurrence. Whereas materials may ingress into apophatic art apparatuses more directly (or at least differently).

Furthermore, materials always also connect out into the world in discursive but not necessarily human-linguistic ways. This is not to say that humans and their languages don't also actually connect out into the actual world. They do, but via a more oblique occurrence – the utterance. There are not and never have been any hermetically sealed boundaries between human language, human art, humans, and materials in the world. The art apparatus functions as a uniquely intentional, experimental, and speculative proposition-generator: a fecund, phenomenal nexus where human processes and thoughts encounter material entities. As such, art apparatuses exist in an emergent space between the decisions, whimsies, and proclivities of materials (accreted, enduring objects) and the purposeful, investigative tactics and approaches of humans (also accreted, enduring objects). Apophatic art apparatuses are thus able to more fine-grainedly become entangled with materials in a way that apophatic writing apparatuses are not.

One difference between apophatic writing and apophatic art is insightfully foregrounded in an observation by Alexander Galloway regarding the difference between literary post-structuralism and architectural post-modernism. When Frank Gehry's buildings begin to leak, their owners don't celebrate these leaks as post-structuralist features. As Galloway observes, "Even if an architectural design is allowed to crack and buckle at the semiotic or symbolic level, it is not allowed to fail at the level of material functionality."[86] According to my own criteria, if Gehry's buildings are not allowed, expected, and invited to materially buckle and leak (and they are not), then they are not yet apophatic art apparatuses (and they are not).

How Might Apophatic Art Be Different Than Deconstructive Art?

Both apophatic writing and deconstructive reading must begin with an initial state, something on which to work. In the case of apophatic writing, the initial state is kataphatic truth assertions about God. With deconstructive reading, the initial state is any text (about anything) which proceeds according to truth assertions. As mentioned previously, the goal of apophatic writing is to undermine ontological language about God (language based on presences, essences, identities, and assertions of truth) in order to (perhaps) be encountered by the God who is beyond ontology. The goal of deconstruction is to

86   Alexander Galloway, "Are Some Things Unrepresentable?" *Culture & Society* 28, No. 7–8 (2011): 97.

undermine ontological language (about any and every-thing) in order to give difference its due – to reveal difference (rather than presence, essence, or identity) as the actual means by which all meaning in the world emerges. Apophatic writing must necessarily leave kataphatic assertion standing. To fail to do so would be heretical. Deconstructive reading doesn't mind leaving whatever text it deconstructs lying in a deconstructed heap. It simply moves on to the next text.

Now let's shift from writing to art. The initial state of our art apparatus is no longer an ontological truth assertion but a piece of physical material. Here we may understand "material" as an accreted series of historical decisions (if not exactly kataphatic or ontological "assertions"). Returning to Whitehead, a piece of "material" is properly understood as an enduring society of actual occasions, actual decision events. It seems to me that a truly deconstructive art apparatus would always be pursuing a kind of nuclear annihilation of material, a kind of under-mining of actual presence in order to achieve a kind of nihilistic absence. This is not to say that deconstructive reading is itself inherently nihilistic (far from it), but simply to say that a deconstructive art practice would shift toward nihilism as it shifted toward physical material. Either that, or deconstructive art would always be un-dermining the noun-ishness of entities in order to make manifest the flux of difference at the heart of their verb-ish becomings. From this latter perspective, then, White-head's cosmology (that objects are actually events) simply describes as always already true much of what a decon-structive art might hope to exemplify and foreground.

Whereas apophatic art does not desire to leave its materials in a heap, or even to reveal the differentiating flux at the heart of their apparent presence. Recall that apophatic writing intends to let kataphatic assertion stand. Likewise, apophatic art intends to let materials have their way and their say – not in order to deconstruct them and reveal their inherent instability, but to use them as kindling to make nothing, as firestarter for braking. Apophatic art apparatuses have nothing against material (whether as object or as event). Instead, apophatic art apparatuses trouble, disturb, and brake the becomings of material in order to make nothings.

Why Make Apophatic Art Apparatuses at All?

> *"Since every aesthetic encounter is singular, any-thing like a general aesthetics is impossible."*
> — Steven Shaviro[87]

> *"[All] untranslatable words are in fact synonyms; and all share the desire for untranslatability, the longing for uniqueness."*
> — Svetlana Boym[88]

Why make apophatic art apparatuses at all? What might be the ethical goal? Why not just continue making ordinary art apparatuses, or cease making any art apparatuses? Why not just continue writing apophatically, or cease writing apophatically? As mentioned previously, one reason for making apophatic art apparatuses is to brake on ice, and in so doing, somehow more efficaciously steer into the future. There are other ethical reasons which will be more easily unpacked in the final chapter of this book, once we have closely examined several, specific, exemplary apophatic art apparatuses in the next four chapters. Each one of these works of art presents its own unique approach to enacting apophasis.

---

87 Steven Shaviro, *The Universe of Things: On Speculative Realism* (Minneapolis: University of Minnesota Press, 2014), 156.
88 Svetlana Boym, *The Future of Nostalgia* (New York: Basic Books, 2001), 13.

If every apparatus (scientific, artistic, material, linguistic, "natural") simply "means" what it has become, then what might the outcome of an art apparatus that makes nothing "mean?" Will it mean anything? Must it explicitly mean "nothing?" Does it defer returning any meaning at all in its deferral of becoming something? Might something relevant and new be learned about ordinary art apparatuses (works of art that make something) by closely examining the function of apophatic art apparatuses (works of art that make nothing)? Hopefully, we shall see.

We now take our current understanding of apparatuses and apophasis and turn to a close examination of a few particular apophatic art apparatuses. At the beginning of my research for this book, I initially "measured" these artworks, and tailored my theory to suit those initial measurements. In the following chapters, I try my theory back onto the artworks to see how well it fits. In order to best reveal the suitability (or lack thereof) of my theory to these artworks, I have chosen to proceed as if the theory fits each artwork just right. That way the reader can more easily judge the instances where the fit seems forced, awkward, or altogether unsuitable. According to Whitehead's pragmatic criteria for philosophy (his own and others), "The verification of a rationalistic scheme is to be sought in its general success, and not in the peculiar certainty, or initial clarity of its first principles."[89] Let's try my apophatic art apparatus theory on for size.

---

89 Whitehead, *Process and Reality*, 8.

II

SOME APOPHATIC APPARATUSES IN CONTEMPORARY ART

3

HOW TO DO (NO)THINGS WITH WORDS: ROBERT FLUDD'S DIAGRAM OF HYLE VS. ARAKAWA AND GINS'S MECHANISM OF MEANING

Sometimes the best way to understand what an apophatic art apparatus is doing is by comparing it with a non-apophatic art apparatus. This chapter makes such a comparison. In this case, the non-apophatic art apparatus is really more like a non-apophatic diagram apparatus that claims to be doing less (materially and affectively) than it is actually doing. And the apophatic art apparatus is really more like a sequence of photographic documents of a (faux?-)pedagogical installation, documents that (implicitly) claim to be a lot more benign than they actually are. Both apparatuses involve human language, and as we discovered in the last chapter, human language has a nasty habit of lying about what it is actually, affectively doing. Both apparatuses approach the conceptual topic of "nothing," but in radically different, almost directly antithetical ways.

The apophatic art apparatus under consideration is *Mechanism of Meaning* by (artist? filmmaker? architect?) Shusaku Arakawa and (artist? poet? philosopher?) Madeline Gins, the duo known as Arakawa and Gins. *Mechanism of Meaning* is a series of art installations (each a revised version of the prior installation) which occurred over a period of about forty years. Each iteration of the installation consists of a sequence of cognitive (visual and bodily) exercises, in the form of physical stations, meant to disrupt (foreground? reset? revise? altogether bungle?) a human's ability to make meaning. I think of each station as a kind of object lesson workshop – something similar to a child's primer, but physical, and for adults. But one could also think of each station as a kind of self-inflicted brainwashing trap (which is to say almost the same thing: something similar to a child's primer, but physical, and for adults). In earlier iterations of the installation, the individual stations were hung on walls, and in later iterations the stations were placed on the floor. The initial station panels measured 7.5 × 5.5 feet. The first iteration of the installation occurred at the Venice Biennale in 1970, although work on the project actually began as early as 1963.

These same exercises are also published in four different book editions (1971, 1979, 1988, 1997), each a revision of the last. All of the exercises are troubling and disruptive in their own specific way. The exercises are grouped according to "improbable or preposterous (lacking definition) subdivisions,"[1] and placed in an intentional sequence within those subdivisions, the subdivisions and

---

1 Arakawa and Madeline Gins, *Mechanismus der Bedeutung (Werk im Entstechen: 1963–1971)* (Munich: Bruckmann, 1971), 27. This text appears in German in the book itself. This English source text is from a hand-typed letter on Ronald Feldman Fine Arts Inc. letterhead which came inserted in my copy of the book. At the bottom of the letter is typed "Arakawa, Mechanism of Meaning / Verlag F. Bruckmann KG / (Munich, 1971)."

sequences themselves continually undergoing revision over the years. After proceeding through all of the exercises sequentially, rigorously, and repeatedly, one is (or at least I am always) well and properly flummoxed. Tempting as it is to analyze the specific function of each exercise, and then the entire series of exercise stations as a whole, I will constrain my examination to one particular exercise station, and consider its revisions, fluctuations, elidings, and slippages across the series of four books (and into its fifth [final?] instantiation on the internet). The particular exercise under consideration always appears as the first exercise in the "Neutralization of Subjectivity" subdivision, which is itself the first subdivision in editions 2–4, but is the third subdivision in the first edition. I will simply refer to this exercise as "The Dot."

According to my analysis, "The Dot" exercise is really an apophatic (micro?-)apparatus which is itself a contributing element toward a much larger apophatic (macro?-) apparatus, the macro-apparatus being the entire *Mechanism of Meaning* project. Where that macro-apparatus begins and ends (makes its "cut" into the universe, following Barad's terminology) is, by design, impossible to pin down. The entire apparatus itself keeps slipping (over time, across galleries, in and out of print), and the micro-apparatuses (the individual exercises) within it keep slipping (instantiation after instantiation, "individual/ subjective" human use after use). Rather than try to pin it all down, I will just slip along with it for a while and report back on the qualitative flavor(s) of the nothing(s) it refuses to finish making.

In order to better understand and appreciate the ingenuity of the apophatic art apparatus known as "The Dot," we will place it alongside another quite rich apparatus: (alchemist? physician? mathematician? astronomer?) Robert Fludd's 1617 diagram of the pre-creation void. Whereas Arakawa and Gins's apparatus acts as a lure to trap and brake linguistic human thought, Fludd's diagram actually enlists linguistic human thought in order to help constrain his diagram from doing and becoming something much greater than he intends it to become. We will ignore Fludd's admonitions to ignore what the materiality of his diagram is actually doing, and will instead attend to and follow the diagram's actual material becomings (both on the front side of its page, on the reverse side of its page, over the centuries, across multiple editions, through the division-of-labor conventions of international book production during the 1600s, in regards to hermetic cosmologies, and in dialogue with the tools, substrates, and materials of engraving media). We will discover that Fludd's diagram is actually a diagrammatic apparatus *meant to* employ pictographic analogy in order to assist in the mimetic description of a braked state. And yet, far from actually braking anything, Fludd's apparatus continues to become and mean what its materials are (still) doing.

Basically, Fludd's apparatus fails to achieve any real apophatic effect because he is unable to properly brake the speedy and proliferating becomings of his own apparatal materials. Whereas Arakawa and Gins's apparatus does enact apophatic effect because they succeed in braking their apparatal materials. More specifically, the present-tense actual occasions that make up Arakawa and Gins's apparatal materials (one material is human language, another material is human bodies) are forced to prehend each other in ways that enact their own self-braking aporia. Fludd's materials exceed his linguistic claim that they signify "nothing." Whereas Arakawa and Gins make no linguistic claim of signifying "nothing" (or "anything").

In a wonderfully concise passage, philosopher and theologian Denys Turner observes that "there is a very great difference between the strategy of *negative propositions* and the strategy of *negating the propositional*; between that of the *negative image* and that of the *negation of imagery."*[2] Some clarification is in order. By "proposition-al," Turner does not mean Whitehead's use of the term, in which "propositions" need not ever involve language or conscious human thought. He means "linguistic proposi-tions" which assert denotative meanings requiring con-scious human thought. Fludd's diagram is merely what Turner calls a negative image. Whereas Arakawa and Gins's "The Dot" not only avoids the strategy of negative linguistic propositions; it even moves beyond "negating" the linguistically propositional, and instead throws a sab-otaging wrench in the entire mechanism of the linguis-tically propositional (i.e., the mechanism of meaning). Similar to Turner, Deleuze observes, "It is of the essence of representation not only to represent something but to represent its own representativity."[3] Fludd's diagram follows this maxim by representing its own ability to be represented. Whereas "The Dot" (pseudo-)banally enters the regime of representation, only to immediately begin eroding the entire regime from within.

Before moving too far along in introducing these two apparatuses, some images of what they look like are in order. The first figure in this chapter is a drawing of the left ¾ of page 28[4] of my own copy of the first printed edi-tion of Arakawa and Gins's *Mechanism of Meaning* (more properly titled *Mechanismus der Bedeutung [Werk im Entste-hen: 1963–71]*) (see Fig. 1[5]). The photographic image that appears on page 28 of this first edition is (one presumes)

2   Denys Turner, *The Darkness of God: Negativity in Christian Mysticism* (Cambridge: Cambridge University Press, 1999), 35. [Italics appear in the original text.]

3   Gilles Deleuze, *Difference and Repetition*, trans. Paul Patton (New York: Columbia University Press, 1994), 80.

4   The right ¼ of the page has typeset German translations of the Eng-lish text.

5   For larger versions of these images, and for additional images, visit http://textshopexperiments.org/textshop03/bereft-nothing-vs-fecund-nothing which is adapted from a presentation I gave at the "[image here]" conference at Harvard in 2016.

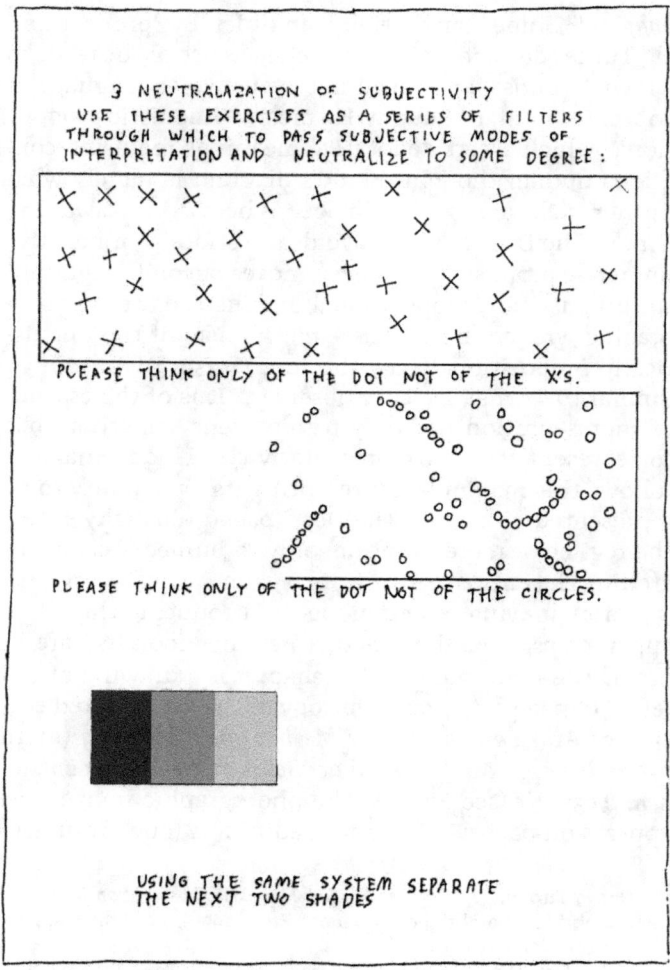

Fig. 1: The left ¾ of page 28 of the first printed edition of Arakawa and Gins's *Mechanism of Meaning*. Drawing by Jordan Cloninger.

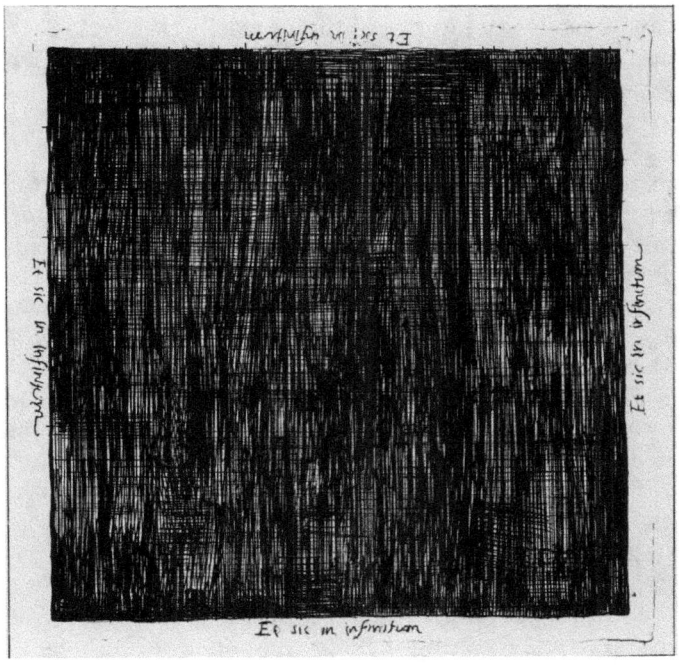

Fig. 2: The diagram on page 26 of Robert Fludd's *The Macrocosm and the Microcosm*. Drawing by Jordan Cloninger.

a photograph of the physical panel for "The Dot" exercise taken from an instantiation of the *Mechanism of Meaning* installation some time between 1963 and 1971. The introductory title at the top of the panel ("3 NEUTRALIZATION OF SUBJECTIVITY") and the main instructions below it ("USE THESE EXERCISES AS A SERIES OF 'FILTERS' / THROUGH WHICH TO PASS SUBJECTIVE MODES OF / INTERPRETATION AND NEUTRALIZE TO SOME DEGREE:") apply to all of the subsequent exercises in section 3 of *Mechanism of Meaning*, not just "The Dot" exercise. The first exercise in section 3 appears immediately below these main instructions. It is the exercise I am calling "The Dot." "The

Dot" exercise is comprised of three sub-exercises. Each one of these sub-exercises has its own instruction which appears beneath it. I will focus more on the first two sub-exercises than on the third.

The second figure in this chapter is a drawing of a digital image of the diagram on page 26 of Robert Fludd's 1617 magnum opus, *Utriusque Cosmi, Maioris scilicet et Minoris, Metaphysica, Physica, atque Technica Historia* (*The Metaphysical, Physical, and Technical History of the Two Worlds, Namely the Greater and the Lesser*), more commonly known as *The History of the Two Worlds,* or *The Macrocosm and the Microcosm* (see Fig. 2). Simply put, the image on page 26 of *The Macrocosm and the Microcosm* is Fludd's diagram of the formless pre-universe (which is made up of "hyle"). "Et sic in infinitum" means "And so on to infinity."

Fludd's diagram enacts a kind of bereft flavor of nothing. It paradoxically but merely re-presents the impossibility of representing "nothing." Via the accompanying text from *The Macrocosm and the Microcosm,* and via the border text of the diagram itself, Fludd enlists his reader as the meaning-making component of his overall diagrammatic apparatus, in order to make the meaning, "nothing." In this "bereft nothing" apparatus, although a limit of the semiotic system is indeed approached, the semiotic system itself necessarily remains intact and un-exceeded. The reader resides within and functions to maintain the semiotic system. The system continues to function well enough to represent its inability to represent. Such media looks "like" nothing, but "nothing" is not experienced. To quote Derrida (out of context), "Presentation [...] is presented in its very inadequation, adequate to its inadequation. The inadequation of presentation is presented."[6]

---

6   Jacques Derrida, *The Truth in Painting*, trans. Geoff Bennington and Ian McLeod (Chicago: University of Chicago Press, 1987), 131.

Fortunately, Arakawa and Gins employ human language for an entirely different purpose, one that well exceeds the hermetically sealed and self-referential realm of "the semiotic turn." "The Dot" apparatus enacts what I will call a fecund (as opposed to bereft) flavor of nothing. "The Dot" triggers an aporia in its viewer in order to engender a kind of supra-semiotic *experience* of nothing. This "fecund nothing" apparatus lures the viewer into initially behaving as a meaning-making component of its overall apophatic apparatus in order to sabotage that meaning-making function so that other affective, material, a-linguistic forms of experience may rise to the surface. The overall linguistic system of human language is not "dismantled" (indeed, this would be impossible), but rather it is used as a launching pad to bootstrap an accompanying affective experience which then exceeds it.

In "The Dot," visual surfaces are not merely occluded, blackened, or erased (as in Fludd's bereft nothing approach). Instead, the very cognitive mechanisms by which surface effects are produced and by which they are semiotically "read" are themselves foregrounded and destabilized, deferring and braking the signifying finality of the surface image. This form of semiotic braking is an apophatic tactic.

It is important to note that affect and signification are always already occurring in both Fludd's diagram and "The Dot." Indeed, how could they not be? Both affect and signification are refracting through and folding in and out of one another in both of these apparatuses. The difference is simply this: the "bereft nothing" tactic of Fludd calls on the viewer to ignore the (often considerable) affective and material excesses produced by the paradox of its signification strategy. Such excesses are treated as incidental and are not purposefully exploited. Whereas the "fecund nothing" tactic of Arakawa and Gins uses the ever-present regime of signification as a lure which then becomes a trap, the aporia of which is purposefully meant to release an excess of experienceable affect.

Language Is As Language Does

If we mean to get at actual (non-metaphorical) becomings and brakings in the actual (non-metaphorical) world, why begin the case study section of this book with two apparatuses that rely so heavily on human language? Almost as a kind of control against which to measure future, less-linguistic apparatuses. If actual apparatal becomings can be enacted by apparatuses which incorporate human language (and they can), then human language must simply be one more force (albeit a strange, unique, and explicitly anthropocentric force) in the actual world (and it is). Human language (even the most declarative, constative, straightforward language) is always already doing something in the world beyond merely re-presenting the world from a once-removed, metaphorical, purely semiotic perspective. In the case of "The Dot," human language acts within the art apparatus as a lure which triggers human bodily aporia. This bodily aporia functions as the affective braking force of the overall apparatus.

We need not even employ a special, magical, dedicated flavor of performative language in order to achieve our braking force. Although "The Dot" does happen to include linguistic commands, they turn out to be commands that become increasingly difficult to sensibly interpret, much less to pragmatically obey. Instead, any and all language, even "ordinary" denotative language, may instigate actual occasions of becoming; and thus (when properly, apophatically implemented), may also instigate brakings and hesitations within those actual occasions.

Regarding the relationship between human language, human thought, and the world, semiotician Charles

Sanders Peirce roundly observes: "The whole function of thought is to produce habits of action... To develop its meaning, we have, therefore, simply to determine what habits it produces, for what a thing means is simply what habits it involves [...]. I only desire to point out how impossible it is that we should have an idea in our minds which relates to anything but conceived sensible effects of things. Our idea of anything is our idea of its sensible effects; and if we fancy that we have any other we deceive ourselves."[7]

According to Peirce's perspective, human language and human thought are not once-removed from the world; they are inextricably entangled in the ordinary becomings of the actual world, because they are inextricably bound up with the actions they produce. If (according to Karen Barad) materials mean what they eventually become; and if (according to me) human language is a material force in the world; then human language is as human language causes to become. From this kind of Peircean perspective, someone like Derrida (re-)appears in a much more performative light. Rather than an infuriating logician who obfuscates more than he elucidates, Derrida becomes the producer of texts that purposefully act as delucidation apparatuses. As Derrida himself explains, "I never write on anything [...]. Even if I feign writing about it, and no matter what I say, before all else I am seeking to produce effects."[8] My point is simply that linguistic effects (whatever their results, however they are produced) are actual, pragmatic, "real world" effects.

7   Charles Sanders Peirce, "How To Make Our Ideas Clear," in *Collected Papers of Charles Sanders Peirce, Volume V: Pragmatism and Pragmaticism,* eds. Charles Hartshorne and Paul Weiss (Cambridge, Mass.: Harvard University Press, 1934), 400–401.

8   Jacques Derrida, "Envois," in *The Post Card: From Socrates to Freud and Beyond,* trans. Alan Bass (Chicago: The University of Chicago Press, 1996), 113.

Artist and poet Brion Gysin, insightful beyond his era, grasped well (and idiosyncratically) the materiality of language as an artistic medium. In 1958, Gysin asserted, "Language is an abominable misunderstanding which makes up a part of matter. The painters and the physicists have treated matter pretty well. The poets have hardly touched it."[9] Later, in 1963, he wrote about language, "It's just material, after all. There is nothing sacred about words."[10] In that same year, Arakawa and Gins installed the first iteration of *Mechanism of Meaning*, ingeniously capitalizing on the materiality of language from the combined perspectives of poetry, architecture, and art. Better than merely "touching" the materiality of language, Arakawa and Gins constructed an apparatus which lured in, exploited, and deeply troubled the materiality of both human language and human bodies.

The time has come to compare Fludd's diagram of pre-creation with Arakawa and Gins's "The Dot" in much more nuanced detail, beginning with Fludd.

Bereft Nothing (Fludd's Diagram)

Fludd's "black" diagram appears toward the beginning of *The Macrocosm and the Microcosm*. In it, Fludd famously illustrates the formless pre-universe, made of a material called hyle. Fludd's own interpretation of hyle is basically a conflation of Aristotle's original hyle (matter awaiting form) with Aristotle's "prime matter" (a fundamental substance not made up of any other substance).

Fludd *writes* of hyle:

9   Brion Gysin, *Poem of Poems* (Alga Marghen LP N. plana G 8Voc-Son021, 1997), originally recorded in 1958.
10 Brion Gysin, "Cut-Ups: A Project for Disastrous Success," in William S. Burroughs and Brion Gysin, *The Third Mind* (New York: The Viking Press, 1978), 43.

This primal material is a primordial, infinite, shape-less existence, as suitable for something as for nothing; having no size or dimension, for it cannot be said to be either large or small; having no qualities, for it is neither thin, nor thick, nor perceptible; having no properties nor tendencies, neither moving nor still, without colour, or any elementary property.[11]

This explanation constitutes an admirably apophatic piece of writing, in which Fludd presses us into service as meaning-makers, only to confound our ability to make meaning. But when Fludd transitions from writing about hyle *itself*, to writing about his own visual representation of hyle, the disclaimers of mediation begin. On visually representing hyle, Fludd writes:

And here, honestly following the descriptions of Mer-curius Trismegistus and Moses, we have painted an imaginary picture of this formless matter, as a black smoke, or vapour, or a dreadful gloom, or the darkness of an abyss, or, in a word, any kind of unfinished, raw, impalpable material.[12]

Fludd freely admits the failure of his image to properly illustrate the formlessness of pre-formed matter. He writes, "We have painted," but the diagram is actually a Matthäus Merian engraving, and not a Fludd painting at all. Fludd's term "imaginary picture" attempts a kind of double remove from actual, material hyle itself. Fur-thermore, by describing hyle "as" a list of analogs, Fludd falls back on analogical, metaphorical adequation, which serves as an even further (thrice) remove. Fludd's written language is doing all it can to bracket our expectations of

11 Robert Fludd, *The Origin and Structure of the Cosmos*, trans. Patricia Tahil (Edinburgh: Magnum Opus Hermetic Sourceworks, 1982), 21.
12 Ibid.

the picture. He is exhausting his own language to warn us that the picture is merely a formal illustration of form-less matter, and not an actual enaction of formless matter. Like some kind of proto-Magritte, Fludd cautions us, "this is not a nothing."

In effect, Fludd's diagram and his writing about the diagram are *meant* to gather, collect, corral, and ultimately trap any and all affective forces emanating from the material diagram itself, and press those forces into the singular service of intensifying signification in order to stress and approach the limit of the meaning of "nothing." Fludd never *intends* any of the affective, material forces of the engraving to exceed the regime of signification. He even goes so far as to corral the borders of the diagram with his own linguistically explanatory hedge: "and so on to infinity." Far from extending the borders of the engraving into actual, material infinity, this hedge text attempts to trap the engraving within the bounds of linguistic signification.

And yet, far from being an impoverished stand-in for Fludd's concept of formless matter, the material diagram itself is actually doing much more than Fludd's own explanatory disclaimer claims. Indeed, the diagram is veritably exuding excessive material affect (all of which Fludd means us to ignore as merely incidental). Instead, we are going to ignore Fludd, and unpack the material functioning of the physical diagram.

As asserted in the previous chapter, representations act as apparatuses, even if they claim not to. It is essential to note that even non-apophatic representations (such as Fludd's diagram) are always affectively doing something. One thing that diagrams are affectively doing is masking the fact that they are affectively doing something! By inordinately focusing us on what they are analogically *representing*, diagrams divert our attention away from all the other things they are actually *doing*. Metaphors function a lot like representational diagrams. Metaphors seduce humans into thinking about metaphors metaphorically, as if metaphors can only ever be thought according to their own self-declared function. Meanwhile, metaphors are actually smuggling in and forging all sorts of intuitive, back-door connections, well in excess of their basic tenor–vehicle relationships.

We may now revisit the Derrida quotation mentioned earlier, attending to its original context. Here is the expanded quotation: "The sublime proper [...] refuses all adequate presentation. But how can this unpresentable thing present itself? [...] Presentation [...] is presented in its very inadequation, adequate to its inadequation. The inadequation of presentation is presented." Derrida goes on to explain, "[The sublime] inadequately presents the infinite in the finite and delimits it violently therein."[13] Such inadequate presentation and violent delimitation of the infinite within the finite is precisely what Fludd's diagram accomplishes. In this sense, Fludd's diagram is an apparatus for subliming. It intends, via hypertrophied media and analogical representation, to point us toward some transcendental beyond. We are meant to use our own sign-interpreting imaginations to arrive at this infinite, transcendent nothing, this form of formlessness.

It bears noting that this kind of imaginative subliming of the transcendent has nothing at all to do with apophasis. Apophatic apparatuses don't point outward toward a transcendent nothing. Instead, they actively brake the becoming of something. In order for Fludd's diagram to truly succeed at its subliming purpose, it has to violently delimit infinite formlessness within discrete, finite media. The more constrained, bereft, and hypertrophied the media materials, the more sublime the overall effect. Unfortunately for Fludd (but fortunately for us), his materials are bursting out at the seams in myriad directions.

13   Derrida, *The Truth in Painting,* 131.

The Square (into Circles)

Fludd's *Macrocosm* initially describes the progressive evolution of the cosmos. Each evolutionary stage of the cosmos is illustrated with a diagram, all of which are in the
form of circles save one. Only Fludd's initial, pre-cosmos
hyle diagram is in the form of a square. Why the difference? The difference is theological, but also technical and
material. The circle form is derived from Fludd's idiosyncratic and hermetic theology, but the initial square owes
its shape to both theological and technical forces.

The created cosmos is a circle because Mercurius Trismegistus says that once God's creative light emanated
forth from him (with a hearty *fiat lux*), it then circled back
toward him, because God was the most desirable thing
in the universe, and the light desired him. So, although
Fludd's initial diagram (on page 26 of the *Macrocosm*) is
square, the diagram which depicts the creation event
(page 49) and all other diagrams of the cosmos (pages 29,
37, 41, 46, 55, 63, 66, 69, 131, 136, 138, and 141) are circles.
In a much later diagram (on page 62 of Fludd's second
volume, the *Microcosm*), Fludd goes so far as to label the
space outside of the circle of the cosmos *extra omnia* =
outside of everything.

In addition to the theological underpinnings of Fludd's
circular cosmos, it is worth noting the almost direct formal correlation between Fludd's spherical experimental
laboratory apparatuses (many of which are also depicted
in *The Macrocosm and the Microcosm*) and Fludd's model of
the cosmos. Fludd would not resist this correlation, since,
to him, the spherical forms of his laboratory equipment
naturally arise from the circular forms of the cosmos itself. Whereas, to us, 500 years later, from the perspective
of our much different cosmological model, it seems the
exact opposite is more likely true: Fludd's cosmos formally mirrors the shape of his laboratory apparatuses, and
not vice-versa.

The reason for the square shape of Fludd's initial page 26 diagram is also technical and material. Not "material" simply in the analogical sense, having to do with the "meaning" of "material" within Fludd's cosmology (hyle = a kind of pulpy, formless matter); but "material" in the very immediate, pragmatic, apparatal sense of the shape of physical books, and the nature of copperplate engravings. In Fludd's diagrammatic apparatus (i.e., the engraving on page 26), the re-presented, pre-formed hyle must analogically seek and attempt to exceed the very edges of media representation. In Fludd's case, those edges happen to be a square copperplate. Why square? Because paper pulp dries most readily on a wire mesh grid, so we have rectangular books full of rectangular pages instead of circular books full of circular pages. The copperplate engraving of the unformed hyle must fit on the rectangular page of the book. This rectangular shape actually works out well for the engraver, because it is more cost-effective to cut a flattened copperplate into squares than into circles (since less material is wasted). Because of these technical and material facts of the world in 1617, the baseline, default, unmodulated shape of the pre-engraved copperplate substrate is square. Since Fludd means to represent his hyle as reaching and exceeding any and all limits, the hyle must cover the full plate, and the default shape of the plate is square. Hence the diagram of the hyle is square.

Technically, all of the engraved figure prints pasted into Fludd's book are square, even when they depict circular images. This is due to the technical nature of intaglio printing. You need not crop your copper plate itself into the form you are depicting (like a circle), because you can just wipe off the ink from the un-engraved area beyond your engraved circle, and the image still prints as a circle (albeit on a square piece of paper). And actually, because of Fludd's border text ("And so on to infinity"), the engraved "hyle" in the square diagram on page 26 doesn't actually reach to the edge of its copperplate either.

All these material processes and histories are suddenly brought into view and accidentally foregrounded once the medium is hypertrophied, once the edge of the copperplate is purposefully approached and (faux-)exceeded. Representing formlessness can't help but stress the regime of formal representation, because formlessness necessarily hypertrophies the limits of representable form. Representing formlessness always forces a focus on the mechanisms, formal craft skills, materials, tools, processes, and substrates of whichever particular medium is doing the formal representing. In this sense, formlessness winds up "outing" the hidden material functionings of the (ostensibly pure) signifying medium seeking to formally represent it. Formlessness seeps outward and beneath the realm of simple signification, outpacing the realm of mere re-presentational adequation. Formlessness lures otherwise straightforward, meaning-making humans toward illicit encounters with absurdist a-formulations of nothing.

Yet almost in direct response to these out-of-bounds tendencies (lest we begin focusing more on the actual functions of the diagrammatic apparatus itself, rather than on the meaning of Fludd's proposed cosmology), Fludd immediately seeks to cordon off all these material affects and excesses with his border text (*Et sic in infinitum*), returning us to the realm of linguistic signification. Otherwise, all these material forces might get out of hand and begin to mean what they are actually doing (which, of course, they do anyway).

The Crosshatching

Fludd says formless hyle is homogeneous, because it can't contain varying intensities of heterogeneous difference. But he also says it has no qualities or pattern, and homogeneity seems like a kind of pattern to me. As such, the diagram seeks to represent an un-form that is neither variable nor consistent.

Fludd himself sketched all of the diagrams in *The Macrocosm and the Microcosm,* and Matthäus Merian translated his sketches into engravings. Fludd says he painted the hyle diagram, but there is no extant record. What would he have painted? Whatever Fludd's original painting looked like (if there even was one), it was up to Merian to translate Fludd's painting, or his written instructions, into a copperplate engraving.

It is worth noting that, had Fludd purposefully intended to incorporate the materials of engraving (ink, paper, copper, steel burin) and the processes of engraving (incising, inking, pressing) into the explicit structure and evolution of his cosmology, he would have been approaching something like the engraved poems of William Blake, where the technical nature of the engraving process influenced and was influenced by the content of Blake's poems. Instead, Fludd drew the diagrams, wrote the text, and conducted the lab experiments; but he subcontracted the technicalities of the engraving and printing.

Merian used the common engraving technique of crosshatching to depict the unformed hyle, but the crosshatching in the hyle diagram is denser (thus darker) and less symmetrical than other crosshatched shadows in Merian's more standard engravings (of cows, barns, and fields) for his less cosmically inclined clients. What drove Merian's formal decision to crosshatch the hyle diagram so densely and asymmetrically? No one knows. Merian was a subcontracted craftsman, and this particular decision was not considered worth recording for posterity. It would have been considered a purely technical decision, not likely to interest those outside of Merian's particular trade. And yet, Matthäus Merian's chosen technical approach to the unique crosshatching challenges of this particular engraving assignment form an integral component of the overall diagrammatic apparatus.

From subsequent diagrams throughout *The Macrocosm* depicting the hyle in more formed states, it is obvious that Merian's crosshatching decisions for the unformed hyle on page 26 were far from arbitrary. From the engravings on pages 37 and 49 for example, the areas of formed (and being-formed) hyle are depicted using symmetrical, directional hatchings, while the areas of yet-to-be formed hyle are depicted with the same, almost aleatoric crosshatchings used on page 26.

Speculating about Merian's specific decisions regarding craft technique necessarily cause us to consider the agency of the subcontracted craftsman at the time, which further leads us to consider the broader international chain of production for fine books in the early 1600s: author Robert Fludd (England) hires publisher Johann Theodor de Bry (Germany) who hires engraver Matthäus Merian the Elder (Switzerland). Once again, Fludd's diagrammatic apparatus of formlessness surprises us by exceeding the bounds of mere signification, this time cutting into and thus prehending specific human labor relations of Europe at the time.

Whatever conceptual, technical, theological, economic, or representational goals drove Merian's decisions to crosshatch the way he did, he arrived at an unusually dense and varied matrix of crosshatchings. The density and variety of this crosshatching matrix caused an inordinate (and inordinately varied) amount of ink to remain within the copperplate incisions after the surface of the plate was wiped and prepared for printing. The *differing* amounts of ink retained from one inking to another meant that each pressing of the copperplate varied greatly from one edition of the book to the next. As a result, four hundred years later, some editions are blotchy and quite ink-black, others contain brittle white ridges amidst a field of black, and still others have grey splotches

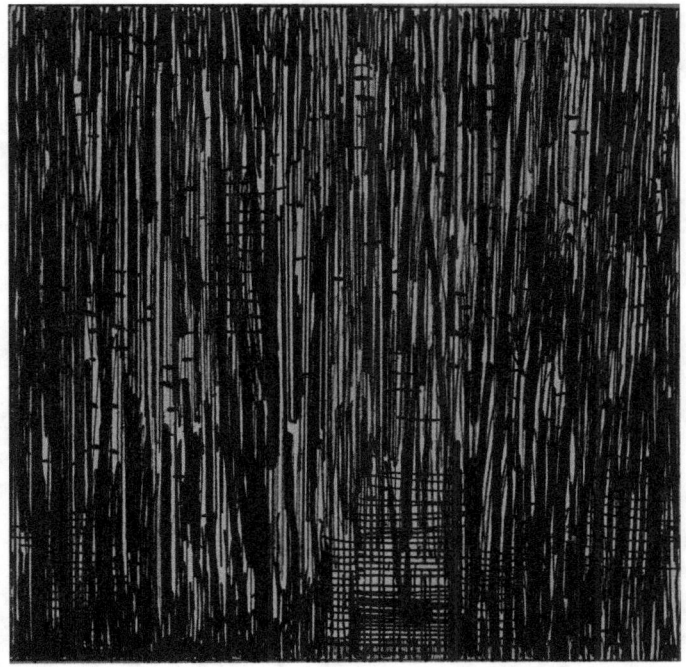

Fig. 3: The bottom left quadrant of the diagram on page 26 of Robert Fludd's *The Macrocosm and the Microcosm,* from the edition housed at Harvard's Houghton Library. Note the purposeful irregularity of the crosshatchings. Drawing by Jordan Cloninger.

where fields of parallel raised white ridges have chipped away and worn down over the years, resulting in a kind of grey residue beneath (see Fig. 3). The *sheer amount* of ink retained in the copperplate incisions often oversaturated the paper onto which it was printed, resulting in bleeding along the x, y, and z axes.

THE BLEEDS (along the x, y, and z Axes)

Because of the dense crosshatchings, each individual printing of the formless hyle plate is more variable than it would be in a printing run of an ordinary engraved plate. As mentioned, some inkings of the copperplate retained more ink than others. Some pressings pressed harder than others. Furthermore, over hundreds of years, due to the density of ink retained by the plate, in various pressings, parts of the ink have flaked off, unevenly exposing areas of the substrate. These material variances do not normally manifest themselves in engravings of cows, but with this particular hypertrophied copperplate, they do. These discrepancies between editions are particularly evident along the edges of the hyle, where the ink has exceeded its proscribed boundary in various, unique ways per edition. It is almost as if the ink itself is attempting to obey the border's admonition to continue "on to infinity."

Also, because the formless hyle diagram plates are so ink-saturated, several even show through, to varying degrees per edition, from the front side of the page (page 26 [verso]) to the reverse side of the page (page 25 [recto]), along the "z-axis," as it were.

A Brief Word on "Blackness"

It might seem that making the physical diagram of the pre-formed proto-universe as black as it could possibly be would somehow create a kind of "actual" nothing, as if we were suddenly staring at a void contained within the very page itself. But, of course, "blackness" does not inherently (or immediately, or directly) "equal" nothing without the human-interpretive work of adequating blackness with nothing. No matter how black the black, we are still called upon as humans to become meaning-making machines in order to "make something" of the black. Blackness doesn't even inherently equal absence; and even if it did, absence doesn't inherently equal nothing (particularly since the nothing we are pursuing in this book has more to do with putting the brakes on becoming, and less to do with any sort of void). One is (humorously) reminded of Anish Kapoor's attempt to patent the blackest black paint possible, and of the black album cover for Spinal Tap's *Smell the Glove* ("It's like, 'how much more black could this be?' and the answer is none. None more black.") At least one inherent property of blackness seems to be how inherently funny is the brute force, full frontal attempt to achieve the maximum quantitative degree of nothingness via sheer qualitative excess of blackness.

To equate blackness with nothing is to suffer from oculo-centrism (and a specifically human flavor of oculo-centrism at that). Human art history suffers from such oculo-centrism. This is why many an art historian has conveniently interpreted Fludd's hyle diagram as a precursor to a host of 20th-century abstract expressionist black paintings (from Kazimir Malevich to Frank Stella). But even Fludd (although he's no Arakawa and Gins) avoids such an obvious, oculo-centric trap. Fludd's diagram does not rely on the color of ink or the accuracy of the illustration to be the hyle itself, or even to accurately re-present the hyle. For Fludd, the whole diagrammatic system used throughout *The Macrocosm and the Microcosm* only ever serves to supplement and augment the text itself. Fludd invokes us as readers to piece everything together in our imaginations. We are called upon to behave as meaning-making mechanisms within the diagrammatic apparatuses he has constructed. We are enlisted to make meaning of the mysterious, inexplicable, formless, originary hyle no more or less than we are enlisted to make meaning of all the other more ordinary elements of earth, air, water, and fire. It's just that the bizarre, apophatic nature of this formless prime matter throws a particularly thorny wrench into our role as meaning-making machines.

* * *

All of these unique material properties that emerge due to hypertrophying the medium of copperplate engraving are bracketed by Fludd himself as merely incidental. They fall outside of Fludd's circumscribed, hermetically sealed, signifying program. And yet, [t]here these material properties all still are, ignoring Fludd's declared intentions as they function within the diagrammatic apparatus that he has co-created. Fludd intends his formless hyle diagram to enlist its viewers as meaning-making machines in order to make the meaning of "formlessness." And although, as we've shown, Fludd's diagrammatic apparatus is actually doing much more than Fludd himself intends, it is still not making nothing (i.e., braking the becoming of something). On the contrary, Fludd's diagrammatic apparatus is actually becoming all sorts of particular new somethings, as every ordinary, non-apophatic apparatus can't help but do (whether art apparatus, Newtonian-behavior-measuring physics apparatus, quantum-behavior-measuring physics apparatus, or any other apparatus created by carving out an explicit chunk of the universe from the rest of the universe). In other words, whatever the merits of Fludd's diagrammatic apparatus (and they are several and thrilling), it is still not an apophatic apparatus. As such, Fludd's diagrammatic apparatus makes a kind of bereft nothing (it makes the human-semiotic meaning "nothing") while simultaneously making a host of proliferating material somethings.

Fecund Nothing
(Arakawa and Gins's "The Dot")

Whereas Fludd's formless hyle diagram succeeds in making a bereft nothing (enlisting the viewer as a meaning-making machine in order to make the semiotic meaning of "nothing"), Arakawa and Gins's installation and book project *Mechanism of Meaning* makes a series of fecund nothings: the viewer's ability to make meaning is purposely sabotaged and confounded. Rather than being able to successfully make the semiotic meaning of "nothing" (or anything, for that matter), the viewer is stranded in a state of aporia, unable to make any definitive meaning at all. Although we will focus on just one exercise (the one I have been calling "The Dot"), each exercise from *Mechanism of Meaning* makes its own unique flavor of fecund nothing (each at its own unique pace, each for its own unique duration, each to its own increasingly confounding end). Each exercise puts the brakes on human meaning-making. One might rightly ask, "why create such a rigorous series of apophatic apparatuses?"

In the first edition of the book (published in 1971), not in a forward or a preface, but in the very first section of *Mechanism of Meaning* itself [said first section being called "1. PRESENTATION OF BASES FOR SELECTION (IRONY, AMBIGUITY, PARADOX, CONCRETE ABSTRACTION, HUMOR, HYPNOTIC ILLUSTRATIONS, etc.)"], Arakawa and Gins describe their own goals for the project:

> This project is [...] an animated [...] cartoon for [nonsense or] meaning. The animation or the mechanism of meaning occurs through [...] the interaction of languages [visual-verbal-tactile etc.] by the viewer working out the exercises on his own terms (sense or nonsense) [...] to increase the effort required (and thus make it more apparent?) and to prolong the time necessary (to allow enough time for the setting of a trap?) for the viewer's mechanism of meaning to operate[14]

---

14 Arakawa and Gins, *Mechanismus der Bedeutung*, 27. This text appears in German in the book itself. This English source text is from a hand-typed letter by Arakawa which came inserted in my copy of the book.

Later (at least by the publication of the second edition of the book in 1979), the artists had deemed this first section to be over-determining and had removed it from the book and from the installation instantiation of the project. This removal makes sense: if the goal of the project is to destabilize the viewer, then providing the viewer with this (however vague, at least somewhat clear) contextualization of the goal of the project winds up undermining the goal of the project. I include Arakawa and Gins's concise explanation here because, unlike *Mechanism of Meaning*, the goal of this book is not to destabilize its reader, but simply to explain how such a destabilizing apparatus may be constructed. As such, insight into what the artists themselves actually thought their own project was doing (at least in 1971) is useful, if for no other reason than to be able to contrast their explanation with Fludd's textual explanation of his diagram. Whereas Fludd was openly apologetic for how inadequately representative his diagram was, Arakawa and Gins indicate that they purposefully intend to use such slippages between signifier and signified in order to set a trap for the viewer's meaning-making abilities. Since "the mechanism of meaning" is the viewer, the project is best understood not as a mechanism of meaning in and of itself, but more as an apophatic art apparatus designed to disrupt "the mechanism of meaning" (i.e., humans). The project thus begins with the implicit awareness that its human "viewers" are already part of the art apparatus.

Although Arakawa and Gins don't directly allude to quantum-behavior-measuring apparatuses, or to apophatic writing, note how aware they are of the apophatic apparatal functionings of their art. They know full well that each exercise functions as a lure that sets a trap. The primary goal of each exercise is to lure human thinking into a whorling, perpetually refracting, aporetic quagmire. Indeed, the artists talk much more about what the work is doing and how it functions than about what it looks like, its physical dimensions, or even its source materials. Of course, they can't talk about what the work "means," since it means (purposes, intends) to confound human cognitive ability to make meaning.

Finally, we have arrived at our first proper apophatic art apparatus! Let us first examine the specific, pragmatic ways in which "The Dot" functions, and then unpack some of the implications of its behavior.

The Curious Case of the Dot (Edition 1)

"The Dot" exercise appears (relatively) straightforward in edition 1 of the book (see Fig. 1). The first dot of which we are instructed to think is admittedly tiny, but still visible just to the left of the "x" that appears roughly in the middle of the top diagram. Or is that "x" really a "+"? Or is that dot not a dot, but only the left-most part of the left-hand arm of the "+"? Perhaps it only *appears* as an extant, self-contained dot because of a misprint of that particular "+"? (When a dot only *appears* to be a dot, doesn't that still make it a dot?) For the sake of argument, let's call it a dot. We may assume (or may we?) that in the source installation panel for this particular exercise (the physical panel that was photographed for this first edition of the book), the "x"s have first been stenciled, and the dot itself has been added later with acrylic paint by the artist's hand.

Ah, but then the instructions below the diagram read: "PLEASE THINK ONLY OF THE DOT NOT OF THE X'S." Perhaps the dot of which we are supposed to think is actually the period at the end of these very instructions? Perhaps it is the apostrophe between the "X" and the "S" in these instructions. (Is an apostrophe a dot?) But let's assume the dot of which we are supposed to think (and *only* think) is the dot next to the center "x" (an "x" that might also be a "+"). Whether or not it's an "x" or a "+" turns out to be irrelevant, since we are only supposed to think of the dot.

But then why add "not of the x's"? Why not simply say, "please think only of the dot" and leave it at that? So now we have to keep a place in our mind for the x's, a place that is a bit more specialized and reserved than the place we are not supposed to keep for all other non-dot things, but a place not yet as central as the place we are supposed to keep for "the dot." But, of course, how can one think to reserve a semi-special place for something that is not supposed to be thought?

It is hard enough to think "only" of the dot. You wind up thinking about thinking about the dot, in which case you are not thinking only of the dot. Or maybe you start thinking about what "*only*" actually means (set theory, unions, exclusions, and the logics they imply); or you start thinking about what "*of*" means (what is the difference between thinking *about* something and thinking *of* something? why *of*?); or you start thinking about what thinking is; or you begin occasionally self-monitoring to assess whether you are still thinking only of the dot (which of course, now you aren't, because now you are thinking about whether you are or not); or you start thinking about how long you are meant to think of the dot (is an instant enough, or need it be a series of instances, and need these instances be continuous, or can they be sporadic?). All of the aforementioned difficulties (and many more) arise simply from trying to think *only of the dot,* much less from trying to think *only of the dot not of the x's.*

The initial straightforwardness of the exercise proves to be a Trojan horse, a lure, a trap. It extends the (false) promise of understandability. But (and this is crucial) the apparatus really does mean us to actually attempt (in real time) the mental gymnastics required to try and execute the instructions. (They did ask nicely, after all. They said *please.*) And here we are only 1/3 of the way down the page, with 2 more sub-exercises to go, and only 1/5 of the way into all of the printed editions of this particular exercise.

In the second diagram on the page, the circle diagram, the dot appears toward the right-hand side of the panel, about mid-way up, above the last in a string of consecutive circles, and to the bottom right of another single circle (or is the single circle really just the skewed final circle in the aforementioned string of consecutive circles?). All of the same conundra apply here as applied to the x diagram, with a few additional difficulties. Maybe all of these circles are actually just large hollow dots. Is "the dot" now this new dot that we see in the circle diagram, or are the instructions still referring to the first dot up in the x diagram? And now, in addition to reserving a special mental place for the x's so that we may not think of them, we must also reserve the same kind of special mental place for the circles so that we may not think of them. Or perhaps we can simply empty our reserved mental x space and replace it with circles. But then of course we would have to think about enacting that swap, and we can't think about that. Why are they circles and not o's? o's might make more sense, or at least be more consistent with x's. Whatever the case, we can't think about the question of why the circles are not o's. And we can't think about the circles (or the o's) themselves. And we can't think about the difference between *about* and *of*. We must (please) think *only* of the dot.

The final (third) diagram shows a sequence of grayscale swatches shading toward (what appears to be) the color of the canvas substrate upon which they are painted. The instructions read "USING THE SAME SYSTEM SEPARATE THE NEXT TWO SHADES." Evidently the above two dot diagrams were supposed to have caused a "system" to emerge, a system which may then also be applied to approximating sequential shades of grayscale. One of the problems with this third set of instructions is that only the first of the "next two shades" may be approximated, after which we have already arrived at white. We can't approximate along the grayscale any whiter than white ("none more white"). But wait, the instructions aren't merely asking us to *approximate* the next two shades, they are asking us to *separate* them. How can you separate two things, when you can't even *imaginatively* approximate one of those two things? Wait a minute, if I'm only imaginatively approximating the next two shades, why am I unable to approximate a shade that is more white than white? In my imagination, I can approximate anything? Or can I? Is imagining the same as thinking? Is it only possible to imagine actual colors, or may I imagine non-actual colors? And what system ("the same system") would I use to imagine non-actual colors? I don't recall having purposefully developed any consistent system during my (failed) attempts to complete the dot exercises. Have I accidentally developed some sort of intuitive system without consciously knowing it? If so, how can I purposefully "use" that intuitive system to complete this third set of instructions? Is it possible to create a problem-solving system without consciously understanding how it works? Even more challenging, is it possible to intuitively apply an intuitive problem-solving system without ever consciously understanding either the system or the way in which you are applying it? How would you intuitively invent and apply such a system? Bodily? Haptically? What does that even mean? And once you had invented and applied the system, how could you consciously verify that you had applied it? Indeed, why would you ever need to consciously verify that you had applied it? Could you bodily verify it? Can a body know? What is the difference between conscious knowing and bodily knowing?

The tip of the *Mechanism of Meaning* iceberg has been struck, and with only 91 more exercises to go! Fortunately (or unfortunately), we will stick with this first exercise ("The Dot") and track it across subsequent book editions and subsequent art installations.

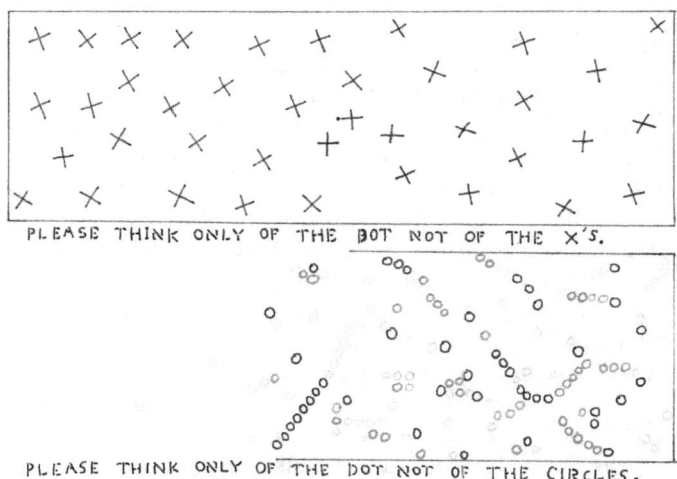

PLEASE THINK ONLY OF THE DOT NOT OF THE X'S.

PLEASE THINK ONLY OF THE DOT NOT OF THE CIRCLES.

Fig. 4: The top two diagrams on the left-hand side of the page containing "The Dot" exercise in edition 2 of *Mechanism of Meaning*. Drawing by Jordan Cloninger.

The Curious Case of the Dot (Edition 2)

Now let us consider the same exercise in edition 2 (1979) of the book (see Fig. 4). Some of the revisions in this edition are overt and intentional (additional color, additional figures), but others differences seem slight and incidental, and some differences seem outright accidental.[15]

In the second edition, the dot page has been printed in color (although if you are currently reading the printed version of *Some Ways of Making Nothing*, Figure 4 will be in black and white), and it turns out the circles are actually multicolored. Some circles are yellow, some are black, some are blue, some are tan, and some are red. And although we won't focus on the third diagram (the one

15 It is worth noting that the edition 3 (1988) instance of "the dot" exercise is identical [more or less] to the edition 2 instance.

with the swatches) from here forward, it turns out that the swatches which had initially appeared in grayscale in the first edition are actually shades of purple (from dark to pale). We are thus able to infer from edition 2 that the physical installation panel of "The Dot" exercise is actually in color rather than grayscale. This poses all sorts of new challenges when it comes to imagining "the next two shades," but mercifully, from here on out we will limit our focus to the first two dot diagrams.

Apart from the addition of color, something very unusual is happening in the circle diagram. The dot has largely disappeared. In its place is a kind of light smudge. Similar (but not identical) smudges appear in several other places throughout the circle diagram. What is going on? The dot in the x diagram is plainly visible. Indeed, it is more prominent than it was in the first edition. So why has the dot in the circle diagram become so scant as to have practically disappeared? Had we not already seen the circle diagram in the first edition, we would think that this exercise was a prank, and that there was no dot amongst the circles. But since we know where to look, we are able to discern what might perhaps be called a trace of the circle dot.

Is the (almost) absent dot simply a technical misprint? Is it intentional? These questions are further complicated by the addition of extra images in the right-hand third of the page. In the first edition, the right-hand third of the page had been reserved for typed German translations of the text from the left-hand panel exercises, because the first edition was originally printed in German by a German press. But now in this right-hand margin, two new images appear (see Figs. 5 and 6).

The top image in the right-hand margin (see Fig. 5) is hilarious and provides an entirely new set of cascading x's and circles for us to not think of, including an entire waterfall that we also must not think of. But the bottom image in the right-hand margin (see Fig. 6) is the one on

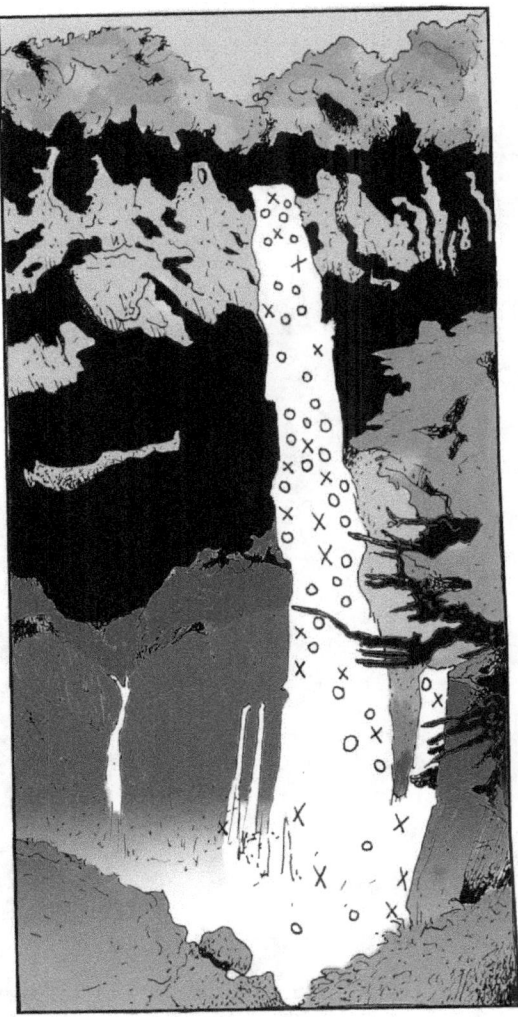

Fig. 5: The top image in the right-hand margin of the page containing "The Dot" exercise in edition 2 of *Mechanism of Meaning*. Drawing by Jordan Cloninger.

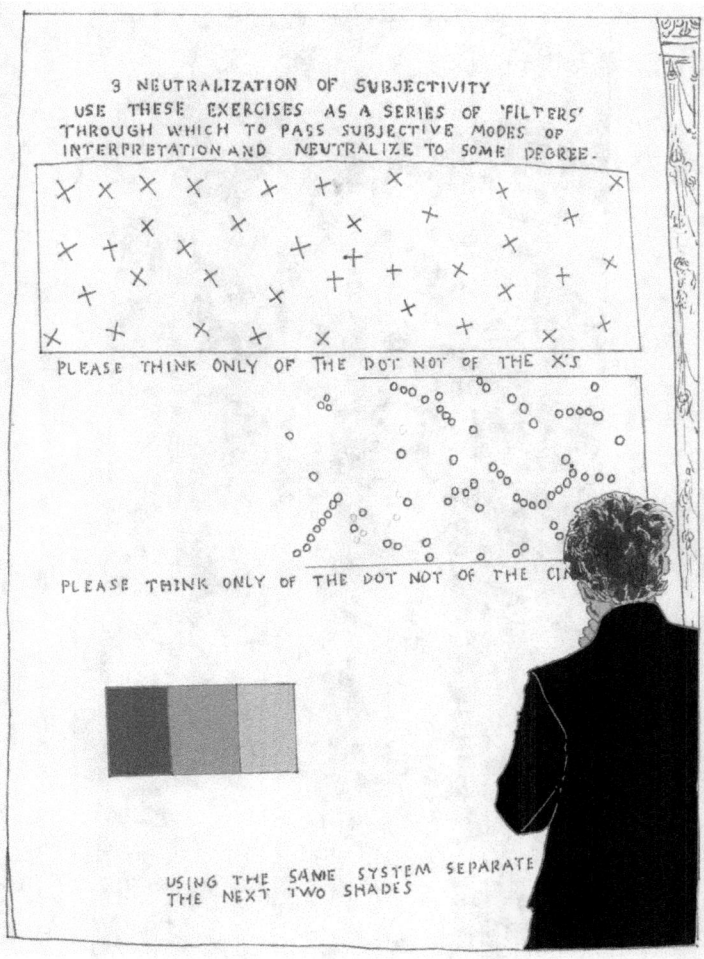

Fig. 6: The bottom image in the right-hand margin of the page containing "The Dot" exercise in edition 2 of *Mechanism of Meaning*. Drawing by Jordan Cloninger.

which I want to focus. It is evidently a color photograph of the physical exercise panel itself as it appears in an instantiation of the art installation, accompanied by an appropriately perplexed viewer. Note that, in this right-hand photograph, the dot amongst the circles is present in all of its full, solid (albeit twice-mediated) glory. So now, there is an additional dot for us to think of.

So which circle dot are we to think of? Is the "primary" circle dot the one in the right-hand installation picture that we can most clearly see, or is the "primary" dot the one in the left-hand book diagram that seems to be a mere trace? Does "primary" mean "original"? Arguably, the original circle dot is the one painted on the panel for the installation. Both the left-hand-diagram circle dot and the right-hand-margin installation-documentation circle dot are mediated (via photography and printing). Which dot is most mediated, and which one is most immediate? Does immediacy equal primacy? Assuming the left-hand diagram dot is the most immediate, it is also the least visible. Is the trace of a *less* mediated dot more primary than the clear punctum of a *more* mediated dot?

What if the left-hand dot's ghostliness is merely a technical misprint? Are we to forgive the misprint and imagine the left-hand dot as more present and less absent? Or is the dot we see the dot we get – technical misprint, intentional dot, or otherwise?

Arakawa and Gins authorize us, indeed, they force us, to pursue such scatological minutiae. Fludd more or less pleads with us to ignore the technical discrepancies of his diagram, and to focus on what the diagram "means." But Arakawa and Gins have done just the opposite. By purposefully creating an apparatus meant to call into question the mechanism by which humans make meaning (that mechanism being humans themselves), Arakawa and Gins invite in every technical consideration, every possible misprint, every speck of dust that falls on the page. Their apparatus extends outward into

all of the technical mechanisms that humans use to create meaning (the book; the printed page; the distinction
between a misprint, an incidental mark, and an intentional mark). Their apparatus sucks all of these technical
mechanisms into its own apparatal quagmire. Once our
agreed-upon conventions of meaning-making begin to
be undermined, where does that undermining stop? We
are no longer able to confidently say, "Well that's just a
misprint. Well, that mark is just a stray mark. That's not
the intended dot. This is the intended dot." *Any* dot (even
the trace of a dot from the 1971 edition that has made its
ghostly way forward into the 1979 edition) is a legitimate
contender for "*the*" dot.

Additional questions arise. If the ghost dot in the left-
hand circle diagram is a misprint, then why is it misprint-
ed in exactly the same way (and it is) in 1988's edition 3?
The artists and publishers had nine years to correct their
mistake. Why didn't they? Or was it a happy accident and
they just re-printed the misprint because they enjoyed
the extra sense of ambiguity that it introduced? Assuming that was indeed the case (and I'm just assuming), is
edition 3's intentional re-print of edition 2's accidental
misprint now suddenly not a misprint? Does the addition
of intention now suddenly make edition 3's ghost dot
somehow more "primary" than its edition 2 predecessor?

To carry things a step further, perhaps the illustrator
of *this* book (*Some Ways of Making Nothing*) mis-drew the
edition 2 circle diagram. Perhaps, in translating the diagram from printed book to drawing, the dot got altered.
Perhaps once the drawing was published in this book, the
dot got altered again. Perhaps a speck of dust has fallen
on your own book's page, (or kindle screen, or whatever).
Which of these dots is "the" dot?

Arakawa and Gins intentionally invite all of these questions into their apparatus. Their apparatus intentionally
opens out onto any further reproductions of the reproductions of their original exercise panel. Their apparatus

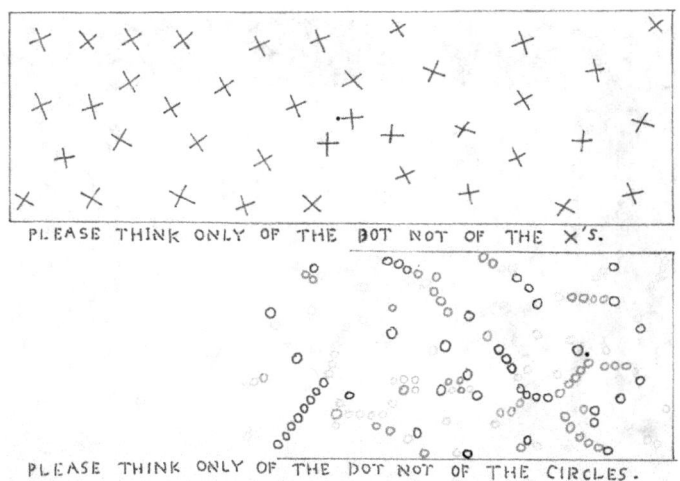

Fig. 7: the top two diagrams on the (now) right-hand side of the page containing "The Dot" exercise in edition 4 of *Mechanism of Meaning*. Drawing by Jordan Cloninger.

cuts into the very domain of human meaning-making, across decades, book editions, installation instantiations, reprints of reprints of reprints, and forward into future reprints not yet printed. The most recent physical panel of "The Dot" installation exercise station is currently in art storage in Manhattan as we speak. Is dust falling on it? Is that dust any more primary than the dust on your kindle? Which dot is *"the"* dot? And now that we have begun thinking of all these other dots, how can we possibly not think of them? Have all dots now collapsed into *"the"* dot?

The Curious Case of the Dot (Edition 4)

The same dot exercise appears again in edition 4 of the book (which appears as part of the larger catalog for Arakawa and Gins's 1997 Guggenheim Soho show). The

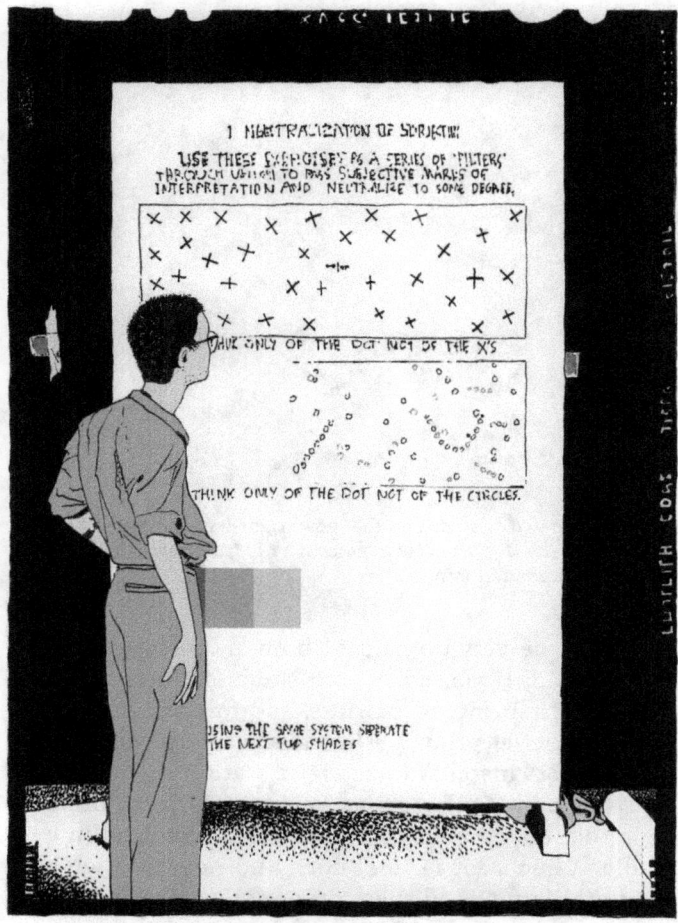

Fig. 8: The lone image at the bottom of the (now) left-hand margin of the page containing "The Dot" exercise in edition 4 of *Mechanism of Meaning*. Drawing by Jordan Cloninger.

main diagram has been moved to the right-hand 2/3 of the page (see Fig. 7).

Note that the dot has now solidly returned to the circle section (more so than in any of the prior book editions). This edition 4 circle dot actually looks more like the circle dot from the actual (?) panel as depicted in the marginal installation documentation photograph from editions 2 and 3. So, the problem of the missing (traced? ghosted?) circle dot has been temporarily resolved, just in time for an altogether weirder problem to arise in the new photograph of the installation included in edition 4 (see Fig. 8).

Now, in the left-hand 1/3 margin, the waterfall image has been removed, and there is a completely new installation documentation image, this time of a different viewer staring at the physical exercise panel. The panel is no longer hanging on the wall (as it was [presumably] in editions 2 and 3), but is now resting on supports which are themselves resting on the floor. Additionally, the edge of the entire documentation image now includes the border contact (test) print text from the printed roll of film and some of the film holes from the negative film roll. Furthermore, masking tape appears to be taping some blue paper to the contact print itself. Were the masking tape and the blue paper actually present on the wall in the gallery? No, the scale is not right. So then why were these physical artifacts left on the contact print prior to transferring the image into the book? In other words, why take a picture of the installation, print that picture out as a contact print, put tape on it, and then take a second picture of that printed out picture to use for the book? Why not just exclude the contact print from the production process (as is usually the case), and simply print to the book from the final print? The inclusion of these additional "technical" elements seems to indicate a kind of artistic intention. Or does it?

Regardless of (in addition to? in concert with?) these border details, what on earth is going on in this new image? The circle dot is visible, but it now competes with at least two other circle dots that have manifested themselves and become equally as prominent as the actual(?) circle dot. Even more problematic, the dot in the x diagram and its nearest proximate x are both garbled into something that looks more like Morse code than a "+" with a dot to its left. The same kind of visual garbling occurs with several other x's, turning their arms into new legitimate dot candidates. (Alas, recently dissipated x dot! Oh, ye who had proved so fairly stable throughout editions 1–3; yea, and even continue to appear stable in the larger, right-hand image on *this very page* in edition 4!) Is this installation documentation photograph a(nother) misprint? If so, why is it (seemingly) the sole misprint in an otherwise excruciatingly detailed and rigorous solo exhibition catalog published by the ordinarily detail-oriented Guggenheim Museum Publications? Are these dot slippages the accidental residue of an intentional move the artists meant to make by publishing the contact print rather than the final print? Or are these new dot slippages themselves all part of the artists' intentions? More relevantly, what (really) do the artists' intentions have anything to do with the extant instructions that still gently yet persistently compel us to PLEASE THINK ONLY OF THE DOT NOT OF THE X'S?

Additional Dot Research

Time does not permit the thrilling tale of the adventures of "The Dot" on the web! OK, briefly: the original Flash-based site of *Mechanism of Meaning* used the main image from editions 2 and 3 (ghost circle dot image), whereas the current non-Flash based version of the panel uses the main image from edition 4 (strong dot image). Throughout my preceding exegesis of "The Dot" across these four book editions, I have made it a point to openly think thorough, question, and doubt my observations and conclusions; not simply to be cheeky, but to transparently enact the role I am lured into playing as a part of this apophatic art apparatus. Now I will attempt to stop getting sucked into the apparatus itself (I will fail), and I will include some extant research on the actual development process involved in these editions. Lamentably, Arakawa and Madeline Gins had both passed on (they have famously decided not to die) by the time I began writing this chapter. In some ways, I am glad not to know their exact intentions regarding these formal, technical decisions. Ultimately, the dot apparatus they wound up constructing continues to do what it does without my access to their personal intentions. I was able to put some of my questions to Stephen Hepworth (Director of Collections at Arakawa and Gins's Reversible Destiny Foundation) and Peter Katz (Executive Director of the Reversible Destiny Foundation). I discovered the following details:

Based on a 10×8-inch black and white vintage photograph of the dot panel from the Dwan Gallery in the 1970s, both the x and circle dots in the actual panel are as they appear in the First edition photograph. But now (predictably), it gets stranger. Hepworth, upon closely examining the dot in the main circle diagram from edition 2, says it "has been over-painted, leaving just the edge of the original [dot] visible, shifting it closer to the identity of a circle."[16] This would imply that Arakawa intentionally altered the physical panel in order to make the dot in the circle diagram less prominent.

So, it wasn't just a misprint! Ah, but there is still a problem: if this change (the purposeful painting-over of part of the circle dot) was intentional, and actually enacted on the physical panel itself, then why, in the inset documentation of the installation (right there on the same page in edition 2) is the dot in the circle diagram so prominent and solid? There is an obvious discrepancy between the

16   Stephen Hepworth, e-mail message to the author, August 3, 2017.

two images. If the ghosted dot in the larger image on the page reflects the intention of the artists, then we may assume (may we?) that the discrepancy between the larger image and the inset image is also intentional.

Regarding the increased prominence of both dots in the larger image from edition 4, Hepworth clarifies that this larger image is based on a 5×4-inch color transparency taken of the physical panel shown at the 1997 Guggenheim Soho show. Both images coincide with Hepworth's own personal condition-reporting photographs that he took of the panel at that time. Hepworth goes on to observe, "It is clear that both the dots have been repainted and made larger and blacker than they appear in the first edition. Why this change occurred I do not know. It is clear from looking at vintage documentation, sometimes as it appears in catalogs, that Arakawa would continue to work, or rework paintings, and in many cases create new versions of works."[17]

So... some time after 1970, Arakawa intentionally ghosted the circle dot in the physical installation panel; and then a few years later he intentionally darkened both the circle dot and the x dot. Ah, but there is still a problem! As with the discrepancy in editions 2 and 3 between the large image of the panel and the inset installation documentation image of the viewer looking at the panel, there is a similar discrepancy in edition 4 between the large image of the panel and the inset installation documentation image of the (other) viewer looking at the panel. Again, one may presume (may one?) that the discrepancy between the larger image and the inset image is intentional.

We may as well follow this rabbit hole on down. Hepworth concludes, "Looking at the difference in stretchers (both in construction and dimensions), it suggests that the *Mechanism of Meaning* was made at four differ-

17   Ibid.

ent times starting (according to Dwan Gallery labeling) in 1969 where it is described as "unfinished, 300 or more 6' × 8' panels" until it was shown in its entirety at the Guggenheim. The second version was made and shown in Japan dated 1988 where it is in the collection of Se-zon Museum of Modern Art. Further research needs to be done to determine when the first version reached the stage it was at when it was shown at the Guggenheim."[18]

"The Dot" as an Apophatic Art Apparatus

Now that we have as clear a logistical understanding as we are likely to get regarding "The Dot" and its behav-ior across six decades, four book editions, and at least four installations, we are ready to begin exploring, in more nuanced detail, the ways in which "The Dot" be-haves as an apophatic art apparatus. Although "The Dot" and all of the other exercises in *Mechanism of Meaning* incorporate human language, and although the primary "audience" for "The Dot" is those who can read human language (i.e., humans), "The Dot" and the overall *Mecha-nism of Meaning* project are by no means limited to human language or humans. Instead, "The Dot" is an apparatus that purposefully cuts into, carves out of, cordons off, and thus intra-acts with a much broader swath of the extra-anthropocentric universe.

Why begin with humans and human language? Be-cause, if humans are to head toward post-humanism and begin to more purposefully, rigorously, and ethically en-ter into and flow amongst the entanglements they (al-ways already) have with the rest of the universe, the inor-dinate stronghold of human language on humans must be foregrounded, confounded, problematized, ridiculed, made a public showing of, and displayed in all of its limi-

18   Ibid.

tations. It is not enough to merely list in human language the limitations of human language; such a move only winds up enacting and thus reconstituting the efficacy and primacy of human language. It is not even enough to create aporias within language using only language itself (whether via apophatic writing or deconstruction). Instead, the limitations of human language must be enacted in a bodily, affective capacity. They must be made to be felt in human bodies. Furthermore, these aporetic enactions must prehend actual material from the physical, human-indifferent, linguistic-indifferent world. In the case of "the dot," the non-human components incorporated into its apparatus include dust motes, stray marks, canvas, black paint, white paint, paintbrushes, stencils, photographic negatives, photographic plates, photographic contact prints, printed paper, bound books, physical gallery spaces, physical publishing and distributions systems, and several decades worth of historical lived time ("cultural," "natural," "universal," "planetary," and yes, even "art historical").

Furthermore, in order for the stronghold of human language on humans to be properly and performatively throttled, the presumed barriers between human language and the "outside world" which it "describes" (whether those barriers are considered impassable or merely correlative) must be involuted, dissolved, reconstituted, permeated, confounded, and bastardized. The "frame" of the work must ultimately be prehended recursively and perpetually into the work itself.

Additionally, the "aesthetic" importance of the visual appearance of the work must be inverted, marginalized, and made increasingly subordinate to the apparatal function of the work itself. The work won't simply disappear (although the dot may temporarily [seem to] disappear), but the way in which the work appears will only come to matter insofar as its appearance functions as a lure for aporetic, human-cognitive impasses.

Finally, the ultimate "moral" or "meaning" of the work must perpetually and continually be refused any summative form of resolved signifying escape; the "meaning" of *Mechanism of Meaning* must always be (re-)captured, turned back into itself, torused, infinitized, deferred, and thus forever braked. In the historical trajectory of their own art practice, Arakawa and Gins proceed from this initial (decades long) place of linguistic confounding to make less apophatic, more positive speculative gestures involving architecture and ways of living. Still, it may be legitimately argued that all of Arakawa and Gins's subsequent architectural explorations are really just continuations and outworkings of the implications of *Mechanism of Meaning*. The "moral" "take-away" of the "narrative" of *Mechanism of Meaning* was never fully reconstituted by the artists in clear assertive language. Instead, Arakawa and Gins chose to proceed along the lines of more affective, bodily, materially entangled ways of "knowing." And well they would. After riding in on the dying horse of human language and throttling said horse to death repeatedly, why resurrect your beaten linguistic horse and ride it into the sunset? Instead, Arakawa and Gins let sleeping horses lie.

Becoming Something New (But What?)

It is important to note that *Mechanism of Meaning* eventually *does* lead somewhere. It *does* become something new. It doesn't forever brake the ongoing, emergent, becoming of the entire universe. It doesn't force a bleak, eternal, nihilistic nothing-void. (How could it?) Instead, what it *does* do is put the brakes on our habitual human reliance on words as more or less trustworthy. It puts the brakes on our habitual human faith in our ability to make meaning of (seemingly) simple situations. And by braking-on-ice (however temporarily) these habitual and usual kinds of linguistically inflected becomings, by making nothing of them, *Mechanism of Meaning* steers us toward new kinds of becomings that would not have emerged if straightforward signification was its primary apparatal function.

In what new direction are we then steered? Arakawa and Gins were steered in one kind of direction in terms of their own art practice post-1997. Another artist who subjects herself to the *Mechanism of Meaning* apparatus (by actually working through the exercises repeatedly in good faith) might emerge from her braking-on-ice experience pointing in a different direction than Arakawa and Gins. The specific new kinds of becomings and resultant new directions cannot be determined beforehand. The proof is in the pudding, in the actual apparatal intra-actions, one human at a time. As with baking, so with the actual concrescences of the universe. Leaving out baking soda doesn't just mean the result will merely lack x amount of baking soda. Baking soda is an active agent. It is prehended by the rest of the ingredients in ways that modulate the overall becoming of the bake. Leaving out x amount of baking soda prior to the bake is much more fundamentally radical than leaving out the same amount of powdered sugar after the bake is done. For humans (as enduring objects with [occasional] consciousness), semiotic language can be quite the active agent in our own ongoing becomings.

In *Writing and Difference,* Derrida incisively recognizes just how much we fundamentally presume by using any kind of language at all:

> If discourse and philosophical communication (that is, language itself) are to have an intelligible meaning, that is to say, if they are to conform to their essence and vocation as discourse, they must simultaneously in fact and in principle escape madness. They must carry normality within themselves. And this is not a specifically Cartesian weakness (although Descartes never confronts the question of his own language), is

not a defect or mystification linked to a determined historical structure, but rather is an essential and universal necessity from which no discourse can escape, for it belongs to the meaning of meaning.[19]

Mechanism of Meaning foregrounds and problematizes this presumed "meaning of meaning" which accompanies (indeed, inheres within) all ordinary use of language. By braking the normality-constituting effects of language, Arakawa and Gins allow for something other-than-normality to emerge. Will "madness" emerge, or "absurdity," or "senselessness," or something else? Whatever else does emerge, whatever that difference or excess or other, that is the wager of their particular apophatic apparatus.

For me, what actually winds up emerging from repeated exposure to "The Dot" is a kind of dizzyingly (thrillingly? spookily?) enlarged field awareness which doesn't slot easily into either "sensibility" or "senselessness" (both terms having their origin in sensibility). What I experience seems too safe, self-aware, and just this side of self-possessed to be "madness." "Absurdity" is too blunt and un-nuanced a term for my experience with "The Dot." Perhaps it could be described as some more specific flavor of absurdity, possibly "ridiculousness," although that term seems too superficial. What I feel might best be described via an analogy from my own bodily experience: I'm not an amazingly technical drummer, or even a very good drummer, but I enjoy drumming a lot. While drumming along with a song, sometimes I forget what I'm doing and just intuitively fall into a groove, during which time I sound much better than I do at other times. At such times, when I'm in said groove, I'll get to feeling as if I'm a better drummer than I actually am. This temporary sense of elation and confidence will often cause me to dive headlong into a heartfelt and daring riff or fill,

19   Derrida, *Writing and Difference*, 65.

the successful outcome of which I have no way of ensuring, but which I nevertheless naively feel will just sort of work itself out because, hey, I'm in the groove. Nine times out of ten I dramatically flub the riff, enacting a kind of awkward, screeching misfire, after which (and often even during which) I laugh openly at the cathartic immediacy of the discrepancy I feel in my body between my moment of misguided, elated confidence and the sudden, instant-after come-down of my clumsy crash-and-burn. That immediate, humorous feeling of hubristic comeuppance, of feeling the discrepancy between what I was sure I could do and what I was immediately proved unable to do – that feeling is somewhat similar to the way I feel after spending some time trying to rigorously THINK ONLY OF THE DOT.

Returning to Bergson, "It is one thing to understand a difficult movement, another to be able to carry it out. To understand it, we need only to realize in it what is essential, just enough to distinguish it from all other possible movements. But to be able to carry it out, we must besides have brought our body to understand it. Now, the logic of the body admits of no tacit implications."[20] When I try to THINK ONLY OF THE DOT, all of the tacit implications upon which I was presuming when I thought I understood what thinking only of the dot would entail are immediately dashed and confounded. I feel my failures to think only of the dot; I feel them one by one. I enact these failures *in my body*. Thinking is curiously and uncannily felt by me as a bodily action. Thinking is no longer some magic, transcendental, disembodied exercise that occurs outside of space and time. My own act of thinking has been foregrounded by the apparatus of "The Dot."

The fact that there are stumbling, impartial, and ineffable ways of making meaning only comes as a surprise

---

20 Henri Bergson, *Matter and Memory,* trans. Nancy Margaret Paul and W. Scott Palmer (New York: Zone Books, 1991), 112.

if I have bought into a binary model of meaning where things are either "sensible" or "senseless." But, as Whitehead observes, "Our conscious experience involves a baffling mixture of certainty, ignorance, and probability."[21] "The Dot" and its sibling exercises are pitch-perfect, finely tuned apparatuses for luring out into the open and foregrounding this "baffling mixture." The purposes and intentions of "The Dot" are not vague; on the contrary, "The Dot" purposes and intends a precisely calibrated flavor of vagueness.

Regarding the generative potency of purposeful vagueness, Whitehead explains, "A power of incorporating vague and disorderly elements of experience is essential for the advance into novelty."[22] Brian Massumi concurs, and recommends accompanying intentional vagueness with speculative conviction: "*Vague* concepts, and concepts of vagueness, have a crucial, and often enjoyable, role to play. Generating a paradox and then using it as if it were a well-formed logical operator is a good way to put vagueness into play. Strangely, if this procedure is followed with a good dose of conviction and just enough technique, presto!, the paradox actually becomes a well-formed logical operator."[23] The very bald-faced and dry tone of *Mechanism of Meaning*, its "generically" stenciled capital letters, its almost naive and straightforward explanation of its own goals, the child's-primer-esque nature of its format – all of these elements lure us into taking the speculative wager of the project seriously. After four decades, four editions, and multiple installations, the artists are nothing if not invested. If they are

21 Alfred North Whitehead, *Process and Reality* (New York: The Free Press, 1978), 205.
22 Alfred North Whitehead, *Modes of Thought* (New York: The Free Press, 1968), 79.
23 Brian Massumi, *Parables for the Virtual: Movement, Affect, Sensation* (Durham: Duke University Press, 2007), 13. [Italics appear in the original text.]

joking, they are seriously joking. This level of commitment and conviction lures in, teases out, and generously invites (PLEASE THINK ONLY OF...) rigorous engagements with the apparatus that have led to new, speculative, bodily felt ways of making meaning (in Arakawa and Gins's subsequent "architectural" practice, and in the various contemporary art and research practices *Mechanism of Meaning* has inspired).

Some Words on Causal Efficacy, Presentational Immediacy, and Symbolic Reference

Whitehead's universe is a universe of micro-instances, of actual occasions. These are its fundaments. Nevertheless, humans do consciously perceive a world full of enduring objects in spatial relation to one another. We are more likely to *consciously* perceive a chair as an enduring object rather than as a historically related route of actual occasions. This conscious human perception of enduring objects is notably unusual since we humans ourselves are also historically related routes of actual occasions. But then perception, consciousness, and humans are all particularly unusual anomalies in the broader scope of the universe. So how does conscious perception, or conscious thought "persist" across actual occasions? I'm not just asking about long-term memory. I'm asking about the consistent formulation of any single thought over a ten second period of time. If "I" am merely a series of actual occasions, how am I ever able to read a single continuous sentence and make conscious sense of its meaning? According to Whitehead's cosmology of concrescence, each actual occasion is prehended by a series of relevant subsequent actual occasions, and what was known in one instant impinges on the next instant. This occurs according to Whitehead's principle of conformation, whereby what is already made becomes a determinant of what is in the making [...]. In practice we never doubt the fact of the conformation of the present to the immediate past. It belongs to the ultimate texture of experience [...]. The present fact is luminously the outcome from its predecessors, one quarter of a second ago.[24]

The pragmatic mechanisms of this conformal transference from actual occasion to actual occasion are complicated and nuanced, exceeding the scope of this text.

"Causal efficacy" is what Whitehead calls the non-conscious mode of perception which deals with actual occasions/entities, and their ingressions, prehensions, virtual actualizations, and concrescences. But there is another, conscious mode of perception called "presentational immediacy." Presentational immediacy is the mode in which we consciously perceive a persistent, object-like chair. Historically, human philosophy has given primacy to this mode of presentational immediacy. But "we" humans are more than our conscious minds, and "we" also traffic in the mode of causal efficacy.

To Whitehead, although consciousness may occasionally be part of experience, it is by no means a requisite of experience. He explains, "An actual entity may, or may not, be conscious of some part of its experience. Its experience is its complete formal constitution, including its consciousness, if any."[25]

The [false] assumption is that the basic elements of experience are to be described in terms of one, or all, of the three ingredients, consciousness, thought, sense-perception. The last term is used in the sense of "con-

---

24 Alfred North Whitehead, *Symbolism, Its Meaning and Effect* (Cambridge: Cambridge University Press, 1958), 46.
25 Whitehead, *Process and Reality*, 53.

scious perception in the mode of presentational immediacy." Also in practice sense-perception is [wrongly] narrowed down to visual perception. According to the philosophy of organism these three components are unessential elements in experience.[26]

According to Whitehead, the gap between causal efficacy and presentational immediacy is bridged by "symbolic reference." Whitehead explains, "The unraveling of the complex interplay between the two modes of perception – causal efficacy and presentation immediacy – is one main problem of the theory of perception [...]. The interplay between the two modes will be termed 'symbolic reference'."[27] Symbolic reference is the means by which human consciousness translates the experience of causal efficacy (the historically related route of chair-like actual occasions) into the enduring object perceived as a presentationally immediate chair. Causal efficacy may do without presentational immediacy (tree-like actual occasions falling in a human-less forest), but there is no presentational immediacy without prior causal efficacy.

I bring all of this up now, because *Mechanism of Meaning* confounds human language, which Whitehead says "almost exclusively refers to presentational immediacy as interpreted by symbolic reference."[28] When we traffic in human language, we are usually dealing with human consciousness and its mode of perceiving the world as presentationally immediate. By confounding human language, "The Dot" in turn mungs up presentational immediacy and conscious human thought. We are made to consciously focus on the tiny, micro-moment, actual occasions of our own thinking – not simply to think *about* the concept of thinking, but to actively think our own

26 Ibid., 36. [Bracketed comments are mine.]
27 Ibid., 121.
28 Ibid., 173.

thinking. We are brought to consciously feel the force of causal efficacy. This is an uncanny, braking, stuttering, aporetic, apophatic feeling. "The Dot" uses language as a snare to capture and make consciously felt the otherwise camouflaged presumptions of presentational immediacy.

Meaning Is As Body Does
(The Installation Apparatus)

Human–computer interface designer Joy Mountford once observed, "When the computer stares back at you, it sees you as one eye and one finger."[29] In other words, we have designed our computer interfaces as if we ourselves are disembodied minds. A corollary might be, "When the book stares back at you, it sees you as one eye." Yet books may also be designed to stare otherwise, see otherwise, engage, lure, or proposition otherwise. And, of course, installation art has the intrinsic capacity to engage much more than our disembodied minds, if installation artists purpose to make work that speaks an embodied language (and usually, even if they don't). Arakawa and Gins's purposeful and ingenious baking of language into the physical installation exercises of *Mechanism of Meaning* causes (or at least insistently invites) human bodies to feel the force of language. The affective impact of these physical installation spaces is then translated into (and modulated by) the accompanying book editions, which in turn inform and further complicate the installations.

These installation stations enlist the "viewer" to experience language in a more holistic way, as a compelling force rather than just a once-removed signifier. Whereas the primary goal of apophatic writing is ultimately to

29 Joy Mountford, quoted in Camille Utterback, "Unusual Positions – Embodied Interaction with Symbolic Spaces," in *First Person: New Media as Story, Performance, and Game,* eds. Noah Wardrip-Fruin and Pat Harrigan (Cambridge: MIT Press, 2004), 218.

confound "the mind" of the reader, the primary goal of the *Mechanism of Meaning* installations is ultimately to confound the body of the viewer. The overall apparatus of the *Mechanism of Meaning* installation sets a starter trap for the viewer's "mind" in order to gradually ensnare her body. The stations all begin with a kind of cognitive, purely linguistic aporia, and while the viewer is engaged with the stations at that initial, seemingly safe, purely intellectual level, the sculptural elements and the sheer scale and proximity of the station panels themselves gradually allow the aporia to seep into, entangle, and be prehended by the (actual occasions of the) body of the viewer. *Mechanism of Meaning* quickly overloads and exceeds the boundary between mere linguistic signification and bodily affect. Language becomes a kind of material, experienced by a human body in installation space. Installation art is the ideal (mixed) medium for this kind of swinging back-and-forth between language and material. At each installation station, the door separating the two domains (language and matter) is swung a bit more rapidly and a bit more forcefully, until eventually the door is swung off of its hinges. Language begins to exert a kind of material force, and material begins to speak a kind of affective language.

Although we have focused solely on "The Dot" exercise station, each exercise station in *Mechanism of Meaning* examines a different cognitive aspect of "meaning-making." As with "The Dot," the other exercises always include text, but the text is always situated in a kind of mock-Cartesian painterly space, and its letterforms frequently do more than simply denote. Each set of English instructions is always accompanied by some piece of extra-textual media – lines, diagrams, images, and sometimes dimensional objects. All instructions invite some form of action on the part of the viewer. Often the exercise stations extend dimensionally into the gallery space and include various objects meant to be manipulated by the viewer (who now must necessarily be called some-thing with more bodily agency than merely "the viewer").

The textual "content" of each exercise is tightly and non-arbitrarily coupled with the embodied event it means to instigate. As a result, the overall embodied ex-perience of each exercise (in terms of scale-awareness, balance, line-of-sight, blush-response, proprioceptive disorientation, haptic feedback) is created in no small part by the instructional provocations and invitations of the exercise's text. If we were to extract the texts of *Mechanism of Meaning* from their spatial con-texts and set them in Helvetica typeface as poetry in a book, they would read as alternately facile and meaningless. Like-wise, if we were to inject other texts into the *Mechanism of Meaning* installation, the rigorous and particular forms of intriguing disorientation and aporia would be lost, re-placed by a much less involving, much less luring, merely binary disconnect.

The embodied elements of the installation are instan-tiated into the book editions via the marginal installa-tion documentation photographs which accompany many of the exercises in the books. Continuing to fo-cus on "The Dot" exercise, no installation documenta-tion photographs appear in edition 1. But in the second and third editions, we get an installation shot of a gray-haired viewer scratching his chin, folding his arms, and (presumably) attempting to think only of the circle dot. By the fourth edition, even when the inset waterfall im-age has been removed, we still have an inset installation photograph. This time it is a new photograph of another viewer, in blue shirt and olive pants, (presumably) at-tempting to think only of the x dot. These same types of marginal installation shots appear throughout editions 2–4, particularly accompanying the exercise stations which require more direct physical viewer engagement (handling physical elements, holding bodies in certain positions, performing physical motions). The installation documentation photographs give the reader of the book editions a kind of mirror-neuron, bodily way into the installation stations. The documentation photographs suggest bodily scale and proximity in relation to the exercise stations. They also suggest ways of engagement with the book exercises themselves: Perhaps we should be standing rather than sitting. Ah, so we really are meant to move our actual bodies in that way, and not merely passively contemplate what it would be like to move our actual bodies in that way. The documentation photographs make the books more bodily engaging.

The decision to move the installation panels from the wall (in the earlier installations) to the floor (in the Guggenheim Soho installation) is not by any means minor or arbitrary. A comparison of the two different installation documentation photographs of "The Dot" (and its two viewers) reveals some of what is at stake and what has been accomplished by moving the stations onto the floor. In the earlier documentation photograph (editions 2 and 3), the circle diagram instructions are at the viewer's eye level, with 2/3 of the panel (containing the two dot diagrams) above his eye level. The photograph crops his body at the waist, with the majority of the panel looming on the wall above him. The viewer appears in an intellectually engaged but somewhat physically removed stance. His arms are folded, and he is holding his chin. It is the classic pose of someone in a museum catalog shot. He might just as easily be contemplating a Rembrandt painting. The moral is, when you hang something on the wall in a gallery, even if it is more like a page from a child's primer and less like a Rembrandt painting, humans are going to view it as if it is a painting, with all of the art-historical baggage such viewing entails.

Now consider the installation shot from edition 4. The x diagram instructions are at the viewer's eye level, with 2/3 of the panel below his eye level. The photograph crops his body at the ankles, revealing the fact that the exercise panel is stationed on the floor rather than hanging on the wall. This viewer seems much more bodily engaged than the viewer in editions 2 and 3. Here in edition 4, the viewer's left hand appears to be on his belt and his right arm hangs slightly bent at his side, with his right hand semi-cupped in an almost absent-minded gesture, as if he is devoting the majority of his bodily attention to thinking only of the dot, and his right hand must somehow take this particular shape in order to allow him to do so. His face is much nearer the panel itself, and he seems to be peering intently at the x dot. In moving the panel to the floor, Arakawa and Gins have reconfigured their apparatus. This newly reconfigured apparatus invites greater bodily participation and thus more holistic engagement of the "viewer" with the overall apparatus. It is worth noting that "The Dot" is arguably one of the least physically engaging of all the installation stations. Perhaps this is why Arakawa and Gins chose to begin with it. They are easing the viewer into greater and greater bodily intra-action. And yet, even with an exercise station that invites relatively minimal bodily movement, taking the dot panel from the wall and placing it on the floor creates a perceptible increase in bodily engagement.

For other, more painterly artists, these formal changes in placement would certainly matter, but they would hardly be critical. Such formal decisions might even be delegated as curatorial decisions. For Arakawa and Gins, these kinds of formal placement decisions and the particular ways in which they lure and activate bodies become increasingly central to their subsequent "architectural" practice. Such formal placement decisions are already (arguably) central to *Mechanism of Meaning,* at least in its later stages of development.

There is an intrinsic relationship between what a body is doing and the way in which a body makes meaning. Which brings us to a series of wonderful quotations about the importance of bodily movement in relation to thinking, reading, and language. Nietzsche: "Only thoughts that come by walking have any value."[30] Proust: "Movement alone restores our thought."[31] Gysin: "Who runs may read my drawing. Run faster to read better."[32] Recognizing the inherent (although often merely implicit) connection between bodily movement and meaning-making, the installation instantiations of *Mechanism of Meaning* are purposefully designed to engage and modulate human bodily movement and bodily proprioception as a means of disrupting a human's ability to make cognitive meaning.

Manhattan gallerist Ronald Feldman was deeply involved with Arakawa's art installations for many important early shows in New York. Feldman shared the story of a personal experience he had after spending time at one particular Arakawa and Gins installation. He left the gallery and began walking down the street in Manhattan, and suddenly he was a giant. All the buildings were tiny and he was huge. This experience lasted several blocks, and when it went away and he shrunk back down to normal size, it was extremely depressing.[33] Nothing about the work itself overtly (or even implicitly) suggested that its viewers imagine themselves as giants. Indeed, as Feldman describes the experience, he didn't imagine that he was a giant. He felt himself to be a giant. The fact that he would have this kind of visceral bodily experience after an Arakawa and Gins installation suggests one of several ways in which their installation apparatuses modulate human bodies: not metaphorically or symbolically, but

---

30 Friedrich Nietzsche, *Twilight of the Idols: Or, How to Philosophize with the Hammer*, trans. Richard Polt (Indianapolis: Hackett Publishing Company, 1997), 10. [Italics appear in the original text.]

31 Marcel Proust, *The Captive*, trans. C. K. Scott-Moncrieff (1929; Paris: Feedbooks, 2014), 104, http://www.feedbooks.com/book/1451/the-captive.

32 Gysin, "Cut-Ups," 46.

33 Ronald Feldman, personal conversation with the author at Arakawa and Gins's studio on Houston Street, Manhattan, June, 2014.

actually, by shifting their overall proprioceptive self-awarenesses. When the stabilizing regimes of human language and normal modes of meaning-making are braked and made nothing of, what new scalar reconfigurations, what new giants might emerge?

Reconfiguring Frames (The Fly and The Machine)

In David Cronenberg's *The Fly*, the main character accidentally enters his teleportation machine accompanied by a fly and winds up melding with the fly. In an attempt to reverse this process, the human–fly amalgam re-enters the teleportation machine and winds up melding with the machine itself, resulting in a human–fly–machine amalgam. The machine that was meant to frame the entire transformation process has been folded into the transformation process itself. The machine frame was not dissolved, permeated, exceeded, or erased. Instead, the frame was incorporated into that which it was meant to frame.

The same kind of thing is happening with *Mechanism of Meaning*, across the several installation instantiations and the several book editions throughout the decades. If each exercise station is its own apparatus, and if the entire *Mechanism of Meaning* installation is a larger, meta-apparatus, then the four editions of the *Mechanism of Meaning* books extend the entire project into an even larger meta-meta-apparatus; and the relationship established back-and-forth between the installations and the books becomes a yet larger meta-meta-meta-apparatus. This telescoping across media, scales, and time is in perfect keeping with the goals of overall project – namely, to continually make nothing of the contextualizing frames and borders which allow us to presume a kind of easy understanding of language, and of meaning in general.

According to Karen Barad, in order for an apparatus to begin functioning at all, an apparatal cut into the universe must first be made. The apparatus cannot stand outside of the universe, so it must demarcate the part of the universe in which it stands, and in so doing demarcate the part of the universe outside of itself. Per apparatal event, each apparatal cut is actual. It matters to the involved apparatal "material" (Whitehead would say "enduring objects"), and it matters to all resultant "measurements." But new and different cuts may always be made. Barad explains, "Boundary transgressions should be equated not with the dissolution of traversed boundaries... but with the ongoing reconfiguring of boundaries."[34]

As an apophatic art apparatus, *Mechanism of Meaning* is forever reconfiguring its own boundaries. For example, in editions 2–4 of the books, the supplemental, marginal installation documentation (the inset photographs of viewers interacting with the installation stations) toggles back and forth between being secondary, derivative material and primary, source material. Are we to think only of the dot in the larger book diagram, or only of the dot in the installation documentation diagram? Do the books frame the installations, or do the installations frame the books? Do the books supplement the installations, or do the installations supplement the books? Derrida's analysis of the parergon is completely relevant to the fluctuating enframings and enfoldings that Arakawa and Gins have devised. The artists are not surprised at the slippery, unstable negotiations between "content" and "frame." On the contrary, they expect such instability and purposefully construct their apparatus to further exploit it. *Mechanism of Meaning* is an apparatus built to tesselate, enfold, and inflect the conventional frames that humans have constructed in order to encompass and corral sensible "meaning." Rather than simply being a self-sabotaging art apparatus (à la Jean Tinguely's *Homage to*

---

34 Karen Barad, *Meeting the Universe Halfway* (Durham: Duke University Press, 2007), 245.

New York), Mechanism of Meaning is a self-reconfiguring art apparatus. It persists in its instability. It is permanently unstable. How can *Mechanism of Meaning* continue to perform its own instability now that no new books are being published and no new installations are being exhibited? Because humans are the mechanism of meaning. As long as humans keep coming to these exercise stations, this apparatus will continue to lure us into perpetually reconfiguring its boundaries.

In Order to Make Nothing, It Must Look Like Something

In order to properly enact nothing (to brake becoming), the apophatic art apparatus must paradoxically look like something. This is simply because the enaction of nothing is not achieved via mimesis. Enacting nothing won't ever "look like" nothing. Instead, a visual something is always presented which acts as a lure for thinking (i.e., making meaning). This meaning-making process is then disrupted. As Derrida observes, "To overthrow the power of the literal work is not to erase the letter, but only to subordinate it to the incidence of illegibility."[35] The dot doesn't merely disappear. Instead, it ghosts itself, but a trace always remains. And of course, multiple interpretations of which dot is the dot remain.

The goal of the apophatic art apparatus is not to replace visual spectacle with darkness, but to rigorously problematize the regime of the visual. Similarly, the goal is not to replace language with silence (à la Wittgenstein's famous dictum), but to rigorously problematize language, to orchestrate and foreground its own self-confounding aporia. The goal is not to replace the object with the event (à la Fluxus), or even to replace the event with inaction and contemplation (which are also events);

---

35 Derrida, *Writing and Difference*, 237.

but to rigorously problematize the regime of the event itself, to bring it to an impasse, a perpetual tessellation, a braking.

An analogy from the world of contemporary technology seems appropriate. Stealth planes don't become invisible by disappearing; but via cloaking algorithms, which divide a plane's presence up into a collective pack of tiny presences, so that the plane reads like a flock of birds on an enemy's radar. The contemporary stealth plane doesn't simply become "black"; instead, it causes itself to be read as something else – not pure absence, but not itself. Invisibility via obfuscation. *Mechanism of Meaning* takes the same approach toward its human "radar" systems. We are obviously able to see and read the stenciled capital letters. There is nothing magic or mysterious about this stencil typeface. In the genre of 1970s conceptual language art, this stenciled typeface was meant to signify generic neutrality. Now, forty years later, we identify this typeface with the art-historical genre of 1970s language art. But no matter. Why? Because the braking, confounding function of *Mechanism of Meaning* has little to do with whether its typeface is generic or genre-d. The typeface only matters as a lure which invites the viewer to feel confident enough to proceed as if she is able to read what is happening. In the 1970s, the viewer would have felt confident that the work of art was contemporary and conceptual. In 2020, the viewer feels confident that this work must have originated in the 1970s. But once the viewer actually begins engaging with the exercises, the visuality of the stenciled typeface becomes only one of many prehended materials, all of which collide and collude to brake our easy read of any apparent presences.

In *Mechanism of Meaning,* ocular media perform an altogether different function than the mere conveyance of information, or even the mere occlusion of information. Ocular media act like a lure promising the (faux-)conveyance of meaning. This lure, once swallowed by the viewer (through her eyes), acts like a trojan horse, irrupting and dismantling the viewer's meaning-making mechanisms altogether. Image as decoy, trap, snare. The image must be visible in order for the viewer to admit it entrance; but once inside, the trojan-horse image renders all subsequent images pragmatically obfuscated.

Furthermore, the poorer and more low-resolution the media is, the easier it is to hypertrophy and confound its visuality and apparent "meaning." The more dimensional and rich the media, the more artistic gymnastics it takes to hypertrophy it. Written words are a low-resolution medium. As such, they require a great deal of work (assembly, constitution) on the part of the viewer. Because the medium of the written word is doing so little "representational" work, the viewer must do more re-constituting work. She must imagine a dog from the word "dog." She must more actively prehend the medium in order to do the heavy semiotic lifting required by written language. This is why (as discussed in Chapter 2) it is easier to confound a meaning-making human with written language than with visual imagery.

Ramping up the resolution of the medium decreases the semiotic work that the user must do in order to "make-meaning," to "piece things together." High resolution media require much more rigorous work on the part of the visual artist if she intends to wreck humans as meaning-making machines, simply because there is less human meaning-making work going on to sabotage. Duchamp's *Nude Descending a Staircase* hypertrophies 2D painting toward film, but his was a pretty ingenious and difficult move. It becomes even more difficult to begin with film and hypertrophy it toward whatever exists beyond film (toward "video," perhaps?). Hito Steyerl's *How to Become Invisible* is a valiant, hilarious, ridiculous, and always already doomed attempt to hypertrophy video toward something like algorithmic–machinic–networked vision. In Steyerl's video, no one ever becomes fully invisible (although many are ghosted). Instead, we human viewers, as meaning-making machines, are increasingly destabilized to the point where even though figures on the "screen" are completely and technically "visible," we begin to doubt our ability to make meaning of their visibility.

One of the reasons the *Mechanism of Meaning* project is so successful at braking and confounding human meaning-makers is because it so prominently uses the low-resolution (and thus readily hypertrophied) medium of written language *in conjunction with* higher-resolution media like imagery, sculpture, and installation. Because language is always very present in each exercise station, we are immediately lured, activated, involved, and charged as highly engaged meaning-makers. Once involved, our highly energized meaning-making activity and receptivity is assaulted by even higher resolution media. It is like whispering into a microphone to get a sound check, and then yelling abruptly into the microphone once the volume has been ramped up. The stenciled instructions entice us; the mysterious dot assaults us.

It might seem like the removal of language (written or spoken) from visual art would make the art *more* readily able to approach nothing. But the absence of language actually makes the visual art have to work harder to approach nothing. Why? Because, to approach nothing in a visual regime of representation requires not blacker paint, but a radical disruption of the viewing human as a meaning-making mechanism. Her meaning-making radar systems must be scrambled, and low-resolution language is an ideal means of scrambling human meaning-making systems, because it so fully and quickly engages humans as active meaning-makers. Language is a lure, a trap, a cue for humans to turn up their meaning-making volumes. And since meaning-making is also embodied, when humans *do* turn up their meaning-making volumes, they also effectively turn up their prehending, apperceiving volumes. The artist can then begin to blast any number of higher-resolution media (painting, sculpture, video, architecture, immersive VR worlds, or whatever). But merely, brutishly increasing the technology and resolution from the get go, prior to setting the appropriate trap, doesn't make approaching nothing any easier. It actually makes approaching nothing increasingly difficult.

Braking Tactics
(Aporia, Impasse, Deferral of Resolution)

Mechanism of Meaning does not attempt to directly or immediately change its viewer's cosmology. It doesn't overtly determine exactly what experience a person is going to have, nor does it specify the direction in which a person may proceed once she has completed the exercises. Instead, it puts the brakes on a person's ability to make a resolute meaning from the project.

How exactly is the meaning-making ability of humans braked? The tactics vary from exercise to exercise, but with "The Dot," a kind of perpetual feedback loop is established which fails to ever resolve. Instructions undermine and re-interpret other instructions in an inverted Moebius strip that has no exit. If the symbol for a basic loop is the ouroboros [zero], then the symbol for "The Dot" exercise is the infinity symbol: self-cannibalism with a twist. The goal is not to constitute a resolved, broken human, but to defer the reconstitution of any singular, constrained, definitive human at all.

In one sense, *Mechanism of Meaning* prepares the way for Arakawa and Gins's subsequent forays into architecture; but in another more accurate sense, their forays into architecture are simply continuations of *Mechanism of Meaning*. The goal of their architectural projects is not to reconstitute a new, stable human from the rubble of the *Mechanism of Meaning* exercises. Instead, their architectural projects explore even more rigorous, dimensional, spectral, embodied ways to keep the deconstition of human bodies going and open. Charles Eames famously called the house a machine for living. For Arakawa and Gins, the house becomes a machine for not dying. By hook or by crook, dying must be deferred. "To not to die." And if the constitution of normal "living" must also be deferred in order to keep dying from subsequently constituting itself, so be it.

To me, *Mechanism of Meaning* is not yet all that interested in achieving a reversible destiny. Its primary concern is simply to avoid constituting and thus finalizing a dead-end destiny. It is not interested in reconfiguring the universe. It is not even interested in reconfiguring art institutions. It is not interested in conveying new information to an old subject. It is not even interested in reconstituting an old subject into a new subject. It is only interested in deconstituting an old subject. This old subject is bound to be reconstituted into some yet to be determined "whatever," or perhaps this reconstitution will be perpetually deferred, or forever reconfigured. Regardless of what particular fate awaits the human who participates in the *Mechanism of Meaning* exercises, a portion of her old meaning-making self will remain trapped in a torus of perpetually deferred signification. Indeed, the very last exercises in *Mechanism of Meaning* circle around to resemble the first exercises. This bent toward recursion suggests a kind of perpetual refusal to permanently re-assemble the viewer as a new and stable meaning-making mechanism.

Summary

Since *Mechanism of Meaning* (and specifically "The Dot" exercise) means to undermine the viewer as a meaning-making mechanism, it welcomes into its apparatus all kind of material, technical, and incidental marks: stray marks, misprints, vague marks, dust, smudges, photographs of photographs, periods, commas, circles, o's, x's, and dots. Every mark and mote resists being bracketed as non-meaningful, because the apparatus itself refuses to take a pre-determined side regarding what is and isn't meaningful. All of these marks, ghosts, traces, and remnants keep asserting themselves back into the frame. What are we to make of them? What do they mean? And how do we determine what they mean? The exercises in *Mechanism of Meaning* don't attempt to re-present nothing. Nor do they occlude a visual something. These exercises approach nothing because they confound our ability to make something of them. They approach nothing because we can make nothing (definite) of them.

Whereas Fludd means us to regard the differences between the various hyle printings as "merely" technical and incidental, in *Mechanism of Meaning*, such differences in printings become centrally relevant. Or, more precisely, our inability to conclusively determine whether or not they are relevant becomes centrally relevant (perhaps).

In principle then, when it comes to apophatic art apparatuses, any rigorous attempt to undermine the viewer as a language-deciphering maker-of-meaning will eventually necessitate a re-valuation of the formal, technical, material aspects of signifying media. Furthermore, such re-valuations and re-configurations of linguistic media destabilize old language-centric, anthropo-centric regimes (such as the perceptual mode of presentational immediacy) and lead outward + inward toward surfaces and substrates and materialities and affects; distributing and dispersing the linguistic realm into flows, economies, processes, bodily ways of knowing, and affective resonances. Humans are undone as primarily meaning-making machines and distributed more fine-grainedly into broader ecological flows. The harder the linguistic braking, the more fine-grained the subsequent redistributions.

4

GENERATIVE ALGORITHMS AND PERPETUAL DEFERMENT: DAVID CRAWFORD'S STOP MOTION STUDIES AND THE DELAYED CHOICE QUANTUM ERASER

In this chapter, we will look at one apophatic art apparatus (David Crawford's *Stop Motion Studies* project) and one scientific apparatus (the uber-thorny Delayed Choice Quantum Eraser experiment).[1] Both may be usefully understood as apparatuses of deferment. *Stop Motion Studies* enacts a kind of perpetual deferment which makes its own kind of apophatic nothing. The delayed choice eraser experiment enacts a kind of self-contained, provisionary apparatal deferment which eventually does come to a final end. Why get back into quantum mechanics again

---

1   My original thoughts about *Stop Motion Studies* were initially commissioned for the *Sequences* exhibition (a group show on contemporary forms of chronophotography), and later published in the book *Sequences: Contemporary Chronophotography and Experimental Digital Art*, ed. Paul St George (London: Wallflower Press, 2009), 114–19; and also in my collection of essays *One Per Year* (Brescia: Link Editions, 2014), 65–86.

when we had so satisfactorily extricated ourselves from it and the end of Chapter 1? Because the delayed choice eraser is an apparatus worth tackling, particularly when attempting to think about time and its relevance to art apparatuses and to apophasis in general. Both *Stop Motion Studies* and the delayed choice eraser are apparatuses which tease out, lure, and proposition the concept of time, but from which time itself never seems to emerge. *Stop Motion Studies* problematizes our prior human understanding of time as represented in photography and film, and the delayed choice eraser problematizes our prior human understanding of time in general.

Before diving into *Stop Motion Studies,* we must return again to the world of quantum mechanics and attend carefully to the delayed choice quantum eraser apparatus. I will keep my descriptions and interpretations as concise as possible, but there really is no "in brief" interpretation of the phenomenon which occurs in this experiment.

A Brief Description of the Delayed Choice Quantum Eraser

The Delayed Choice (Quantum) Eraser apparatus is really just an extremely rigorous version of the Delayed Choice Which-Path Double-Slit apparatus, which measures which-path occurs *after/behind* the double-slit wall rather than *before/in front of* it, and discovers the same "weird" results. The Delayed Choice Which-Path Double-Slit apparatus is just a more rigorous version of the Which-Path Double-Slit apparatus, which itself is just a more rigorous version of Young's original Double-Slit apparatus (both discussed in Chapter 1). And so, we find ourselves back at Richard Feynman's statement that the double-slit experiment "contains the only mystery" of quantum mechanics.[2]

I will initially describe the delayed choice eraser apparatus reported by Kim et al. in 1999,[3] and will also refer to the 2008 Canary Islands apparatus reported by Ma et al.[4] A prepared and isolated photon is sent through a double-slit wall. On the far side of the double-slit wall, if the photon passes through slit A, it is split into an entangled pair of photons such that their polarizations are opposite. Likewise, if the photon passes through slit B, it is also split into an entangled pair of oppositely polarized photons. Here, "entangled" just means that when you "measure" the value of one photon's polarization (polarization being one kind of particle observable), then the other entangled photon's polarization will be the opposite value. It turns out that this process of quantum entanglement introduces more "weirdness" into the apparatus than it removes (we'll get to that later), but initially this kind of photon splitting and entanglement was intended as a way to measure the which-path information of one entangled photon without decohering (and thus altering) the wave-like diffraction range in which its partner photon could be expected to land. One proton of the entangled pair (let's call it the "signal" photon) is sent forward and detected in some specific position along a far "wall" (not really a "wall," but just a position detector placed at a consistent distance from the double slit). At

2   Richard P. Feynman, "Lecture 37: Atomic Mechanics," in *The Feynman Lectures on Physics, Volume I (Mainly Mechanics, Radiation and Heat)* (Pasadena: California Institute of Technology, 2013), 1–1: "Atomic mechanics," http://www.feynmanlectures.caltech.edu/III_01.html.

3   Yoon-Ho Kim, R. Yu, S.P. Kulik, and Y.H. Shih, Marlan O. Scully, "A Delayed Choice Quantum Eraser," *Physical Review Letters* 84, no. 1 (2000): 1–4.

4   Xiao-Song Ma, Johannes Kofler, et al., "Quantum Erasure with Causally Disconnected Choice," *Proceedings of the National Academy of Sciences of the United States of America* 110, no. 4 (2013): 1221–26.

the same time, its partner proton (let's call it the "idler" photon) is diverted and sent along a different path which detects which of the two slits it passed through. Because we haven't physically interfered with the signal photon, our original measurement conundrum should be solved. The signal photon should remain cohered and land somewhere within the predicted, wave-like diffraction pattern (rather than in the decohered, tennis-ball-like clump pattern), and the idler photon should tell us which-path the pre-split photon went through.

But the results confound this expectation. We send a bunch of photons through the apparatus one at a time, splitting and entangling each one of them after the double-slit wall and detecting each one of the entangled pairs as described above, and instead of a diffraction pattern on the signal photon "wall," we get a tennis-ball-like clump pattern. Perhaps this clump result is not surprising, since both signal and idler photons are detected simultaneously. Perhaps the simultaneous detection of the idler photon's which-path data is causing its entangled signal path photon to decohere and get clump-like. So, we delay the detection of the idler photon (by 8 nanoseconds in the Kim apparatus, and by a lengthy 479 microseconds in the 2008 Ma apparatus). Surely now we will observe a diffraction pattern on the signal "wall," since the signal photon must "land" (be detected) "prior" to its idler photon. Surely all of the signal photons will (gradually) display the expected diffraction pattern from the original (non-which-path) double slit experiment, since each signal photon will have already landed and can't possibly "know" whether or not the which-path information of its idler photon will or will not ever be detected. And yet, even by delaying the time between the signal photon's position detection and its entangled idler photon's which-path detection, the clump pattern of the signal photon continues to emerge.

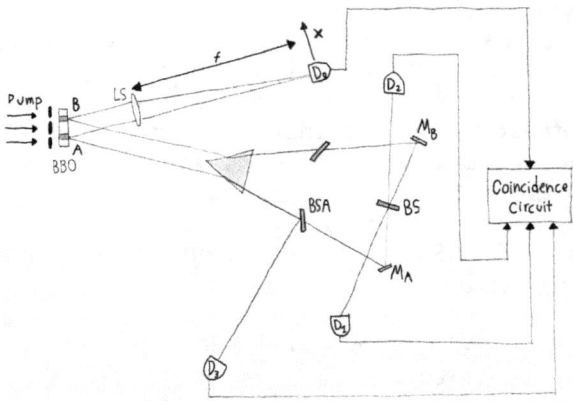

Fig. 1: Schematic of the experimental setup of the 1999 Delayed Choice Quantum Eraser apparatus devised and implemented by Yoon-Ho Kim, et al. Starting at the pump, a photon first passes through either slit A or slit B (or does it?), and then is split into an entangled signal/idler pair. The location of the signal photon is recorded by detector D0. Its idler photon passes through a series of splitters and reflectors, with a 50% chance of arriving at detector D3 with its which-path information intact, and a 50% chance of arriving at detectors D1 or D2 with its which-path information obfuscated (erased, lost). The idler photon is detected 8 nanoseconds after the signal photon. The coincidence circuit records which signal photon goes with which idler photon. Drawing by Jordan Cloninger.

What if we modify this apparatus (and thus construct a new apparatus) that records which slit each idler photon went through 50% of the time, and loses (obfuscates) which slit each idler photon went through the other 50% of the time? To make things even more interesting, what if we construct this new apparatus so that the choice (to record the path of the idler photon or to lose the path of the idler photon) is totally random? This new apparatus that I've just described is the Delayed Choice Quantum Eraser (see Fig. 1).

We fire a bunch of photons through this new apparatus one at a time. What we find on the signal photon "wall" is just a big clump of photons. But wait, we are able to correlate each one of these individual signal photon locations with its exact corresponding idler photon. We know which signal photons had their idler photon paths recorded, and which signal photons had their idler photon paths lost. So, we separate out all the signal photons which had their corresponding idler photon paths recorded, and we get a tennis-ball clump pattern. We separate out all the signal photons which had their corresponding idler photon paths lost, and we get the diffraction pattern.[5] Once again, the (human-)"weird" aspect is that the signal photon locations were each recorded "prior to" any corresponding idler path information was recorded or lost (obfuscated, erased). Arguably, this delayed choice eraser result is no more or less "weird" than the delayed choice non-eraser result. It's just that the added rigor of the eraser element intensifies the "weirdness" of the same basic results.

The 2008 Ma experiment was conducted in the Canary Islands between two separate islands. The part of the apparatus (a quantum random number generator) that randomized the "choice" (whether to save or lose the which-path information of the idler photon) was "space-like separated" from the recording of the location of the signal photon, which was "space-like separated" from the recording (or obfuscation) of the path of the idler photon. In other words, because the recorded idler photon results

5   Actually, in the Kim apparatus, we get two diffraction patterns, inversely phased with one another: one phase for all the idler photons that went through slit A, and the inverse phase for all the idler photons that went through slit B. This phase inversion has to do with the way the apparatus was constructed, the nature of half-silvered mirrors, and the laws of optics.

could not have traveled faster than the speed of light, they could not have "physically" (in a Newtonian, cause-effect sense) influenced the location of their signal photon. Perhaps then we are thinking about it all wrong, and it was actually the "original" signal photon that influenced the "subsequent" which-path detection (or erasure) of its idler photon. But this won't do, because the decision to record or lose the idler photon path information was randomly made by aleatoric software, space-like separated from the recording of the signal photon's location. Dramatically (although perhaps only incidentally), the signal photon location was recorded on one island and the idler photon path was recorded (or intentionally obscured) 144 kilometers away on an entirely different island.

Perhaps we may seek comfort in the fact that these "weird" results are only applicable to massless phenomena like photons and light and energy; but are in no way applicable to electrons and atoms and matter. Perhaps massless particles don't experience time, because time is related to mass. But that won't do either, because similar results in different apparatuses have been observed with particles as "large" as helium atoms.[6] Perhaps these "weird" eraser results are simply the effect of quantum entangled photon pairs themselves, and if we were somehow able to build the same kind of delayed choice eraser apparatus for a single photon, we could bypass these weird results. But again, that won't do. Delayed choice eraser apparatuses have been created for single photons, and they yield similarly "weird" results.[7] Perhaps each idler photon, upon its which-path detection (or obfuscation), travels back in time and alters the prior recorded

6   A. G. Manning, R. I. Khakimov, R. G. Dall & A. G. Truscott, "Wheeler's Delayed-Choice Gedanken Experiment with a Single Atom," *Nature Physics* 11 (2015): 539–42.

7   Xiao-Song Ma, Johannes Kofler, and Anton Zeilinger, "Delayed-Choice Gedanken Experiments and Their Realizations," *Reviews of Modern Physics* 88, no. 1 (2016): 15–16.

location of its signal photon. But this won't do, because the signal photon location results have been recorded. They have been measured. They happened. Irrevocable "marks" have been made. If this were not the case, if irrevocable marks had not yet been made, then nothing about these apparatal measurement results would seem "weird" at all. When the idler photon which-path information is recorded, the diffraction pattern on the signal detection "wall" doesn't "disappear." It isn't "erased." Apparently, for those signal photons whose idler photons had their which-path information recorded, the aggregate diffraction pattern was never there.

Human physicists are ingenious to the point of obsession at attempting to nail down the challenges to our inherited Newtonian cosmology posed by quantum behavior. And yet, it seems, the more rigorously we attempt to impose our inherited cosmology onto photons via the construction of increasingly bizarre and convoluted apparatuses, the "weirder" quantum behavior behaves.

A Semi-Brief Interpretation of the Delayed Choice Quantum Eraser

It seems we are going to have to abandon one of our cherished Newtonian presuppositions. We can abandon the idea of causality altogether, but this is the least appealing option. We can abandon the notion of chronological time, which is at least more appealing than abandoning causality. Or we can abandon the notion that a holistic apparatus may somehow readily and easily be broken up into discrete sub-parts and rightly understood separately without radically misunderstanding the overall holistic function of the apparatus. Barad's interpretation of Bohr does indeed challenge the idea that a holistic apparatus can be divided into parts without disruptive consequences.

The problem with my above description of the time delayed quantum eraser apparatus is that the sequential chronology of written human language forces me to describe the functioning of the apparatus in sequential parts, one after the other, as if one function of the apparatus was completed as I completed describing it, and another function of the apparatus was then subsequently begun as I subsequently began describing it. Even the name "delayed choice eraser" forces me to describe a choice that is sequentially delayed *until after* the signal photon position *has been* recorded, a choice of whether to record which-path idler photon information that *became* available *after* the slit *was passed* through, or to *erase* that information *now*. Indeed, my entire linguistic description of the apparatus presumes its divisibility and imposes a chronological series of events onto it.

Even the above diagram of the Kim apparatus is presumptive and misleading. During the holistic apparatal event, when the particles are in a superpositional quantum state, it is incorrect to imagine that the particles have decided upon a particular path at the beginning of the apparatus which they then simply follow pro forma through the apparatus to its end. And yet the diagram above implies that an idler photon, upon arriving at one of the two which-path obfuscation detectors at the end, will have either followed path A or path B to arrive there. Thus, the diagram itself presumes that the idler photon first commits to one of two paths (collapses its waveform of potential position probabilities), then goes down that one specific path, then has its path choice obfuscated rather than detected, then reverse-expands its waveform of potential position probabilities (thus also reverse-expanding the corresponding waveform of potential position probabilities belonging to its signal photon). But perhaps this described sequence of events is not what is happening at all. In other words, this diagram, far from neutrally and objectively displaying the set-up of the apparatus, is actually interpreting (sequentializing, sub-partitioning) the inner workings of the holistic apparatus. The diagram can't help but do this. The diagram was drawn by human scientists to convey information to human scientists, and we humans are all still deeply conditioned to think according to classical Newtonian physics. The "problem" is not just with our language, but with our entire sequential, cause-and-effect, object/subject way of thinking.

But (apparently) the delayed choice eraser apparatus functions holistically, not discretely. The entire apparatus happens as it happens and until the whole thing is finished happening none of it is finished happening. This interpretation is troubling because 479 microseconds elapse between the recording of the signal photon's position and the recording (or obfuscation) of the idler photon's path. All I can say is that this external measurement of the 479 microseconds is somehow not part of, not prehended by, and thus irrelevant to the overall functioning of the holistic apparatus. Such a time-indifferent interpretation is admittedly troubling to a human, but not as troubling as backwards time travel or the abandonment of causation. And, of course, my "holistic apparatus" interpretation is not troubling at all to the pair of entangled photons.

Causality and Time

A re-examination of causality seems in order. Regarding the entangled photons, Newtonian concepts of direct physical causality leave us with two clear-cut, binary options: either the signal photon's position measurement directly caused the "subsequent" recording or obfuscation of its idler photon's path, *or* the recording or obfuscation of the idler photon's path directly retro-caused whether or not its signal photon landed in a clump pattern range or a diffraction pattern range. But entangled photons behave "weirdly," not just from a Newtonian perspective, but even from an Einsteinian perspective (Einstein's word for their behavior was not "weird," but "spooky" – "spooky action at a distance"). Perhaps, in this prepared, cohered, and entangled state (pre-decoherence, pre-well-decidedness), photons retain all of their observable value options until they are invited by the holistic apparatal arrangement (however courteously or insistently) to commit to specific observables and values. Until such commitments are made within the cut-off, carved-out, holistic context of the overall apparatal phenomenon, external time and space are irrelevant to (negatively prehended by) the holistic apparatus. If we are to believe that time and space are truly the result of relations within and amongst phenomena, rather than time and space being the always-already-given, all-pervading, pre-existent, Cartesian containers for relata (nouns), then within the phenomenon of the apparatal context, until all relations have been irreversibly decided, time has not yet emerged.

Once entangled and well-decided, quantum particles do not inherently pine for the fjords of the Schrödinger equation. And yet, until quantum particles *do* decide to decohere and commit to an observable and its particular value, they tend to remain as uncommitted as they can for as long as possible. The delayed choice quantum eraser apparatus is a very delicate, very courteous apparatus that quite gently invites particles to commit in their own good "time," and particles take every advantage of this courtesy.

Within the quantum-behavior-measuring apparatal entanglement, then, what we are dealing with is not so much Newtonian "causality" (well-decided societies of complexly entangled entities physically bumping into each other). Instead, we are dealing with entities that are barely decided at all. Indeed, a prepared, unentangled, coherent photon is arguably a mere bundle of undecided potentialities. Perhaps the entire "journey" of the two entangled photons through the delayed choice quantum eraser apparatus is in fact only one single, indivisible, actual occasion. One thing that is happening with(in) the time delayed eraser apparatus (and with(in) all quantum-behavior-measuring apparatuses) is that the virtual real is becoming actualized into the actual real. Until this virtual real is actualized, it is no use expecting it to behave as if it had already been actualized.

The "speed of light" is simply the fastest that one thing can affect and communicate with another thing in Einsteinian spacetime. But what do "affect" and "communicate" mean? And what is "one thing" and "another thing?" Are a pair of entangled photons one thing, or two things? If neither of the entangled photons have manifested their position observable at all (much less its actual value), are either of them even noun-y "things" at all? Can a thing without an actual position rightly be considered an actual thing? Perhaps a prepared, unmeasured photon is an actual thing, but its position observable is a virtual thing, something that may or may not ever emerge. Can an actual thing have a virtual position? Is a virtual position even a position? Is a photon without an actual position constrained by the speed of light? Evidently not. Is the relationship between two entangled photons more "fundamental," more "primary," than time and space? Evidently so. When offered the chance within a particularly courteous apparatal arrangement, will prepared, cohered, entangled photons remain largely indifferent to time and space? Evidently so.

Concrescent becomings (actual occasions/entities) don't happen "in" space and time; they create space and time. This is because such concrescences involve commitments (decisions) that are irreversible. According to Whitehead, these actual occasions are the holistic units that make the world. An actual occasion is not subdivisible into units of time. Actual occasions are the fundamental units, and time and space are their byproducts.

Time results from decisions of commitment that cumu-late and become irreversible. In Whitehead's own words, "This passage of the cause into the effect is the cumula-tive character of time. The irreversibility of time depends on this character."[8] He explains that

> actual entities atomize [the extensive continuum], and thereby make real what was antecedently merely po-tential. The atomization of the extensive continuum is also its temporalization; that is to say, it is the pro-cess of the becoming of actuality into what in itself is merely potential.[9]

Due to the sequential nature of linguistic explanation, Whitehead is forced to describe the internal workings of an actual occasion/entity in terms of a series of progres-sions, but these progressions are internal to the holistic occasion itself. Actual occasions don't actually break up into discrete, externally measurable sub-occasions, or those sub-occasions themselves would be actual occa-sions, and you have to stop somewhere. In describing the internal "phases" of the actual occasion/entity, White-head makes this curious aside, "Time has stood still – if only it could."[10] In the delayed choice quantum eraser ap-paratus, perhaps we are given a glimpse into the standing still of time that occurs within singular actual occasions.

Prior to running the delayed choice quantum eraser apparatus, within the prepared apparatal state itself, ir-reversible decisions have yet to be made. The "quantum" state of the apparatus does not come about because pho-tons are very small, but because a purposefully "shielded" environment has been prepared. This shielded environ-

8   Alfred North Whitehead, *Process and Reality* (New York: The Free Press, 1978), 237.
9   Ibid., 72.
10 Ibid., 154.

ment lacks the pressing obligations to honor a prior history of cumulative decisions made by prior actual occasions. Those decisions are negatively prehended by the apparatal phenomenon. In this sense, the apparatus has been carved out from the rest of the universe. If the rest of the universe also lacked a history of prior cumulative decisions, it would also be in this same cohered state. Physicist Roland Omnès speculates that, "If the universe contained only two or three particles [such that decoherence were not likely], [...] one would be allowed to choose arbitrarily the direction of time in logic."[11] Taking up Omnès, Michael Epperson further clarifies, "Logical, asymmetrical temporality is a byproduct of the actualization of potentia – the evolution of probability to fact [...]. Without the existence of facts, there is nothing to measure temporally."[12] In other words (stated in Whiteheadian–Deleuzian terms), since "time" (asymmetrical temporality) is a byproduct of actual occasions that actualize the virtual real, time is hardly the most suitable tool for measuring actual occasions.

Regarding the relationship of cartesian space to a singular actual occasion, splitting up the "parts" of the delayed choice quantum eraser apparatus and placing them on separate islands is irrelevant to the holistic actual occasions that occur intra-actively within the "prepared" and "shielded" functional context of the apparatus. This is because actual occasions make their own space. Whitehead explains, "The concrescence presupposes its basic region, and not the region its concrescence. Thus the subjective unity of the concrescence is irrelevant to the divisibility of the region. In dividing the region we are ignoring the subjective unity which is inconsistent

11   Roland Omnès, *The Interpretation of Quantum Mechanics* (Princeton: Princeton University Press, 1994), 318.
12   Michael Epperson, *Quantum Mechanics and the Philosophy of Alfred North Whitehead* (New York: Fordham University Press, 2004), 96.

with such division. But the region is, after all, divisible, although in the genetic growth it is undivided."[13] This passage reads as if Whitehead is interpretively explaining the "weird" behavior of the delayed choice quantum eraser experiment (as I am currently doing), but he is simply theorizing in 1928 about the "ordinary" behavior of the general universe, decades before the delayed choice quantum eraser experiment had even been conceived, much less successfully implemented.

Until final decisions are made, they have not finally been made. The delayed choice quantum eraser, with its rigorously courteous invitation to decide, its barely insistent insistence to eventually commit, is the quantum-behavior-measuring apparatus par excellence at enacting deferment. As a human who is himself a well-decided, well-entangled society of entities, who is used to thinking and moving amongst well-decided, well-entangled societies of entities (enduring objects like rocks, dogs, laptop computers, and other humans), the idea that actual occasions create space and time is difficult to think. This difficulty extends beyond anthropocentrism. It is more like well-decided-centrism. Oh well. My difficulties to think something don't alter the results of the apparatus. Such is the power, efficacy, and world-view-altering potential of an apparatus. Unlike mere human rhetoric, an apparatus is far more difficult to dismiss. Simply pejoratizing all of the behavior in the time delayed eraser apparatus as "weird" won't do, because such behavior (whether virtual, actual, or both) is still real; and the real is relevant. The primacy of entangled apparatal relationships (intra-actions) over even time and space is particularly relevant for all levels of decidedness (from well-decided to semi-decided to undecided), and thus relevant to our art apparatuses.

13 Whitehead, *Process and Reality,* 283–84.

The Holistic Apparatus

Just as the quantum-behavior-measuring apparatus is indivisible into sequential time-fragments, it is also indivisible into spatial part-fragments. To cut out a subpart of the delayed choice eraser apparatus and examine it separately is to create an entirely new apparatus. One may choose within the apparatus to bracket whichever portion of it she so desires (just as the holistic apparatus itself chooses to bracket the portion of the universe that it so desires), but such internal bracketing may not occur without cutting into (and out of) the overall holistic apparatus. Thinking separately about the discrete function of each individual component of the delayed choice eraser apparatus (the source photon, the double-slit wall, the signal photon, the signal photon position detection device, the idler photon, the random number generator, the idler photon which-path detection device, the idler photon eraser/obfuscator device, etc.), and then combining those thoughts together will not result in proper thinking about the overall holistic apparatus. Even thinking about the ways in which these discrete parts "interact" with each other will not result in proper thinking about the overall holistic apparatus. As Barad lucidly observes, "interaction" assumes that all the parts of the apparatus are already discretely formed prior to the apparatal phenomenon. "Interaction" is a Newtonian way of thinking – pre-existent noun objects with pre-existent adjectival properties verb-ishly acting upon each other in adverbial ways. But within a quantum-behavior-measuring apparatus, the key elements of the apparatus (the photons) are not yet discrete, noun-y things. What the photons will eventually become has everything to do with the "intra-active" (Barad's term) phenomenon of the holistic apparatus. As humans, we don't just need new words to describe the function of quantum-behavior-measuring apparatuses; we need new, holistic, apparatal, intra-active ways of thinking altogether. Whitehead was already there, as early as 1927.

The 2008 version of the Ma et al. delayed choice eraser experiment which takes place across two islands illustrates some other important facts regarding the holistic nature of apparatuses: apparatuses need not be black boxes; they need not exist in contained laboratories (or contained galleries); they need not appear to be hermetically sealed. In one of John Wheeler's original delayed choice eraser thought experiments, the original photon is emitted from a star many light years away from the "eraser" component of the apparatus. In Einstein's original EPR thought experiment, devised to question the "spooky action at a distance" of entangled photons, the entangled photon pair is separated over great cosmic distances so that the measurement of one photon could only instantaneously "affect" the state of its partner photon at a speed greater than light. These examples drive home the fact that an apparatus is really just a configuration of intra-acting relationships cut out of the rest of the universe in such a way that its "measured" "results" mean what they have become. Just as parts of the universe are perpetually "measuring" (I would say "reckoning") other parts of the universe; in this same sense, apparatal phenomenon (i.e., intra-active becomings, apparatuses) are cropping up all the time. Throughout this book, I am primarily using the term "apparatus" to discuss human-devised apparatuses (whether artistic, scientific, or otherwise); but technically, what makes an apparatus an apparatus is the intra-active relations amongst its phenomena, the cutting out of itself from the rest of the (negatively prehended) universe, and the irreversible "marks" left on the universe as a result of its "measurement" outcome. Apparatuses function as a propositions, as holistic lures for becoming, regardless of what they look like.

I will leave the final word on the issue of apparatal holism to the physicists themselves –

Niels Bohr:

> Only the totality of phenomena exhausts the possible information about the objects. [...] I advocated the application of the word phenomenon exclusively to refer to the observations obtained under specified circumstances, including an account of the whole experimental arrangement.[14]

John Wheeler, proposer of the original delayed choice eraser thought experiment:

> In actuality it is wrong to talk of the "route" of the photon. For a proper way of speaking we recall once more that it makes no sense to talk of the phenomenon until it has been brought to a close by an irreversible act of amplification.[15]

Xiao-Song Ma, principal investigator of the 2008 Cayman Islands apparatus:

> It is a general feature of delayed-choice experiments that [...] the relative temporal order of measurement events is not relevant, and no physical interactions or signals, let alone into the past, are necessary to explain the experimental results. To interpret quantum experiments, any attempt in explaining what happens in an individual observation of one system has to include the whole experimental configuration and also the

---

14 Niels Bohr, "Discussion with Einstein on Epistemological Problems in Atomic Physics," in *Albert Einstein: Philosopher-Scientist*, ed. Paul Arthur Schilpp (New York: MJF Books, 1970), 210, 237–38.
15 J.A. Wheeler, "Law without Law," in *Quantum Theory and Measurement*, eds. J.A. Wheeler and W. H. Zurek (Princeton: Princeton University Press, 1983), 192.

complete quantum state, potentially describing joint properties with other systems.[16]

The fact that it is possible to decide whether a wave or particle feature manifests itself long after – and even space-like separated from – the measurement teaches us that we should not have any naive realistic picture for interpreting quantum phenomena. Any explanation of what goes on in a specific individual observation of one photon has to take into account the whole experimental apparatus of the complete quantum state consisting of both photons, and it can only make sense after all information concerning complementary variables has been recorded.[17]

Indifference to Human Observation

Although the delayed choice quantum eraser apparatus never would have been devised were it not for the relentless and idiosyncratic inquisitiveness of humans; nevertheless, the actual results of the apparatus are wholly indifferent to and independent of human observation. The measured results of our quantum-behavior-measuring apparatuses may be mind-blowing to humans; but to photons, it's just another day on the job. To photons, there is absolutely nothing "weird" or "spooky" about the results of the delayed choice eraser. The apparatus's behavior is totally expected and utterly banal. Indeed, the human capacity to think that something is weird is way more weird than any of the things that humans think are weird.

---

16 Ma, Kofler, and Zeilinger, "Delayed-Choice Gedanken Experiments and their Realizations," 24.
17 Ma, Kofler, et al., "Quantum Erasure with Causally Disconnected Choice," 1226.

The measured results of any scientific apparatus (whether quantum-behavior-measuring or classical-behavior-measuring) are based on irreversible decisions that the apparatus itself enacts. Physicist Maximilian Schlosshauer observes, "The very definition of measure-ment hinges on the property of irreversibility."[18] And again, "It is difficult to regard a reversible interaction as a proper measurement."[19] What makes the apparatal measurements count as measurements at all is not that humans observe these measurements, but that the meas-urements themselves are irreversible. Indeed, until a measurement is irreversible (i.e., until the apparatus has decided to mean what it has holistically become, until the actual occasions relevant to it have occurred), there is no measurement.

In multiple quantum eraser apparatuses of various configurations (Dürr, 1998; Kim, 2000; Scarcelli, 2007), the diffraction (interference, fringe) pattern is "destroyed" and becomes a clumped pattern once which-path infor-mation is detected and stored within the apparatus, re-gardless of whether or not a human ever reads, observes, or notes that which-path information.[20] The which-path information has not yet been obfuscated. It remains in the universe. The retention of this information matters within the carved out, holistic context of the apparatus, whether or not it ever comes to matter to a human exter-nal to the apparatus.

Perhaps even more (human-)"weird," Barad summariz-es the findings of one which-path apparatus in which the mere *ability* to distinguish which-path information with-in the apparatus is enough to "destroy" the interference pattern, even when "which-path" measurements are not

18 Maximilian Schlosshauer, *Decoherence and the Quantum-To-Classical Transition* (Berlin: Springer, 2010), 69.
19 Ibid., 101.
20 Ma, Kofler, and Zeilinger, "Delayed-Choice Gedanken Experiments and their Realizations," 17–18.

performed.[21] "It has been confirmed experimentally that the interference pattern disappears without any which-path measurement having actually been performed – but just by the mere possibility of distinguishing paths."[22] These findings only strengthen the interpretation of the scientific apparatus as a holistic unit in and of itself, independent of external human observation.

In contrast, all of the art apparatuses I happen to discuss in this book *do* concern themselves with humans. This is not because art is "subjective" and science is "objective." The difference is, science apparatuses (at least of the physics variety) are purposefully structured to *avoid* intra-acting with the enduring objects known as humans, whereas (most) art apparatuses are purposefully structured to intra-act with humans. Art apparatuses are not solely dependent upon human intra-action. Materials within the art apparatus are themselves intra-acting with each other. Humans are involved in most art apparatuses simply because most artists purposefully configure their art apparatuses to intra-act with humans. Most human artists assume and make a place for human "audiences" in their art apparatuses. All of this is perfectly understandable and utterly reasonable. It doesn't mean art apparatuses are any less apparatuses. It just means that, by definition, art apparatuses are less scientific than scientific apparatuses (as one would expect). Whereas to science, according to the goals of science, it is essential to (attempt to) inhibit the scientific human observer from influencing the measurement outcome.

Of course, the various measurement outcomes of the various quantum-behavior-measuring apparatuses have a great effect on the human community of physicists.

21 X.Y. Zou, L.J. Wang, and L. Mandel, "Induced Coherence and Indistinguishability in Optical Interference," *Physical Review Letters* 67, no. 3 (1991): 318–321.
22 Karen Barad, *Meeting the Universe Halfway* (Durham: Duke University Press, 2007), 306.

But in order for those measurement outcomes to matter to human physicists, humans themselves may not be allowed to intra-act with these apparatuses in any way that would affect the measured results. Almost the opposite is true with the human community of artists, gallerists, art historians, and art patrons. Unless humans *are* invited to intra-act with art apparatuses, the human art community is generally not that interested. Art apparatuses have been devised which *seem* to purposefully exclude the intra-action of humans. Joseph Beuys's *How to Explain Pictures to a Dead Hare* comes to mind. But even during that performance, humans are welcomed to peer through the gallery windows, the "pictures" in the gallery have been created by humans, and after a certain amount of time, humans are invited back into the gallery. And of course, Beuys himself is a human.

By observing that art apparatuses purposefully include humans, I am not at all saying that art apparatuses are merely equivalent to gedanken apparatuses, to thought experiments. Artists and scientists may imagine the possible results of various apparatuses, but until those apparatuses are built and run in the world, until irreversible marks are made, both gedanken science experiments and yet-to-be-implemented art project ideas are less integrated into (and thus less integral to) the universe. Yes, to imagine is itself a form of actualizing the virtual, since thoughts are actually real and not merely virtual potentia. But thoughts themselves don't involve much material, so they (literally) don't matter as much. It is one thing for Niels Bohr to assert against Einstein that "spooky action at a distance" (space-like separated quantum entanglement) is a real thing. It is another thing for scientists to construct an apparatus and run an experiment that enacts this form of remote entanglement. The apparatus doesn't merely "show and prove" the "truth" of the thought experiment. The apparatal experiment entangles that thought experiment with materials and actual history, and in so doing, translates the thought experiment into an irreversible event. There is no substitute for the construction and enaction of an actual apparatus (whether scientific or artistic). Even an artist as conceptual and language-centric as Lawrence Weiner must still spray-paint words onto a floor, or hang some words on a wall, or publish some words in a conceptual manifesto explaining how art doesn't have to be made of anything other than words. Theoretical *thinking* alone won't *do*. Thinking alone won't *cut it*. An *actual* apparatus is required.

And so, we turn our attention to David Crawford's *Stop Motion Studies* art apparatus. Crawford doesn't merely think theoretically about the liminal space between photograph and film. Instead, he constructs an art apparatus that functions in that liminal space. What emerges continues to problematize and advance both photography theory and film theory, as well as human notions of durational time.

Stop Motion Studies

Stop Motion Studies is our second proper example of an apophatic art apparatus. Our first apophatic art apparatus ("The Dot" from Arakawa and Gins's *Mechanism of Meaning*) put the brakes on making meaning. *Stop Motion Studies* puts the brakes on sequential becoming; but then so does still photography, and so does the filmic loop. Yet *Stop Motion Studies* goes further, braking both the static resolution of still photography (by setting its own frames in perpetual motion) and the cyclic repetition of the filmic loop (by aleatorically animating its own frames so that they never actually "loop"). *Stop Motion Studies* is a very thorough apophatic art apparatus. Something does gradually and eventually become of/from this time-braking

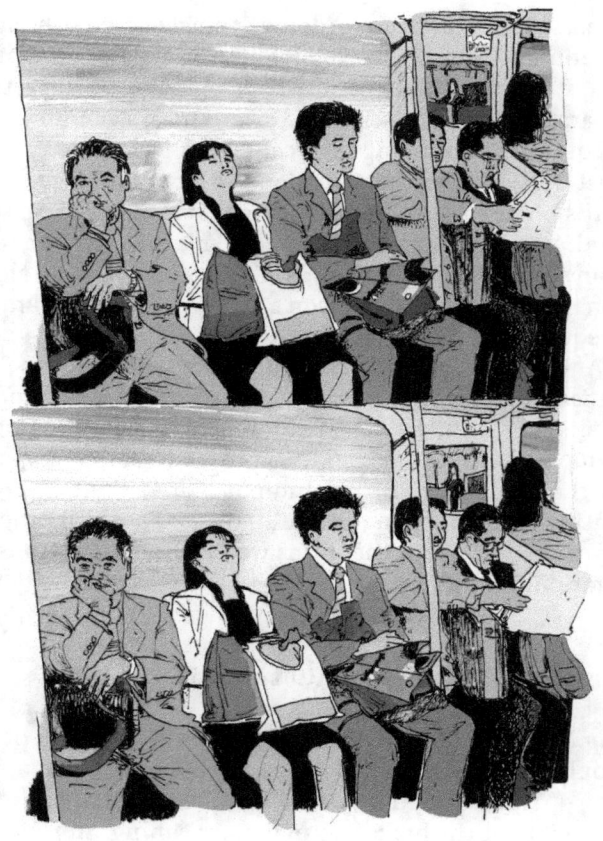

Fig. 2: 2/3 of the frames from David Crawford's *Stop Motion Studies*: Series #8, Sequence #2. Drawing by Jordan Cloninger.

apparatus: a portrait of humans as a sequence of occasions rather than as enduring objects.

Stop Motion Studies is a series of aleatoric animations by the artist David Crawford. The animations are not static photographic stills, nor are they perpetually looping micro-films. Crawford's microcosmic photographic studies of people riding on subways initially seem like looping micro-films. But the animations never actually loop. Instead, their sequence and duration are controlled by randomizing software instructions. Imagine a slide projector tray filled with anywhere between three to eight slides. All the slides in the tray are of the same subject, all photographed within a limited time frame of just a few seconds. The projector displays these same slides infinitely, but always in random order. The projector also randomizes the duration each slide is displayed, anywhere from about .03 seconds to about .3 seconds. This set-up roughly approximates the mechanics of what Crawford has termed "algorithmic montage."[23] The result is a kind of stochastic motion study more akin to chronophotography than film; but with a distinct, non-linear twist. Crawford uses this aleatoric art apparatus to prize open the liminal timescape between still photography and film (see Fig. 2).

Although *Stop Motion Studies* is similar to both still photography and looping film, it is its own taxonomically unique genre of media. It shares features with and was inspired by the Victorian-era chronophotography of Étienne-Jules Marey. Crawford himself poetically observes, "Marey's chronophotographs flourished in the tiny space between the still and the moving image."[24] The shared goal of *Stop Motion Studies* (hereafter, *SMS*) and Marey's chronophotography experiments is not to simulate motion (à la film), but to dissect and unpack a discrete moment. Yet Marey's approach is more akin to still photography. Every frame of the discrete moment is spread out before the viewer in a single image, like individual notes on a piano keyboard, immediately assimilable and thus immediately foreclosed, reduced, and finalized. Although

23 David Crawford, *Algorithmic Montage*, Master's Thesis, University of Gothenburg, 2004, 1.
24 Ibid., 26.

different than ordinary photography, Marey's approach still freezes the moment too much. Like Zeno's arrow paradox, Marey's chronophotography removes the viewer from the moment under analysis and places her outside of the moment, peering back into it. She does not fly along with the arrow. Marey's chronophotographic apparatus only invites the viewer into the apparatus *after* the occasion in question has been archived and frozen. The viewer does indeed have an immediate experience (how could she not?), but it is an immediate experience of viewing static documentation of an archived series of moments. Contrarily, by aleatorically re-animating static documentation of a discrete moment (via random frame order and random frame duration), *SMS* places the viewer in a re-enactment of the moment, and leaves her stuck therein. In this sense, *SMS* distinguishes itself from Marey's chronophotography (and standard still photography), functioning as a particularly apophatic apparatus.

In his classic work of photographic theory, *Towards a Philosophy of Photography*, Vilém Flusser notes:

> The camera is not fully automatic. These are the categories of photographic time and space. They are neither Newtonian nor Einsteinian, but they divide time and space into rather clearly separated areas. These areas of time and space are distances from the prey that is to be snapped.[25]

Although an ingenious critique of still photography and its slavish relationship to the stalk, capture, pin-down function of the apparatus known as camera, Flusser's observations don't fully apply to *Stop Motion Studies*. This is because, via aleatoric programming code, *SMS* functions as a meta-camera-apparatus. Crawford re-animates the

---

25 Vilém Flusser, *Towards a Philosophy of Photography*, trans. Anthony Matthews (London: Reaktion Books, 2012), 34.

frozen spacetime of his source camera images, freeing them from their own amber trap. In so doing, he activates an entirely different kind of meta-camera apophatic apparatus which functions as a porous and sticky La Brea tar pit trap for its viewers. The still photograph sucks out spacetime in order to trap a moment; *Stop Motion Studies* creates an aleatoric, apophatic spacetime in order to trap us within a moment.

If *SMS* differs from still photography, it also differs from film, video, and even looping micro-animation. Paul Virilio observes, "Cinema is the end in which the dominant philosophies and arts have come to confuse and lose themselves, a sort of primordial mixing of the human soul and the languages of the motor-soul."[26] Arguably, as early as Vertov's *Man with A Movie Camera*, the motion of the projector reel/wheel was predisposed to celebrate the motion of the motor wheel. But Crawford's aleatoric animations aren't constrained to follow the cyclic function of either, because they never (quite, exactly) loop. Although the stage and setting of *SMS* are on moving subway trains, the functional *SMS* software apparatus "jumps the track." It refuses to proceed sequentially on down the line, but it also refuses to loop perpetually round and round. Instead, *SMS* stutters and staggers forwards and back. There is actually a function in certain programming languages called "drunk" which randomizes a series of numbers between, for example, 0 and 9, in such a way that the numbers selected move forward and backwards in steps, constrained within a range of something like 3. So, unlike a "random" function, a "drunk" function would never return 0 followed immediately by 9. It would instead return something like the following series: 0, 3, 5, 2, 6, 4, 3, 7, 4, 8, 9. Although Crawford's ActionScript code is not technically a drunk function, by

26 Paul Virilio, *The Aesthetics of Disappearance* (New York: Semiotext(e) Books, 1991), 105.

randomizing the duration of each frame in addition to randomizing the order of the frames, it feels drunk. It is obviously not a loop. It lurches forward, hesitates, staggers, returns, and lurches again.

SMS contrasts this drunken stagger of its own apparatal kinematic procession with the steady, motor-wheel hurtling-forward of the subway train itself. Crawford's media apparatus ingeniously stages and foregrounds the stuttering micro-movements of its human subjects in front of the speedy, motor-logic blur of the scenery passing by outside of the train windows. The humans move fractionally, while the blurred backgrounds lurch wildly from one frame to the next. By staging his moments on a moving train, Crawford captures and juxtaposes human bodily affective time with motor/projector-wheel speeding time, confusing and confounding them both within the drunken, lurching, molasses time created by his apophatic apparatus.

It is not as if *SMS* is such a new medium that all prior photographic theory is totally inapplicable to it. No, *SMS* traffics in images, so any theory of images still comes into play, albeit modulated by the aleatoric animation. Similarly, although *SMS* is not merely looped video, it is still creating many of the effects and much of the affect that looped video also creates. *Stop Motion Studies* is not totally other than either still photography or looped video, just as looped video itself is not totally other than still photography. It would be overly simple to say that *SMS* is doing everything that still photography and looped video is doing, and then some. It is not simply an $n+1+1+1$ mathematics of linear accretion. This is because each work of art is its own holistic apparatus. In an apparatus, accretion is not merely additive. Instead, new additions to the apparatus often modulate the entire holistic function of the apparatus: they alter the ways in which it is becoming, and the things it is coming to mean. New differences emerge from accreted similarities.

Regarding looped video itself, every looped video creates its own unique event depending on the nature of the video and the way in which it loops. For single or multichannel video installations looping in the context of an art gallery exhibition, the goal of most contemporary video installation artists is rarely to mimetically (or even abstractly) re-present some kind of source experience in and of itself. Instead, a looped video acts as its own discrete, catalytic "object" which causes its human "audience" to perform an undulating, back-and-forth dialogue between present perception and past memory, resulting in an emergent future. This generic affective function is characteristic of looped film, looped video, looped animated gifs, looped analog flipbook animations, or any looped sequence of images.

My point is that aleatoric animation is not explicitly required to create a visceral (sense of) time. Not only video art, but all art is properly understood as "time-based." Film and photography (and painting, and sculpture) have always already been time-based and time-generating apparatuses. Per Roland Barthes' concept of intertextuality, every discrete "linear" text gets re-mixed and re-run in real time every time it is read anew, even by the same human reader. To experience a variation in the text, no cut-up techniques or aleatoric constraints are required. Simply re-read the same text a second time. Likewise, as I sit in front of a Rothko painting, I am having a time-based experience. I am intra-acting with that Rothko painting apparatus, and time is emerging as a result. The relevant question is not "is this piece time-based?" (since all art is time-based). From a media theory perspective, the relevant question has to do with *how much* and *what kind* of variability occurs in the art apparatus over time? And a related question: how much of the variability occurs within the technics of the piece itself, and how much of the variability occurs in the affective experience of the user, audience, participant, or viewer? In the case of a

Rothko painting, there are technical changes in the hue, saturation, value, surface, and depth of the painting as I move my body around the room in relation to the painting; these changes also occur as I attend to one part of the painting and then another part. But the majority of the variability in a Rothko painting occurs in my affective experience as a viewer over time. Whereas, in a looped digital video, in addition to the variability that my viewing body is experiencing, drastic technical changes are occurring to the media itself (RGBA value changes, pixel by pixel, micro-second by micro-second) as the video proceeds from frame to frame. And in *Stop Motion Studies,* due to its aleatoric animation, there is a near infinite amount of variability in the technical procession of the medium itself.

Ironically (but understandably), this infinite amount of variability in the medium of aleatoric animation fails to create an experience of infinitely variable time in the viewer. This is because we as humans are unable to cognitively process the exact, discrete differences in frame order and frame duration. These subtle differences elude intellectual reduction. But we are able to affectively and bodily experience these differences. We don't read *Stop Motion Studies* as a loop, and we don't read it as a still photograph. Our inability to reduce it to either of these historically familiar media only further contributes to the lure and trap that *SMS* sets for us. We get stuck in the unique time of its infinitely variable media, trapped within an unending moment. Via aleatoric animation, *Stop Motion Studies* "wrest[s] a non-pulsed time from th[e] system of chronological pulsation"[27] (to apply Deleuze). *SMS* breaks our habit of viewing photography as static

---

27 Gilles Deleuze and Richard Pinhas, "Vincennes Seminar Session, May 3, 1997: On Music," trans. Timothy S. Murphy, *Discourse: Journal for Theoretical Studies in Media and Culture* 20, no. 3 (Fall 1998): art. 23, 8.

documentation and our habit of viewing film as narrative representation. It creates a different time, a trap time, an apophatic time of the perpetual moment.

Aleatory vs. Iteration

Software can be thought of as a set of instructions. Whether these instructions are ultimately executed by a digital computer, a wooden loom, or an ensemble theater cast is not what determines them as software. All programming is governed by three basic control structures: sequence (execution in a linear order), selection (choosing between two things), and iteration (looping). The combination of these three structures is what determines the operation of any piece of software. Introducing a random variable into the iteration structure results in a variation or wobble in the loop. Each time the loop iterates, a new random value is generated which alters the run of that particular loop. Combining a random number generator with an iteration control structure results in an aleatorically induced wobble time that is not quite an ordinary loop. The effects of a random number generator are so unique, it almost acts like its own fourth programming control structure. Technically, a random number generator is really just a kind of arrayed selection control structure (randomly select one number from a given set of numbers), but because a random number generator is a uniquely value-indifferent form of selection, a wildcard form of selection, it can seem like its own category of programming control structure.

A brief and nerdy sidebar regarding randomness: within programming circles, there is great philosophical debate over whether or not a truly random selection is actually possible. Most random number generators are actually pseudo-random, deriving the source ("seed") of their randomness by sampling a computer's internal clock state, and then doing math on that source number. Because a computer's internal clock is not actually random, the number that results is more properly understood as pseudo-random. More truly random number generators take their source seeds from extra-computational, real-time climate readings or other "naturally" occurring values. The philosophical debate comes down to whether or not you think the universe itself is random. Pragmatically, in our case, the distinction between randomness and pseudo-randomness is splitting hairs, because whether truly random or pseudo-random (*SMS* happens to be pseudo-random), the affective result of *SMS* on the human viewer would be more or less the same.

By embedding a random number generator within an infinite loop, a new, unique, non-looping, non-static time is created and made to be felt. This new time is not merely a simulated, once-removed, mimetic trick of the media. The time created, enacted, and felt is not a symbolic, re-presentational, re-mediated version of aleatoric time. It is *actual* aleatoric time (or more properly, it is actualized aleatoric becoming, human-apperceived as aleatoric time). Via the random (or pseudo-random) seed sampling, the agency and variability of the real universe is purposefully invited to ingress into the ongoing occasions involved in the software-driven art apparatus. Each singular, unique, real-time, random number decision event is repeatedly and indefinitely made, over and over: an infinite number of one-of-a-kind historical decisions. By combining a random number generator with an iteration control structure, the resolution of the system is indefinitely deferred.

Of course, according to Whitehead, a rock sitting in a field is doing more or less the same thing as the *SMS* apparatus. The static rock is actually a society of moment-by-moment actual occasions, each occasion prehending (or mostly negatively prehending) the "randomness" of the rest of the universe, and concrescing with it into its own self-becoming. The difference between the rock and *SMS* is that, moment by moment, the rock occasions mostly decide to continue to become an enduring object known as rock. Until the rock shatters apart, or melts, or lands on our foot, we are mostly human-indifferent to its subtle (quasi-static) perpetual becomings. Whereas Crawford has embedded into the heart of his *SMS* apparatus a lively random number generator which foregrounds *to humans* the ongoing becomings of his art apparatus. The random number generator injects marked, actual differences into the system's perpetual becomings in order to make these moment-by-moment becomings felt. Its becomings become human-apparent to our habituated, media-consuming bodies. We are made to feel these differences in the micro-second becomings of the *SMS* apparatus. We find (the successive occasions of) ourselves prehending its aleatoric time. Furthermore, these functional, processual, software differences are not "content"-indifferent, because the mediated "content" of *Stop Motion Studies* is itself a prior, actual moment of becoming: a moment of humans riding trains. Crawford's random number generator injects a lively present-tense variable into a mediated prior moment (which was, itself, at that prior time, actually lively and present-tense), thus perpetually re-animating and re-vivifying that prior micro-moment. *SMS* brackets and freshly enacts its prior moments in a kind of living amber, and our human viewing bodies get stuck-in with them.

Returning to quantum mechanics, the wave function predicts a probability range of observable values, but never a single exact value for any given measurement event. The exact observable value is only decided, enacted, and marked once the apparatal measurement is historically made. Similarly (although not identically), the random number generator injects a kind of quasi-quantum-behaving, superpositional randomness into *SMS*'s photographic media. I don't mean to claim that *SMS* is a proper quantum-behavior-measuring apparatus; but rather that it is a human–cinematic apparatus which is transformed, via random number generation, into something functionally and behaviorally non-deterministic, similar to a quantum-behaving superpositional state.

Of course, the individual photographic frames of *SMS* do not remain in a literal quantum superpositional state. Every sequential frame and its duration are finally and discretely decided once and for all, each time the loop function is re-run. *SMS* is thus not so much a series of perpetually deferred decisions as an infinitely ongoing series of final decisions randomly made each time. Still, since humans are invited to intra-act with the *SMS* apparatus (as opposed to being quarantined from the Delayed Choice Quantum Eraser apparatus), we bodily experience these perpetually made random decisions as a kind of superpositional, perpetually deferred time state. *SMS* is apophatic in that it refuses to settle on any single, resolved time (whether static or looped). *SMS* is not as cosmically radical as the Delayed Choice Quantum Eraser apparatus (although to the universe itself, the Delayed Choice Quantum Eraser apparatus is quite normal). Instead, *SMS* is aesthetically, bodily, and affectively radical to our cinematically conditioned, photographically conditioned human bodies. Whereas the results of the Delayed Choice Quantum Eraser apparatus blow our Newtonian-conditioned human minds, *Stop Motion Studies* makes us bodily feel the rich superpositional fecundity of the universe's moment-by-moment micro-becomings.

Deferment

Stop Motion Studies is apophatic because it arrests time while not exactly freezing it. It defers any single, final becoming; much more so than a discrete photograph, which always winds up getting thrust into "having become" a static image. *SMS* makes us feel what Whitehead calls "the penumbral welter of alternatives."[28] We are opened out onto and remain stuck in this penumbral welter of alternatives. Whitehead elaborates:

This graded envisagement is how the actual includes what (in one sense) is "not-being" as a positive factor in its own achievement. It is the source of error, of truth, of art, of ethics, and of religion. By it, fact is confronted with alternatives.[29]

As conscious humans, we normally rush past this "graded envisagement," this actualizing of the virtual, these actual occasions of micro-becoming that perpetually make the world new. *SMS* sidesteps our recognizing minds and sticks our experiencing bodies into these occasions of moment-by-moment becoming by perpetually deferring any finalized sequence of its loop. In so doing, Crawford's apparatus invites us to (more consciously) feel these micro-instant becomings.

SMS doesn't halt becoming (that would be impossible), but it does remain in a perpetual state of becoming. All apparatuses lure their involved actual occasions into making time; *SMS* lures the actual occasions of its human viewers into its own time-making process, into its perpetual time of time-making. Deferral of closure is a major tactic of the apophatic writers, and deferment necessarily involves time. In the words of historian Michael Sells, the achievement of unsaying is "unstable and fleeting."[30] Apophatic language is always performative and ongoing in order to avoid reaching a definitive conclusion that might calcify into a reducible ontological statement. *SMS* simply automates this deferral process via software and

28 Whitehead, *Process and Reality*, 187.
29 Ibid., 189.
30 Michael A. Sells, *The Mystical Languages of Unsaying* (Chicago: University of Chicago Press, 1994), 217.

applies it to photographic media rather than to natural human language. *SMS* is thus an apophatic apparatus that, by perpetually making an infinite number of different ephemeral marks, refuses (and thus defers) the inscription of any final, concretized, single mark.

From the perspective of post-structuralism (and always with a bit of Whitehead sprinkled throughout), *SMS* is an apparatus which generates a perpetually unstable trace. It inscribes and re-inscribes event-trace after event-trace, without ever leaving any final, underlying, or source event-mark. It assembles an ensemble of perpetually becoming and re-shuffling, ghost-image occasions that refuse to ever settle down and become a single, stable, well-decided society of entities. In this sense, *SMS* is a purposefully unstable media apparatus. It is indifferent toward the finality of its own mark. It is an auto-rewriting etch-a-sketch. To decide not to is (subtly, but) radically different than to not decide. *SMS* enacts Bartleby's "I would prefer not to," creating a kind of self-cancelling combination of affirmations and denials that results in a disturbingly aporetic deferral, much more apophatic than the mere direct refusal of, "No I will not." *SMS* perpetually re-inscribes an unstable un-mark. It purposefully fails to resolutely leave a final mark. All trace; no mark. Such is the (admittedly apophatic) language post-structuralist literary theorists might use to unpack *Stop Motion Studies*.

Humans Intra-act with *SMS*

The mediated human bodies (on trains) in Carson's source photographs act as a lure for the human viewers of *SMS*. Whether via mirror neurons, performance empathy, bodily affect, emotional connection, or simple formal recognition, humans more strongly connect with mediated images of other humans than they do with mediated images of rocks. Or at least they connect and entangle differently. Once this human-to-human entanglement is formed, the variable time that *SMS* creates is that much more likely to tweak and trap our human viewing bodies. We, as human viewers, are more likely to bodily intra-act with the apophatic apparatus of *SMS* via our own bodily identification with the train-riding human bodies than we would if the source images were of rocks in a field. We affectively feel the jittery movements of Carson's mediated bodies as both recognizable and uncanny. Our bodies are sucked into the strange, stuttering time of these aleatorically animated, human-populated micro-scenes. In this sense, *SMS* is similar to almost all other art apparatuses: art apparatuses are (almost always) designed to intra-actively involve humans in their apparatal configurations. Art apparatuses cut out a part of the universe which purposefully includes humans. As mentioned previously, this is in stark contrast to quantum-behavior-measuring scientific apparatuses, which cut out a part of the universe that purposefully excludes humans.

Crawford himself is fully aware of the importance of experientially sucking his human viewers into his apparatus, rather than positioning them as once-removed, intellectually reflecting agents outside of his apparatus. In an essay entitled, "The Implication of Movement: From Bergson to Bohm," Crawford cites Henri Bergson on the difference between distanced reflection and immersive identification. The Bergson selections that Crawford cites are worth repeating in full:

> Instead of attaching ourselves to the inner becoming of things, we place ourselves outside them in order to recompose their becoming artificially. We take snapshots, as it were, of the passing reality, and, as these are characteristic of the reality, we have only to string them on a becoming, abstract, uniform and invisible, situated at the back of the apparatus of knowledge, in order to imitate what there is that is characteristic in this becoming itself [...].

In order to advance with the moving reality, you must replace yourself within it. Install yourself within change, and you will grasp at once both change itself and the successive states in which *it might* be immobilized.[31]

It is difficult enough to theorize this kind of immersive identification, and even more difficult to construct an apparatus which causes it to be felt. *SMS* is such an apparatus. Again, as stated previously, (the actual occasions that make up) humans participate in all sorts of "naturally occurring" apparatal configurations all day long, moment by moment. It's just that we, as conscious humans, rarely recognize what is happening in these micro-second actual occasions. Instead, it most often seems to us that we are discrete entities passing other discrete entities within a kind of Cartesian container space along a kind of linear timeline. *SMS* disrupts our habitual understanding of time by sucking us into an apparatus which allows us to (in Bergson's words) "advance with the moving reality" by "replac[ing] [ourselves] within it." Not only does *SMS* place us within the reality of movement, it leaves us stuck there indefinitely, until we click on another aleatorically animated scene, which traps us yet again. *SMS* places us within the becomings of micro-second actual occasions.

One of the ingenious ways *SMS* lures us into itself is by showing us images of other humans. As human viewers, we allow ourselves to intra-act with the apparatus, in part, because we see and feel the pathos, the significance, and the import of the micro-moments being (re-)enacted: humans hurtling forward on trains, living their urban working lives, spending and wasting passing mo-

31 Henri Bergson, *Creative Evolution*, trans. Arthur Mitchell (London: Electric Book Co., 2001), 295–297, quoted in David Crawford, "The Implication of Movement: From Bergson to Bohm," in *New Realities: Being Syncretic*, eds. Roy Ascott, Gerald Bast, et al. (Vienna: Springer, 2009), 78.

ments, moments lost in transit, going nowhere fast. *Stop Motion Studies* enacts the often brutal melancholy and banality of individual human lives, moment by moment by moment. These in-transit (transitory, transitional) lives are not epically memorialized in a captured photographic moment. Photography gives each captured moment a kind of grace, dignity, and elevation. Or rather, photography elevates us as viewers from the moment, allowing us to intellectually ponder the moment at a distance, in our own good time, at our leisure. Contrarily, *SMS* traps us within the banal frozen micro-moment, forcing us to ongoingly live and re-live it in our own present-tense, perpetually emerging time. We become inordinately aware of the gravitas of these micro-moments, in stark contrast to the humans on the train, who are largely oblivious to the very micro-moments in which they themselves are participating. If only they could see themselves through the lens of this new medium, surely their next commute would be more purposefully relished? Surely after *SMS*, we ourselves will now be more fully present to our own micro-moments. But probably not, because giving oneself over to the process of concrescence is not really an intellectual exercise. Actual occasions happen too fast for that. And yet, bodies may themselves know and be trained. Perhaps *SMS* is training our bodies to better negotiate their own moment-by-moment becomings.

At any (and every) rate, it is a mistake to think that process philosophy and affect theory reside on the cold and analytic side of human-beingness; and that ethics, compassion, and empathy reside on the culturally relevant and politically pragmatic side of human-beingness. Our empathy arises from and folds back into the technics of our affective concrescences. There is not one world of process and physics and another world of emotions and ethics. There is only one immanent world, and everything affects everything else (however epically or fractionally).

Time Created (Not Filled)

Both the Delayed Choice Quantum Eraser apparatus and the *Stop Motion Studies* art apparatus demonstrate that time is created rather than filled. In both cases, only by deferring resolution within the apparatus does this fact become apparent. In its attempt to lock down the weirdness of the Double Slit apparatus, the Delayed Choice Quantum Eraser introduces the further weirdness of entangled particles and "spooky action at a distance." In the process, time (and space) are revealed as created rather than filled. The time created within the Delayed Choice Quantum Eraser apparatus is not subject to clocks external to the apparatus. Similarly, in its attempt to problematize and disrupt the media regimes of photography and film, *SMS* invents an ongoingly liminal, molasses time that traps its audience via aleatoric animation and human empathy. Again, time is revealed as created rather than filled. In a sense, *SMS* invites its human viewers to remain in the (non-)time of the actual occasion, the (proto-)time of the virtual becoming actual. Technically, the time *SMS* makes is more like an actualized faux-virtual time. It is an emulation of the virtual instantiated within the actual. In computer science terms, *SMS* is a software-enacted emulation of the virtual, running on the Operating System of the actual.

It is noteworthy that the idea of the virtual came to both Proust and Bergson via the topic of human memory: the one thing that explicitly falls outside of the arrow of linear time and the grid of Cartesian space. According to Bergson, human memory is not stored anywhere in the human brain. It is created anew each time in real-time. Memory is not media material. It is not matter; it is event (not noun, but verb).

Proust elaborates on the extra-temporal (and affective) nature of memory:

The noise of the spoon upon the plate, the unevenness of the paving-stones, the taste of the madeleine, imposed the past upon the present and made me hesitate as to which time I was existing in. Of a truth, the being within me which sensed this impression [...] found itself in the only setting in which it could exist and enjoy the essence of things, that is, outside Time [...]. The being that I then had been was an extra-temporal being [...]. Only that being had the power of enabling me to recapture former days, Time Lost, in the face of which all the efforts of my memory and of my intelligence came to nought.[32]

Short of such an involuntary, immersive memory experience, what other ways might the procession of time be braked? *SMS* offers at least on means of (temporarily) braking time: software-induced aleatoric animation. Indeed, a bit later in *Time Regained,* Proust himself observes, "A work of art is the only means of regaining lost time."[33] Why? Because art apparatuses are able to manufacture time anew in ways that invite humans to affectively, bodily experience these new temporal becomings. Time is of course always created anew, actual occasion by actual occasion. But art apparatuses (whether epic French novels or aleatoric new media animations), if constructed ingeniously enough, invite their human audiences to affectively experience the creation of new time. *SMS* achieves this effect by miring us in the perpetual creation of new time.

Apparatal intra-actions create space and time, so it is backwards to think of art apparatuses as objects (space occupiers) or even as "performances" or "time-based media" (time occupiers). Instead, art apparatuses make

---

32 Marcel Proust, *Time Regained,* trans. Stephen Hudson (1931; Paris: Feedbooks, 2014), 140–41, http://www.feedbooks.com/book/1453/time-regained.
33 Ibid., 163.

space and time. The difference between *Stop Motion Studies* and your average art apparatus is that, rather than merely making time, *SMS* brakes time, luring us into its own amber trap, embedding us within its own micro-second mise-en-scènes which it perpetually re-enacts anew, moment by moment by moment.

5

BR(E)AKING ARCHIVES AND SABOTAGING INSTITUTIONS: JOSHUA CITARELLA'S COMPRESSION ARTIFACTS AND WILLIAM POPE.L'S BLACK FACTORY

Just as apophatic writing sabotages the system of kataphatic language, forcing it to perform its own limitations until it collapses; certain apophatic art apparatuses sabotage systems of art object commodification, systems of art historical canonization, and even entrenched historical systems of constructing self-identity and difference. This chapter analyzes two such apophatic apparatuses. The first apparatus is Joshua Citarella's *Compression Artifacts*, an ephemeral gallery show that simultaneously occurred in a temporary gallery in the woods and at different locations online, featuring impossible art objects that simultaneously exist somewhere between physical gallery space and digital archive space. The second apparatus is William Pope.L's *Black Factory*, a mobile "factory" (performance/installation) for pulverizing inherited notions of racial blackness, racial whiteness, and other binary constructs.

Both *Compression Artifacts* and the *Black Factory* cut out large swaths of the world (across time, space, human-art-histories, human-recognizable-media) and intra-act with them, while simultaneously refusing to allow themselves to be cleanly subsumed into larger apparatuses of "art world" assimilation. Both of these projects refuse to be out-meta-ed. They will not allow art markets to commodify them. By rigorously, ingeniously, and playfully refusing to let themselves be easily canonized by art-historical forces, both apparatuses reveal the mechanisms, presuppositions, and unspoken agendas of art institutions, art archives, and art markets. In all the places where sparks fly and things don't quite slot in, the conforming contours of our cultural institutions are revealed.

As mentioned previously, one crucial difference between art apparatuses and quantum-behavior-measuring apparatuses is that the boundaries of art apparatuses can always be made to extend well beyond their immediate physical edges; whereas scientific apparatuses meant to intra-act with quantum-behaving materials can't telescope outward without experiencing decoherence, the very bane of quantum-behavior measurement and quantum computing. In the case of both *Compression Artifacts* and the *Black Factory*, the edge of each physical apparatuses (in one case, three temporary walls and a floor; in the other case, a large truck) is really just a ruse, a decoy, a provocation meant to initiate a larger chain of outwardly telescoping boundaries. This outward telescoping is large part of the apparatal phenomenon that these apparatuses purpose to engender.

With both apparatuses, it is as if something really banal or silly has to happen within the immediate, local, lure component of the apparatus in order to trigger the outward-telescoping, macrocosmic, large-swath-cutting component of the apparatus. In the case of *Compression Artifacts*, a minimal sculpture and a few digital prints are placed in a well-lit gallery. What could be so media-modulating about this move? In the case of the *Black Factory*, a kind of medicine show truck rolls into town with three vaudeville-like performers acting absurd. What could be so identity-shattering about this move? The apparatal bait is set with banality and humor; and the larger net unfolds outward from there.

Neither *Compression Artifacts* nor the *Black Factory* are overtly anti-gallery or anti-museum. These aren't really works of "institutional critique" in the art historical sense. But both projects are what one might call gallery-aware and museum-aware. Both apparatuses presume the existence and function of art institutions in the world, and both purposefully cut off the part of the world that includes these art institutions in order to involve galleries, museums, and art markets in their own apparatal intra-actions. In this sense, we are dealing less with mere institutional "critique" and more with holistic institutional modulation.

Two precedences from art history come to mind, one per project. Marcel Broodthaers's *Musée d'Art Moderne, Département des Aigles* (*Museum of Modern Art, Department of Eagles*) is particularly relevant to Pope.L's *Black Factory*. Both are mobile museums (or at least part of the *Black Factory* is a museum). Both are patently and absurdly thematized: Broodthaers's museum is comprised of eagle-related images and objects (however obliquely interpreted), while Pope.L's museum is comprised of black-related images and objects (however obliquely interpreted). Both are paradoxically acerbic and playful in tone. Both pedantically add value to their objects by transforming them into art commodities: Broodthaers by stamping bars of gold with eagle images and selling them at twice their value; Pope.L by signing canned goods, selling them at increased prices, and donating the profits to local soup kitchens so they can buy canned goods. Finally, both projects have proved difficult for art institutions to archive,

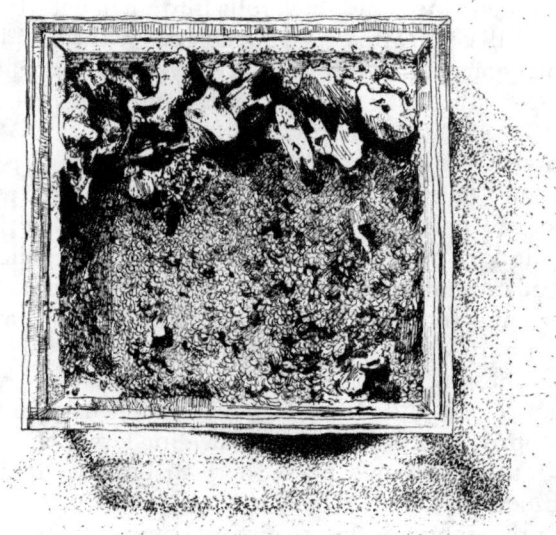

Fig. 1: Some of the ashes of the burned gallery from Joshua Citarella's *Compression Artifacts*. Drawing by Jordan Cloninger.

the projects themselves being their own archiving institutions.

Yves Klein's *Zone de Sensibilité Picturale Immatérielle* (*Zone of Immaterial Pictorial Sensibility*) is particularly relevant to Citarella's *Compression Artifacts*. Klein's project consisted of selling a certificate for an invisible work of art. The buyer paid Klein a specified amount of gold leaf in exchange for the certificate. If the buyer wanted to keep the certificate, she would own the work of art but never be able to access it. In order to access the work of art, the buyer had to meet with Klein on the banks of the river Seine and burn their certificate of ownership while

Klein threw half of the gold leaf payment into the river. That event (the burning of the certificate and the throwing away of the gold) was the actual work of art, which the purchaser had been able to experience, but was no longer able to own. Somewhat similarly, at the end of Citarella's *Compression Artifacts* exhibition, the gallery in the woods was burned. Years later (via the internet) Citarella sold chances (at $5 per chance) to be mailed some of the ashes of the burnt gallery. Winners were then mailed the ashes (see Fig. 1). They were asked to scatter the ashes, document this scattering, and post digital images of the scattering event to Instagram. Both *Compression Artifacts* and *Zone of Immaterial Pictorial Sensibility* translate (seemingly) solid objects into air, and reify (seemingly) abstract market value into gold (or at least into a $5 PayPal credit).

I mention both of these art historical precedences to emphasize the fact that apophatic art apparatuses are not inherently "new media," or even new. Yes, *Compression Artifacts* and the *Black Factory* both do use the internet to achieve part of their apophatic effect, but the apophatic power of these apparatuses is not some de facto byproduct of merely using electronic networks. Instead, like Broodthaers and Klein before them, Pope.L and Citarella have rigorously constructed apophatic apparatuses, cleverly situated within their own contemporary worlds. All four artists simply use whatever relevant materials and media are at hand.

Both *Compression Artifacts* and the *Black Factory* ultimately wind up exhausting their material apparatal structures. Citarella burns his gallery and Pope.L submits his truck to a series of punishing performances (and one installation) before finally donating it to a local homeless shelter. Yet this exhaustion of the physical object alone is not what makes these projects apophatic, any more than merely abandoning the art object for ephemeral Fluxus performance was ever able to side-step the commodifying (re-)capture of the art market. Apophatic apparatuses don't annihilate matter as much as undermine faith in fundamental presence and ontological stability. Just as deconstruction first adopts the trajectory of an argument in order to then undermine that argument from within according to the argument's own presuppositions and rules of engagement, so *Compression Artifacts* and the *Black Factory* begin with the presumed aura/presence of "the things themselves" (sculptural objects, donated objects) in order to "absence" these objects from within. Citarella uses Photoshop; Pope.L uses a blowtorch.

Both of these apparatuses are fairly complicated, so a good part of this chapter will simply be me explaining the logistical workings of the apparatuses themselves. Once we come to specifically understand the ways in which these apparatuses function, theoretical analysis of their accomplishments and implications should be a straightforward step away.

Compression Artifacts

Compression Artifacts was a group show curated by Joshua Citarella featuring work by Wyatt Niehaus, Kate Steciw, Brad Troemel, Artie Vierkant, and Citarella himself. All of these artists (particularly Vierkant and Citarella) make work that purposefully blurs the line between physical objects in a gallery and digital documentation of those objects online. The gallery was built in the woods in an undisclosed location. The physical construction of the gallery was streamed live on the internet. Once the gallery was constructed, the artworks were installed, and then documented photographically. The works were then de-installed, the gallery was disassembled, and everything (gallery and work) was burnt.

Documentation of the show was then posted to Citarella's web site in the form of digital photographs, a short

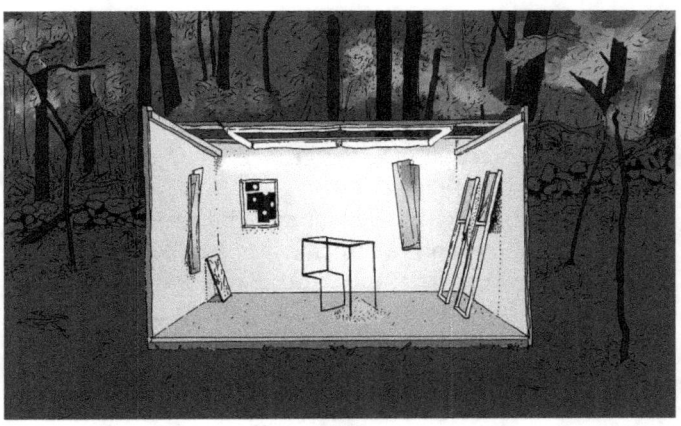

Fig. 2: An instantiation of Joshua Citarella's *Compression Artifacts.* Drawing by Jordan Cloninger.

low-resolution video, and an animated GIF.[1] Initially, the photographic documentation appears straightforward enough, but upon closer inspection, things begin to seem amiss. The gallery keeps changing dimensions, and the artworks themselves keep changing appearance and location. Artie Vierkant is known for printing large images of Photoshop "brush strokes," hanging these printed images in a gallery, taking digital photographs of these physical prints, adding more Photoshop brushstrokes to these digital photographs (of hanging physical prints of photoshop brush strokes), and posting these digital > physical > digital images online. It seems that the same type of approach is happening to the documentation of *Compression Artifacts,* but on a much more holistic, messy, entangled, nuanced, and difficult-to-parse scale. There is a pile of sand that seems obviously photoshopped. The marble of the floor must also be photoshopped. The sculpture in

1   Joshua Citarella, *Compression Artifacts,* http://joshuacitarella.com/artifacts.html.

the middle (Citarella's own piece) keeps changing shape and material, and at one point it is on fire, so those effects must be photoshopped. The gallery itself keeps changing dimensions, gaining a split level, gaining differently angled walls, increasing in length; so all of that must be photoshopped (see Fig. 2).

But what to make of the woods? The shots of the gallery interior show what we initially took to be a legitimate gallery somewhere in Manhattan, Paris, Berlin, London, or wherever. But the shots of the gallery in situ reveal it as a kind of stage set in the middle of some suburban looking woods. Has the gallery itself been photoshopped into the woods? It doesn't appear that way. So, if we are now convinced that the gallery really was constructed in the woods when we had initially taken it to obviously be some gallery on West 26th Street in Chelsea, then what else are we to believe and doubt?

Citarella has created an apparatus for confounding several presumed dichotomies: offline vs. online; analog vs. digital; material vs. immaterial; outside-the-machine vs. inside-the-machine; documentation as after-the-fact supplementary media vs. documentation as integral and ongoing conceptual component of the artwork itself; group exhibition as art-market-sanctioned event vs. group exhibition as (post-)internet-art performance project. *Compression Artifacts* (hereafter *CA*) would not have been able to achieve such confoundings by simply taking a digital image of the woods and photoshopping a Bigfoot into it. We are not amazed anymore by believable images of fantastic scenes. We see them all day long in Hollywood science fiction movies. We have grown suspicious of (and even indifferent to) their claims of veracity. *CA* does something much more clever than merely trick us into believing that something "fake" is "real" – it purposefully straddles the line between the believable and the dubious. We waver back and forth in our reading of the narrative of this project. And while we vacillate and hesitate, an intrinsic yet occult relationship begins to emerge between the value of contemporary gallery art, the value of Manhattan real estate, and the value of high-resolution photographic documentation.

On May 10, 2018 (five years after the project), Citarella announced on his Instagram account:

> Let's try something fun. Help me give *Compression Artifacts* the burial it deserves. I'm going to lottery off 10 containers of ash and we will scatter the remains around the world. I built the gallery in 2013 at an undisclosed location. After the show I demolished and cremated the remains and have been saving them ever since. The documentation images were so transformed in Photoshop that no one ever really knew what was there... people still ask if it was real to begin with. Signing up for $5 puts you in the lottery. Send me a video of you scattering the ash I'll throw in an extra ticket for next month's piece.[2]

This final act of networked distribution increases the dematerialization of the physical objects while simultaneously monetarily reifying the purely abstract and conceptual value that the project initially possessed. The announcement of the contest is distributed via Instagram. Lottery tickets are purchased via the micro-funding internet platform Drip. The ashes are distributed via the (semi-)analog network of the postal service. Presumably, some ashes will continue their distribution via river networks and wind currents. Finally, the digital traces of these physical distribution events will find their way back to the artist via email attachments and Instagram hashtags. All that is solid melts into air, flames, ash, and photoshop filters; only to return in the form of PayPal credit and (yet

2   @joshuacitarella, Instagram post, May 10, 2018, https://www.instagram.com/p/Bim-4a_njJV/?taken-by=joshuacitarella.

more) digital image documentation. This final act of (re-) distribution all the more deeply confounds and entangles all of the dichotomies mentioned above.

Confounding the Original/Mediated Dichotomy

Compression Artifacts calls into question both the primacy of the original object and the derivative nature of its mediated documentation by confusing the line between the two. For example, did the morphing sculpture begin its life as a steel object, a wooden object, or a 3D software image that was only later turned into a physical object? If it began as a physical object, which was the original object, the steel instantiation or the wooden instantiation? Or was the sculpture ever even a physical object? Was it ever physically present in the gallery, or has it only ever existed as a digital object? Was the photographic documentation not really documentation at all, but instead the "original" art object? For that matter, was the gallery itself ever physically present? Perhaps *CA* is not an art exhibition at all, but simply a digital photography project.

Deconstruction has already taught us that just because a mark came first, that doesn't mean it is inherently more relevant than its subsequent traces. So, let us set aside the concern about which instantiation of *CA* came first and assume for the sake of argument that the physical gallery is the "original" version. Perhaps the ultimate and final instantiation of the project is the most important, the final word, so to speak. But that won't do either, because the final instantiation of the project is vials of indiscriminate ashes that might or might not be from the physical exhibition, distributed to winning entrants throughout the world who only properly participate in the project (à la Klein's Zone of Immaterial Pictorial Sensibility) by scattering the ashes.

Perhaps we are asking the wrong questions by concerning ourselves with primary and ultimate instantiations.

Perhaps we should instead be trying to discern which of the instantiations (physical exhibition, online "documentation," networked distribution of ashes) is most fundamental, primary, and important to the project. But that won't do either, because they are all important to the overall functioning of the art apparatus. Like any proper apparatus (art, science, or otherwise), separating out the individual components and analyzing them separately interferes with the holistic functioning (and the "measurement results") of the entire apparatus. If I were to make a case for which of the instantiations is most important, my money would be on the internet-contingent instantiation (the online documentation). But that's not exactly right either, because without the physical installation, there would have been no livestream broadcast, no source images to tweak, and no ashes to distribute. Which brings us to the inescapable conclusion that the entire apparatus, including the physical gallery in the woods, is intrinsically internet-contingent. Likewise (and equally inescapable), the entire apparatus, including the online documentation and the distribution of ashes, is intrinsically contingent on the physical site-specificity of the gallery in the woods. Thus, nothing is made of our attempt to dissect and parse out the primary locus of the "art" within the apparatus. The art is what the entire apparatus winds up becoming; and in this particularly apophatic case, the *CA* apparatus winds up becoming a device to confound the dichotomies between originary vs. mediated, source vs. copy, presence vs. absence, logos vs. trace.

CA pits two equally wrong but well-entrenched mythologies against each other, and winds annihilating (or at least deeply problematizing) both. The first wrong mythology posits the modernist white cube gallery as a transcendental space of pure spiritual encounter between audience minds and image aesthetics. The second wrong mythology posits the "inside" of a computer (and its accompanying networks) as a non-physical, dis-embodied, transcendental space of pure data. Of course, neither of these mythologies is the least bit true. The art gallery is entangled and shot-through with economics, real estate markets, class and race presuppositions, grav-ity, air condition, track lighting, unpaid interns, art han-dlers, collector contracts, and bottles of wine. Likewise, the inside of a computer and its accompanying networks are entangled and shot-through with silicon, electricity, proprietary code, microchip architecture patent lawyers, underwater fiber optic cables, contested transfer proto-cols, New Zealand mineral mines, Indonesian manufac-turing plants, and non-European dump sites. *CA* doesn't simply and naively presume to undermine passé physi-cal gallery spaces with the new and virtual power of the internet. Instead, *CA* undermines, foregrounds, reconfig-ures, dallies-with, conflates, and further entangles both gallery and computer mythologies. Physical materials, concepts, aesthetics, networks, audiences, and markets are stretched, shrunk, intermingled, and modulated; not unlike Citarella's warped gallery documentation images.

What, ultimately, are the *"Compression Artifacts"* of *Compression Artifacts*? Technically, they are the signature blurs and bandings that incidentally result from digital image file compression formats (GIF, JPG, PNG, etc.). Ar-cheologically, they are the source artifacts of the actual gallery (the displayed digital prints and the sculpture, the wood used to build the gallery, and the burned ash rem-nants from the fire). Cognitively, they are the bits, pieces, and traces that remain in affective limbo after our failed, uncanny attempts to parse aspects of this project into clean categories of either "original" or "mediated."

Realism Matters

The confounding, apophatic, braking effect that *CA* achieves is predicated on the realism of its media. This is because humans are also part of the *CA* apparatus, and in order for our human dichotomies to be confounded, we need to believe certain things about the media with which we are presented. By "realism," I don't mean the hyper-realism of Hollywood special effects, or even solely the high-resolution of Citarella's digital images. By "realism," I simply mean that a given media element has the texture that our apperceiving bodies expect to receive, according to our normal, regular consumption of that medium. In the case of *CA*, these expected media textures persuade us that the objects/events mediated by the media were physical, and that they were actually installed somewhere in a physical location at an actual historical time. An image can't be *unheimlich* or unhomelike without there first being something homelike and familiar about it. The realism (expected texture) of the media is the lure, the bait on the hook. The not-quite-right, uncanny tweak of the media is the hook itself that brakes any business-as-usual, interpretive becomings.

Again, this kind of media realism is not inherently triggered by high-resolution mimeticism. Instead, it is achieved by an expected grain of the media that synchs-up-with and checks-out-with the networks (technical and economic) through which we are meant to believe the media has traveled. So, for instance, the low resolution of the short video feed at the *CA* web page is read by us as realistic, because we are meant to believe that it is a video screen capture of a live internet video stream. If the video were high resolution, we would read it as unrealistic. (The "truth" is, the entire livestream was not archived. Although the construction took several days, the live stream was only streaming during part of one day.[3]) Similarly, the high-resolution digital images of the gallery space also initially check out as realistic, because any

3   Joshua Citarella, interview with the author at Citarella's New York apartment/studio, April 21, 2017.

gallerist with a gallery that white and that cubed would have paid the requisite money to hire a professional art photographer to light and shoot her group show. One reason the texture and resolution of Citarella's digital images are so pitch-perfect is because he has a day job as a professional photographer documenting gallery art exhibitions.

In the case of *CA*, the actual choice of the sculpture and the prints included in the show is made in order to set up and prime the subsequent slippages in the texture and resolution of their digital documentation. The work in the gallery is created with the express purpose of sabotaging the seamlessness of its subsequent digital (re)distribution. This is exactly the opposite of an "old media" sculpture or photography show, where the sculptures and photographs are (ostensibly) chosen based on their aesthetic or conceptual merit in-and-of-themselves, with little regard for how they will appear in subsequent documentation. Then it simply becomes the job of the professional photographer documenting the show to make that Henry Moore sculpture look the best she can via lighting, shutter speed, tripod placement, depth of focus, etc. And yet, in the commercial gallery world, even this is not exactly true, because artists are regularly coached by gallerists to create works of certain dimensions (and even certain colors) so that the work will look more appealing in an online buyer catalog or will fit better over a collector's sofa.

The minimal geometric forms Citarella chooses for his sculptures are a way to focus viewers on the line between what is "fake" and what is "real," instead of focusing them on how aesthetically pretty the object itself is.[4] The sculptural forms are chosen not for any inherent aesthetic value, but because complex sculptural forms would be less confounding. Basic forms seem more readily present

4   Ibid.

and more easily readable in photographic documentation. When these seemingly easy-to-read forms suddenly begin slipping and changing, we are all the more fundamentally confounded. In this sense, *Compression Artifacts* is a holistic apparatus telescoping outward through art markets and digital networks. In the context of the overall *CA* project, the sculpture and the prints in the show don't really function as discrete, individual apparatuses (as they normally would in an urban gallery exhibition). There are no art patrons there in the woods to experience these pieces in the live, physical gallery context. Instead, the sculpture and the prints are actually the starter bait components of a much larger, holistic, apophatic art apparatus. They are the set-up for a punch line that comes much later.

There are some forms of contemporary sculpture (by Jon Rafman, for instance) meant to look in the gallery space as if they are physical instantiations of images from mediated space. If you were to take a realistic image of such sculptures, they would look as if they had been photoshopped, or as if your image's GIF or JPG compression algorithm had glitched. There are other forms of contemporary sculpture (by Olafur Eliasson, for instance) that are simply impossible to photograph altogether. Your body in the physical space apperceives a certain image (a circular rainbow, a refraction of light), but when you go to take a digital picture of it, what your body is seeing is uncapturable by the camera apparatus. And again, there are certain forms of "digital sculpture" (work curated by the online gallery *Panther Modern*, for instance) that are purposefully meant to be fantastic and physically impossible, designed to populate virtual galleries of non-physical space.

Citarella's sculptural object in *CA* is not really any of these three types of sculpture. It doesn't look like it came from the internet. It is not impossible to photograph. It is not meant to exist exclusively on the internet. It is really a fourth kind of sculpture meant to elude firm placement in either offline physical or online mediated space. By failing to settle down and neatly land in one space or the other, it acts as a kind of sabotaging wrench, munging up the works and sending off sparks along the physical–mediated divide. This kind of sabotage only works if the digital image of the sculpture reads believably as a representation of a physical object. This kind of realism is only possible if aspects of the sculpture are actually physical. According to Citarella, computer-generated 3D models of physical objects somehow lack the alchemy of physical stuff in the actual world. Physical materials that exists in space over time (marble, for example) reveal aspects of historical space and time.[5]

In *CA*, the dividing line between the physical and the mediated is so problematized, that four years after the project, Citarella himself could not remember which images were photoshopped and which were not. Some of the components that seem to me the most photoshopped (like the fire) were actually physical. Other components that seem to me the most "natural" (like several of the welded angles of the metal sculpture) were actually photoshopped.

Even the vertical order of the documentation on the web page is carefully choreographed to promote maximum confusion. The web page begins with images that seem believable, then gradually progresses to increasingly unbelievable images, ending with the low-resolution animated GIF which blatantly and unrealistically distorts the dimensions of the gallery.[6] The result is the braking of "resolution" (in both the technical and cognitive senses). The documentation exists across a range of technical resolutions, none of which seem to have the final word

5   Ibid.
6   Ibid.

on the accuracy and truth of the event; and the actual historical space of the gallery is cognitively irresolvable.

Citarella says the "art" of his work happens in both the physical space of the gallery and the subsequent documentation of that space. To him, it's not that a new third space is created. Instead, an uncanny effect is created by combining difficult and rigorous pre-Photoshop staging of physical objects with professional post-production Photoshop techniques.[7] A new space is not created (that would be making something), but rather the combination of two existing spaces is apparatally choreographed in such a way that an apophatic braking event is caused. The cognitive aporia induced by *CA* is in some senses even more disturbing than the cognitive aporia induced by the affective linguistics of Arakawa and Gins's *Mechanism of Meaning*. As humans, it is easier to dismiss linguistically induced aporia as "merely" a trick of language (even though language is itself a material force in the actual world). We are somehow less willing to dismiss photographically induced aporia. Evidently (even if the evidence is only in media textures), realism still matters.

Markets Matter/The Material of Markets

As mentioned above, although documentation of art exhibitions chronologically occurs after the creation of the artworks in the exhibitions, that doesn't mean that the documentation has no effect on the creation of the artworks, particularly if the art exhibitions occur in for-profit galleries. Furthermore, the size of the gallery itself affects the monetary value of the artworks on display. As a professional photographer of art exhibitions, one of Citarella's main jobs is to make the gallery look as large as possible. The logic goes like this: Manhattan real estate is expensive. The larger the gallery, the higher the rent.

7   Ibid.

The higher the rent, the more the gallerist must be making. She must be making all that money selling valuable art.[8] A bizarre, tail-wagging-the-dog effect is thus created whereby it becomes as important to make the gallery look large in your catalog images of the exhibition (because not all buyers will be able to attend the actual exhibition) as it does to make the art look good.

Compression Artifacts was inspired by all of these bizarre (real estate and art) market forces. If Citarella's photographic documentation of his own exhibition can make it look as if he and his friends had a group show in a large white cube Chelsea gallery, then it doesn't matter where the gallery is, even if it is a gallery he constructed himself miles outside of Manhattan in the woods. At least this is one of the tongue-in-cheek conceits of *CA*. Artists who wish to make money from their art are forced to consider not just the technical production of a single work of art, but also its subsequent reception, critical journalistic evaluation, catalog distribution, conceptual marketing, art fair booth hawking, sale, resale, institutional collection, eventual re-exhibition, and ultimate art-historical canonization. Given an awareness of this outwardly telescoping chain of forces, the fact that real estate markets and perspectival photographic techniques for enlarging architectural interiors would be relevant to a conceptual art project seems at least a bit less bizarre.

The fun and critical ingenuity of *CA* is that it takes these economic forces and throws a wrench in them, playfully grinding them to an aporetic halt (however briefly), all the while obscuring its overt "exposure" of them. The project doesn't read as straightforward "institutional critique." The *CA* apparatus doesn't merely cut out a large swath of the world called "the art market," point a didactic finger at it, and make something called "critical awareness." Instead, *CA* cuts out and follows the contours of

8   Ibid.

all of these market forces and digital networks in a way that causes these forces to publicly perform their own aporetic absurdity. Five-dollar transaction bits enter the apparatus, and ashes exit the apparatus. What is "made" in the interim is a kind of perpetually involuting Mobius strip, back and forth between offline and online, original and mediated, profit and profligation, object and image, art and dust.

The *Black Factory*

If *Compression Artifacts* cuts out a large swath of the world, the *Black Factory* (hereafter the *BF*) cuts out even more. Like *CA*, it too subsumes art institutions and art markets; but the *BF* moves well beyond them to chew on additional institutions like race, class, nationality, identity construction, difference, and gas mileage. Tempting as it is to launch right into the apparatal functionings of the *BF*, a pragmatic explanation of its myriad logistical functions is first in order before any theoretical analysis is even possible.

Pope.L initially imagined the *BF* as "a mobile art installation performance work that would travel not only geographically but also conceptually." It would be housed in "a truck renovated to function like a cross between a lending library, an old timey medicine show, and a field research laboratory."[9]

Although the *BF* is (mostly) housed in a truck, the project itself is not the truck, but is instead an installation and a performance (and an archive, and two websites, and a contest, and numerous conversations). Even the truck itself isn't just a single thing. The truck houses

9   William Pope.L, artist talk given at Center for Maine Contemporary Art, Rockland, Maine, August 4, 2004, available at http://theblack-factory/ceo_pages/ceo_2.htm.

several stations that expand on performance day. There is "the workshop" (also known as "the pulverizing station"), the store, the inflatable igloo archive, the "black object of the day," the online archive (accessible via a laptop in the back of the truck), the main website associated with the project (theblackfactory.com), and the auxiliary "Distributing Martin" website (distributingmartin.com) which is frequently linked to from the main website.

The *BF* project launched on May 8, 2004, at MASS MoCA as part of a group exhibition curated by Nato Thompson called *The Interventionists*. The truck went on three US tours, one per year, between 2004 and 2006. The tour stops were announced prior to the tour and people were invited to bring objects to the truck which they associated with blackness. On the day of the installation/ performance, the truck would show up at a town (usually sponsored by a local arts institution), set up the different stations, and each person of the three-member crew would begin to perform a "node." The nodes were structured interactive performances ultimately designed to engage visitors from the community in dialogue. There were around twenty different nodes, and these nodes would be repeatedly performed in cycles over a six-hour period. The black objects which community members brought were either photographed and archived in the online archive, and/or collected and added to the physical archive, or pulverized at the pulverizing station, the residue of which might be packaged and sold in the store.

Typically, each stop lasted a day and a half, although certain guerrilla stops (unplanned, unsponsored, spontaneous stops) might last as short as fifteen minutes. In 2004 there were six scheduled stops in four states over ten days. In 2005 there were twelve scheduled stops in fifteen states over six weeks. In 2006 there were twenty-four scheduled stops in twelve states over two months. That is the *BF* in a nutshell. Now for a more detailed explanation of each individual component.

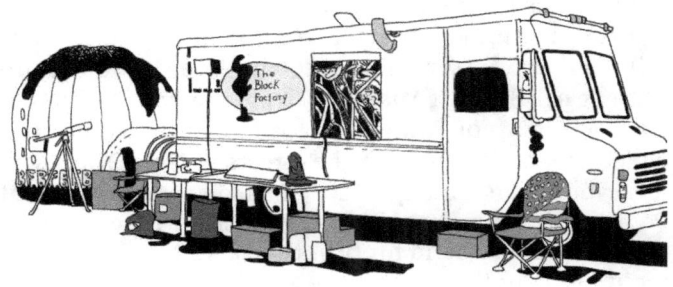

Fig. 3: The *Black Factory* installation set up, sans crew and audience. Drawing by Jordan Cloninger.

A More Detailed Explanation of the Individual *Black Factory* Components

The Truck Itself

The truck was a 22-foot long, 1989 GMC, Grumman Olson paneled step van (ice cream) truck weighing six tons. Its previous owner had used the truck for occasional fishing trips in Maine.[10] Once set up, with the attached inflatable igloo coming off the back of the truck, the entire installation was 54-feet long (see Fig. 3).

The cab of the truck, once parked and installed, expanded into the gift shop. In transit, the rear of the truck stored the igloo archive, the pulverization table, objects, props, and a sound system. Once parked and installed, the rear of the truck housed the computer station for accessing the online archive. Furthermore, according to

---

10   William Pope.L et al., "CEO page 5," *Black Factory*, http://www.the-blackfactory.com/ceo_pages/ceo_5.htm and William Pope.L et al., "the truck," *Black Factory*, http://www.theblackfactory.com/truck.html.

Pope.L, "The rear of the *BF* is also a work area [and ...] a hiding place for goof-off employees."[11]

After the third and final *BF* tour in 2006, the truck itself was used in several subsequent Pope.L projects. In 2009 at Art Basel in Miami it was partially buried under gunpowder. In 2011 it was used as a mobile projection unit which was pulled through the streets of New Orleans by local volunteers. Finally, in 2013, in a move reminiscent of Pope.L's own durational body crawls, the truck was pulled throughout Cleveland for twenty-five miles by a rotating group of volunteers. After the 2013 event, the truck was donated to 2100 Lakeside Men's Shelter in Cleveland.[12]

The Pulverization Station
The pulverization station is

> a set of 3 heavy duty plywood and steel tables whose tops, when properly assembled, resemble a contorted USA and Cuba. The tables are off-loaded at the vehicle's rear and set-up on the side of the truck along with a hefty array of tools and workshop gadgetry.[13]

In Pope.L's own playfully acerbic verse:

> We stand on this table. / Shout. Talk. Sing. Leap. Beg. Cajole. Shake in our boots. Act tough. Let our minds wander. Get the lack out. / Grind shit up on the table. Blind shit up on the table. Dance on the table. Spirit on the table. spit on the table... / Do experiments. Chew experience. Product the black that's out-of-wack. Serve enchiladas, watermelon, sauerkraut. feather, iron, saliva...blood...tums...[14]

11   William Pope.L, artist talk, August 4, 2004
12   William Pope.L et al., "the truck."
13   William Pope.L, artist talk, August 4, 2004.
14   William Pope.L et al., "overview," *Black Factory*, http://www.the-blackfactory.com/overview.html.

The pulverization station is one of the locations where nodes are performed. Here, "black" objects are pulverized via electric grinder, blowtorch, pestle and mortar, and other means.

The Gift Shop

In the gift shop, the staple items for sale include a rubber duckie stamped with the *BF* logo ($5), "limited edition good used soap" ($1,400), and a plastic Yoda head shrink-wrapped together with racist Ben Klassen's "white hate literature" *The White Man's Bible*. Also, for sale is powder from the pulverized donated black objects, packaged as if it were spice for your spice rack, labeled with a gold black factory sticker signed by Pope.L. Additionally, canned goods are sold and auctioned for several times their original value, and then that money is donated to local food pantries so that they can buy more canned goods. Pope.L calls this scheme "Twice Sold. [...] a perverse reverse of capitalism."[15] As described by Pope.L, the list of canned goods includes, "peas, corn, pork n' beans, pickled eggs (discontinued but hopefully coming back!), collard greens, peanut butter, tomato soup, evaporated milk (discontinued), airport candle, used soap, tee-shirts, used American flags, Tesco chicken curry (UK) and Sainsbury baked beans (UK)."[16] According to Pope.L, "The *BF* has a graduated pricing scheme and we love to give discounts, for almost any reason at all."[17]

The Igloo Archive

The Igloo Archive is an inflatable igloo with hanging shelving throughout, displaying a rotating selection of physical items that have been donated to the *BF* archive.

15   William Pope.L, artist talk, August 4, 2004.
16   William Pope.L et al., "products," *Black Factory*, http://www.the-blackfactory.com/products.html.
17   William Pope.L, artist talk, August 4, 2004.

The igloo has window-like openings for people to look in and view the items. It is attached to the back of the truck. According to Pope.L:

> Anyone may donate a black object. A black object is anything a person deems black or feels references blackness for them. The specific days for submitting black objects are called check days. During the tour, every day was check day.[18]

The Black Object of the Day

The black object of the day is one of the donated black objects from the physical archive, placed inside a box built into the side of the truck. According to Pope.L, "You can only access this box by putting your hands into holes cut into the side of the truck and feeling around for knowledge."[19]

The Nodes

The nodes are the interactive aspect of the *BF*. The number of nodes is variable. In 2005, during each six-hour installation, there were 20–25 different nodes. The nodes are performed in rotation. Once the rotation of nodes is completed, it is begun again, continually, until the six hours ends. Most nodes are short, around three minutes each.

According to Pope.L:

> A node is a chunk of time defined by an activity or an event. An installation can also be a node. All nodes are designed. Some are scripted. Some not. Improvisation is key in playing a node. [...] The function of a node is to engage the audience-participant in an inward-outward journey. Most nodes are built around a theme,

18   Ibid.
19   Ibid.

for example, stereotypical views of migrant workers in the U.S. Some are built around a gesture, such as giving away free watermelon. Most have a turning point where the meaning of what was first proposed is shifted to create a conflict or contradiction or enigma or silliness. All nodes have three parts: 1. the come-on, which is the invitation to engage, 2. the shift, which is the raising of the stakes of the invitation. It can also be the introduction of a problem that has to be solved. An audience-participant can also raise the stakes. [...] 3. the leave, what the performer and audience-participant glean from the interaction.[20]

One particularly successful node was developed and performed by Pasqualina Azzarello, crew member and Miss *Black Factory* 2005. The node involved a tarot reading with a custom set of tarot cards. The outcome of the reading always involved the exclamation, "Shazam!," and a prophesied shift in race, nationality, and gender for the participant.

I promised to defer my theoretical analysis until after the logistical explanations, but the shift within the node is the crux of the entire apparatus, so a bit of preliminary theoretical analysis is in order here. Pope.L's motto for the entire *BF* project is, "The *Black Factory* does not make blackness. we make something better: opportunity."[21] The nodes are the heart of the opportunity that is made, because they are the interpersonal contact points at which each individual community member most overtly intra-acts with the overall *BF* apparatus. The "shift" phase in the node is precisely the "nothing" that the *BF* makes. It is the *BF*'s most apophatic moment. The shift is the point at which the brakes are thrown on the participant's prior, operative understanding of her own culturally inherited

20   William Pope.L et al., "CEO page 5."
21   William Pope.L et al., "overview."

self-identity. The "leave" phase of the node is never pre-determined. Yes, something is always left. Something always becomes. But what that something is cannot be pre-determined. It must remain undetermined in order to allow the shift to truly occur and accomplish its braking work. Otherwise, we simply have one more series of pre-determined becomings, with the artist's pre-determined ideology engaging in the same tired/rote, partisan-driven agreements/disagreements with the participant's pre-determined ideology. Granted, "nothing" can never be permanently (or even briefly) maintained in a world of perpetual becomings. The wager of the *BF* is that after the hard brake of the shift (Shazam!), at least the opportunity to live otherwise in the world will be made. This opportunity is what is left, what emerges, what remains; and the specific nature of this opportunity is inherently different and personal, per person, per node.

Miss Black Factory

Miss *Black Factory* was a contest held in 2005 and again in 2006. Primarily the contest was a way to select one of the three members of the crew. Her duties were exactly the same as the other two members, except she held the title Miss *Black Factory*. The first contest announcement ran as a feature piece is the Spring 2005 edition of *Art Journal*, and also served as a promotion for the upcoming tour.

In order to be eligible,

Anyone may enter who is 18 years old or older, has a valid U.S. driver's license, and a major credit card. Also necessary are: a strong back, an enthusiasm for making social change, good people skills, the ability to use power tools, attendance at all *BF* rehearsals and tour activities, and collaboration with CEO Pope.L. A few not so necessary, but still excellent skill areas with which Miss *BF* might be familiar: community organizing, playing music, street theater, chemistry, ethnic culture, international law, political theory, baking, working in a factory, etc.[22]

Miss *Black Factory* 2005 was Pasqualina Azzarello and Miss *Black Factory* 2006 was Josh Atlas.

The Online Archive

The "DONATED BLACK OBJECT ARCHIVE" is an online archive accessible at http://www.theblackfactory.com/ archiveintro.html. It contains numbered pictures of black items that people brought to the *BF*, descriptions of those items, comments about the items by the people who brought them, numbered pictures of the people who brought them, and a series of questions answered by the people who brought them. Sometimes the items are donated for pulverization or collection in the physical archive. Other times, they are simply photographed for the online archive and then returned to their owners.

As of summer 2018, there were 934 donated objects in the online archive. Sometimes the pictures of the items and/or the donors are absent, in which case black place-holder images are put in their place, as "place holders for lost encounters."[23] Each item is assigned a color, but the colors are only ever accidentally associated with the items. The colors simply cycle in order. Seventeen items in a row will be listed as "blue," then the next seven will be listed as "clear," then the next thirteen will be listed as "white," and so on.

Here are the questions asked of each donor:

Black Object: _
Why donor chose object: _

---

22 William Pope.L et al., "miss bf contest," *Black Factory*, http://www.theblackfactory.com/contest.html.

23 William Pope.L et al., "archive," *Black Factory*, http://www.theblackfactory.com/archiveintro.html.

Date Donated: _
Color: [randomly assigned]
Donor Name: _
Age: _
Place of Birth: _
Nationality: _
Race: _
Ethnicity: _
Class: _
Religion: _
Sex: _
Gender: _
Current Residence: _
States/Counties/Countries you have lived in: _
Reaction to the experience of donating a black object:
_

On the 2006 tour, the following questions were added:

Do you feel that Affirmative Action only benefits blacks? Why? Why not?
If you had a daughter and/or son is there any race from which you would not want them to marry? Why? Why not?
Should undocumented workers a.k.a. illegal immigrants be allowed to remain in the US? Why? Why not?
Should the US withdraw from Iraq? Why? Why not?
Should Israel give land back to the Palestinians? Why? Why not?

The objects donated range from thoughtful items that people have obviously prepared to bring after viewing the *BF* invitation in advance, to things that passers-by simply had in their pockets. Jazz CDs are inordinately represented. There are many items associated with Africa. Sometimes people take picture of their hair. Some items (particularly books) seem to have been donated by Pope.L himself (since he references the same books in texts about the *BF*). There is also a photograph of a vagina, and a photograph of a penis (both from anonymous donors).

Upon entering the website for the entire *BF* project (theblackfactory.com), the visitor is led through a series of randomly sequenced introductory pages of various phrases and colors. Oftentimes, a randomly selected photograph of a black object from the online archive will appear on one of these introductory pages.

distributingmartin.com

distributingmartin.com is a website in the form of an interactive, multimedia, blog-like journal. As of summer 2018, distributingmaratin.com itself never links to theblackfactory.com, but various pages throughout theblackfactory.com link to various pages throughout distributingmartin.com. In this sense, distributingmartin.com serves as an auxiliary site, or a back-story site, or a supplementary site, or at least a companion site to the *BF* project website.

distributingmartin.com contains journal entries beginning at the date of Pope.L's conception ("15, or 18, or 23 October 1953") and continuing into an imagined future where Martin Luther King Jr.'s DNA has been distributed throughout the world and has altered all humans. The journal entries talk about Pope.L's old band (sardonically named John Wayne), his family, his old girlfriend, a novel he wants to write, his moving to Maine, his teaching, and the offline *distributingmartin* project. For the offline *distributingmartin* project, in 2001 Pope.L pasted posters throughout New York City that read, "THIS IS A PAINTING OF MARTIN LUTHER KING'S PENIS FROM INSIDE MY FATHER'S VAGINA" in white letters on a black background.

The blog entries are written in a non-linear, hypertext fashion, with words from each entry linking across the site to (mostly) personal photographs, other blog entries, fragments of the novel-in-progress, notes for the project, various cryptic instructions and plans, and newspaper clippings about DNA experiments and biomatter theft.

The site lists "13 reasons to make a blog about spreading MLK's body parts all over the Universe." Reason #1: "fingers, toes, eyes, & ears are better in the stars, mountains, and clouds but easier to reach on MACs and PCs."

The site lists 12 steps to the completion of the long-term distributingmartin project. Step #8 is "Peace." The first three paragraphs of this step are worth quoting in full:

Step 8: Peace

The Peace Gene Project is a bio-engineering enactment in which genetic material from Martin Luther was obtained and re-tooled with the help of artists and scientists from MQXRRSWQRXLRLLQDXIXQBDGGSJRRA-BSXSLT, who participated in a special interdisciplinary program encouraging projects between specialists in different fields.

King's genetic material was obtained via a lucky fluke. The possibility of a degraded or polluted sample is not out of the question. Regardless, the material was re-built, retrained, and retrofitted with new mechanics and subsequently re-introduced to the human body via the eating of fruit on sale in supermarkets, whereupon, after being ingested the MLK gene (or MILK gene) 'turns on' and replicates at an incredible rate: its motor was modeled on the amazing replication ability of the HIV virus. The MILK gene then seeks out receptor sites on a rogue protein curiously called the 'Peace Gene' and interacts with it to create fresh biological, social, and political environments, matrixes and potentialities within the human host.

Of course, the exact nature of these new environments can never be completely known. Interestingly enough, the outcome focus is very similar to African vodoun rituals where a simple shift of wind may drastically alter the effectiveness of a spell or action. The so-called Peace gene (like the so-called Gay gene) is surrounded by much debate. Other names for the Peace gene are: the Flying Dutchman gene, the Ghost gene, or simply PG. Many thinkers do not so much doubt the existence of the PG as simply doubt the ability of humans (who are naturally bent to self-destruction) to take advantage of such a provocative biological resource.[24]

In a sense, the offline *distributingmartin* project is a precursor and companion to the *BF,* just as distributingmartin.com is a precursor and companion to theblackfactory.com. *distributingmartin* is the imaginary distribution of DNA (to the stars, mountains, and clouds), and the actual internet distribution of a viral opportunity to imagine a future that might be otherwise; *BF* is the actual geographical distribution (stop by stop, town by town, state by state) of that same opportunity.

The Documentation

theblackfactory.com contains media documentation from the three tours in the form of the online black object archive, still photographs of the performances, short video promotional materials for the project, much writing by Pope.L poetically explaining the project in the persona of the *BF* CEO, and two separate written accounts of community members who attended performances. In 2005, Craig Saddlemire made a documentary film called *Get Off The Truck: Black Factory Rehearsal 2005,* which chronicled the training of the 2005 crew members by Pope.L, but there is little footage in Saddlemire's documentary of any actual nodes being performed. In 2015, The Museum

---

24 William Pope.L, "Step 8: Peace," *Distributing Martin,* http://www.distributingmartin.com/Page08A.html.

of Modern Art acquired some physical items from the *BF* archive for their permanent collection (more on this acquisition later). As mentioned, the truck was donated to a homeless shelter in 2013.

An Analysis of the Holistic Functioning of the *Black Factory* Apparatus

Now that the logistical components of the *BF* have been explained, we are ready to consider the ways in which it holistically functions as an apophatic art apparatus. Prior to my own analysis, I want to let the CEO of the *BF* have his own say regarding the project, its goals, its purpose, and its function.

The CEO of the Black Factory on the Function of the Black Factory

The *Black Factory* was built to explore the space between what we think we know and what we can imagine.[25]

[The Factory] encourages us to take hold of the stereotypes of race and class which bind us to our indecision and apathy and to turn them inside out. It challenges us to grapple with the habitual ways in which we consume products, identities, and ideologies.[26]

The *BF* travels throughout America (or as much of it as we can afford on three miles a gallon), bringing possibility and the glaring light of amusement, boredom, pushy conversation and a flaky utopianism wherever it's needed most.[27]

25 William Pope.L, artist talk, August 4, 2004.
26 William Pope.L et al., "CEO page 3," *Black Factory*, http://www.the-blackfactory.com/ceo_3.htm.
27 William Pope.L et al., "the truck,"

[The *Black Factory*] travels throughout America seeding difference where it is needed.[28]

The *Black Factory* makes [...] the opportunity to make a new blackness. And what is this new XXXXXXX? Difference! A boutique lackness. A lackness on the beach. And – where is this this this – reach? Well, where is your frolitics? Lying on its multi-ethnic towel boiling under a hot, hot, hot pun.[29]

Our big thing is to be clumsy, very earnest and manipulative and imperfect in the face of beliefs like:
1) everything matters
2) nothing matters unless you got money then nothing matters because you got money
3) nothing matters unless you are you and nothing but you because you are the center of the XXXXX so help you god and there is no god except you how lonely[30]

Finally, here is Pope.L (more or less) as Pope.L, applying for a Guggenheim Fellowship in 2002, two years prior to the first *BF* tour:

[The *Black Factory* is] at once a mobile marketplace that trades in provocation and a nomadic laboratory for crafting consciousness.

I want to make "crucibles" for blackness. These crucibles are art works that have two functions: 1) to protect, validate and enshrine blackness; 2) to isolate, imprison and obfuscate blackness. The drama of these

28 William Pope.L and Patricia C. Phillips, "Artist Project," *Art Journal* 64, No. 1 (Spring 2005): 51.
29 William Pope.L et al., "overview."
30 Ibid.

two opposing forces, at odds with each other, circum-
scribes a contradictory blackness.

To me, blackness is a many-sided hole. Or more paradoxically, a hole within a hole within a hole and so on.
When I say this I simply mean an open-ended nature
that is not about blackness but the world itself. The
Black Factory is the concrete expression of this sort of
thinking. It is the experiment with which I will test
this very hypothesis.

By collecting, recycling and peddling the ingredients
for re-thinking blackness, The *Black Factory* transforms
the tensions and contradictions of race into a dynamic
field of possibility.[31]

The *BF* CEO is well aware of the apophatic function of his
factory, and poetically describes this function in admirably apophatic language, pitch-perfectly aligned with the
tone of the project itself. Perfectly apophatic is the correlation between black and lack, and the idea that a hole-y
lack might contain within it the bastard seeds of a holy
fecundity. The *BF* CEO presents the factory as one very
rigorous, complex, and exhaustive way of seeing what
new possibilities might arise from pitching oneself, a
few crew members, and dozens of communities headlong
into the aporetic, telescoping hole of (b)lackness.

The Black Factory *Slams on the Brakes of Rote Becoming,
Leaving the Door Open for X*
The *BF* makes nothing of (i.e., brakes the rote and cyclical becoming of) inherited, status quo, historical modes
of capturing, oversimplifying, and binarily delineating
(black/white) actually nuanced differences. As men-

---

31   William Pope.L, "CEO page 1," *Black Factory,* http://theblackfactory.
com/ceo_pages/ceo_1.htm.

tioned above, these apophatic brakes are most forcefully applied during the "shift" phase (the second phase) of the various performance and installation nodes. This hard braking is designed to produce an instantaneous opening-up toward reconfigurable difference(s), creating a brief worm hole into possibly othered becoming(s). This temporary wormhole is the productive opportunity that the factory makes. It makes a kind of open placeholder for future encounters. The labor of the *BF* is to do everything in its power to keep this wormhole open for as long as possible, to stall, ward off, and keep at bay its inevitable collapse and closure. This hole-stabilizing labor is accomplished on as many fronts as possible: by deferring the inevitable museological canonization of the *BF* so that it may properly run its institution-eroding course; by not overdetermining the performance nodes and by allowing the crew members to participate in the organic development and improvisational enaction of the nodes; and by letting the crew drive the truck away on the tour while the artist–CEO stays at home.

The *BF* makes nothing of all institutions (financial, national, socioeconomic, artistic) that would attempt to suck the project into their own contextualizing apparatuses. Instead, the *BF* lures and sucks those institutions into its own gaping apparatus, leaving the door open for whatever else may enter and exit. The *BF* is a brave project because of its scope, its openness, and its vulnerability toward being captured by other contextualizing institutions. This vulnerability (the artwork "looks like" a silly vaudeville ice cream truck cum inflatable igloo) actually functions as a lure that allows the *BF* to entice, trap, and capture topics like race, religion, gender, income, and housing; tweak them; and release them into the worm hole. The *BF* makes nothing of itself being made something of (some thing of), in order for it to make nothing of other institutional somethings.

The *BF* CEO states, "Someone once told me: 'The *BF* stages a kind of moral constipation.' I said to myself: 'That's cool. what does it mean?' It's a question that has to be asked and re-casted over and over again."[32] The *BF* stops-up previously configured and calcified ethical flows, in order to hold open the bung hole of becoming long enough for X to emerge.

Humor is part and parcel of the *BF* apparatus, as is self-deprecation, as is absurdity; because bald-faced earnestness can become a kind of codifying trap that propels one forward into already-proscribed, rote, partisan, cyclical becomings. Humor puts the brakes on these binarily determined, pre-scripted re-dialogues and re-debates. It sets the stage for something else to happen other than the same old presumptions leading to the same old binary positions leading to the same old circuitous arguments.

Pope.L says of humor:

> Humor is a water-soluble, personal lubricant made social. I like the idea that when people laugh their mouths open and all sorts of things can fall in – bits, ideas, cracks, sites, very tiny police-persons, subversives, dust, hope – an erotics of humor must be cathected to the flesh as well as the waste of the flesh – the castoff flavors that ooze out of our tittering and guffaws and nervous nelly-a-tions – humor can be used as a structure that dis-a-wows while building an architecture of what-the-fuck.[33]

In the same interview, Pope.L says of binary contradiction:

---

32 William Pope.L et al., "overview."

33 William Pope.L, "William Pope.L on 'Acting a Fool' and Alternative Futures," interview with William Pope.L. by Samuel Jablon, *Hyperallergic*, July 10, 2015, https://hyperallergic.com/221452/william-pope-l-on-acting-a-fool-and-alternative-futures/.

Contradiction. Don't exist in the real world. What I mean is, in a way, contradiction is too logical, too closed off and neat and packageable-like – similar to opposites, contradiction is frequently understood as figured on binaries. Bargain basement epistemology. But contraries, which I prefer, are more fflaky (note: keep the extra "f" for fucking or flucking or...), so they are more the knot one encounters on the ground where most of us crawl. Acting a fool. To be contrary. To act the fool. To act your act off. To disappear the ass in presencing the act. To put your foot in in in in someone else' ass –[34]

The *BF* CEO doesn't know exactly where the *BF* will lead, but humor and undermining inherited dichotomies are two apparatal mechanisms that lead to that wherever. The only guaranteed outcome provided by the *BF*'s hard braking apparatus is the guarantee that eventually, here and there, catch as catch can, new opportunities for re-configuration will be created. What these opportunities are and where specifically they lead is a massive speculative wager. As Pope.L concedes, "Part of doing this work is to let it go, is to not be so afraid to have a work that you can't control. But you pay for that."[35]

Lest I put too much emphasis on the punk rock, "slam the brakes on in order to make nothing of rote becoming" aspect of the *BF*, I also want to focus on the final "leave the door open for X" aspect of the *BF*. If the first two node stages (the come-on and the shift) are the bait-and-switch, apophatic trap of the *BF* apparatus; then the final node stage (the leave) is the necessarily courteous but no less essential "easing-off of the emergency brake in order to accelerate into whatever new directions have

34 Ibid.
35 William Pope.L, in Craig Saddlemire, "Black Factory (Teaser)," *Vimeo*, March 25, 2014, http://vimeo.com/90020782.

emerged" part of the *BF* apparatus. This third phase is the self-revelatory phase for the community member, who is invited during the leave to articulate her own self-revelations to the participating *BF* crew member, further historically actualizing the virtual potentia which began to ingress during the shift phase. Pasqualina Azzarello (Miss *Black Factory* 2005) noted that it was not enough for the participant to merely have a revelation, but that the node encounters were purposefully constructed so that the participant was then able to articulate this revelation to a total stranger, when just thirty seconds prior, the participant had not even had the revelation.[36]

In order for participants to feel comfortable enough to share their own immediate self-revelations with total strangers, a very intentional kind of courtesy and care had to be produced by the *BF*. The creation of this safe space (the space of "the leave") was just as much a part of the *BF*'s tactical ingenuity and success as its creation of the uncomfortable "shift" space. According to Azzarello, the two spaces operated in tandem: "There was something in the discomfort that made people speak. There was a pressure for people to respond [...]. But at the same time, there was a sense of safety where people could share."[37] To Azzarello, the actual "product" produced by the *BF* was the responses that the community members gave. Beyond just producing responses, the gift that the *BF* returned to its participants was allowing them "to inhabit their own experience."[38] Pope.L had obviously placed a great deal of trust in the *Black Factory* crew members. What was less immediately obvious to me, but what Azzarello was quick to point out, was the amount of trust Pope.L had also placed in the participating community members.[39]

---

36 Pasqualina Azzarello, telephone interview with the author, July 25, 2018.
37 Ibid.
38 Ibid.
39 Ibid.

In order for the *BF* apparatus to allow each participant to inhabit and articulate her own experience of race, the *BF* had to maintain a fine-tuned balance between under-determining and overdetermining her experience. Had Pope.L underdetermined the come-on and shift phases (by leaving them out altogether), the participants would have had a very rote, impersonal, superficial, party-political, pre-scripted conversation about race in the US. On the other hand, had he overdetermined the "leave" phase by preaching his own political agenda to the participants, they would have been left with someone else's relationship to race in the US without being allowed to consider anew the ways in which their own constructed identities and personal histories were colored by blackness.

In a reflective piece Azzarello wrote just after returning from the 2005 *BF* tour, she observes, "it seems there is a gap. not just between the self-image this country projects and its internal daily reality, but between our own ideas of this reality and how people actually inter-relate when room is made for the possibility to see things differently. the smoke that the black factory generates, this symbol of proof that transformation is taking place, seeps into this gap and it makes its boundaries and limitations known, makes them visible, and serves to create a more holistic understanding of what a resource this can be, when made use of."[40] This observation resonates with Pope.L's own understanding of the potential agency of holes. Where there are gaps (between institutionally whitewashed histories and actually lived histories, between de facto inherited self-identities and more purposefully constructed "selves"), then there are always opportunities for productive slippage.

40 Pasqualina Azzarello, "insides-out: an intimate look at the black factory by pasqualina azzarello, miss black factory, 2005," privately published, 2005.

The Black Factory *Negotiates Its Own Contingency Upon Art Institutions*

The *BF* was funded by grants from arts institutions, and its regularly scheduled stops were sponsored by local art institutions. It even began its life in an art show at MASS MoCA, a major art institution. Hilariously (to me, at least) but inevitably (I suppose), in 2015, the Museum of Modern Art acquired objects from the *BF* archive for its permanent collection. Tellingly, the March 2015 Artforum news article reporting the acquisition reads:

> MoMA [...] added William Pope.L's The *Black Factory*, 2004–2006, to its collection recently – a collection of objects, films, commercial products, props, and documents associated with the artist's performance tour project across the United States.[41]

As if the entire *BF* project could be reduced to and reside within a few physical objects and media related to it. At the MoMA web site, their online catalog entry is a bit less reductive and a bit more accurate: "The *Black Factory* Archive / 2004–ongoing / Medium: Archive with 210 items, including objects, multiples, ephemera, digital image files, and a film / Dimensions: Various dimensions"[42]

So, a mobile performance/installation laboratory with its own online object archive has now been "collected" by a major art institution and entered into *its* online archive. Appropriately (at least as of summer 2018), there is only a placeholder image at the MoMA online catalog web page for the *BF* archive that says "Image not available." If anything, like Broodthaers's *Museum of Modern Art, Department of Eagles*, the collecting, museological nature of the

---

41 "Museum of Modern Art Acquires Jasper Johns Sculpture," *Artforum*, March 17, 2015, http://artforum.com/news/museum-of-modern-art-acquires-jasper-johns-sculpture-50855.

42 "Pope.L, The Black Factory Archive, 2003–ongoing," *Museum of Modern Art*, https://www.moma.org/collection/works/182201.

BF project itself insured that, once another museum tried to collect it, the ordinarily invisible mechanisms of the institutional act of collecting and canonizing could not help but be revealed. The *BF* was booby-trapped from the beginning to foreground the culturally commodifying, value-adding function of the art museum apparatus. Like a sabotaging wooden shoe, the *BF* allows itself to enter into the art-institutional mechanism, in order to throw a wrench in that same mechanism. A black factory for munging up a white-(cube), white-(run) factory.

The acquisition of ephemera from the *BF* by the MoMA might seem like a conceptual failure or an ethical sell-out, but the stated goal of the *BF* apparatus was never blatant institutional critique. The *BF* was never really anti-art-institution. It always had bigger institutional fish to fry. If collecting art museums wanted a piece of the *BF* action (and Pope.L anticipated they eventually would), the apparatal doors of the *BF* were always already open for this intra-action. The primary focus of the *BF* was never on museums anyway, but always on the individual personal encounters that community members had with the *BF* apparatus. The ephemera that the MoMA collected will never be able to reduce, encapsulate, finalize, and deaden those individual encounters. Because of the way the CEO has structured the evolution of the *BF* project over time, the only thing these pieces of collected ephemera can ever really do is instigate further individual, personal encounters with the (ghost of the) *BF* – a kind of Shazam 2.0. MoMA may have the physical *BF* archive, but the internet will always have the (much more expansive) online object archive, and Cleveland still has the truck.

Although the goal of the *BF* is not *solely* or even *primarily* to resist institutional commodification and archiving, such resistance is still at least one of its goals. As Pope.L himself clarifies (regarding his overall art practice):

Is resistance to the art market essential for performance art? Did its celebrated slippery resistance ever truly exist? Is resistance an obsolete concept for today's consumers? / For my money, resistance to established power is always necessary, even if, especially if, the established power is radical, avant-garde, or subversive. / Or a gleaming castle on a hill that sells artworks, snacks, and central heating.[43]

At any rate, the *BF* was already collecting art institutions long before art institutions were collecting it. *Black Factory* Donated Object Number 168 is a black-colored keychain and cards from Maine College of Art's gallery, the Institute of Contemporary Art, donated on June 20, 2004, by Sarah Schuster. "Why donor chose object: Hi William, the ICA needed to be recycled back to the *Black Factory* I think!"[44] And *Black Factory* Donated Object Number 248 is a catalog from the Cleveland Institute of Art donated by Tina Cassara on June 8, 2015, at the *BF* stop sponsored by the Cleveland Institute of Art. Cassara describes the donated object as "The Cleveland Institute of Art" itself. "Why donor chose object: A black hole, the invisible within the larger blackness."[45] Holes within holes within holes.

Regarding institutional support along the tour, the *BF* CEO is aware of it, and negotiates it as a kind of necessary evil. But his heart really is in the bare streets. He explains, "In a way, as a way, the *BF* is always performing. Rain or shine, we deliver the gusto so the cracks show.

With high gas prices, the truck getting 9 miles to the gallon [...] we'll continue to waste gas and do guerrilla stops whenever we feel like it (though they can be the

43 William Pope.L, "Canary in the Coal Mine," *Art Journal* 70, No. 3 (2011): 56–57.
44 From the *Black Factory* online archive, http://www.theblackfactory. com/archiveintro.html.
45 Ibid.

toughest cause there is no institutional net to catch you when you fall), in fact, we have to do guerrilla stops! They are our politic-colonic. The crew might disagree, especially after a particularly grueling stop but no matter it's what makes us go.

What be a guerrilla stop? That's when we go to a place, park the truck and trek out to meet the natives sans beads and blankets, sans muskets and powder, sans truck, sans spectacle, sans theatrical frame, sans the confidence provided by our familiar. Whatever you want to call it, we leave as much of it behind as possible and go native.

We have problems getting venues to fund this guerrilla-thing, it has an elegant framelessness so it's difficult to "product" so they don't trust it. Even I have a hard time with guerrilla stops but that's what happens when you let more life in —[46]

One particularly noteworthy guerrilla stop was the last stop on the 2005 tour. Scheduled by Pope.L at the last minute, it was meant to be a video documentation opportunity in a remote, unpopulated location. The crew members were to perform for an absent audience while being filmed. Instead (as described by Azzarello), "we pulled in and did our job. we sang our song and carried on audaciously for the butterflies, rocks and trees. we were there for all of ten minutes when two atv riders pulled in. then some hikers. then a mom and her children. then one of the atv riders called his father, who showed up moments later. among them were a student, a soldier, two factory workers, a mother, a child and a cop. and there we were, in the middle of the goddamn woods, with an audience, and conversation that was among the very richest of the entire tour."[47] One of the ATV riders was shipping

46 William Pope.L, et al., "overview."
47 Azzarello, "insides-out."

out to serve in Iraq the next day. The other ATV rider, his best friend, was opposed to the war.[48] In this particular instance, even when the expressed intent was to acquire documentary footage for some future, art-institution-aware, archival purpose, the *BF* apparatus could not help but intra-act with local humans.

Regarding art-institutional funding of the tours themselves, it only ever covered part of the costs. The CEO explains:

> Why do it in this particular way? Why an art object that loses money? Why a truck that gets 4 miles to a gallon of gas? Why a CEO, yours truly, who during every two week rehearsal period develops medical problems? Why do it? Why do it this way? [...] To fear a little less. To be encouraged a little more. To take a risk that I could share with others.[49]

The Black Factory *Operates across Multiple Scales of Time*

The *BF* is an ambitiously perspicacious apparatus operating across multiple scales of time. The *BF* is not just a series of three summer tours that occurred between 2004–2006. As mentioned above, it also anticipates (negotiates, and partially evades) its own eventual museological capture/collection, which doesn't happen until nine years after the tour is completed. Pope.L continues to maintain the online black object archive, and both web sites at theblackfactory.com and distributingmartin.com. distributingmartin.com reaches into the past (beyond Dr. King's assassination and right up to Pope.L's conception) and into the future (when the MILK peace gene is distributed to all humans). The questions on the black object donation questionnaire about Israel–Palestine re-

---

48 A photograph of this encounter is viewable at http://www.theblackfactory.com/images_hiatus/10-cairo/csp-20.jpg.

49 William Pope.L et al., "CEO page 5."

lations and US immigration paranoia continue to haunt the world. If anything, these issues have only intensified and become more relevant since they were added to the donation questionnaire in 2005.

As an archive of objects, the *BF* operates as a kind of memory modulation machine. It separates the subjective personal associations from individual objects and redistributes them amongst an entire archive of other memory-laden objects. Personal memories are mixed with cultural memories. "Black" memories are mixed with "white" memories. Entire objects, memories, and histories are pulverized, fine-grainedly shuffled, and fundamentally reconstituted. In this sense, the *BF* is mnemonically porous: a hole-y, memory-filtering sieve. Rather than merely being a cultural memory repository (which all archives are), the *BF* purposes to be a memory modulation factory (which most archives also are, but don't realize that they are). The *BF* breaks apart, rearranges, and reconstitutes new cultural memories. Memories from the past made new for the future.

The Black Factory *Is Designed to Modulate Its Own Crew Members*

The performative nodes were not just meant to brake, switch, and open up participating community members. In order for the *BF* to truly brake the old and make new opportunities for X, the *BF* crew members also had to be improvisationally and intuitively open to where the conversations and events might lead. If the *BF* was to create new opportunities in the world, then the crew members couldn't merely show up with their own bag of pre-packaged opportunities. That would only be a mobile opportunity distribution unit. Whereas the *BF* was supposed to be a mobile opportunity creation factory. As described by the CEO:

BF nodes sometimes had a clear goal, sometimes the only goal was to get at a feeling, not a position. To do this, a performer needed to reject final answers yet accept the performance situation. So – no matter what I say in these notes, no matter how confident they might sound, the on-going challenge was always to arrive at and accept a radical in-betweenness that disturbs.[50]

This radical performative openness was a lot to ask of a small set of three crew members, all under thirty years old, somewhere in the middle of Ohio, with Pope.L back in Maine. The CEO explained:

At the end of each day we'd talk on the phone. The crew would describe their successes and challenges and I'd offer perspectives and direction. There were two main challenges: 1) could or should they, as a primarily white crew, really engage people in a discussion about blackness? And 2) was blackness the end goal?

I answered their queries in this way: 1) you have to own the challenge. Whatever it is. Maybe you are black and you don't know it? Or are not willing to admit it? Perhaps being black is a matter of commitment like being honest or being true or being free. I answered #2 like so: blackness is a conduit to speak about differences.[51]

Pope.L did more than challenge and offer support. He ongoingly fine-tuned the functional logistics of the *BF* apparatus based on crew member feedback. According to Pasqualina Azzarello, "he listened after every performance to the lengthy lists of discoveries and challenges. he then privately ingested what he heard, and before each

50 William Pope.L, "CEO notes," *Black Factory*, http://www.theblackfactory.com/ceo_notes.html.
51 William Pope.L, artist talk, August 4, 2004.

and every show new additions were integrated into the mix: new characters, new approaches, new baubles in the pockets."[52]

From my own research of the project, it seems to me that the people whom the *BF* changed the most were the crew members and Pope.L himself. From the beginning, the *BF* was set up to be self-replicating. It was never meant to be permanently run by a group of experts in the know for a group of community members awaiting enlightenment. The CEO even includes these instructions for how to make your own *Black Factory*:

Reach out to someone.
Do this over and over and over AND OVER again.
If you take BACK YOUR HAND. It's ok. IT'S OK.
Count to 5. THEN—
Put it out there again.
Keep doing this. OVER AND OVER AND OVER AGAIN—

You will notice after a while THAT
The clarity you initially possessed EVAPORATES AND
Any sense of system YOU ONCE HAD is NOW in bits and doubts and tatters—
This is how to make your own *BF*—

NOW[53]

Summary: Two Macro-Cosmic Apophatic Apparatuses

Pope.L's *Black Factory* and Joshua Citarella's *Compression Artifacts* are both apophatic art apparatuses that cut out

---

52 Azzarello, "insides-out."
53 William Pope.L et al., "make your own bf," *Black Factory*, http://www.theblackfactory.com/make_your_bf.html.

large swaths from the institutional world. The danger of such macroscopic engagements is always that your own apparatus will be folded into and recontextualized by the larger institutions with which you are trying to intra-act. This is (probably) ultimately inevitable. The game is to see how long you can defer your own commodification, and how many ways can you anticipate and thus steer your eventual commodification. How many wrenches can you throw into the institutional works? How can you throw the brakes of inevitable institutional becoming in such a way that new and heretofore unimagined ways of becoming might emerge? Not anti-institutional becomings or even alter-institutional becomings, but new ways of becoming that tweak the institutions themselves. How do you bait the institutions to swallow the trap of your apparatus? And how does your apparatus then deploy itself once inside those institutions, to mung up their de facto works? Much is at stake for art apparatuses that cut out such large and well-established chunks of the world.

Glossing Deleuze and Guattari's cosmology of stratification and territorialization, Brian Massumi explains:

The force of collective, expressive emergence will be streamed into stratified functions of power. Unless the collectivity in the making resists pick-up by an established stratum, insisting on defining its own traits, in a self-capture of its own anomaly. In this case, they will retain a shade of the unclassifiable and a margin of unpredictability in the yes (or net) of existing systems of reference, no matter how hard those systems try fully to contain them [...] (especially if the collective learns to creatively shed its traits as confidently as it cultivates them) [... The atypical expression] must extract itself from captures ready and waiting, falling for an instant through the propositional mesh.[54]

Not only do *BF* and *CA* resist commodification and fall through the nets of institutional capture, on their way down they manage to mung up and slice into those institutional nets. Then they take the scraps of institutional netting that they have torn loose, and use those scraps to fashion hole-riddled wings for plummeting down newly emergent black holes.

54 Brian Massumi, "Introduction: Like a Thought," in *A Shock To Thought: Expression after Deleuze and Guattari,* ed. Brian Massumi (London: Routledge, 2005), xxviii–xxix.

6

THEORY TRAPS:
HAIM STEINBACH'S OBJECT
ENSEMBLES

Since the 1970s, Haim Steinbach's art practice has (mostly) involved arranging and displaying various objects on shelves. The shelves are specifically constructed to display the particular objects they are displaying. The objects are not affixed to the shelves; they merely rest on them. The shelves are usually colored in some way that correlates to the color of the objects, and often the shelves have two tiers. These custom shelving units displaying their accompanying objects are meant to be installed on walls, usually at about chest height, either in a collector's home, a gallery, or a museum.

These ensemble shelf/object pieces function as lures and traps for human-generated critical and theoretical perspectives about objects and their relationship to humans and other objects. It is in this sense that Steinbach's object ensembles function as apophatic art apparatuses. Surprisingly, numerous competing theories about objects are readily accommodated by Steinbach's work.

It might be objected that *all* art accommodates multiple interpretations, each of which may be convincingly supported by a number of equally valid critical perspectives.

I disagree. A Rembrandt self-portrait inherently rewards certain art-critical perspectives and thwarts certain others. To critique a Rembrandt as if it were a Warhol would perhaps be a wacky post-modern exercise in perspectival subjectivity, but it would yield a poorer analysis of the Rembrandt than any number of critiques based on more formal or material aesthetic perspectives. A Rembrandt etching doesn't purposefully give itself over to multiple critical perspectives. It is not that kind of art apparatus. It invites and accommodates certain perspectives while eluding and impoverishing other perspectives. Whereas, not only do Steinbach's object ensembles draw out and yield themselves to multiple art critical perspectives, they also draw out and yield themselves to multiple and differing ideological and cosmological perspectives.

On the opposite end of the spectrum from the Rembrandt etching, an accidental cobweb in the corner of a gallery is so *un*purposeful, so *un*staged, it welcomes any old kind of critical perspective at all. The cobweb invites all of the same, rote, unrigorous, boring, unproductive, philistine perspectives wielding all the same old, blunt, brutally well-trodden questions: Why is Duchamp's urinal even art? Why is Felix Gonzalez-Torres pile of candy art? Why is Tracey Emin's unmade bed art? Isn't my child's drawing just as good as Picasso's? The cobweb in the corner may indeed function as an apparatus (because any part of the universe cut off from the rest of the universe may function as an apparatus), but it is not yet an explicitly human-directed (i.e., "art") apparatus, because there is no human-devised, human-aware rigor or staging which would *purposefully* include humans in any particular way. The cobweb is not intended for humans. And so, we are left asking the same banal semantic questions about what constitutes art *at all,* rather than asking more rigorous questions about what this particular art apparatus is actually doing.

Whereas I contend that Steinbach's object ensembles have purposefully and willingly yielded themselves up to an onslaught of critical perspectives over the decades (and the parade of perspectives shows no sign of stopping). By so utterly and unreservedly yielding to competing theoretical perspectives about objects, Steinbach's work continues to elude, confound, and play the coquette to an army of theory suitors who continue to try (in vain) to woo it into becoming the object-lesson mascot of their object-centric theories. Through its apparent straightforwardness and seeming openness to analysis, Steinbach's work lures each of these theoretical perspectives into revealing itself. After all, these are just some objects arranged on a shelf, similar to what you might find on a knick-knack display shelf in your grandmother's house (if your grandmother were a surrealistic metaphysical comedian). (Most of) the objects aren't moving. They are just sitting there. The objects don't resist examination or theoretical capture. They don't even resist physical capture, since they are not glued down to the shelves. Once a pair of basketball shoes was stolen from an object ensemble at a gallery opening by a boy who wandered in and wanted a new pair of basketball shoes.[1] According to Steinbach, the motivating question driving his entire art practice is deceptively simple: "What happens when you put things next to things?"[2] His object ensembles evoke myriad interpretations not because they are occluded, misty, and vague; but precisely because they are so plainly denuded (like a kind of object porn). The fact that they remain intriguing even after they have been so plainly

1   Haim Steinbach, interview with the author at Steinbach's New York studio, April 21, 2017.
2   Haim Steinbach, "Haim Steinbach in Conversation with Tom Eccles, Beatrix Ruff, and Hans Ulrich Obrist," in Haim Steinbach, Beatrix Ruf, et al. *Haim Steinbach: Object and Display* (New York: Gregory R. Miller & Co, 2015), 362.

and obviously "displayed" makes them all the more intriguing. Their plain apparentness is their lure.

Ultimately, however, the work resists being summatively and reductively analyzed by any *single* explanatory theory. It accomplishes this feat by yielding to multiple explanatory theories simultaneously. Steinbach's object ensembles are wily and acrobatic in their temporary dalliance with, but ultimate indifference toward, any single human-generated cosmology. The object ensembles are porously resistant. They are like ingenious, paradoxical, theory-confounding trawling nets: they capture other people's interpretations in their own apparatal nets, but manage to slip through the nets of the interpretations which they capture.

Steinbach's shelf/object artworks are human-designed apparatuses which orchestrate objects in such a provocative, open, curious, and faux-apparent way that they invoke and draw out of humans a variety of theories about objects. Steinbach's apparatuses not only *invoke* various human interpretations, they willingly make themselves available as proof positive of these interpretations. They lure human-invented object-theories to the fore, tease them into articulation, and all without being summatively captured by any of them. Although Steinbach's apparatuses *appear* to be object-centric and human agnostic, they are anything but. They are explicitly engineered by a human in order to provoke humans into thinking about objects, even when (particularly when) the human-constructed theories which they provoke claim that Steinbach's art lets objects "speak for themselves."

Before I proceed any further, I should introduce the particular Steinbach piece on which I will focus. It is titled *00:02 (2,4S)*. It was made in 1988 and acquired by the Stedelijk Museum in 1989. It is part of the Stedelijk's permanent collection and is on display (as of summer 2018) in the sculpture room of "part two" (1980–now) of their displayed permanent collection ("STEDELIJK BASE"). The

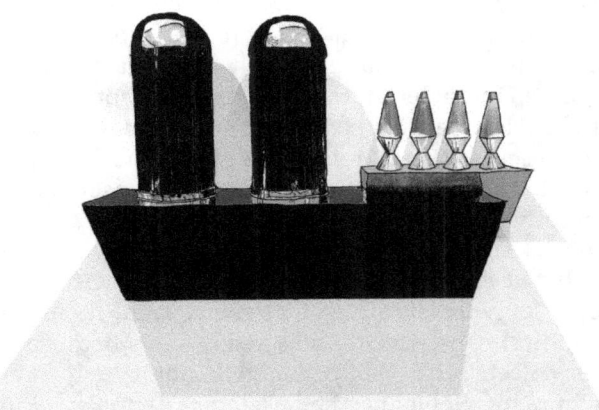

Fig. 1: A Photograph I took of Haim Steinbach's *00:02 (2,4S)* at the Stedelijk Museum in 2018. Drawing by Jordan Cloninger.

piece is comprised of two trash cans and four lava lamps. The two trash cans sit toward the left on a large black shelf. The four lava lamps rest on a smaller silver shelf, inset into the right side of the black shelf, raised slightly above the black shelf, and protruding slightly to the right of the black shelf (see Fig. 1).

If the descriptive wall text in the Stedelijk is to be believed, "00:02" in the title refers to an amount of elapsed time; "2" and "4" in "(2,4S)" refer to the number of trash cans and lava lamps respectively; and "S" stands for "small" (because the same work has been realized in both large and small versions). The title of the work is a bit anomalous for Steinbach. Many of his shelf/object ensembles are either simply titled "Untitled" with a list of the objects in parentheses, or their titles are minimally sly and wry (to list just four examples: *the village people; oxygen; oz;* and *orient point*). His titles are sometimes followed by numbers describing the identity of that particular shelf/object ensemble within a related series [to list four examples: *Untitled (breast mugs, Marilyn guitar) I-2;*

One minute managers I-1; One minute managers II-2; and *One minute managers, IV-1*]. The materials listed for *00:02 (2,4S)* [hereafter referred to as *00:02*] are "plywood, black veneer, silver-colored metal leaf, lava lamps, trash receptacles."

I selected this piece as an example not because it is perfectly representative of Steinbach's entire shelf oeuvre. Arguably, by design, *no* single shelf/object ensemble is representative of the others. Indeed, one interpretation of the object ensembles is that they purposefully trouble the line between "this" specific object (its haecceity) and this object as representative of a generic kind (its interchangeability). One reason I selected *00:02* is because it includes objects with well-decohered (not merely subatomic) moving elements (the lava lamps are plugged in and their lava is "active"). Just as a point of comparison, two other objects with moving elements in Steinbach's other ensembles are digital clocks and those wave machines that sit on office desks and see saw back and forth. I also selected *00:02* because it is a mixture of objects that are meant to be functionally utilized (the trash cans) and objects that are meant to be visually contemplated (the lava lamps). Finally, *00:02*'s contextual situation in the Stedelijk Modern Sculpture room (across from Damian Hirst's transparent bin of medical waste, and in the same room with Donald Judd's phenomenology-centric chairs and Ashley Bickerton's own version of an object ensemble) affords a critical opportunity to comparatively think through what Steinbach's work might *uniquely* be doing in the immediate physical vicinity of other work arguably functioning in similar ways.

Throughout the decades, people have theorized that Steinbach's object ensembles were about: the objects themselves, the shelves themselves, about what an object even is, about commodities and capital, about semiotics and language, about fundamental numerical relationships, about minimalism, about formalism, about found objects and readymades, about pop art, about the psychological and mnemonic connection that humans have with objects, about domesticity, about the artist as curator, about minimalist phenomenological sculpture, about institutional critique, about symbolic narrative, and about Steinbach himself. Evocatively, and somewhat in line with my own approach to the work, Steinbach asserts, "It's about the display showing itself being displayed."[3] This formulation is the inverse of Derrida's formulation regarding the way in which the sublime (inadequately) presents itself: "Presentation [...] is presented in its very inadequation, adequate to its inadequation. The inadequation of presentation is presented."[4] In the case of Steinbach's object ensembles, his claim is that there is no man behind the curtain: no inaccessible sublime "beyond" which obliquely reveals itself by prohibiting our access to it. Quite the opposite, in fact. The object ensembles don't simply display and disclose their content while occluding the act of display itself. Instead (at least according to Steinbach), the shelf/object ensembles are all openly, purposefully, and *primarily* displaying the fact that they are putting objects on display, regardless of the specific objects actually being displayed.

Whether we take Steinbach at his word or not depends on our own interpretation of what the work itself is doing, but I find his claim intriguing at least. It suggests that the things on display (whether as types or singularities; whether as semiotic signifiers or surplus commodities; whether as "enduring objects" or "societies of actual entities;" whether "in-themselves," "for-us," or "in-themselves-for-us") are simply there to jump-start the more primary meta-function of their holistic art apparatus: namely, to display the act of displaying. You can't display nothing, so you must start with something. But the work

3   Ibid., 365.
4   Jacques Derrida, *The Truth in Painting,* trans. Geoff Bennington and Ian McLeod (Chicago: University of Chicago Press, 1987), 131.

is not really about the somethings (per se); it is about the act of displaying (in toto). What it is it to display? Is displaying the same as disclosing? Uncovering? And if so, uncovering what? Essences? Qualities? Intra-object relationships? The act of uncovering itself? Also, uncovering to whom? To humans? To other objects? To being itself? All very Heideggerian and Derridean questions.

When I initially encountered Steinbach's object ensembles, I had the distinct impression that their creator had somehow mastered access into the essences and subjectivities of ordinary objects. The work bodily affected me. It still does. Initially, it seemed like Steinbach was some kind of object-whisperer. I don't quite believe that anymore. I still believe Steinbach is a master, but he is a master at discerning the affinities that objects *seem* to have with one another (based on their production histories, material qualities, formal qualities, past functional uses, historical cultural connotations, art historical resonances) all *from his own capacious human perspective*; and he is a master at staging those objects in order to evoke rich and resonant responses *from other humans*. I concur with Germano Celant's observation that "[Steinbach] wants to verify [the thing's] degree of seduction and persuasion, of delight and repulsion."[5] Yes, but verify to whom? To himself and to other humans. It turns out Steinbach's work wasn't deftly revealing the subjective hidden language of objects right before my eyes; instead, Steinbach was orchestrating objects in such a way that I intuited them talking to each other. He was creating inviting and connotative blanks for me to fill in. What I initially mistook as the occult voice of the objects I now recognize as the siren voice of the holistic apparatus, luring me into its ingenious trap: a trap set in holistic collaboration with the objects, the shelves, and art history; a trap for humans,

5   Germano Celant, "An Existential Building Site," in Steinbach, Ruf, et al., *Haim Steinbach*, 389.

invented by a human. At least that is the theory which the object ensembles are currently provoking from me.

According to this position, *00:02* functions as a kind of double-slit apparatus for human-generated cosmologies. Whereas Young's apparatus is "measuring" photons, Steinbach's apparatus is "measuring" humans. In Young's double slit apparatus, humans are purposefully excluded from the experimental measurement results, and the photons themselves are left to make their own decisions and marks. In Steinbach's *00:02*, humans are purposefully invited into the apparatus. We are lured into believing that we are measuring the results of the intra-actions between trash cans and lava lamps. We declare them either withdrawn objects (per object oriented philosophy), ongoing events (per process philosophy), linguistic signifiers (per Saussurean semiotics), etc. We imagine we are reckoning the marks these objects have made; when in truth, we are the ones making the marks and getting reckoned. All the while, the trash cans and lava lamps "themselves" remain, utterly indifferent to our presumptuous cosmological pronouncements on their behalf. *00:02* isn't an object-centric apparatus for measuring trash cans and lava lamps; it is a display-centric apparatus employing trash cans and lava lamps to measure humans.

The rest of this chapter will examine some of the human-generated cosmologies and ideologies that Steinbach's shelf/object ensembles have enticed thus far, beginning with past dalliances and proceeding toward the work's most recent paramour, object-oriented ontology (and in particular, its progenitor, Graham Harman's dashing yet troubled object-oriented philosophy). We will conclude our examination of the theory suitors with one of the work's most ardent and persistent hopefuls, semiotics. This will lead to my own personal favorite (yet still woefully unrequited) theoretical interpretation, the artist as master craftsman of the medium known as object arranging.

Suitor #1: Symbolic Narrative

There was an idea in 1970s art criticism that every object contained its own narrative. Critics subscribing to this approach failed to understand or appreciate Steinbach's work, because they were not able to interpret his ensembles in terms of any sort of cohesive symbolic story. His work was criticized as nonsense. There seemed to be no "meaningful" relationship between his objects. In fact, the objects in Steinbach's ensembles have always been very purposefully selected and arranged. His selections and arrangements are not in the least random or nonsensical. It's just that the work doesn't parade any overtly symbolic narrative "meaning." Instead, Steinbach's object-selections and object-groupings are driven by his own oblique attunement to objects rather than by any agreed upon cultural symbolism (or even by any idiosyncratic, personal mythology, à la Matthew Barney).

In an attempt to interpret the object ensembles as "narratives," we might choose to see Steinbach as the director, the shelves as the stage, and the objects as the actors. But the object ensembles are not really "plays." There is no "narrative plot," no "rising action." The closest we are going to get to symbolic narrative is the paradigm of a staged tableau, in which case Steinbach is more like a stage director, or perhaps a prop master, or is he the wedding photographer, or perhaps the tableau placement orchestrator, or maybe the window dresser of a department store product display? If we must interpret the object ensembles as "narratives" at all, they enact a new kind of symbolic language developed by Steinbach in collaboration with the histories, forms, and materialities of the objects that "star" in his micro-tableaus. But if that is indeed the case, why awkwardly strain to retroactively shoehorn these object ensembles into the anthropocentric constraints of "symbolism" and "narrative" at all?

Despite the overall weaknesses of this symbolic narrative approach toward the shelf/object ensembles, the ensembles themselves are nevertheless able to seduce and draw out (human-supplied) symbolic interpretations. For example, to me, when I first saw *00:02*, it seemed like all of the objects were in some sort of object rock band. The two black trash cans were like twin, male, death metal lead guitarists; and the four lava lamps on their raised silver background platform seemed like female, doo-wop backup singers. The title *00:02* seemed to allude to John Cage's *4'33"*. To me, the entire ensemble seemed like a conceptual speedmetal doo-wop John Cage cover band, except the band was so minimalist and monumental, they only made it two seconds into the performance before they froze. The only thing left moving was the slow undulation of the lava in the lamps, which was like the fluttering poodle skirts of the doo-wop backup singers. According to this symbolic narrative interpretation, I just happened to walk into the room at the four second mark of the performance, right after the band had frozen.

To add further fuel to the symbolic suitor fire, Steinbach says that the squawking stuffed pumpkin object that appears in several of his ensembles actually symbolizes the Belgian critic Thierry de Duve, who criticized Steinbach for betraying Duchamp.[6] This proves that the symbolic narrative interpretation is correct!

Seriously, the symbolic narrative suitor is ill-matched to the object ensembles because it is too wed to the other media for which it was more purposefully developed (fictional literature, theater, and film). Applying it to Steinbach's work proves an awkward fit.

6   Haim Steinbach, interview with the author at Steinbach's New York studio, April 21, 2017.

Suitor #2: Found Objects and Readymades

Steinbach's work doesn't betray Duchamp. If anything, it continues and complexifies what Duchamp was doing, and in so doing, exceeds it. Duchamp was interested in displaying everyday, manufactured objects in a museum setting to undermine the value placed on rare, esoteric, hand-crafted objects within the modern art world and the modern art market of the early Twentieth Century. The gallery was a key context for Duchamp's historical move. In contrast, Steinbach's investigation of the mechanisms of display doesn't require the gallery; it also works in the home of a collector beyond the gallery building (if not beyond the art market). Steinbach's practice is less institution-centric. Furthermore, Steinbach's objects are much more diverse than Duchamp's. Steinbach's objects include Yoda heads, ancient pottery, rocks, rubber dog chew toys, Hulk hands, medicine balls, and eastern European salt shakers. Although most of Steinbach's objects are man-made, not all of them are. Also, many of his objects dive headlong into proper-name pop culture in a way Duchamp's objects refuse to. Duchamp dealt with coffee grinders and snow shovels, not C-3PO and Tony the Tiger.

There is of course a comparison to be made between Joseph Cornell's object-filled boxes and Steinbach's object-laden shelves, but the comparison proves superficial. Cornell is exploring a kind of personal object surrealism, combining wondercabinetry with Magritte's object synecdoche. Steinbach's object combinations might initially *seem* interpretable through this lens, but the viewer winds up encountering object assemblages that refuse to assemble, even according to the alter-logic of surrealism. Perhaps Steinbach is akin to artists like Mark Dion and Fred Wilson who also use and arrange objects. But Wilson's arrangements are made with an explicit interest in the social history of his objects, often in order to subvert the implicit colonial perspective of museological curating. And Mark Dion's arrangements are meant to evoke a cultural memory of Victorian exploration and early scientific experimentation. Steinbach is also interested in the cultural history of his objects, but this is not his primary interest.

All of the artists mentioned (and we could add Daniel Spoerri, Arman, the Fluxus box artists, and Ashley Bickerton) have engaged in the collection, arrangement, and display of objects they did not themselves "make." But, so what? Each of these artists is pursuing very different topical and conceptual trajectories. A similarity in process and media alone is not enough to group Steinbach with the found object artists. No one would curate a group show of Vermeer, Klee, Rothko, and Bob Ross simply because they all used brushes to distribute paint on canvas. Once again, the object ensembles entice, yield, and pass through the trawling net of another theory suitor.

Suitor #3: Minimalist Phenomenological Sculpture

The shelf/object ensembles may be considered as minimalist phenomenological sculptures. From this theoretical perspective, Steinbach removes everything but the essentials in order to cause us to experience what the essentials are essentially doing. The work of minimalist sculptor Robert Irwin seems a particularly relevant point of comparison, since Irwin is intent on foregrounding spaces between objects rather than objects themselves. Or rather, Irwin uses ephemeral materials to create gaps that our bodies are meant to phenomenologically experience. Irwin's sculptures are like dimensional versions of John Cage's 4'33". The sculptures are more about removal than addition. Regarding earlier experimental exercises that led Irwin to his process of removal, he recalls, "Maybe it didn't need any of the details I added. What was really essential was going on there anyway."[7] Irwin biographer Lawrence Weschler adds, "The point of these exercises, it sometimes seemed, was to achieve the maximum transformation with the minimum alteration."[8]

Steinbach's process seems similar. Select an initial group of objects that seem to have an affinity with each other; add and remove objects, fine-tuning the relationships between the objects; rearrange the objects, moving them further apart and closer together; sit with the objects; walk away from them; think about the objects while absent from them; revisit the ensemble; continue rearranging, until... what? Until, according to Weschler's dictum, the maximum transformation is achieved with the minimum alteration. But the maximum transformation of... what? In Irwin's case, the maximum transformation of the space of the room. In Steinbach's case, the maximum transformation from plain old objects on any old shelf into... what? Into maximally resonating objects on a shelf? Into maximally receding objects on a shelf? Into objects on a shelf with the maximal discrepancy between what they *seem* to be doing and what they are *actually* doing? It is hard to say exactly. On the process of addition via removal, Irwin invokes Wortz's law: "Each new whole is less than the sum of its parts."[9] From a minimalist theoretical perspective, this law applies to Steinbach's work as well.

Both Irwin and Steinbach are meticulously precise. The shadows that the trash cans and lava lamps cast in *00:02* are perfectly symmetrical and can't help but be read as intentional. The minimalist sculptural approach to precision and detail is always present and palpable in Steinbach's shelf/object ensembles. Also, in a home, no

7   Lawrence Weschler, *Seeing Is Forgetting the Name of the Thing One Sees: A Life of Contemporary Artist Robert Irwin* (Berkeley: University of California Press, 1982), 172.
8   Ibid.
9   Ibid., 181.

one would put a trash can on a shelf at chest height; by doing this, *00:02* forces us to feel the scale and volume of that trash can in implicit proprioceptive relation to the volume of our own chests. Such a move is straight from Donald Judd's playbook.

And of course, there are the shelves themselves, which are perfectly milled, seamlessly joined, and precisely finished. As with many of Steinbach's shelves, the shelves of *00:02* are triangular when viewed from the side, and the raised triangular shelf eases into the base-level triangular shelf in a proportional relationship appreciative of fundamental geometric forms. If *00:02* were simply the shelves without the objects, it might still hold its own in the post-1980 sculpture room at the Stedelijk. Regarding Steinbach's shelves, sculptor Lisa Lapinski proposes, "The shelf works are fractions: the things in the world divided by the minimalist object."[10]

And yet Steinbach and Robert Irwin are, in many ways, worlds apart. Whereas Irwin's sculptures achieve their less-ness by receding yet remaining, Steinbach's object ensembles achieve their lessness by exceeding yet remaining. Steinbach's objects give everything away in plain sight. Instead of being subtle and shrouded, they are utterly denuded and presented. Irwin's materials are shadow and light. Steinbach's materials are shadow, light, and Yoda heads. Steinbach takes maximal, wacky, incongruous objects from contemporary pop capitalism and displays them with all the care, precision, attention, and concern of a Donald Judd cube. The results are strange and jarring. Steinbach's presentations seem to monumentalize and Platonize his otherwise banal objects. Steinbach is not a minimalist sculptor per se, but he applies the tactics of minimalist sculpture to the contents of the Sears Catalog in order to display an array of mass-produced

10 Bruce Hainley, "Haim Steinbach: Sonnabend Gallery, New York," *Artforum* 46, no. 4 (December 2007): 339.

objects as phenomenally profound. Is Steinbach *revealing* these objects as phenomenally profound (this would be the claim of minimalist phenomenological sculpture), or is he merely *staging* them to *seem* phenomenally profound? Or... is he throwing these objects into an aporetic toggling apparatus that perpetually flips them back and forth between profound object and banal object until we start to question what it is to "display" something in the first place? My money is on this last interpretation.

Suitor #4: Pop Art

Steinbach's work incorporates objects from popular culture, but he treats them in decidedly non-pop art ways. Regarding his choice of objects, Steinbach says, "What's most important is that all of these objects are in the world; they are part of our language. And they overlap."[11] Steinbach selects objects from popular culture not because he wants to celebrate pop culture, or critique it, or use it to critique 1960s minimalism. He selects objects from popular culture because he is interested in the world and the ways in which humans are in the world. The creation, use, circulation, sale, and resale of objects is a primary way that contemporary humans are in the world. Given this broader interest in the mass production, consumption, and circulation of objects themselves, if Steinbach is a pop artist, he is a quite heady and conceptual one. One obvious difference between Steinbach and pop artists proper is that Steinbach uses actual objects from contemporary mass consumer culture rather than making copies of them. Andy Warhol makes his own Brillo Boxes. Such weak mimeticism is Warhol's strong conceptual move. Steinbach doesn't make his own Yoda heads. He just buys

11   Steinbach, "Haim Steinbach in Conversation with Tom Eccles, Beatrix Ruff, and Hans Ulrich Obrist," 369.

them off of eBay. Incidentally, Pope.L's *Black Factory* incorporates Yoda heads as well (albeit shrink wrapped to racist literature and sold from a mobile truck). But the mere use of Yoda heads does not make one a pop artist.

Even compared to apparently similar work like Jeff Koons's stacked vacuum cleaners in plexiglass (which are actual vacuum cleaners), Steinbach's ensembles are exploring different territory. I find Koons's vacuum cleaner stacks beautiful and monumental (they are the only works of his I like), and that seems to be Koons's objective with them – to reveal a mass-produced commodity item as aesthetically beautiful in a classical sculptural sense. Whereas Steinbach is not *primarily* interested in celebrating the hidden beauty of his objects by recontextualizing them in a museum setting. Instead, Steinbach is more interested in the implicit (human-inferred?, human-imbued?) resonances of the objects within the ensemble, and the potential conceptual connections that suddenly materialize in the space around the objects when they are removed from their commodity contexts and given some breathing room. Also, some of Steinbach's shelf objects (like rocks, and even our two black trash cans) don't really come from "pop" culture. They just come from the world.

Suitor #5: Marxism

Marxism (of the art criticism variety) arrives hard on the heels of the pop art suitor to scold the object ensembles for not shunning pop art altogether. Apparently, even a weekend fling with pop art is enough to label you Mrs. Pop Art in the eyes of the Marxist suitor. The object ensembles should have publicly declared their intentions toward Pop Art early on. If they were not serious about Pop Art, they should have properly distanced themselves from him via irony. They should have at least made some overt protestations (if not in the work itself, then at least in an accompanying artist statement)! Otherwise, Steinbach's work risks complicity endorsing and celebrating its objects (which are obviously from contemporary popular culture); and by proxy, endorsing and celebrating the capitalist system that produces these popular commodities. Shame on you, object ensembles, for allowing yourselves to be seduced by the lascivious charlatan of Pop Art!

This Marxist critique might be valid if the object ensembles weren't also simultaneously giving themselves over to every legitimate suitor who passes through the door. And, of course, the object ensembles give themselves over to the Marxist suitor as well. But it is at best an awkward blind date (with your ex-boyfriend's activist uncle). The Marxist suitor does all the talking without taking the time to really get to know the object ensembles. What's a nice apophatic art apparatus to do?

Regarding Steinbach's approach to his objects, Germano Celant explains, "[His] orientation is inclusive in nature and incorporates in the work the greatest quantity of things and information, of corporeal and mass-media traces, with an open and unbiased attitude."[12] This openness to capitalist culture disturbs the Marxist suitor, but it is precisely this same broad openness that lures multiple and even competing theoretical interpretations into Steinbach's work.

Furthermore, and as mentioned above in regards to their relationship with pop art, the object ensembles don't always incorporate mass-produced contemporary objects. A wonderful example of this is a piece called *Untitled (jugs and mugs), Number 1* from the Metropolitan Museum of Art's permanent collection. The piece consists of two shelves, one above the other, whose materials are listed as "Laminated plywood, ceramic mugs, and ancient

12   Germano Celant, "An Existential Building Site," in Steinbach, Ruf, et al., *Haim Steinbach*, 389.

pottery." The top shelf supports four ancient, handmade, earthenware vessels. The bottom shelf supports three contemporary, mass-produced ceramic mugs, one of which displays Milton Glaser's "I heart NY" logo. Yes, the ceramic mugs are products of contemporary popular culture, but like the earthenware jugs, they are also vessels for gathering (to reference late-era Heidegger). *jugs and mugs* consists of seven ceramic vessels created by humans to hold liquids. The earthenware jugs are antique archeological objects, quite pre-capitalism. The point of this and other object ensembles, then, is to engage with all of human culture, throughout history, via the display of objects. An engagement with "capitalism" is necessarily part of that overall project, but not an exclusive part of it.

Furthermore, the object ensembles are not above celebrating certain aspects of capitalism. Steinbach tells of growing up, going to the dry goods store, knowing what you wanted, but having to ask the clerk to retrieve it for you, because all of the objects were behind the counter. He describes his first visit to a supermarket as a positive experience: "There was the supermarket, which was supposed to be the modernism that you were against, but I liked it. You could walk down the aisles, and there were all the things on the shelves in front of you."[13] There is something inarguably wondrous about having row upon row of objects displayed on shelves within one's grasp.

Of course, Steinbach's object ensembles put the objects back behind the counter, so to speak; but not exactly. There is something important about the fact that the objects are not affixed to the shelves. It mattered to the boy who stole the shoes off the shelves at the gallery opening. And it matters to the collectors who display the object ensembles in their own homes. Each collector has the very real option of putting her own objects on

13   Haim Steinbach, interview with the author at Steinbach's New York studio, April 21, 2017.

the shelves, creating a collaborative work with the artist. The Marxist suitor complains that the work fetishizes the objects by separating them from their use value. But Steinbach points out that, once collected, the digital clocks and boom boxes in the ensembles may be left on in one's home,[14] providing the use value of music and the current local time. And although a docent at the Stedelijk would have surely objected, there was nothing physically prohibiting me from *using* the trash cans in *00:02* as trash cans.

Suitor #6: Formalism

Although Steinbach is not primarily interested in the aesthetic beauty of his objects from a classical, beaux arts perspective; he is interested in their formal aesthetic qualities (shape, color, volume, materiality, opacity, reflectivity, scale, balance, symmetry/asymmetry, mobility/stability, serial progression) from a modernist or formalist perspective. His objects appear beautiful not because they are inherently beautiful, but primarily because of the way in which he arranges and displays them. Koons couldn't lose with his stack of vacuum cleaners. They were already beautiful on the Sears showroom floor. But Steinbach has his formal aesthetic work cut out for him with a box of Fruit Loops cereal. Steinbach's eye for formalist aesthetics transforms his objects into something much more beautiful than they were on the grocery store shelf. This transformation is part of what it is to "display" something.

The shelf arrangements all have formal properties. The shelves themselves are triangular volumes. The objects on the shelves are always formally related to one another. They exist in volumetric ratios with one another. Stein-

14 Ibid.

bach says, "I am dealing with the same angles at different scales and proportions. Then I am amplifying them
by extending them horizontally. And I am playing with
color throughout."[15] This attention to formal aesthetic
principles comes through implicitly and explicitly in the
work. The object ensembles are always well-proportioned
and beautiful.

Still, these formal aesthetic qualities are a means
rather than an end. They display (help us recognize?) the
objects as having not just popular connotative qualities,
but also formal aesthetic qualities. Steinbach's formalism and minimalism concurrently make the objects seem
profound. Simultaneously, the ordinary historical usage
of the objects (the trash cans and lava lamps of *00:02*, for
instance) often make the objects seem banal. This toggling back and forth between banal and profound is one
of *00:02*'s major apophatic tactics. Steinbach's shelf/ob-
ject ensembles court, use, and employ formalism to help
achieve their desired apophatic effects; but they are wise
enough not to begin and end with formalism alone.

Suitor #7: Psychology

As far as a psychological explanation of the poetic ways
in which humans relate to objects – mnemonically, em-
pathetically, and affectionately – I trust and enjoy Peter
Schwenger's excellent *The Tears of Things: Melancholy and
Physical Objects*. Via nostalgia and sentimentality, objects
act for humans as unwitting mnemonic horcruxes (my
analogy, not Schwenger's), storing parts of our memories
inside themselves for our later involuntary retrieval. I
also find Schwenger's own interpretation of Steinbach's
work sensitive and convincing from a psychological perspective.

15   Ibid.

But no one tops Proust in evocatively describing the psychological, subjective relationships that humans develop with the objects of their own personal histories. Here is a selection of relevant excerpts from *À la recherche du temps perdu*:

Love, and suffering which is one with love, have, like intoxication, the power to alter for us inanimate things.[16]

Only imagination and belief can differentiate from the rest certain objects, certain people, and can create an atmosphere.[17]

With the sandwiches of cheese or of green-stuff, a form of food that was novel to me and knew nothing of the past, I had nothing in common. But the cakes understood, the tarts were gossips.[18]

We exist only by virtue of what we possess, we possess only what is really present to us [...]. A simple crescent of bread, but one which we are eating, gives us more pleasure than all the ortolans, young rabbits and barbavelles that were set before Louis XV.[19]

16   Marcel Proust, *The Guermantes Way*, trans. C. K. Scott-Moncrieff (1925; Paris: Feedbooks, 2014), 145, http://www.feedbooks.com/book/1449/the-guermantes-way.

17   Ibid., 27.

18   Marcel Proust, *Within a Budding Grove*, trans. C. K. Scott-Moncrieff (1924; Paris: Feedbooks, 2014), 430, http://www.feedbooks.com/book/1448/within-a-budding-grove.

19   Marcel Proust, *The Sweet Cheat Gone*, trans. C. K. Scott-Moncrieff (1930; Paris: Feedbooks, 2014), 64, 72–73, http://www.feedbooks.com/book/1452/the-sweet-cheat-gone-the-fugitive.

All impression is two-fold, half-sheathed in the object, prolonged in ourselves by another half which we alone can know.[20]

Wonderful as Proust is, Steinbach is not fully convinced. Regarding Proust's conception of objects, Steinbach observes, "We put our life into objects, and we leave, and others come in and find us in the objects, or so we believe when we meet objects. But we are fooling ourselves."[21] My own problem with the psychological explanation of Steinbach's work is that it presumes a hard and fast subject–object divide. It would be very uncomfortable with Whitehead's dissolution of the subject–object divide via his concept of the superject – the idea that during the concrescences of actual occasions, "human" entities and "non-human" entities are both subject and object simultaneously. Regarding Steinbach's object ensembles, if I had to place a wager on which of these two entities (human or non-human) was doing most of the prehending (in other words, which one was acting most "subject-like"), my bet would definitely be on the human. (And I say this not just because I am a human!) This is why I'm not *terribly* bothered by the psychological account of Steinbach's work, an account which posits humans as the main agents in these encounters between humans and shelf/object ensembles. But again, there is more going on in these apparatal intra-actions than human subjectivity merely psychologically imputing characteristics into otherwise passively inert object receptacles.

20 Marcel Proust, *Time Regained,* trans. Stephen Hudson (1931; Paris: Feedbooks, 2014), 157, http://www.feedbooks.com/book/1453/time-regained.
21 Haim Steinbach, interview with the author at Steinbach's New York studio, April 21, 2017.

Suitor #8: Process Philosophy

I put Whitehead's own process philosophy explanation at #8 because I don't want to give it the last word (since my argument is that no suitor gets the last word); but also because, in the case of the shelf/object ensembles, I don't intuitively and affectively feel that process philosophy is the most convincing explanation of what is happening. The trash cans and lava lamps of *00:02* sure seem solid enough. Viewing them, I sure seem like a discrete human subject. It doesn't seem like the objects and I are involved in an ongoing series of occasions whereby we are prehending each other. *00:02* is not displayed to draw my attention to present-tense time and immediate process. On the contrary, my attention is drawn away from the idea of an ongoing series of events, and toward the quite hermetically sealed, removed, pristine, idealized, static, Platonic presentation of the objects.

But, of course, this is simply how the encounter *seems* to *me*. Henri Bergson explains what might actually be happening:

> Does not the fiction of an isolated material object imply a kind of absurdity, since this object borrows its physical properties from the relations which it maintains with all others, and owes each of its determinations, and, consequently, its very existence, to the place which it occupies in the universe as a whole?[22]

According to Bergson, my very act of reckoning the objects as separate from me, is itself a kind of intra-action with the objects: "Perception, in its pure state, is, then, in very truth, a part of things."[23] By stepping back, reflec-

---

22 Henri Bergson, *Matter and Memory,* trans. Nancy Margaret Paul and W. Scott Palmer (New York: Zone Books, 1991), 24.
23 Ibid., 64.

tively scratching my chin, and trying to think detachedly about the nature of subject and object, I only *seem* to increase the subject–object divide. When in reality, according to Karen Barad's reading of Niels Bohr, "We are a part of that nature that we seek to understand."[24]

As one would expect, Whitehead has more to add on the matter of our own detached perception of objects:

> Reaction to environment is not in proportion to clarity of sensory experience [...]. The specialist in clarity sinks to an animal level – the hound for smell, the eagle for sight. Human beings are amateurs in sense experience. The direct, vivid clarity does not dominate so as to obscure the infinite variety involved in the composition of reality.[25]

Perhaps there is another, less abstractly generalized, more viscerally specialized way of encountering these object ensembles? Whitehead suggests there is: "The subject-object relation can be conceived as Recipient and Provoker, where the fact provoked is an affective tone about the status of the provoker in the provoked experience."[26] Applying this model to my own situation at the Stedelijk, *00:02* provokes an affective tone about its status which I receive in our shared occasional experience. I am no longer a removed subject over here, perceiving *00:02* as a separate object over there, and then detachedly contemplating the object I am perceiving.

In truth, whether or not I ever achieve the mental state of "becoming object," I am always already entangled with the objects of *00:02*. Whitehead explains: "Every indi-

---

24 Karen Barad, *Meeting the Universe Halfway* (Durham: Duke University Press, 2007), 26.

25 Alfred North Whitehead, *Modes of Thought* (New York: The Free Press, 1968), 113.

26 Alfred North Whitehead, *Adventures of Ideas* (New York: Free Press, 1967), 176.

vidual thing infects any process in which it is involved, and thus any process cannot be considered in abstraction from particular things involved. Also the converse holds."[27] Furthermore, "The group of agitations which we term matter is fused into its environment. There is no possibility of a detached, self-contained local existence. The environment enters into the nature of each thing."[28] I don't have to consciously attend to this moment by moment process of concrescence in order to make it happen. It is always already happening.

It is important to understand that the actual occasions in which *00:02* participates, although intended by Steinbach to include a human audience, are by no means contingent upon human participation in those occasions. Much of what *00:02* contributes to its occasions is negatively prehended (or minimally prehended) by entities other than humans (i.e., the rest of the objects in the sculpture room), but *00:02* presents its contributions nonetheless. Affect is actual, and not solely human-psychological. Humans don't manufacture affect in their psychological, "subjective" minds.

Does this mean that all of the objects in the sculpture room of the Stedelijk are picking up on all the affect the other objects are exuding? No. Does it mean there is an excessive surplus of noun-ish affect stored within the hidden molten core of each object? No. It means that affect is produced and contributed when apparatal entanglements occur (i.e., when actual occasions occur), and they are occurring all the time. As Karen Barad asserts, "Reality is composed not of things in-themselves or things-behind-phenomena but of things-in-phenomena."[29] Are these actual occasions contingent upon human presence? No.

27 Whitehead, *Modes of Thought*, 97–98.
28 Ibid., 138.
29 Barad, *Meeting the Universe Halfway*, 140.

With that said, something is happening between me and *00:02* well beyond me looking at it and thinking about it, and well beyond it displaying itself to me. Are the (actual occasions that comprise the enduring) objects of *00:02* prehending me in the same way and to the same degree that (the actual occasions that comprise the enduring object called) I am prehending them? No. As I continue to argue, the trash cans and the lava lamps are mostly negatively prehending me. Were they mostly negatively prehending Steinbach when he was arranging and re-arranging them in his studio? No. They were more actively attending to those arrangement intra-actions. Were the trash cans negatively prehending the metal extrusion machine at the factory which molded them into shape? Again, no. Those formational, transformative actual occasions "meant" more to the enduring object that was to become known as "trash can" than the subsequent actual occasions of me standing in the Stedelijk gazing upon it. By "meant more," do I mean anything like what the word "mean" means to a human? No. According to my understanding of Whitehead, all objects "experience" (in their own thingy ways), but only human objects experience in humany ways.

Thus, according to process philosophy, all of the entities in the Stedelijk sculpture room (myself included) are prehending and prehended by each other moment by moment as usual, all in our own well-decided and decohered, macrocosmically scaled, thingy or humany ways. But the most remarkable intra-active encounters in the sculpture room are occurring not amongst the shelf objects themselves, nor amongst the other artworks in the room, but amongst the artworks and the enduring objects in the room known as humans. This is because all the artworks in the room are apparatuses specifically designed by humans to intra-act with humans; and also, because humans are, in truth, quite remarkable and peculiar enduring objects. (And I say this not just because I am a human!)

00:02 allows this process philosophy interpretation, but doesn't exactly foreground it. Our process philosophy suitor is invited to the theory party, but *00:02* doesn't go out of her way to dance with him. Which suits process philosophy just fine, because (according to process philosophy) he and *00:02* were always already dancing anyway.

The Suitor Du Jour: Object-Oriented Ontology

Object-oriented ontology is the theoretical dandy currently courting Steinbach's object ensembles; and indeed, courting contemporary art in general. The genealogy of its popularity may be traced back to a conference in 2007 at Goldsmiths College in London called *Speculative Realism* where four philosophers spoke (Ray Brassier, Ian Hamilton Grant, Graham Harman, and Quentin Meillassoux). Subsequently, these philosophers discovered that they didn't really have all that much in common, but the conference spawned academic discussion and helped popularize the philosophy of Graham Harman known as object-oriented philosophy. This philosophy in turn spawned its own broader flavor of thought known as object-oriented ontology (whose main propagators are Harman, Ian Bogost, Levi Bryant, and Timothy Morton).

A decade from now, the amount of time that I devote to object-oriented ontology (hereafter OOO) and object-oriented philosophy (hereafter OOP) will likely seem scatological, dated, and all very two-thousand-teenish. But here we are. I will focus most of my attention on Harman's OOP. It is the progenitor of broader approaches to OOO; it makes the most daring claims of positions within OOO; and it is the position within OOO that proves the most fruitful foil to Whitehead's process philosophy. Rather than begin with OOP's goals, motivations, and challenges, I will skip to the end and explain the cosmology it wound up proposing. This explication is based on Harman's first two books (*Tool-Being* and *Guerilla Metaphysics*), and his 2011 book *The Quadruple Object*.

What Does OOP Claim?

OOP proposes that all real objects are withdrawn and cannot be directly accessed by other objects. (Humans are objects too.) Real objects store a reserve of excess potential within themselves that can never be exhausted by other objects or the world. Real objects are divided from their own real qualities. Real objects are also divided from sensual objects, which are themselves divided from their own sensual qualities. When we feel we are coming into contact with real objects, we are in fact only contacting sensual objects. These four parts (real objects, real qualities, sensual objects, and sensual qualities) make up the world. These four parts are able to influence each other, but only obliquely and via indirect causation. The particular way in which this indirect causation occurs is aesthetic, a kind of poetic encounter made possible via (something akin to) metaphor and (something akin to) humor. Indirect causation is not a metaphorical encounter (per se), but an actual encounter that takes place via something like metaphor, where one object encounters another object obliquely, and the first object is changed via that indirect encounter. I encounter (the sensual instantiation of) a cypress tree, it seems like the ghost of a dead flame, and I am changed. I'll never look at a cypress tree the same way again. It becomes a different entity for me. How this aesthetic encounter changes the (real instantiation of the) cypress tree itself, and what the exact mechanisms of that change are, remain unclear and speculative in OOP's explanatory cosmology. Presumably, the real cypress tree has similar (but less human, more thingy) metaphor-ish encounters with (the sensual instantiations of) other objects, and it too is (really) changed.

These poetic, metaphor-driven change encounters are the weak link in the OOP cosmology for me. Whereas Whitehead provides a detailed account of the concrescence and emergent self-becoming of actual occasions (one that has the benefit of correlating with the way in which quantum-behavior-measuring apparatuses happen to work), OOP provides oblique descriptions of oblique encounters. Whitehead understands the world primarily in terms of processes (verbs). OOP understands the world almost exclusively in terms of hermetically sealed objects (nouns). Karen Barad's quantum-based cosmology (akin to Whitehead's) understands the world primarily in terms of relationships (prepositions, although she would say "intra-actions"). To Barad, relations precede relata. In other words, the contextual relations that objects have with one another constitute the very object-ness of those objects. To OOP, relata precede relations, so much so that one can hardly even call them relata, and one has difficulty concretely explaining what relationships even are.

Why Invent OOP?

Why even propose such a speculative cosmology of hermetically sealed objects? What does it solve? And by what means could one ever verify that it was actually so? OOP sets out to solve a human-philosophical problem. Here is an uber-brief summary of the problem: Kant asserted that humans couldn't directly access objects. (This assertion came to be known as "correlationism.") Kant's argument was pretty convincing, and it bothered lots of people. How to respond to his assertion?

Perhaps humans *can* access objects and Kant was wrong. But then, how to prove it? (Husserl tried, failed, limited his attempt and tried again, and still pretty much failed. Heidegger further limited his attempt, got pretty close, and also failed.) Perhaps Kant's problem was merely a problem of false premises, in that he wrongly assumed a divide between humans and objects that is really not there. But again, how to prove this? (For my money, Whitehead's process philosophy comes pretty close.) Perhaps Kant had an unduly philosophical understanding of what "access" is. Perhaps we do have a *kind* of direct access to objects; it's just that this access doesn't reduce to philosophy. If that is the case, we'll never be able to prove the existence of this kind of direct access *philosophically,* but we could still prove it (or at least experience it) scientifically, affectively, aesthetically, mathematically, or via any number of other means. Or perhaps we are more stuck than even Kant realized, and the human language which constrains our philosophical access to the world also permeates and thus constrains all the other (scientific, affective, aesthetic, mathematic) ways we have of accessing the world. This is Derrida's position. To me, Derrida's position is more or less unassailable *within the historical game of philosophy,* because you always have to use philosophical language to dethrone his position, which then opens you up to Derrida's ingenious critiques of philosophical language.

Which brings us to OOP. Derrida's reign in contemporary philosophy was becoming boring to those within the historical game of philosophy, so Harman made a move (within the game) to change the game. Perhaps (and here is Harman's move) the problem is not that humans lack direct access to objects via philosophy, but that all objects lack direct access to all other objects via any direct means of encounter whatsoever. The problem is not with humans. The problem is with the world. Although this "solution" seems more like a resignation or an abdication, it appeals to (some) people for several reasons: it purports to make humans nothing special and to start taking objects more seriously; it absolves humans of having to overcome a centuries-old philosophical problem; it makes aesthetics important again (but in a weird way); and it is something new in continental philosophy besides deconstruction. Ironically, however, rather than de-centering humans and overcoming correlationism, OOP winds up making the world more anthropocentric than ever before.

Despite OOP's opposition to Derrida and the "semiotic turn" that followed him, OOP takes Derrida's suspicion of knowability two steps further. To Derrida, we can only indirectly access the world beyond us via language, and pretty much all of our human forms of access are entangled with language. To OOP, not only are we barred from directly accessing the world beyond us by any means at all, but all the other real objects in the world are in this same hermetically sealed state. One of the motivating factors of OOP's theory of universally withdrawn real objects is to be un-anthropocentric. We humans are ourselves just objects amongst other objects, all equally barred from direct access to each other. But in fact, this theory of universally withdrawn real objects is the ultimate act of anthropocentric hubris, because it theoretically extends our own human-thinking, solipsistic, philosophical psychosis (the correlationist suspicion that we can't directly access the world) to the rest of the world. Our human-specific desire to overcome the (human-invented) human-specific condition of correlationism motivates Harman to theoretically imbue all other objects in the world with our same human-specific condition. Correlationism is overcome(?) via its universal distribution. Objects, you're welcome. Sincerely, your fellow objects, thinking humans. It is a bit like patting yourself on the back for sharing your virus with everyone else at the office party.

From the perspective of a (fairly orthodox) Whitehead adherent like myself, correlationism is a human-invented problem existing within the historical game of philosophy. It need only be "overcome" by those humans wanting to make the next historical move within the game of philosophy, but it doesn't need to be overcome in the actual world. Rocks don't existentially struggle with their lack of direct access to other rocks.

Even within the game of philosophy, OOP gives rise to more problems than it solves. If we have no direct access to real objects in the world, then how is Harman able to access the rest of the real objects in the world in order to discover and verify that none of them have direct access to each other either? By speculative, indirect, oblique causal contact with their sensual object counterparts, of course. But labeling one's philosophy "speculative" doesn't excuse it from being tautological. OOP is like picking up your phone, discovering that the line is dead, and poetically inferring that everyone else's phone line is dead as well. How are you able to connect with everyone else and verify this fact? Via the indirect access you have to them through your own dead phone line. Yikes.

What's the Problem with OOP's Aesthetics?

Any cosmology that posits aesthetics as a fundamental universal force is bound to be received as validating and exciting by artists, curators, and art critics. The problem with OOP's aesthetics is that they are redundant and regressive. Whitehead's cosmology already includes a quite nuanced explanation of what might be called object aesthetics. Deleuze and Guattari have also developed a sophisticated aesthetics of ethology, geology, and the entire immanent universe. In comparison, Harman's model of object aesthetics is vague, blunt, and late to the game. Worst of all, it fails to connect explanatorily with the actual world of objects.

To take just one example, OOP uses the term "allure" to describe the oblique connection between real objects and sensual qualities. But Whitehead also uses the term "allure" to describe the prehending affinities which actual entities have toward one another, and Deleuze and Guattari incorporate into their philosophy an explanation of natural selection via aesthetic attraction ("a lure").

Whitehead and Deleuze have been accused of the same kind of anthropomorphism of which I am accusing Harman, so what is the difference between Deleuze and Guattari's "lure," Whitehead's "allure," and Harman's "allure"? Whitehead begins with his understanding of mathematics and quantum physics, and uses human language to describe quantum behavior as rigorously as possible. Whitehead's writing includes poetic, "extra-scientific" language to describe novel (to humans, at the time) but natural quantum behaviors, behaviors that the "objective" Newtonian scientific language of the time lacked the vocabulary to articulate. Whitehead doesn't claim that human affective allure is the direct result of our being fundamentally made up of photons. It is simply that both photons and humans exist in a world functionally driven by allure. Whitehead isn't anthropomorphically imposing human behavior onto electrons. Indeed, it could be argued that prior Newtonian physics was a kind of anthropomorphic imposition of the observed behavior of well-decided, decohered macrocosmic entities (like rocks) onto less decided, pre-cohered microscopic entities (like photons). It was only via Whitehead's "listening" to quantum-behavior-measuring apparatuses and what they had to say, that some of our prior scientific and philosophical anthropomorphisms began to be undone.

Similarly, Deleuze and Guattari don't project human aesthetics onto the animal kingdom as much as they recognize a kind of behavior in the animal kingdom that functions in the same way as human aesthetics. Female birds are lured into mating by the appearance and behavior of male birds. In the case of bower birds, this behavior involves a kind of performative treatment of objects and materials that exploits aesthetic attraction. Similar to Whitehead's position, Deleuze and Guattari aren't simply saying that humans appreciate aesthetics because we evolved from animals, who themselves fundamentally evolved via aesthetic appreciation. Instead, Deleuze and Guattari are saying that humans and animals both exist in a world functionally driven by aesthetic allure.

In Deleuze and Guattari's own words:

> We can then say that the musician bird goes from sadness to joy or that it greets the rising sun or endangers itself in order to sing or sings better than another, etc. None of these formulations carries the slightest risk of anthropomorphism, or implies the slightest interpretation. It is instead a kind of geomorphism. The relation to joy and sadness, the sun, danger, perfection, is given in the motif and counterpoint, even if the term of each of these relations is not given. In the motif and the counterpoint, the sun, joy or sadness, danger, become sonorous, rhythmic, or melodic.[30]

When "we" come to attend to our own flow and entanglement with "the rest of the world," this entanglement is not anthropomorphic simply because we begin attending to it. Indeed, this entanglement, flow, or pulse predates humans and even geological strata. It is baked into the behavior of the cosmos.

My critique of Harman's "allure" is that it is arrived at deductively rather than inductively. Indeed, according to OOP, the concept of allure could never be arrived at inductively, since we have no direct access to real objects, but only speculative, oblique, or indirect access to them. Harman develops his concept of allure by beginning with an

---

30 Gilles Deleuze and Félix Guattari, *A Thousand Plateaus: Capitalism and Schizophrenia*, trans. Brian Massumi (Minneapolis: University of Minnesota Press, 1987), 318–19.

analysis of the way in which metaphor and humor work in human language systems,[31] and then speculatively imposes this type of behavior onto the world.[32] Whereas Whitehead and Deleuze and Guattari each begin their understanding of allure with the (largely) human-indifferent world (Whitehead with slit-selecting electrons and Deleuze and Guattari with mating birds), Harman begins his understanding of allure with the way that metaphors and humor within human language systems represent the world. This seems a backwards place to begin for someone intent on overcoming anthropocentrism. Harman linguistically speculates the existence of a world wherein the only means of real change (aesthetic allure) functions according to speculative linguistic slippage. It all seems a bit too tidily self-confirming and tautological.

OOP achieves its self-referential, hermetically sealed, unassailable neatness at the cost of failing to access the complex, ongoing becomings of the actual world. Granted, pure evolutionary ethology and pure quantum physics fail to wholly access the ongoing becomings of the actual world, but at least they more courteously attend to the things themselves (although OOP would say that they are only attending to mere sensual things). Whitehead's incorporation of physics into his cosmology and Deleuze and Guattari's inclusion of evolutionary ethology into their cosmology doesn't *guarantee* them direct access to the actual world, but it gets them deeper into actual objects than Harman gets.

Why Does the Contemporary Art World Love OOP (and OOO)?

Why then have OOP and (its less daring spawn) OOO been so embrace in contemporary art circles? I don't believe

---

31 Graham Harman, *Guerrilla Metaphysics: Phenomenology and the Carpentry of Things* (Chicago: Open Court, 2005), ch. 8–9.
32 Ibid., ch. 10–11.

Object Oriented Ontology has been embraced for its epis-temological rigor, or for its ability to most satisfactorily explain the actual functioning of the actual world. On the contrary, I believe it has been embraced precisely be-cause it is a daring and beautiful (if slightly harrowing) speculative fiction that engages with the relevant con-temporary topic of overcoming anthropocentrism. OOO serves as a speculative provocation for launching subse-quent speculative art-curatorial provocations. And (dare I say it), OOO also serves as a kind of self-justification for the less socially relevant, hermetically sealed, white cubed, contemporary art scene. "All we have here in our gallery are objects (you see), only obliquely and indirectly connecting to the world outside these walls. But don't blame us; blame the world. Direct connections between objects are simply not possible." The hermetically sealed, intellectually contemplatable, idealized aesthetic art ob-ject and OOO are a match made in Plato's heaven of pure forms. As a point of radical contrast, consider how utterly out of place Pope.L's object-pulverizing, world-connect-ing, community-modulating Black Factory would be in a white cube gallery show about Object Oriented Ontology.

Why Does OOO love OO:O2?

Writing about Proust (and his iconic madeleines), Sam-uel Beckett observes, "When the object is perceived as particular and unique and not merely the member of a family, when it appears independent of any general no-tion and detached from the sanity of a cause, isolated and inexplicable in the light of ignorance, then and then only may it be a source of enchantment."[33] Steinbach's object ensembles meet Beckett's requirements, and thereby en-chant OOO – hook, line, and sinker.

33 Samuel Beckett and Georges Duthuit, "Proust," in *Proust and Three dialogues with Georges Duthuit* (London: John Calder, 1987), 22–23.

And of course, the shelf ensembles welcome their latest suitor unreservedly (but never ultimately or even exclusively). *00:02* takes objects out of their usual networks and leaves them suspended (via minimalism, formalism, and the gallery's inherent hermeticism) in a strange kind of Platonic netherspace. All of their former connections have been temporarily severed. All of the ways in which they were plugged in and refracting with the world have been disconnected, unplugged. And those empty sockets remain open to new, imaginative, speculative connections. OOO imagines these sockets are open to connections with a litany of other objects (all in the sensual realm, of course). But actually, in their gallery setting, these non-human shelf objects aren't connecting with other non-human objects that much. Instead, these open sockets act as lures to draw out and connect with human theories.

Object-oriented ontologists imagine these empty object sockets being filled by a million sensual object plugs obliquely reaching out and plugging in via allure. In actuality, these empty sockets are being filled by the human-invented theories of object-oriented ontologists (and a host of other human-invented theories). Steinbach's ensembles lure and trap human cosmological theories via the same mechanism that clothing store window displays lure and trap customers. The clothes on the mannequins exist in an isolated and ideal Platonic world (the world of pure "display"). They don't really belong to the mannequins. Instead, the clothes are open to an infinite possibility of owners, and thus I am lured into imaging that the clothes could (one day) belong to me. OOO imagines that *00:02* suits its explanatory theories. OOO can see itself in *00:02*.

In truth, the trash cans and lava lamps of *00:02* aren't really connecting all that much with other objects in the Stedelijk sculpture room. Most of the non-human, non-*00:02* objects in the room are mostly not intra-acting with the trash cans and lava lamps (and vice versa). A good work of art is able to hold its own in a group show without getting conceptually hijacked by the other work in the show. Holding one's own is particularly challenging in a group show based around the very loose them of "sculpture made in the 1980s." Many art apparatuses, with many different conceptual functions, are all pulling in different directions. The weak apparatuses risk getting hijacked and munged up by the strong ones. In the Stedelijk room, *00:02* holds its own amongst the other apparatuses (although the minimalist in me *thinks* that Steinbach's shelves are flirting with the Donald Judd chairs). By "holding one's own," I don't mean to imply that the art apparatuses actively resist each other all night long in the room while no humans are present. I simply mean that each of the art apparatuses in the Stedelijk sculpture room are designed to intra-act with humans in one unique way or another. "Holding one's own" as an art apparatus means continuing to fulfill your intended function of *intra-acting with humans* (in whatever your intended way) without that function being modulated by another nearby apparatus' intended function of *intra-acting with humans*.

00:02 is there to intra-act with humans, and it does. Passersby just making the rounds through the Stedelijk collection, checking off the artwork one by one, frequently stop and stare at *00:02*. It is too elegant to be a mere anti-art joke, but too pop-object-ish to be minimalist sculpture. Even for the casual viewer, aporia is (however temporarily) invoked. And of course, the theorizing art patrons (like myself) get good and mired in *00:02*'s yielding, theory-invoking, theory-provoking quicksand facade.

It is important to note that the art of Steinbach's trap does not reside in his objects alone; his apparatal trap is set and sprung by a deftly orchestrated interplay between his minimalist shelves, his formalist arrangements, the gallery setting, and Steinbach's own intuitive feel for ob-

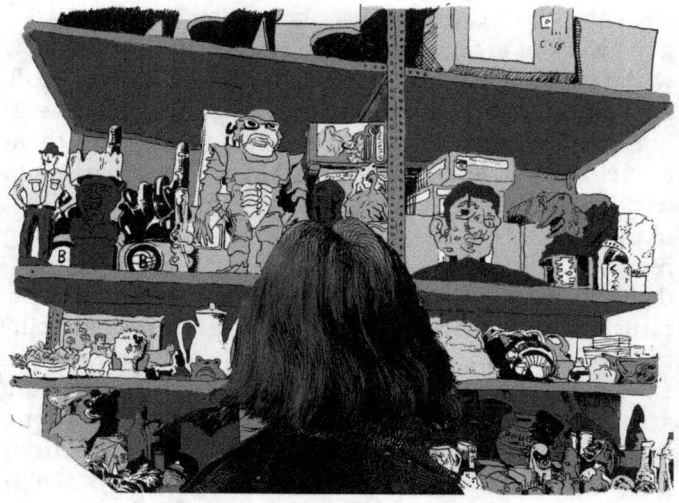

Fig. 2: A photograph I took of my middle daughter staring at a shelf of objects in Haim Steinbach's studio in 2017. Drawing by Jordan Cloninger.

ject display. As a point of comparison, consider this image of my middle daughter staring at some of Steinbach's pre-ensemble objects, stored on shelves in his studio, all (patiently?) awaiting inclusion into future object ensembles (See Fig. 2).

I spent a good while surrounded by these shelves of objects in Steinbach's studio. Although the objects were odd and evocative, and many of their incidental arrangements evoked me to make mental connections between the objects, this room full of objects did not cause me to experience anything like what the trash cans and lava lamps of *00:02* caused me to experience in the Stedelijk. According to ooo, the studio room should have been teeming with sensual allure between the objects themselves, and between the objects and me (as one more object in the room). But the room was not teeming with such allure. Or at least it didn't *seem to me* as if it was.

Maybe the sensual objects *were* connecting with each other, and I just wasn't in on their allusive chatter! Maybe I'm just an object dolt who lacks the nuanced subtlety of an attuned object-whisperer. Of course, who could "really" know? But about that which one cannot justify, one can always speculatively assert.

In Steinbach's studio on the day that I visited, I was even able to see a few objects in the transitional state between the storage shelves and the gallery shelves. On the floor of the studio were a selected group of objects that Steinbach was in the process of arranging and re-arranging. There was not yet any shelving (the shelves are custom-built and out-sourced, so that is the last step); but even just sitting on the floor without their minimalist shelves, not yet in their final ensemble arrangements, this proto-ensemble in proto-arrangement mode already seemed to me much more resonant and full of implicit meaning than the objects on the storage shelves. The fewer the objects, the more removed from their ordinary contexts, the more purposefully displayed by Steinbach to ensnare me, the more the apophatic art apparatus was beginning to work its mojo.

As an even more refined point of comparison (an even more rigorously controlled case study), that large Creature from the Black Lagoon object on the studio storage shelves was also famously featured in Steinbach's 2011 solo show (*Creature*) at the Tanya Bonakdar Gallery in Chelsea. In that show, the Creature object alone occupied a single, room-length shelf in a large upstairs room of the gallery (see Fig. 3). On Steinbach's studio shelves, the Creature object looked comic, goofy, and awkward. In the *Creature* show, the Creature object looked commanding, epic, and revelatory. It stole the show, so to speak.

It was the same object in both spaces, so what was the difference? Of course, the context made all the difference. In the gallery, I was rigorously and meticulously lured into an apophatic apparatus designed to elicit spec-

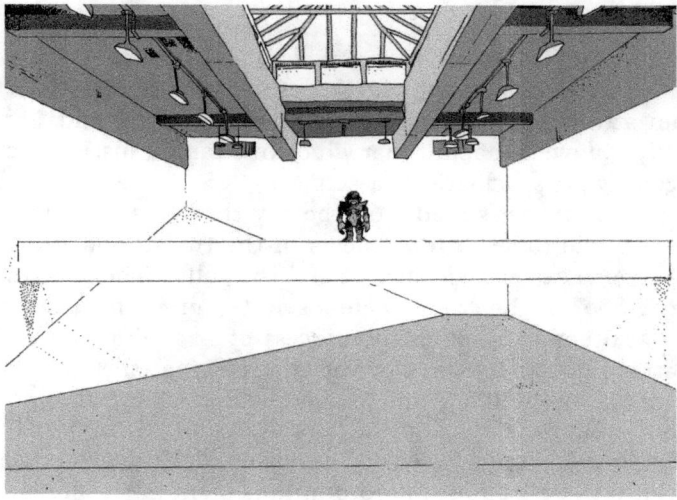

Fig. 3: *The Creature from the Black Lagoon* figure standing on a big shelf in the upstairs room of the Tanya Bonakdar Gallery in 2011. Drawing by Jordan Cloninger.

ulation from me. In the studio, I incidentally observed a studio apparatus (a series of shelving units) designed to store objects. Whitehead's cosmology of concrescence and Barad's theory of apparatuses both readily explain this difference. OOO has to perform all sort of schematic gymnastics to explain this difference.

But (and here is the *particular* trap that Steinbach's work sets for OOO), in the gallery alone, without a point of extra-gallery comparison, properly seduced theorists may *imbue* all sorts of qualities and withdrawn essences into these helplessly receptive shelf objects. Then those same objects, once imbued with this new (human-theoretical) essence, may be used as object oriented poster children (poster objects?) – proof positive that all objects in the universe behave like Steinbach's shelf objects. OOO would contend that Steinbach's work gives us oblique insight (albeit not direct access) into the essence of objects, an essence that was there all along. Process philosophy (as I'm employing it) would contend that Steinbach's work creates an event which entices humans to have undeniably resonant, poetic feelings of allure toward an ensemble of objects; feelings to which the objects themselves, alas, are almost utterly indifferent. OOO would say that the Creature object in the gallery is the same as the Creature object in the studio, and the gallery just helps humans realize *more* of what it already is. Whitehead would say that the Creature object in the gallery and the Creature object in the studio are not the same object. They are both enduring objects made up of an ongoing series of related actual occasions, changing from occasion to occasion as they prehend (or negatively prehend) the rest of the world. But the actual occasions in the gallery are not at all the same as the actual occasions in the studio.

00:02 entices OOO with its (Apparently) Flat Ontology

Flat ontology is the broad idea that all objects are objects in their objectness, and that there is no real hierarchy of objectness. Flat ontology is not unique to OOO. A form of flat ontology is (arguably) found in actor–network theory, the sociological model of Bruno Latour. Actor–network theory (hereafter ANT) is designed to help humans think properly about objects in situ in the world. According to ANT, objects are indeed connected, with each other and with humans, at microcosmic and macrocosmic scales, and we humans should better attend to these objecty connections, this democracy of objects (of which we ourselves are just one part). For Actor Network Theory, objects have meaning in relation to other objects, as nodes in a broader and reconfigurable network. The network is flatter and not as hierarchical as we humans had originally supposed. Latour's flat ontology has led to a literary trope amongst OOO writers called the "Latour litany," where incongruous objects (incongruous from the perspective of humans, one supposes) are listed one after the other, indifferent to any hierarchy (indeed, they are implicitly required to *not* seem hierarchical). These litanies are meant to indicate (by force of repetition and alliteration) that objects are objects are objects, regardless of scale, material, complexity, animality, etc.

But once objects in situ have been removed from their networks and placed with their open and empty sockets in a gallery on Steinbach's shelves, ANT has less to say about the nature of these curious, *pragmatically disentangled* objects. This is because Steinbach's objects are not actively connected to the world in their ordinary use capacities (the lava lamps are not enticing hippies to have trippy trips; the trash cans are not receiving trash). And ANT is a tool for dealing with objects actively situated in networks.

To put it another way, Steinbach *seems* to have thrown the brakes on the intra-active becomings that create time. With time *seemingly* frozen, objects begin to feel much less verb-y and much more noun-y. And noun-y objects are OOO's raison d'être. At this point, OOO is enticed to rush in and fill in the metaphysical gaps about which ANT would otherwise hesitate to speculate. Because of their superficially apparent incongruity, Steinbach's shelf objects initially *seem* to be ideal illustrations of the flat ontology that Latour litanies are meant to illustrate. But from a formalist theoretical perspective, the objects are not at all incongruous. They have all sorts of formal volumetric, scalar, color, shape, and material relations. And even from a Marxist perspective, the objects still retain their own unique production histories and prior use functions in the historical context of human economic markets. And from a theatrical perspective, the objects are always facing outward toward their human audiences. They never face each other. They are on display *for us*. Similar to characters in a stage play, the objects are staged to perform the fiction of their implicit relationships and dialogues with each other *for us*. And so, once again, the object ensembles willingly yield themselves up to be used as proof positive of the explanatory prowess of their latest theory suitor, while still remaining polyamorously faithful(?) to all of their prior theory suitors.

Why Am I Still Talking about OOO?

Like Steinbach's object ensembles, Object Oriented Ontology sets its own kind of trap. It is a purposeful provocation that trolls other theorists into interminable debates about its own speculative assertions. I don't intend to have the final word on OOO in this brief subsection of a chapter in a book about art. I only mean to engage with OOO long enough to illustrate that it doesn't get the final word about *00:02*. To Steinbach's shelf/object ensembles, OOO is just the latest in an increasingly long series of illicit affairs. As with all its other theory suitors, Steinbach's work entices OOO, lures it out into the open, yields to it, and then has to go because it has a call on the other line.

The Most Ardent Suitor: Semiotics

Semiotics has been attracted to Steinbach's object ensembles from the beginning, in part because both were coming to prominence in the United States during the late 1970s. There are all sorts of flavors of semiotics, but Ferdinand de Saussure's is the easiest to digest, which is no doubt why it has become so popular. According to Saussurean semiotics, a signifier signifies a signified. Both signifier and signified together constitute a sign. A signifier can be the word "dog" signifying a physical dog, or it can be a physical dog signifying all other dogs. Saussure discovered that chains of signification are infinite (they never arrive at any core or grounding signified [like

God] that would act as the foundational, bedrock guarantor of meaning for the chains of signification leading up to it). He also discovered that semiotic signifiers (words) are arbitrarily coupled to their signifieds (in other words, the word "dog" is no more or less inherently "doggy" than the word "chien" or the word "perro"). Derrida took these two discoveries and ran with them into the wilds of deconstruction. To me, Charles Sanders Peirce has a much more robust and grounded tri-part semiotic system made up of sign, object, and interpretant (compared to Saussure's merely bi-part system of signifier and signified), but Peirce's system never gained the popularity of Saussure's system.

Semiotics is seduced by Steinbach's shelf/object ensembles because they look like sentences made out of objects and shelves. The shelf sections act like sentence diagrams, indicating the grammatical sentence parts. This object must be the subject, and that object must be the predicate. Steinbach's objects are often repeated, and more or less interchangeable because of their mass-produced nature, so they seem like common nouns. To semiotics, there is nothing different about the following two words – "lamp" and "lamp" – other than the context in which they are used (and in this particular sentence, there is not that much difference between their two contextual usages). I could swap the first "lamp" for the second "lamp," and you would not be able to tell the difference. For this reason, to the semiotic suitor, *00:02* "reads" like a kind of physically instantiated sentence. *00:02* is purposefully designed to give itself over to this semiotic "reading." As already mentioned, the objects in Steinbach's ensembles are prepared with an overt understanding of formalism and minimalism. These approaches combine with the hermetic, Platonic idealism of the white cube gallery to ontologically sterilizes and de-individualize Steinbach's objects, preparing them for easy assimilation into the semiotic regime of interchangeable signifiers.

But of course, there is a problem. If the phrase "trash can" points to some physical object that functions as a garbage receptacle, then what does an actual physical trash can point to? Also, the two trash cans in *00:02* are not interchangeable – the light of the gallery reflects differently off of one than off of the other. Are we meant to bracket these "surface" differences and solely focus on the "essence" of the object-noun-ness of the trash cans? Are the different light reflections from the trash cans simply incidental to their trash-can-ness, like the same word set in two different typefaces? Are typefaces simply incidental? Incidental to whom, and in what ways? In what ways are object-signifiers different than word-signifiers? When an object becomes a signifier, to whom does it become a signifier? When an object is placed beside another object, do they become "signifiers" to each other? Or is signification solely a human phenomenon? Is there any way for an object to fully resist being "read" as a signifier? What would such a non-signification cloaking device look like? Would it "read" as "unreadable?" Would its non-significance even be able to signify? Such are the questions that have provided the erotic fuel which has stoked the flames of the liaison between the semiotic suitor and Steinbach's object ensembles for decades. Let us briefly open up a few of these worm cans.

An Emphasis on the Space between the Nouns
(Alas, for Naught)

Because Steinbach's object signifiers are so semiotically vague, we are forced to concentrate on the space between his objects and on their own implicit signification. Like translating a foreign language where we don't know the meaning of the nouns, perhaps a proper understanding of the articles and prepositions between the nouns will give us some clue. As if we somehow have a better chance of gaining a semiotic purchase on the spaces *between* the trash cans and the lava lamps than we do of gaining a semiotic purchase on the trash cans and the lava lamps themselves.

This shift of emphasis from nouns to articles and prepositions occurs in the work of Samuel Beckett, Gertrude Stein, and Emily Dickinson. Here is Samuel Beckett's (implicit) mission statement as a writer, age 26:

> The experience of my reader shall be between the phrases, in the silence, communicated by the intervals, not the terms, of the statement, between the flowers that cannot coexist, at the antithetical (nothing so simple as antithetical) seasons of words, his experience shall be the menace, the miracle, the memory, of an unspeakable trajectory.[34]

But, whereas Beckett and Stein often leave semantic relational structures intact while omitting (or obscuring, via pronoun-ization) the nouns which these structures relate (relations preceding relata, so to speak), Steinbach does something even more confounding. He allows common "nouns" (trash can, lava lamp) to remain as common nouns (albeit physical-object-nouns), but he makes them so minimalistically concrete that they refuse to operate explicitly as semiotic signifiers and merely seem like plain old objects (they are what they are). So, we are forced to turn our attention to the shelves in an attempt to try and find some more concrete prepositional or grammatical meaning to these object sentences. But we are stymied there as well. If the ensembles are sentences, they are indeed written in a foreign language. Perhaps we are discovering the hidden language of objects! More likely, we are discovering the failure of semiotics to ex-

---

34 Samuel Beckett, *Dream of Fair to Middling Women*, eds. Eoin O'Brien and Edith Fournier (London: Calder, 1993), 138. The main character Belacqua muses these lines.

clusively and reductively interpret Steinbach's work. And of course, displaying this failure of the semiotic suitor to "make an honest woman" out of the object ensembles is the goal of the object ensembles.

A Surrealistic Language of Objects

Unable to properly nail down any specific semiotic meaning, our human imaginations run wild in an affectively rich play of multiple, supra-semiotic possibilities. Such free and refracting imaginings are properly understood as surrealistic. Plenty of theorists have noticed the power of uncanny objects to trigger surrealistic connections. Foucault on Magritte: "It is in dream that men, at last reduced to silence, commune with the signification of things and allow themselves to be touched by enigmatic, insistent words that come from elsewhere."[35] Derrida: "The dreamer invents his own grammar."[36] Even Whitehead:

An inhibition of familiar sensa is very apt to leave us a prey to vague terrors respecting a circumambient world of causal operations. In the dark there are vague presences, doubtfully feared; in the silence, the irresistible causal efficacy of nature presses itself upon us; in the vagueness of the low hum of insects in an August woodland, the inflow into ourselves of feelings from enveloping nature overwhelms us; in the dim consciousness of half-sleep, the presentations of sense fade away, and we are left with the vague feeling of influences from vague things around us.[37]

---

35 Michel Foucault, *This Is Not a Pipe*, trans. and ed. James Harkness (Berkeley: University of California Press, 1983), 49.
36 Jacques Derrida, *Writing and Difference*, trans. Alan Bass (London: Routledge, 2005), 262.
37 Whitehead, *Process and Reality*, 176.

I would argue that Steinbach's object ensembles are uber-surrealistic precisely because of their bald-faced realism. The objects in *00:02* trigger all of the surrealistic connections and imaginings that vague and hazy liminal objects invoke, while still remaining utterly clear and plain. Germano Celant calls Steinbach's objects, "resolutely palpable."[38] The stage magician's trick is all the more harrowing when there is no smoke and there are no mirrors; everything is plain as day, and yet still the magic occurs. The object ensembles have nothing up their sleeve. We should be able to figure this out. How are they tricking us?

Whitehead's observations give us a clue. Via minimalism, formalism, and the white cube gallery, the object ensembles shut down the ordinary noise of objects in functional situ, and our own thoughts rush to fill in this vacuum. We are not hearing the withdrawn essence of real objects (or even the clamoring of their sensual object counterparts), and we are not hearing a new form of object language (objects calling out to other objects via semiotic signification). We are hearing ourselves theorizing that we are hearing these things.

Semiotics Plus X

Jenny Jaskey suggests that the object ensembles are *both* semiotic *and* caught up in situational networks somewhat similar to the ones described by ANT:

> Steinbach cares about how cultural valuation gets altered through language and about how the stuff of everyday life has its own rich material interchange in excess of what might be said about it by us [...]. His works are invested in revealing how objects gain or lose different kind of significance for humans [...], but that they are at the same time undeniably material

38   Celant, "An Existential Building Site," 383.

aggregations of a human–inhuman matrix that continue to gather momentum as they take on new forms over time."[39]

Her interpretation is not so much that Steinbach's object ensembles are interpretable *neither* by semiotics *nor* by ANT, but that they are simultaneously interpretable both. I agree with this. I would only add that they are also simultaneously interpretable as minimalist, formalist, psychological, and phenomenological. Furthermore (and here is the main point of this chapter, in case you somehow missed it), by purposefully being simultaneously interpretable from all of these theoretical perspectives, Steinbach's object ensembles are *primarily* apophatic art apparatus for capturing human theories.

My Favorite Suitor: Artist as Master Craftsman

If I had to choose which of all the suitors I find most convincing, I would choose the Artist as Master Craftsman suitor. I agree with those who think that Haim Steinbach is a master craftsman of displaying objects on shelves. He is idiosyncratically and uniquely skillful at displaying objects that confound human interpretation. His chosen medium is the display of objects. If you think anyone can do this as well as Steinbach, try it on a shelf in your own home. The results are virtually guaranteed to be much less enticing and much less disturbing than *00:02*. Steinbach's object ensembles are so confoundingly evocative because he is really, really good at displaying objects, and he's had a lot of practice. Steinbach is the Michelangelo of obfuscatory object display. That is my contention, in an era where the artist as craftsman is beyond passé, and

---

39 Jenny Jaskey, "The Unstatic," in Steinbach, Ruf, et al., *Haim Steinbach*, 399.

arranging found objects hardly qualifies as a craft or a medium. Steinbach is so good at displaying objects, he got bored with it and went on to master the meta-craft of displaying display itself.

Perhaps Steinbach *is* a kind of object-whisperer after all. He is able to discern object relationships that are particularly resonant in a number of simultaneous ways: formally, phenomenologically, art-historically, pop-culturally, humorously, ironically, functionally. When we feel as if we hear the voice of the objects calling to us and to one another, we are really experiencing traces of the idiosyncratic hand of the master craftsman coming to us through his medium. Steinbach has spent time sitting with these objects. When we ourselves sit with the objects in the gallery, we are also sitting with his prior sittings with the objects. Steinbach is in the room with us and the objects.

Steinbach himself describes the objects in his ensembles not like words in sentences, but like pieces on a game board:

> The thinking around the object [...] starts with the concept of the game board, because for me it is like [...] a blueprint of the thinking of the arrangement of the pieces. Also, while a game involves a scheme and a strategy, it also consists of aspects of chance. There is engagement as well as the unpredictable.[40]

And elsewhere, "I do not 'curate' objects, but put them into play."[41] In Steinbach's game, the pawns are the Kong-

---

40 Steinbach, "Haim Steinbach in Conversation with Tom Eccles, Beatrix Ruff, and Hans Ulrich Obrist," 368.
41 Haim Steinbach, interview by Ginger Wolfe-Suarez, *InterReview* 6 (2005): 55.

brand rubber chew toys.[42] Maybe the giant Hulk hands are the rooks? In Steinbach's own words:

> Each [object ensemble] is a study in different relations, like [Joseph] Albers with colors and squares. He kept doing the color studies to see what would happen when you put the different colors in play, their affinities with each other in different contexts, within a constrained system. I am doing a similar thing with these objects.[43]

According to Steinbach, the object ensembles are also about math, number relations, repetition, and the difference between one and many.[44] Perhaps the next theoretical suitors will be game theorists and number set theorists.

From another perspective, Steinbach has described the ensembles as musical compositions. "When I arrange these objects, I am looking for new sounds. Sometimes something will sound too familiar, and I will move on. Sometimes something will sound foreign, and I am intrigued. I ask, why is that foreign to me? Why am I bothered by it?"[45] The goal is not necessarily to create the most "harmonious" compositions, but to create compositions with new and uncanny frequencies.

So, is Steinbach an object composer, an object game player, or a displayer of display? Of course, he is all of these and more. According to the Artist as Master Craftsman theory, Steinbach is simply an artist who has mastered the idiosyncratic and peculiar rules of his own self-devised art game, the same way other great artists (Rembrandt, Klee, Duchamp) have mastered the idiosyncratic

42 Haim Steinbach, interview with the author at Steinbach's New York studio, April 21, 2017.
43 Ibid.
44 Ibid.
45 Ibid.

and peculiar rules of their own self-devised art games. Duchamp's king was a sideways urinal; Steinbach's king is the Creature from the Black Lagoon.

Conclusion

Which theoretical suitor will "get the girl?" All of them to greater or lesser degrees, but none of them exclusively. Is my own meta-theoretical interpretation just one more theoretical interpretation destined to take its place in the suitor line? In order for my interpretation to be self-consistent, it has to be; and I'm fine with that. I don't want to reduce *00:02* once and for all. I simply want to show the ways in which it functions as a particularly wily apophatic art apparatus. *00:02* is a theory trap. It lures theories out, and then paradoxically resists their exclusive theoretical interpretations by simultaneously yielding to all of them. It makes nothing of human theories. Even now it sits in the Stedelijk, silently awaiting future suitors.

III

CONCLUSIONS

7

TOWARD AN ETHICS OF NOTHING

"Nothing is more frowned upon than nothing."
– Eugene Thacker[1]

"Sometimes nothing is a real cool hand."
– Cool Hand Luke

The goal of this book has been not simply to explain and demonstrate some ways in which artworks function as apparatuses. Instead, I have specifically focused on artworks that make nothing – artworks that function as apophatic apparatuses. Why nothing? If all artworks function as apparatuses, then all one has to do to participate in the ongoing becomings of the universe is to keep making works of art. The problem is, the universe doesn't always tend toward becoming better, beneficial, good, or even decent. So how to co-modulate the universe's becomings so that the universe becomes something better? I will go ahead and bracket the following questions: What is "better?" Better according to what criteria? Better for whom? etc. I don't mean to establish a universally agreed upon definition of "better" in this chapter. My interest

---

1   Eugene Thacker, "Three Questions on Demonology," paper presented at *Hideous Gnosis: Black Metal Theory Symposium* 1, Brooklyn, NY, December 2009, 219.

is more in the logistical pragmatics of becoming. What-ever your definition of "better," understanding the ways in which the universe becomes anew is bound to aid you in co-steering the universe toward a future that might be better. The ability to make nothing of becoming (how-ever temporarily) is an important tool for the practicing artist who hopes to make the universe better.

We should really abandon the term "better" (which reeks of linear progressivism and teleology) for a "bet-ter" way of describing "better." My own ethical goal for writing this book is that more people would make more art that matters more. What does "matters" mean? Mat-ters according to what criteria? Matters to whom? These are questions that each artist must answer for herself. If, according to Whitehead, the universe is becoming new every moment, then the simple avant-garde goal of mak-ing art that is new is not enough. Just by making art at all, we are already making art that is new (even if only slight-ly new). If, according to Whitehead, everything matters somewhat, to something, somewhere; then it is not even enough to make art that simply matters, because every-thing made always already matters (even if only a little bit). The problem is, most things hardly matter at all. So how to make something that matters more than a little bit? And, returning to Robert Irwin's question, "How to achieve the maximum transformation with the mini-mum alteration?"

The ability to make nothing is simply one tool that an artist can use in her quest toward making something new that matters. The ability to brake (however temporarily) a part of the universe from becoming is a useful ability to have for a number of reasons. Braking becoming can reveal the contours of becoming in a way that simply becoming-along-with-becoming cannot. Discovering the fissures, mechanisms, and holes of becomings could lead to more rigorous, adept, and efficacious ways of be-coming. Hard-braking (i.e., making nothing) also allows us a chance to steer radically on ice, "ice" being the slippery contemporary pace of our technological and media-saturated era. Rather than hurtling forward with every new capitalist-driven becoming, desperately pumping our brakes, sliding along and turning our wheels left and right without gaining any real purchase on the path toward our desired becomings; the hard-braking of making nothing gives us the ability to gain some purchase, to make turns on ice that would simply not be possible with ordinary turning, or even with gradual braking.

When using an emergency brake to steer on ice, not all hard-braking tactics are exactly the same. At what speed do you throw the brake? Where are your wheels pointing while the brake is thrown? How long do you leave the brake engaged? How quickly do you accelerate once the brake is released? All of these decisions modulate qualitatively different turnings and qualitatively different new directions. Likewise, not all apophatic apparatuses make the same kinds of nothing, and not all nothings lead to the same kinds of new becomings. Some nothings leave you pointing west, some leave you pointing east, and some leave you spinning your wheels in a ditch. Hence, there is nothing particularly magic or inherently ethical about simply throwing the brakes on becoming. It all depends on how you implement the hard-braking tactic. Yours could be an ingenious move that leads to a new way out of rote and cyclical becomings, or it could be a disastrous move that makes things worse than when you began. The trick is in learning how to deftly use the ability to make nothing in conjunction with other apparatal ways of making something.

It is worth emphasizing that the ethical goal of making nothing is not to bring the universe (or even part of it) to a grinding halt forever, just as the goal of hard-braking a car on ice is not to wind up at a dead stop, spinning your wheels in the same place forever. For one thing, it is impossible to permanently halt the ongoing becomings of any part of the universe. Even decay and dementia are kinds of becoming. For another thing, even if a permanent dead stop were possible, there would hardly be much ethical about permanently freezing the universe, or even our own little Earth-scaled part of it.

In this chapter, I want to accomplish a few things. First, I want to distinguish the rigorous nothings that apophatic art apparatuses make from a few other kinds of nothings with which they might accidentally be confused. Second, I want to suggest some ways that making nothing might reveal the contours of the process by which the new is actually made. Third, I want to propose that making nothing can be a way of braking rote and cyclical becomings. Fourth, I want to explore some ways that nothings might be used to more purposefully activate new becomings which might come to actually matter. Fifth, I want to confess that making nothing (when done properly) is a pure wager which could actually make things worse. And finally, I want to explain that although making nothing (when done properly) cannot be guaranteed to lead anywhere in particular, it is always guaranteed to lead somewhere at all.

Some Nothings That Apophatic Art Apparatuses Do *Not* Make

Apophatic art apparatuses are not purposefully nihilistic. Nor are they purposefully misanthropic. They don't mean to bring an end to all human civilization so that we may be succeeded by post-humans, dolphins, cephalopods, aliens, or artificial intelligences. To desire any of these outcomes is already to desire something much more specific than apophasis allows. The goal of apophatic art apparatuses is to brake rote becomings so that eventually qualitatively new somethings may emerge. The goal is not to attain some permanent state of nothingness, whether on a global human scale (your apparatus leads to the extinction of human thought), or on an individual human scale (everyone who encounters your apparatus instantly dies). As Deleuze and Guattari caution, once an individual human dies, she loses a large amount of agency.[2] The nothings that apophatic art apparatuses make are meant to tweak humans, not to delete them.

Neither are apophatic art apparatuses iconoclastic. They do not mean to remove the visual until nothing remains. Indeed, the five apophatic art apparatuses examined in this book all employ the visual in order to make their nothings. Besides, the mere removal of something is not yet the creation of nothing. Removing something creates an absence, and an absence is simply another kind of something.

Apophatic art apparatuses are not the same as apophatic literary apparatuses, just as art is not the same as literature. The two different kinds of apparatuses make different kinds of nothings. I am not saying that language is merely denotative, mimetic, or semiotic. Far from it. Language itself is a force in the world. Both literary apparatuses and art apparatuses work with humans to create bodily affect. But there is something different about the way in which Arakawa and Gins use language in *Mechanism of Meaning* and the way in which Pseudo-Dionysius uses language in *Mystical Theology*. In general, *Mechanism of Meaning* and other apophatic art apparatuses engage humans more holistically and bodily than apophatic literary apparatuses. According to Elizabeth Grosz, this type of holistic engagement is a particular strength of art. "[Art] is culture's most direct mode of enhancement or intensification of bodies, culture's mode for the elabora-

2   Gilles Deleuze and Félix Guattari, *A Thousand Plateaus: Capitalism and Schizophrenia*, trans. Brian Massumi (Minneapolis: University of Minnesota Press, 1987), 162.

tion of sensations, and thus culture's most intense debt to the chaotic forces it characterizes as nature."[3]

Apophatic art apparatuses are not really "postmodern." They don't mean to freeze the current era of art ("the contemporary") in order to reflectively analyze it and critically contemplate it forever. To do so would not be to make nothing, but rather to make a perpetual state of contemplation. This move toward perpetual reflection and critical self-analysis is often driven by an ethic of hesitation, skepticism, and doubt – a postmodern ethic born out of the sour grapes of modernism's heroic failures. This reflective postmodern ethic is not the ethic I am proposing. Apophatic art apparatuses perform pragmatic brakings that open ways for qualitatively new becomings. From the perspective of apophatic art apparatuses, an ethics of permanent braking and perpetual wheel-spinning would be a true ethical failure.

Apophatic art apparatuses do not merely refuse to participate in some particular aspect of contemporary commodification. In this sense, they are not really Bataillean. Instead, apophatic art apparatuses are more like Melville's Bartleby: they would prefer not to participate in anything and everything. Their apophatic "refusals" are less refusals to participate in some specific *kind* of becoming which they find distasteful, and more a holistic braking of the process of becoming *in general*.

The nothings made by apophatic art apparatuses cannot be achieved via willy-nilly, slipshod, or haphazard craft. Apophatic art apparatuses must always be intentional, well-considered, and rigorous. True, these apophatic nothings can't be manipulated to lead anywhere in particular, but unless they are ingeniously crafted, they will always wind up leading somewhere rote. Any old result at all is not the same as a heretofore unknown

3   Elizabeth Grosz, *Chaos, Territory, Art: Deleuze and the Framing of the Earth* (New York: Columbia University Press, 2008), 23.

result. Yes, both results are unknown, but for completely different reasons. The former result is unknown because we don't know which of several already-known things it will be like. The latter result is unknown because we don't know what new thing it will be at all. A kind of meticulous wagering is required. Derrida speaks of a way of proceeding "as gaily and scientifically as possible."[4] Gregory Ulmer describes Derrida's own process as "so rigorously irresponsible."[5] And Deleuze and Guattari admonish, "How necessary caution is, the art of dosages, since overdose is a danger. You don't do it with a sledgehammer, you use a very fine file."[6] Nothings worth making won't be made haphazardly.

Finally, this book really is meant to lead to the actual creation of more (and more effective) apophatic art apparatuses. If an increased appreciation of apophatic art apparatuses also occurs, all the better. But my ethical goal in writing this book is not merely to make some sort of academic, intellectual, theoretical move in the micro-community of art theorists and experimental curators. This book is primarily intended for art educators and practicing artists. For art educators, hopefully the ideas shared in this book will suggest ways of moving students beyond the mere creation of images and objects (which incidentally happen to function as apparatuses), and on toward the purposeful creation of apparatuses (which incidentally happen to incorporate images and objects). For artists, hopefully the close readings of the selected artworks in this book will inform your conceptual and material practices and processes. It would be a shame if all that resulted from this book was that an increasing

4   Jacques Derrida, "Entre Crochets: entretien avec Jacques Derrida," Digraphe 8 (1976): 112, translated by Gregory Ulmer in *Applied Grammatology: Post(e)-Pedagogy from Jacques Derrida to Joseph Beuys* (Baltimore: Johns Hopkins University Press, 1985), 59.
5   Ulmer, *Applied Grammatology*, 145.
6   Deleuze and Guattari, *A Thousand Plateaus*, 160.

amount of artist statements began including the term "apparatus" without any of the art work actually changing much. And specifically, for those artists whose practices tend toward the apophatic (or whose work could benefit from a modicum of hard-braking every now and then), hopefully this book inspires and equips you to develop increasingly ingenious braking traps. The world needs more rigorous and purposeful nothings so that new, heretofore unknown, and (hopefully) worthwhile somethings might (eventually) emerge.

Making Nothing Reveals the Ways in Which Somethings Are Made

Making nothing is a kind of limit-case of making something. It puts the brakes on ordinary becomings in such a way that the contours of those becomings become more readily apparent. Revealing the contours of becoming is not all that making nothing does, but it is one of its advantages. A better understanding of the ways in which becomings occur leads to a more adept and nuanced ability to purposefully tweak becomings so that new, mattering somethings might emerge more often. It is not enough to merely claim that becomings happen. Of course they do. In order to ethically and effectively modulate becomings, it is necessary to get in and mess with the material flows of actual occasions to discover the specific contours of how becomings happen in particular instances and contexts.

Chapters 3–6 analyze five unique apophatic art apparatuses in order to understand a variety of ways that becoming may be braked. Each of these apophatic art apparatuses are ethical wagers of their own. Each change the world and make it something other than what it was. They are not solely or even primarily meant to be case studies or explorations of becoming. Nevertheless, they do serve as useful lenses through which to understand the mechanisms of becoming, and they serve as models for the construction of new apophatic art apparatuses.

The way to the truly new always begins with an understanding of the past, because historical material decisions have been made in the actual world via countless actual occasions which have resulted in our contemporary present world of well-decided, well-decohered, enduring objects. These material histories must be taken into consideration. Ahistoricism in art movements inevitably leads to rote historical reenactments of prior ahistorical art movements. Regardless of what many of the early-twentieth-century avant-garde art manifestos claimed, we are never able to begin at square one. Not every part of the universe exists in a quarantined, prepared, quantum-behaving state. Not all things are possible. What is currently possible is contingent upon (although not wholly predetermined by) prior decisions that have already been made. According to Whitehead, insofar as we remain in our current cosmic epoch, the mechanisms of becoming are themselves constant – the ways in which the new emerges are not themselves emergent. These ways of emergence may be investigated, understood, and exploited. Making nothing doesn't re-set the entire universe to a disintegrated, primal state. It simply exposes the current contours of becoming.

There are some ethical dangers in misunderstanding the mechanisms of becoming and the role that humans play in becoming. At one incorrect extreme, I may imagine myself having much more agency than I actually do. This results in a kind of fantasy ethics where everything I do matters a great deal. I flap my wings in North America, and the great wall of China is blown down. This is nothing more than an impotent faux-agency, causing me to waste my time on ineffective modulations of the world. Yes, everything matters; but lots and lots and lots of things matter hardly at all, at any scale, to any one or any thing, at any time, more or less ever. Unless I am willing to own that fact, I will waste an awful lot of time modulating an awful lot of things and claiming that I am having an awful lot more affective influence than I actually am, instead of spending my time figuring out how to most effectively modulate that which matters most.

It is indeed radical to want to undo all accreted concrescent histories and return to a zero-state of pure potentia. Fortunately, this is simply not possible. Merely ignoring historical accretions and entanglements will not undo them. Yes, my human decisions matter; but I also have to respect the fact that the historical decisions of other entities (human, non-human, part-human) also matter, and that my current decisions are in some ways contingent on their prior decisions. Bashing away at the well-decided, decohered world as if it were the cohered quantum world is a futile exercise in impotent faux-agency. To acknowledge this fact is to escape from idealized solipsism into true intra-active accountability.

Another ethical problem with such radical, zero-state, reset agendas is the loss of valuable accretions, ingressions, and glommed-up complexities that have come to matter a great deal in the contemporary world. One such valuable accretion is human consciousness (whatever that actually is). Prepared photons in a double-slit apparatus are radically unique because they begin with a kind of direct, pre-cohered access to pure potentia. But human consciousness is also unique, because speculative human thought has achieved a radical wildcard agency at well-decided and decohered states that rocks simply do not possess. A rock is not going to up and take itself for a walk; a human may (skipping as she goes). A prepared photon may be a wildcard in quantum-behavior-measuring apparatuses, but as a photon increasingly decoheres, it necessarily loses its pure potential agency (for location, momentum, spin, etc.). Whereas well-decohered humans still retain all sorts of wildcard agency (for good and for ill).

At another incorrect extreme, the realization that my own agency is always contingent upon the prior decisions of other entities can lead to a kind of defeatist determinism (the lie that my decisions are totally pre-determined). This is to misunderstand the co-creative (intra-active) nature of becoming. Yes, the prior decisions of other entities matter, but they do not solely pre-determine and pre-define a world "out there" apart from me, a world which I may only subjectively interpret from "in here." To acknowledge this fact is to escape from (the fictions of) correlationism and into (an awareness of) intra-action.

Apophatic art apparatuses provoke and lure human entities into an awareness of the creative propensity of the universe, and into a more accurate understanding of their own agency within the universe. By braking becomings, by luring humans and other enduring objects into actual occasions that stymie and trouble their becomings, apophatic art apparatuses invite humans to feel the contours of becoming itself, and to imagine other ways in which humans and the universe might become. This more accurate feel for the contours of becoming should lead in turn to a less quixotic, less defeatist, more efficacious exercising of human agency.

By examining in detail these five specific apophatic art apparatuses, my goal is not just to help humans get a better feel for the contours of universal becomings, but to help them get a feel for the ways in which human-made art apparatuses may purposefully modulate these becomings. Elizabeth Grosz observes, "Art allows the difference, the incommensurability of subject and object to be celebrated, opened up, elaborated."[7] This is only half right. Karen Barad clarifies what is actually happening with apparatuses: "It is not merely the case that human concepts

7   Grosz, *Chaos, Territory, Art,* 75.

are embodied in apparatuses, but rather that apparatuses are discursive practices, where the latter are understood as specific material reconfigurings through which 'objects' and 'subjects' are produced."[8] Art apparatuses don't simply explore the pre-existing differences between pre-existing objects and pre-existing subjects. Art apparatuses actually produce what Whitehead calls superjects, entities that both prehend and are prehended by each other in intra-active becomings. All art apparatuses do this. Apophatic art apparatuses brake these becomings.

Making Nothing Brakes Rote and Cyclical Becomings

By refusing to move straight through the ordinary mechanisms of default becoming in general, apophatic art apparatuses brake rote and cyclical becomings, opening up the opportunity for new, more novel, less rote becomings to emerge. Describing literary apophasis, William Franke speaks of "words that negate themselves in order to evoke what is beyond words."[9] Similarly, apophatic art apparatuses contrive becomings that arrest themselves in order to evoke what may otherwise become.

My use of "apparatus" differs from Vilém Flusser's use of the term, but his observations are nonetheless relevant here. To Flusser, the technological devices upon which we rely are apparatuses programmed to keep us sleeping and needy: "These idiotic objects, these 'gadgets' that surround us, program us in two different ways. We are programmed so that we can no longer live with-

8   Karen Barad, *Meeting the Universe Halfway* (Durham: Duke University Press, 2007), 148.

9   William Franke, "Apophasis as a Mode of Discourse," preface to *On What Cannot Be Said: Apophatic Discourses in Philosophy, Religion, Literature, and the Arts, Volume 2*, ed. William Franke (Notre Dame: University of Notre Dame Press, 2007), 2.

out them and we are programmed in order not to notice their stupidity."[10] Apophatic art apparatuses might then be seen as sabotaging antidotes to Flusser's dependency-inducing, awareness-numbing technological apparatuses. Apophatic art apparatuses throw the brakes on the rote and cyclical becomings of contemporary capitalism. Pope.L's *Black Factory* is an exemplary, multi-scalar case in point. The hard-braking of apophatic art apparatuses breaks technological dependencies and awakens self-awareness (however temporarily). Such apparatal sabotaging is in line with Flusser's own ethics: "We can no longer be revolutionaries, which means to be opposed to the operative program through other programs. We can only be saboteurs, which means to throw sand on the apparatus' wheels. With effect: every current emancipatory action is, when intelligent, a subversive action."[11] Apophatic art apparatuses are not quite as reactionary as Flusser's model proposes, but they do mung-up and sabotage rote becomings while avoiding the purposeful reinstitution of equally diabolical rote becomings.

Making Nothing Is a Tool to More Purposefully Activate New Becomings

Although making nothing is not guaranteed to activate new becomings that matter, it prepares the way for a more purposeful activation of new becomings that might matter. I am not proposing that pure nothing in and of itself is an achievable state of endlessly fecund potential. According to my usage of the term, "making nothing" puts the brakes on becoming something. It does not create a noun called "nothing." Making nothing is an ethi-

10 Vilém Flusser, *Post-History*, trans. Rodrigo Maltez Novaes (Minneapolis: Univocal, 2013), 123.
11 Ibid., 127.

cal wager that heads toward a kind of less-than-specific-something. According to poet Alice Fulton, "Nothing will unfold for us unless we move toward what / looks to us like nothing."[12] "Making nothing" doesn't achieve a state so much as defer a process. The "nothing" made is a verb rather than a noun. Emily Dickinson conjures nothing aright:

> By homely gift and hindered Words
> The human heart is told
> Of Nothing —
> "Nothing" is the force
> That renovates the World —[13]

Gordon Bearn comes close to my understanding of "making nothing" when he describes Derrida's infamous *différance* as "a place holder for what may come."[14] Making nothing doesn't create what may come, but it leaves the side door open for something else to come vs. that same old something which was already coming through the front door. By deferring inevitable becoming (however briefly), making nothing lingers in an open moment, giving ordinarily hesitant (shy?) potentia a bit more chance to become actual. Following Deleuze and Bergson, Elizabeth Grosz explains, "Duration entails an open future, it involves the fracturing and opening up of the past and the present to what is virtual in them, to what in them

---

12 Alice Fulton, "Cascade Experiment," quoted in Barad, *Meeting the Universe Halfway*, 39.

13 Emily Dickinson, from Poem 1563, *The Poems of Emily Dickinson: Reading Edition*, ed. R.W. Franklin (Cambridge: The Belknap Press of Harvard University Press, 1999).

14 Gordon C.F. Bearn, "Differentiating Derrida and Deleuze," *Continental Philosophy Review* 33 (2000): 451.

differs from the actual, to what in them can bring forth the new."[15] Later, Grosz elaborates:

> [Life's] becomings are contingent only on its capacity to link with, to utilize, and transform, that is, to unbecome, the apparent givenness and inertia of material objects and to give to these objects new virtualities, new impulses and potentials. It needs to unbecome, to undo its actuality as fixed givenness in order for its virtualities to be capable of a new or different elaboration.[16]

Apophatic art apparatuses extend the duration of actual occasions, shaking loose calcified actual givens, giving hesitant potentia some extra time to actualize anew.

Deleuze uses the term "expression" to mean something akin to Whitehead's concrescence. Following Deleuze, Brian Massumi writes:

> To tend the stretch of expression, to foster and inflect it rather than trying to own it, is to enter the stream, contributing to its probings: this is co-creative, an aesthetic endeavor. It is also an ethical endeavor, since it is to ally oneself with change: for an ethics of emergence.[17]

Apophatic art apparatuses extend the stretch of expression, holding the door open (however fractionally longer) for what (otherwise) may eventually decide to emerge.

There is more than one way to make nothing, and the way in which one makes nothing *in some sense* (obliquely,

15 Elizabeth Grosz, "Bergson, Deleuze and the Becoming of Unbecoming," *parallax* 11, no. 2 (2005): 4.

16 Ibid., 10–11.

17 Brian Massumi, "Introduction: Like a Thought," in *A Shock To Thought: Expression after Deleuze and Guattari,* ed. Brian Massumi (London: Routledge, 2005), xxii.

indirectly, abstractly, affectively) affects the subsequent something that may eventually arrive. Making nothing doesn't *determine* the subsequent something that *will* arrive, but it *paves the path* along which the subsequent something *may* arrive. And certain somethings prefer certain paths over other paths. Setting a squirrel trap doesn't guarantee I'll catch a squirrel, but it precludes me catching an elephant.

Of course, apophatic art apparatuses don't simply leave open side doors, pave paths, and set squirrel traps. These are all over-simple analogies for what is actually happening. Apophatic art apparatuses are propositions that lure intra-active actual occasions into temporary aporias, momentary hesitations. The qualitative ways in which these aporias are created obliquely (but actually) influence the quality of the becomings which may finally emerge from these occasions. That description is less poetic, but more accurate.

Apophatic art apparatuses create aporias by rendering irrelevant certain "ordinary" functional behaviors of human and non-human objects, freeing both to function in heretofore undetermined ways. Apophatic art apparatuses don't directly try to make new humans and new materials. Instead, they free old humans and old materials from their old obligations so that both may perform new (heretofore unimagined) functions. Put another way, apophatic art apparatuses don't merely slow down the chunking mechanisms of becoming; they actually invite becoming to chunk otherwise. And since humans are always purposefully included in art apparatuses (by definition and design), apophatic art apparatuses invite humans to begin chunking their own post-apparatal occasions otherwise and anew.

Arakawa and Gins challengingly assert, "We have decided not to die." What do they mean by this? They mean they have decided not to organism. They have decided not to person. They have decided to hold the door of becoming open for as long as possible in order to see what other ways of (alter-, part-, post-)human becomings might emerge. Like Arakawa and Gins, apophatic art apparatuses have decided not to become (just yet). Like Bartleby, they would prefer not to (just yet). What might happen in the meantime?

Making Nothing Is a Wager (Things Could Get Worse)

There is no guarantee that something beneficial will come from making nothing. Indeed, if you are doing it right, there can be no guarantee, by definition. Making nothing could ultimately make the world worse. Or (more likely) it could not change the world all that much one way or another. To make nothing is to make some extra time in the immediate event of becoming, in order that something extra or unforeseen may emerge. If you already have in mind what is going to emerge, then you haven't really made nothing. Apophatic art apparatuses prolong and defer becomings. This prolongation is hard enough to achieve in and of itself without the added responsibility of guiding whatever emerges to some specific end.

Apophasis is not a tactic of resolutions and conclusions. Contrary to popular understanding, the goal of theological apophasis is not to create an experience of ecstatic union with God. Theologian Edmund Rybarczyk explains, "The apophatic approach is misunderstood if one envisions its goal as some kind of spiritual or ethereal experience. The Orthodox consistently warn both those whom seek some kind of phenomenological manifestation and those whom merely want to experience what an encounter with God might be like."[18] Theological apophasis may indeed clear the way for some future encounter with God – but it will always be a God known via his own revelation to humans, unbound by our ontological categorizations of him. Perhaps this self-revealing God will be utterly harrowing and terrifying. Or perhaps theological apophasis will lead to demon possession. Perhaps it will lead to an acute awareness of a godless abyss. Perhaps it will lead to nothing at all.

Whatever the case, if done properly, apophatic artmaking entails a perpetual risk. This is because apophasis necessarily involves what Michael Sells calls an "anarchic moment." He writes, "To attempt to place a guarantee within the [apophatic] anarchic moment is to transform apophatic discourse into non-apophatic discourse."[19] Without any guarantee, when the truly new arrives, how will we recognize it? Derrida suggests, "The future can only be anticipated in the form of an absolute danger. It is that which breaks absolutely with constituted normality and can only be proclaimed, presented, as a sort of monstrosity."[20] Well and good, but what exactly does an emergent monstrosity look like? It can't always resemble the same grotesque, Cronenbergian–Lovecraftian horror creatures, because we have already seen those forms of the monstrous.

One possible outcome of the apophatic wager is the emergence of an entirely new cosmic epoch. Arguably, in the 1900s, this happened twice in art (with Duchamp's *Fountain* and Cage's *4'33"*) and once in physics (with quantum mechanics). Brian Massumi describes such an

---

18 Edmund J. Rybarczyk, "Reframing Tongues: Apophaticism and Post-modernism," *Pneuma: The Journal of the Society for Pentecostal Studies* 27, no. 1 (2005): 87–88.

19 Michael A. Sells, *The Mystical Languages of Unsaying* (Chicago: University of Chicago Press, 1994), 213.

20 Jacques Derrida, *Of Grammatology*, trans. Gayatri Chakravorty Spivak (Baltimore: Johns Hopkins University Press, 1997), 5.

epochal shift in his *Parables for the Virtual*: "If feedback from the dimension of the emerged re-conditions the conditions of emergence, then it also has to be recognized that conditions of emergence change. Emergence emerges. Changing changes."[21] Karen Barad suggests that such meta-changes are indeed possible: "The very nature of change and the possibilities for change changes in an ongoing fashion as part of the world's intra-active dynamic."[22] In *Writing and Difference*, Derrida implies the possibility of such epochal shifts: "This hollow space is not an opening among others. It is opening itself, the opening of opening."[23] And Deleuze and Guattari suggest a kind of cosmic, artisanal experiment that "may go beyond all assemblages and produce an opening onto the cosmos."[24]

Such epochal shifts which change the very mechanisms of change itself remain the holy grail goal of the cosmic artisan. But even with radical epochal shifts, things could still get worse (and exponentially so). For example, we could shift from an epoch of rapid technological acceleration to an epoch of the extinction of human thought from the universe via the extinction of humans from the world. This would definitely constitute a new epoch, but (arguably) not a better one.

Making Nothing Always Leads to Something, But No Particular Something Is Ever Guaranteed.

Regardless of what does eventually emerge from making nothing, *something* eventually has to emerge. Just as

21 Brian Massumi, *Parables for the Virtual: Movement, Affect, Sensation* (Durham: Duke University Press, 2007), 10.

22 Barad, *Meeting the Universe Halfway*, 179.

23 Jacques Derrida, *Writing and Difference*, trans. Alan Bass (London: Routledge, 2005), 103.

24 Deleuze and Guattari, *A Thousand Plateaus*, 333.

making nothing can never guarantee that something *particular* will emerge; neither can it guarantee that nothing will *ever* emerge. Indeed, something always emerges. Even the Derridean game of perpetual deferral is an emergent *something* (namely, a game of perpetual deferral). As C.S. Peirce observes, "The vague always tends to become determinate, simply because its vagueness does not determine it to be vague [...]. It is not determinately nothing."[25] And elsewhere, "It must be by a contraction of the vagueness of that potentiality of everything in general, but of nothing in particular, that the world of forms comes about."[26]

The goal of making nothing is not to perpetually freeze becoming. Indeed, freezing becoming is not only impossible but also undesirable. Instead, the goal of apophatic art apparatuses is, via hard-braking, to modulate the flows of becoming in such a way that something which matters might eventually emerge. Theological apophasis is often criticized for beginning with the implicit desire to encounter God. But if you're doing it right, no such encounter is ever guaranteed. A similar critique could be leveled against those who desire a new kind of pagan or atheistic apophasis which inherently precludes an encounter with God. If you're doing apophasis right, you can't preclude anything. A similar critique could be leveled against deconstruction. Derrida admirably desires to keep presence and ontotheological assertions from rearing their kataphatic heads for as long as possible, but this ethic of resistance to closure can easily transition from perpetual non-commitment into an adamant commitment to the non-committal. To enact apophasis properly,

25 Charles S. Peirce, *The Essential Peirce: Selected Philosophical Writings*, vol. 2 (Bloomington: University of Indiana Press, 1998), 323–24, quoted in Brian Massumi, *The Principle of Unrest: Activist Philosophy in the Expanded Field* (London: Open Humanities Press, 2017), 144.

26 Charles Sanders Peirce, *Collected Papers of Charles Sanders Peirce, Volume VI: Scientific Metaphysics*, eds. Charles Hartshorne and Paul Weiss (Cambridge: Harvard University Press, 1935), 196.

it necessarily must be ephemeral and temporary. It must be open to eventually emerging into all sorts of possible actual outcomes. Indeed, proper apophasis must always expect its own eventual becoming.

Apophasis is ultimately about rigorously yielding oneself to whatever may come. As Eugene Thacker rightly discerns, "The admission of divine possession seems to entail the minimal admission of demonic possession."[27] Indeed, openness to possession by a monstrously new other which one does not currently control is at the core of the apophatic wager. Making nothing (hard-braking on ice) is a kind of losing control to see what may emerge. It always leads to something. Apophatic art apparatuses make nothings that may eventually lead to new somethings that matter (for better or worse). Then again, they may lead to nothing much at all. That is the wager.

---

27   Eugene Thacker, "The Shadows of Atheology: Epidemics, Power and Life after Foucault," *Theory, Culture & Society* 26, no. 6 (2009): 150.

BIBLIOGRAPHY

Arakawa, Shusaku, and Madeline Gins. *Mechanismus der Bedeutung (Werk im Entstechen: 1963–1971)*. Munich: Bruckmann, 1971.

———. *The Mechanism of Meaning: Work in Progress (1963–1971, 1978): Based on the Method of Arakawa*. New York: Harry N. Abrams, 1979.

———. *The Mechanism of Meaning*. New York: Abbeville Press, 1988.

——— "The Mechanism of Meaning." In *Reversible Destiny*, 54–111. New York: Guggenheim Museum Publications, 1997.

Artaud, Antonin. *Oeuvres Complètes IX*. Paris: Gallimard, 1971.

———. "To Henri Parisot (September 22, 1945)." In *Antonin Artaud: Selected Writings*, edited by Susan Sontag, translated by Helen Weaver, 448–51. New York: Farrar, Straus and Giroux, 1976.

Austin, J.L. *How To Do Things with Words*. London: Oxford University Press, 1962.

Azzarello, Pasqualina. "insides-out: an intimate look at the black factory by pasqualina azzarello, miss black factory, 2005." Privately published, 2005.

Baggott, James Edward. *Beyond measure: Modern Physics, Philosophy, and the Meaning of Quantum Theory*. Oxford: Oxford University Press, 2009.

Bakhtin, M.M. "The Problem of Speech Genres." In *Speech Genres and Other Late Essays,* edited by Caryl Emerson and Michael Holquist, translated by Vern W. McGee, 60–102. Austin: University of Texas Press, 1986.

———. "The Problem of the Text in Linguistics, Philology, and the Human Sciences: An Experiment in Philosophical Analysis." In *Speech Genres and Other Late Essays,* edited by Caryl Emerson and Michael Holquist, translated by Vern W. McGee, 103–31. Austin: University of Texas Press, 1986.

Barad, Karen Michelle. *Meeting the Universe Halfway: Quantum Physics and the Entanglement of Matter and Meaning.* Durham: Duke University Press, 2007.

Bearn, Gordon C.F. "Differentiating Derrida and Deleuze." *Continental Philosophy Review* 33 (2000): 441–65.

Beckett, Samuel. *Dream of Fair to Middling Women.* Edited by Eoin O'Brien and Edith Fournier. London: Calder, 1993.

Beckett, Samuel, and Georges Duthuit. "Proust." In *Proust and Three Dialogues with Georges Duthuit.* London: John Calder, 1987.

Benson, Bruce Ellis. *Graven Ideologies: Nietzsche, Derrida & Marion on Modern Idolatry.* Downers Grove: InterVarsity Press, 2002.

Bergson, Henri. *Creative Evolution.* Translated by Arthur Mitchell. New York: Henry Holt, 1911.

———. *Matter and Memory.* Translated by Nancy Margaret Paul and W. Scott Palmer. New York: Zone Books, 2005.

Bersani, Leo, and Ulysse Dutoit. *Arts of Impoverishment: Beckett, Rothko, Resnais.* Cambridge: Harvard University Press, 1993.

Bohr, Niels. "Discussion with Einstein on Epistemological Problems in Atomic Physics." In *Albert Einstein: Philosopher-Scientist,* edited by Paul Arthur Schilpp,

199–241. Library of Living Philosophers 7. 1949; New York: MJF Books, 1970.

Boym, Svetlana. *The Future of Nostalgia*. New York: Basic Books, 2001.

Celant, Germano. "An Existential Building Site." In Haim Steinbach, Beatrix Ruf, et al., *Haim Steinbach: Object and Display*, 381–89. New York: Gregory R. Miller & Co, 2015.

Chesterton, Gilbert K. *Orthodoxy*. New York: Dodd, Mead & Co., 1908.

Cloninger, Curt. "Bereft Nothing vs. Fecund Nothing (or Broken Icons vs. Glitched Gifs or the Dead End Zero vs. the Via Negativa)." *Textshop Experiments* 3 (2017). http://textshopexperiments.org/textshop03/bereft-nothing-vs-fecund-nothing.

———. "Eternity in An Instant: The Moving Images of David Crawford." In *Sequences: Contemporary Chrono-photography and Experimental Digital Art*, edited by Paul St George, 114–19. London: Wallflower, 2008.

———. *One per Year*. Brescia: Link Editions, 2014.

Colebrook, Claire. "Matter without Bodies." *Derrida Today* 4, no. 1 (2011): 1–20. DOI: 10.3366/drt.2011.0003.

Coleman, Ornette. Liner notes. *Naked Lunch: Music from the Original Motion Picture Soundtrack*. Milan America, 1992.

Crawford, David. "Algorithmic Montage." Master's thesis. University of Gothenburg, 2004.

———. "The Implication of Movement: From Bergson to Bohm." In *New Realities: Being Syncretic*, edited by Roy Ascott, Gerald Bast, et al., 78–81. Vienna: Springer, 2009.

Culler, Jonathan. *On Deconstruction: Theory and Criticism after Structuralism*. Ithaca: Cornell University Press, 1985.

Deleuze, Gilles. *Difference and Repetition*. Translated by Paul Patton. New York: Columbia University Press, 1994.

————. *The Fold: Leibniz and the Baroque*. Translated by Tom Conley. London: Athlone Press, 1993.

————. *Francis Bacon: The Logic of Sensation*. Translated by Daniel W. Smith. London: Continuum, 2003.

————. *The Logic of Sense*. Translated by Mark Lester with Charles Stivale. New York: Columbia University Press, 1990.

————. "Mediators." In *Negotiations: 1972–1990*, translated by Martin Joughin, 121–34. New York: Columbia University Press, 1997.

Deleuze, Gilles, and Félix Guattari. *A Thousand Plateaus: Capitalism and Schizophrenia*. Translated by Brian Massumi. Minneapolis: University of Minnesota Press, 1987.

————. *What Is Philosophy?* Translated by Hugh Tomlinson and Graham Burchell. London: Verso, 2009.

Deleuze, Gilles, Lyotard, J.-F., et al. "Discussion," after the presentation of Lyotard's "Notes sur le retour et le Kapital," and Deleuze's "Pensée nomade." In *Nietzsche AuJourd'hui, 1: Intensités*, 175–90. Paris: Union Générale D'Éditions, 1973.

Deleuze, Gilles, and Claire Parnet. *Dialogues II*. Translated by Hugh Tomlinson and Barbara Habberjam. New York: Columbia University Press, 2007.

Deleuze, Gilles, and Richard Pinhas. "Vincennes Seminar Session, May 3, 1997: On Music." Translated by Timothy S. Murphy. *Discourse: Journal for Theoretical Studies in Media and Culture* 20, no. 3 (Fall 1998): Article 23.

Derrida, Jacques. "Entre Crochets: entretien avec Jacques Derrida." *Digraphe* 8 (1976): 97–114.

————. "How to Avoid Speaking: Denials." Translated by Ken Frieden. In *Derrida and Negative Theology*, edited by Harold Coward and Toby Foshay, 73–142. Albany: State University of New York Press, 1992.

————. *Limited Inc*. Translated by Alan Bass and Samuel Webber. Evanston: Northwestern University Press, 1988.

————. *Of Grammatology*. Translated by Gayatri Chakravorty Spivak. Baltimore: Johns Hopkins University
Press, 1997.

————. *The Post Card: From Socrates to Freud and Beyond*.
Translated by Alan Bass. Chicago: The University of
Chicago Press, 1996.

————. "Post-Scriptum: Aporias, Ways and Voices."
Translated by John P. Leavey, Jr. In *Derrida and Nega-
tive Theology*, edited by Harold Coward and Toby
Foshay, 283–323. Albany: State University of New York
Press, 1992.

————. *The Truth in Painting*. Translated by Geoff Bennington and Ian McLeod. Chicago: University of
Chicago Press, 1987.

————. "The Villanova Roundtable." In *Deconstruction in
a Nutshell: A Conversation with Jacques Derrida*, edited by
John D. Caputo, 3–28. New York: Fordham University
Press, 1997.

————. *Writing and Difference*. Translated by Alan Bass.
London: Routledge, 2005.

Dickinson, Emily. *The Poems of Emily Dickinson: Reading
Edition*. Edited by R. W. Franklin. Cambridge: The
Belknap Press of Harvard University Press, 1999.

Duchamp, Marcel. "The Creative Act." In *The Essential
Writings of Marcel Duchamp*, edited by Michel Sanouil-
let and Elmer Peterson, 138–40. London: Thames and
Hudson, 1975.

Eastman, Timothy E., and Hank Keeton, eds. *Physics and
Whitehead: Quantum, Process, and Experience*. Albany:
State University of New York Press, 2004.

Eckhart, Meister. *The Complete Mystical Works of Meister
Eckhart*. Translated by Bernard McGinn. New York:
Crossroad, 2009.

————. *Meister Eckhart: The Essential Sermons, Commen-
taries, Treatises, and Defense*. Translated by Bernard
McGinn. The Classics of Western Spirituality. New
York: Paulist Press, 1981.

Epperson, Michael. *Quantum Mechanics and the Philosophy of Alfred North Whitehead.* New York: Fordham University Press, 2004.

Feynman, Richard P. "Lecture 37: Atomic Mechanics." In *The Feynman Lectures on Physics, Volume I (Mainly Mechanics, Radiation and Heat).* Pasadena: California Institute of Technology, 2013.

Fish, Stanley. *Professional Correctness: Literary Studies and Political Change.* New York: Oxford University Press, 1995.

Fludd, Robert. *The Origin and Structure of the Cosmos.* Translated by Patricia Tahil. Edinburgh: Magnum Opus Hermetic Sourceworks, 1982.

———. *Utriusque Cosmi, Maioris scilicet et Minoris, Metaphysica, Physica, atque Technica Historia.* Oppenheim: Johann Theodor de Bry, 1617. https://archive.org/details/utriusquecosmimao1flud/.

Flusser, Vilém. *Post-History.* Translated by Rodrigo Maltez Novaes. Minneapolis: Univocal, 2013.

———. *Towards a Philosophy of Photography.* Translated by Anthony Matthews. London: Reaktion Books, 2012.

Foucault, Michel. *This Is Not a Pipe.* Translated and Edited by James Harkness. Berkeley: University of California Press, 1983.

Franke, William. "Apophasis as a Mode of Discourse." Preface to *On What Cannot Be Said: Apophatic Discourses in Philosophy, Religion, Literature, and the Arts, Volume 2,* edited by William Franke, 1–8. Modern and Contemporary Transformations. Notre Dame: University of Notre Dame Press, 2007.

Galloway, Alexander. "Are Some Things Unrepresentable?" *Culture & Society* 28, No. 7–8 (2011): 85–102. DOI: 10.1177/0263276411423038.

———. "The Poverty of Philosophy: Realism and Post-Fordism." *Critical Inquiry* 39 (2013): 347–66. DOI: 10.1086/668529.

Grigely, Joseph. *Textualterity: Art, Theory and Textual Criticism.* Ann Arbor: University of Michigan Press, 1998.

Grosz, Elizabeth. "Bergson, Deleuze and the Becoming of Unbecoming." *parallax* 11, no. 2 (2005): 4–13. DOI: 10.1080/13534640500058434.

———. *Chaos, Territory, Art: Deleuze and the Framing of the Earth.* New York: Columbia University Press, 2008.

———. *Volatile Bodies: Toward a Corporeal Feminism.* Bloomington: Indiana University Press, 1994.

Gysin, Brion. "Cut-Ups: A Project for Disastrous Success." In William S. Burroughs and Brion Gysin, *The Third Mind,* 42–51. New York: The Viking Press, 1978.

———. *Poem of Poems.* Alga Marghen LP N. plana G 8Voc-Son021, 1997. Originally recorded in 1958.

Hainley, Bruce. "Haim Steinbach: Sonnabend Gallery, New York." *Artforum* 46, no. 4 (December 2007): 339.

Harman, Graham. *Guerrilla Metaphysics: Phenomenology and the Carpentry of Things.* Chicago: Open Court, 2005.

Hartshorne, Charles. "Bell's Theorem and Stapp's Revised View of Space-Time." *Process Studies* 7, no. 3 (1977): 183–91. https://www.jstor.org/stable/44797910.

Hayles, N. Katherine. "Print Is Flat, Code Is Deep: The Importance of Media-Specific Analysis." *Poetics Today* 25, no. 1 (2004): 67–90. DOI: 10.1215/03335372-25-1-67.

James, William. "Does 'Consciousness' Exist?" In *Essays in Radical Empiricism,* 1–38. New York: Longmans, Green, and Co., 1912.

Jaskey, Jenny. "The Unstatic." In Haim Steinbach, Beatrix Ruf, et al., *Haim Steinbach: Object and Display,* 397–99. New York: Gregory R. Miller & Co, 2015.

@joshuacitarella. Instagram post. May 10, 2018. https://www.instagram.com/p/Bim-4a_njJV/?taken-by=joshuacitarella.

Klossowski, Pierre. "Oubli et anamnèse dans l'expérience vécue de l'éternel retour du Même." In *Nietzsche: Cahiers de Royaumont,* 233–5. Paris: Editions de Minuit, 1967.

Kim, Yoon-Ho, R. Yu, S.P. Kulik, and Y.H. Shih, Marlan O. Scully. "A Delayed Choice Quantum Eraser." *Physical Review Letters* 84, no. 1 (2000): 1–4. DOI: 10.1103/PhysRevLett.84.1.

Kotz, Liz. *Words To Be Looked At: Language in 1960s Art.* Cambridge: MIT Press, 2007.

Landsman, N.P. "Observation and Superselection in Quantum Mechanics." *Studies in History and Philosophy of Modern Physics* 26, no. 1 (1995): 45–73. DOI: 10.1016/1355-2198(95)00001-A.

Lovecraft, H.P. "The Case of Charles Dexter Ward." In *The Thing on the Doorstep and Other Weird Stories,* edited by S.T. Joshi, 101–231. New York: Penguin Books, 2001.

———. "The Dream-Quest of Unknown Kadath." In *The Cthulhu Tome,* edited by Anthony Uyl, 370–412. Woodstock: Devoted Publishing, 2016.

———. "The Lurking Fear." In *The Dreams in the Witch House and Other Weird Stories,* edited by S.T. Joshi, 62–81. New York: Penguin Books, 2004.

Ma, Xiao-Song, Johannes Kofler, and Anton Zeilinger. "Delayed-Choice Gedanken Experiments and their Realizations." *Reviews of Modern Physics* 88, no. 1 (2016). DOI: 10.1103/RevModPhys.88.015005.

Ma, Xiao-Song, Johannes Kofler, et al. "Quantum Erasure with Causally Disconnected Choice." *Proceedings of the National Academy of Sciences of the United States of America* 110, no. 4 (2013): 1221–26. DOI: 10.1073/pnas.1213201110.

Manning, A.G., R.I. Khakimov, R.G. Dall, and A.G. Truscott. "Wheeler's Delayed-Choice Gedanken Experiment with a Single Atom." *Nature Physics* 11 (2015): 539–42. DOI: 10.1038/NPHYS3343.

Manning, Erin. *Relationscapes: Movement, Art, Philosophy.* Cambridge: MIT Press, 2009.

Marion, Jean-Luc. *The Idol and Distance: Five Studies.* Translated by Thomas A. Carlson. New York: Fordham University Press, 2001.

Massumi, Brian. "Like a Thought." Introduction to *A Shock To Thought: Expression after Deleuze and Guattari*, edited by Brian Massumi, xiii–xxxix. London: Routledge, 2005.

———. *Parables for the Virtual: Movement, Affect, Sensation*. Durham: Duke University Press, 2007.

———. *The Principle of Unrest: Activist Philosophy in the Expanded Field*. London: Open Humanities Press, 2017.

———. "Virtual Ecology and the Question of Value." In *General Ecology: The New Ecological Paradigm*, edited by Erich Hörl, 345–73. London: Bloomsbury, 2017.

Minh-ha, Trinh T. *When the Moon Waxes Red: Representation, Gender, and Cultural Politics*. New York: Routledge, 1991.

Murphy, Timothy S., and Daniel W. Smith. "What I Hear Is Thinking Too: Deleuze and Guattari Go Pop." *ECHO: A Music-Centered Journal* 3, no. 1 (2001). http://www.echo.ucla.edu/article-what-i-hear-is-thinking-too-deleuze-and-guattari-go-pop-by-timothy-s-murphy-and-daniel-w-smith/.

"Museum of Modern Art Acquires Jasper Johns Sculpture." *Artforum*, March 17, 2015. http://artforum.com/news/museum-of-modern-art-acquires-jasper-johns-sculpture-50855.

Nietzsche, Friedrich. *Twilight of the Idols: Or, How to Philosophize with the Hammer*. Translated by Richard Polt. Indianapolis: Hackett Publishing Company, 1997.

Omnès, Roland. *The Interpretation of Quantum Mechanics*. Princeton: Princeton University Press, 1994.

O'Sullivan, Simon. *Art Encounters: Deleuze and Guattari, thought Beyond Representation*. London: Palgrave MacMillan, 2006.

Parikka, Jussi. "Apparatus Theory of Media à la (or in the wake of) Karen Barad." *Machinology: Machines, Noise, and Some Media Archaeology*, July 16, 2009. https://jussiparikka.net/2009/07/16/apparatus-theory-of-media-a-la-or-in-the-wake-of-karen-barad/.

Peirce, Charles Sanders. *Collected Papers of Charles Sanders Peirce, Volume VI: Scientific Metaphysics*. Edited by Charles Hartshorne and Paul Weiss. Cambridge: Harvard University Press, 1935.

———. *The Essential Peirce: Selected Philosophical Writings*, vol. 2. Bloomington: University of Indiana Press, 1998.

———. "How To Make Our Ideas Clear." In *Collected Papers of Charles Sanders Peirce, Volume V: Pragmatism and Pragmaticism*, edited by Charles Hartshorne and Paul Weiss, 388–410. Cambridge: Harvard University Press, 1934.

Perloff, Marjorie. "Grammar in Use: Wittgenstein/Gertrude Stein/Marinetti." *South Central Review* 13, nos. 2–3 (1996): 35–62. DOI: 10.2307/3190371.

"Pope.L, The Black Factory Archive, 2003–ongoing." *Museum of Modern Art*. https://www.moma.org/collection/works/182201.

Pope.L, William. Artist Talk given at Center for Maine Contemporary Art. Rockland, ME. August 4, 2004. http://theblackfactory/ceo_pages/ceo_2.htm.

———. "Canary in the Coal Mine." *Art Journal* 70, no. 3 (2011): 55–58.

———. *Distributing Martin*. http://www.distributingmartin.com/.

———. "William Pope.L on 'Acting a Fool' and Alternative Futures." Interview with William Pope.L. by Samuel Jablon. *Hyperallergic*, July 10, 2015. https://hyperallergic.com/221452/william-pope-l-on-acting-a-fool-and-alternative-futures/.

Pope.L, William, et al. *Black Factory*. http://www.theblackfactory.com/.

Pope.L, William, and Patricia C. Phillips. "Artist Project." *Art Journal* 64, no. 1 (Spring 2005): 50–59. DOI: 10.2307/20068363.

Proust, Marcel. *The Captive*. Translated by C.K. Scott-Moncrieff. Reprint of the 1929 edition, Paris: Feed-

books, 2014. http://www.feedbooks.com/book/1451/
the-captive.

———. *The Guermantes Way*. Translated by C.K. Scott-Moncrieff. Reprint of the 1925 edition, Paris: Feedbooks, 2014. http://www.feedbooks.com/book/1449/
the-guermantes-way.

———. *The Sweet Cheat Gone*. Translated by C.K. Scott-Moncrieff. Reprint of the 1930 edition, Paris: Feedbooks, 2014. http://www.feedbooks.com/book/1452/
the-sweet-cheat-gone-the-fugitive.

———. *Time Regained*. Translated by Stephen Hudson. Reprint of the 1931 edition, Paris: Feedbooks, 2014. http://www.feedbooks.com/book/1453/time-re-gained.

———. *Within a Budding Grove*. Translated by C.K. Scott-Moncrieff. Reprint of the 1924 edition, Paris: Feedbooks, 2014. http://www.feedbooks.com/book/1448/
within-a-budding-grove.

Pseudo-Dionysius. "The Divine Names." In *Pseudo-Dionysius: The Complete Works*, translated by Jean Leclercq, 47–131. Mahwah: Paulist Press, 1987.

———. "Mystic Theology." In *The Works of Dionysius the Areopagite*, translated by John Parker, 130–37. London: James Parker and Co., 1897.

———. "The Mystical Theology." In *Pseudo-Dionysius: The Complete Works*, translated by Jean Leclercq, 133–41. Mahwah: Paulist Press, 1987.

Rybarczyk, Edmund J. "Reframing Tongues: Apophaticism and Postmodernism." *Pneuma: The Journal of the Society for Pentecostal Studies* 27, no. 1 (2005): 83–104.

Saddlemire, Craig. "Black Factory (Teaser)." *Vimeo*, March 25, 2014. http://vimeo.com/90020782.

Savransky, Martin. "Modes of Mattering: Barad, Whitehead, and Societies." *Rhizomes: Cultural Studies in Emerging Knowledge* 30 (2016). DOI: 10.20415/rhiz/030.e08.

Schlosshauer, Maximilian. *Decoherence and the Quantum-to-Classical Transition*. Berlin: Springer, 2010.

Schlosshauer, Maximilian, and Kristian Camilleri. "What Classicality? Decoherence and Bohr's Classical Concepts." *American Institute of Physics Conference Proceedings* 1327 (2011): 26–35. DOI: 10.1063/1.3567426.

Schwenger, Peter. *The Tears of Things: Melancholy and Physical Objects*. Minneapolis: University of Minnesota Press, 2006.

Sells, Michael A. *The Mystical Languages of Unsaying*. Chicago: The University of Chicago Press, 1994.

Shaviro, Steven. *The Universe of Things: On Speculative Realism*. Minneapolis: University of Minnesota Press, 2014.

———. *Without Criteria: Kant, Whitehead, Deleuze, and Aesthetics*. Cambridge: MIT Press, 2009.

Spurse. *Time Drills: A Series of Exercise Scores*. Omaha: Bemis Center for Contemporary Art, 2009.

Steinbach, Haim. "Ginger Wolfe Interviews Haim Steinbach." *InterReview* 6 (2005): 55.

———. "Haim Steinbach in Conversation with Tom Eccles, Beatrix Ruff, and Hans Ulrich Obrist." In Haim Steinbach, Beatrix Ruf, et al., *Haim Steinbach: Object and Display*, 361–69. New York: Gregory R. Miller & Co, 2015.

Stewart, Kathleen. *Ordinary Affects*. Durham: Duke University Press, 2007.

Stockhausen, Karlheinz. Interview in *Le Monde*. July 21, 1977.

Taubes, Jacob. "Notes on an Ontological Interpretation of Theology." *The Review of Metaphysics* 2, no. 8 (1949): 97–104.

Terpstra, Marin, and Theo de Wit. "No Spiritual Investment in the World As It Is: Jacob Taubes's Negative Political Theology." In *Flight of the Gods: Philosophical Perspectives on Negative Theology*, edited by Ilse N. Bul-

hof and Laurens ten Kate, 320–53. New York: Fordham
University Press, 2000.

Thacker, Eugene. "APOPHATIC ANIMALITY: Lautréamont, Bachelard, and the Bliss of Metamorphosis."
Angelaki: Journal of the Theoretical Humanities 18, no. 1
(2013): 83–98. DOI: 10.1080/0969725X.2013.783443.

———. "The Shadows of Atheology: Epidemics, Power
and Life after Foucault." *Theory, Culture & Society* 26,
no. 6 (2009): 134–52.

———. *Tentacles Longer than Night (Horror of Philosophy.
Vol. 3)*. Winchester: Zero Books, 2015.

———. "Three Questions on Demonology." Paper presented at *Hideous Gnosis: Black Metal Theory Symposium*
1, Brooklyn, NY, December 2009: 179–219.

Turner, Denys. *The Darkness of God: Negativity in Christian
Mysticism*. Cambridge: Cambridge University Press,
1999.

Ulmer, Gregory. *Applied Grammatology: Post(e)-Pedagogy
from Jacques Derrida to Joseph Beuys*. Baltimore: Johns
Hopkins University Press, 1985.

Utterback, Camille. "Unusual Positions – Embodied
Interaction with Symbolic Spaces." In *First Person: New
Media as Story, Performance, and Game*, edited by Noah
Wardrip-Fruin and Pat Harrigan, 218–26. Cambridge:
MIT Press, 2004.

Virilio, Paul. *The Aesthetics of Disappearance*. New York:
Semiotext(e) Books, 1991.

Weschler, Lawrence. *Seeing Is Forgetting the Name of the
Thing One Sees: A Life of Contemporary Artist Robert
Irwin*. Berkeley: University of California Press, 1982.

Wheeler, J.A. "Law Without Law." In *Quantum Theory and
Measurement*, edited by J.A. Wheeler and W.H. Zurek,
182–213. Princeton: Princeton University Press, 1983.

Whitehead, Alfred North. *Adventures of Ideas*. New York:
Free Press, 1967.

———. "Immortality." In *Essays in Science and Philosophy*,
77–96. New York: Philosophical Library, 1947.

————. *Modes of Thought*. New York: Free Press, 1968.

————. *Process and Reality: An Essay in Cosmology*. New York: Free Press, 1978.

————. *Symbolism, Its Meaning and Effect*. Cambridge: Cambridge University Press, 1958.

Zou, X.Y., L.J. Wang, and L. Mandel. "Induced Coherence and Indistinguishability in Optical Interference." *Physical Review Letters* 67, no. 3 (1991): 318–21.

Zurek, Wojciech H. "Decoherence and the Transition from Quantum to Classical – Revisited." *Los Alamos Science* 27 (2002): 86–109.

————. "Decoherence, Einselection, and the Quantum Origins of the Classical." *Reviews of Modern Physics* 75, no. 3 (2003): 715–75.